THE RUSES FOR
WAR

• •

THE RUSES FOR

AMERICAN INTERVENTIONISM SINCE WORLD WAR II

• •

JOHN QUIGLEY

 Prometheus Books

59 John Glenn Drive
Amherst, New York 14228-2197

Published 2007 by Prometheus Books

Inquiries should be addressed to
Prometheus Books
59 John Glenn Drive
Amherst, New York 14228–2197
VOICE: 716–691–0133, ext. 207
FAX: 716–564–2711
WWW.PROMETHEUSBOOKS.COM

11 10 09 08 07   5 4 3 2 1

Library of Congress Cataloging-in-Publication Data

Quigley, John B.
     The ruses for war : American interventionism since World War II / John Quigley.
          p. cm.
     Originally published in 1992.
     Includes bibliographical references and index.
     ISBN 978–1–59102–516–0 (alk. paper)
     1. United States—Foreign relations—1945–1989. 2. United States—Foreign relations—1989– 3. United States—Foreign relations—Citizen participation. 4. United States—Military policy. 5. Intervention (International law) I. Title.

E744.Q54 2007
327.73009'045—dc22   2007000018

Printed in the United States on acid-free paper

To Shirley Adele Shank

who didn't have to save me in Cambodia

CONTENTS

List of Abbreviations   11

Preface to the Second Edition   13

1. Secrets of Government   17

2. How It Began   21

3. Korea: Whose War?   31

4. Korea: The Russians Are Coming   47

5. Korea: The Chinese Hordes   55

6. Guatemala: Deception and Timing   71

7. Indonesia: Caught in a Coconut Tree   79

8. Lebanon, Iraq, and Jordan: Cokes on the Beach   87

9. Cuba: We Were Not Involved   97

10. Laos A Free-Fire Zone   105

11. Vietnam: What Were Those Bleeps?   117

12. The Congo: Trouble Out East   129

13. The Congo: Another Cuba?   137

14. The Dominican Republic: Bullets in the Embassy Window   147

15. The Dominican Republic: Seeing Red   155

16. Cambodia: Fish in the Craters   163

17. Angola: A Global Monroe Doctrine   173

18. Shaba: A Congolese Reprise   183

19. Iran: Hostages Will Die   191

20. Nicaragua: Who Is Contra?   197

21. El Salvador: A Textbook Case   205

22. Lebanon: Death on the Beach   215

23. Grenada: An Ocean Venture   221

24. Grenada: Saving Our Students   229

25. Grenada: The Cubans Were Ferocious   241

26. Libya: Qaddafi's Air Conditioner   253

27. The Philippines: Shoring Cory   263

28. Panama: Slaying a Monster   269

29. Panama: Explaining Why   283

30. Liberia: Just in Case   293

31. Iraq: Blood for Oil?   299

32. Somalia: Blackhawk Down   311

33. Baghdad: Missiles with a Message   317

34. Sudan: Pharmaceutical Fiasco   329

35. Iraq: Low-Intensity Intervention   335

36. Kosovo: Credibility Above All   349

37. Afghanistan: End to Terror?   359

38. Iraq: Regime Change   367

39. Why Not Tell the Truth?   377

40. Why Intervene at All?   385

41. Won't the Media Protect Us?   391

42. Won't Congress Protect Us?   397

43. Interventions of the Future   403

44. The Price of Fraudulent Intervention   411

Bibliography   417

Name Index   429

LIST OF ABBREVIATIONS

Abbreviations are used in the notes for a few frequently cited sources.

DSB   United States, Department of State Bulletin

FRUS   Foreign Relations of the United States

GAOR   United Nations, General Assembly Official Records

SCOR   United Nations, Security Council Official Records

Full publication data on the major works cited in the notes appears in the bibliography.

Preface to the Second Edition

When the first edition of *The Ruses for War: American Interventionism Since World War II* was published in 1992, the topic of military intervention initiated on premises other than those stated by the U.S. government was not prominent in the public view. One of my aims in writing the first edition was to bring about an awareness that when a president of the United States intervenes militarily in another country, the reasons that the White House or the Pentagon gives may not be the actual ones. The first edition demonstrated that in none of the military interventions undertaken after World War II had the public been given a full and truthful account of the reasons.

As of 2006, the situation is different. The media has covered in detail the frailty of the reasons President George W. Bush gave in 2003 for committing troops in Iraq. The public understood that the country had been taken to war for a purpose that turned out to have no reality. As a result, this second edition appears in the context of a public understanding that differs from what obtained in 1992. Public skepticism is now aroused when a president gives reasons for committing troops. At the same time, the phenomenon of intervention for reasons other than those stated continues to be a blot on the level of democracy under which we live. Through the 1990s, and into the early years of the new century, presidents, as before, have intervened militarily abroad. And, as before, they have failed to apprise the public of the true reasons for intervention. If democracy is to work, the public must know what the government is doing and why.

This second edition brings the account of U.S. interventions up to date. It also incorporates new information that has become available about the interventions discussed in the first edition. I am grateful in preparing this edition, as I was in preparing the first edition, to the Michael E. Moritz College of Law, Ohio State University, for research support. I am grateful, in particular, to Linda Poe of the library, who made heroic efforts to locate source material, and to Jenny Pursell, who taught me what I needed to know about software, and who overcame horrific formatting glitches to produce a readable text.

The military interventions recounted in the first edition occurred in the context of the Cold War. At times, we intervened quietly, denying afterward that we had done so. At times, we intervened openly. In both situations, the purposes typically involved supporting or opposing a government that was on one side or the other in the Cold War. Even if a president lied to the public about the reasons, the president could think he was doing the "right thing," because he was working against the Soviet adversary.

After 1992, the context changed. The Cold War took its place on the shelf in history libraries. The reasons that were behind those military interventions seemed to have no relevance any longer. Yet a strange thing happened: the United States continued to intervene with some frequency, and the reasons presidents gave still did not comport with the factual situations they faced.

This second edition asks why it is that military intervention has continued and why presidents are still apparently unable to explain the actual reasons. The bottom line is that the uncomfortable fact portrayed in the first edition still holds true—that the public is not given a full and accurate account of the reasons for interventions or of the circumstances that lead to them.

This book explores U.S. military actions abroad over the past half century. We look in each instance at what the president and his aides said, and what reasons they gave. Then we examine the situation in light of what is known today to determine whether the administration was truthful.

In a developing crisis, the public gets its information from the media. The media gets its information from the White House, the Defense Department, and the State Department. If troops are sent into combat, the president appears on television. "My fellow Americans," he says solemnly, "it is my duty to inform you that at dawn this morning our forces landed in far off Ruritania."

Then the president explains that civil order in Ruritania has broken down, or that the tyrant who runs Ruritania has threatened the United States or our allies in his region. If there are Americans living in Ruritania, he may say that their lives are at stake. The media and the public typically have little independent information to assess the president's statement.

Whatever the scenario, can the public rely on this kind of information from the president? Do presidents explain the true reasons for the military action they take, or do they shade the truth to get public support? The evidence presented in this book suggests that presidents do not always divulge the truth, at least not the whole truth. In the interest of gaining public backing, they omit inconvenient details and exaggerate hazards.

A president may act in what he perceives to be the best interest of the country, even if he feels he must embellish facts to make his case. Or he may be inventing a story he knows has no reality in order to intervene for entirely different reasons. Domestic political considerations may be behind a president's decision, but if they are, the president is not likely to mention them.

If presidents do shade the truth when they send troops into combat, the implications for our system of governance are serious. A premise of democracy is that the public keeps tabs on the government. If we don't like an administration, we throw it out at the next election. If a president can deceive us, we cannot properly assess his conduct. Democracy fails.

John Quigley
Columbus, Ohio

1. SECRETS OF GOVERNMENT

In 1971, when several American newspapers sought to publish documents colloquially known as the *Pentagon Papers*, which showed what lay behind the policy of the United States in Vietnam, federal authorities tried to stop them. The government said it needed to maintain the confidentiality of how decisions were made relating to a war still in progress. The newspaper editors said that the public had a right to know. The matter wound up before the Supreme Court. It decided against the government. Justice Hugo Black penned the court's opinion. "In the First Amendment," wrote Black, referring to the free speech clause of the Constitution, "the Founding Fathers gave the free press the protection it must have to fulfill its essential role in our democracy. The press was to serve the governed, not the governors. The Government's power to censor the press was abolished so that the press would remain forever free to censure the Government."

Black explained that one purpose of freedom of speech is to keep the government from going to war without explaining why:

> The press was protected so that it could bare the secrets of government and inform the people. Only a free and unrestrained press can effectively expose deception in government. And paramount among the

responsibilities of a free press is the duty to prevent any part of the government from deceiving the people and sending them off to distant lands to die of foreign fevers and foreign shot and shell.

The newspapers, Black continued, were carrying out the purpose of the free speech clause by publishing the *Pentagon Papers*: "In my view, far from deserving condemnation for their courageous reporting, the *New York Times*, the *Washington Post*, and other newspapers should be commended for serving the purpose that the Founding Fathers saw so clearly. In revealing the workings of government that led to the Vietnam war, the newspapers nobly did precisely that which the Founders hoped and trusted they would do."[1]

Nothing could be worse, Black thought, than for an administration to deceive the public about the need to get into a war. The administration's reasons might be valid or invalid, but those fighting the war should not be sent to their graves for a cause they do not understand.

After World War II, the United States became the world's leading power. France had fallen from its perch as a great power and had not been a major factor in the war. Britain survived the war with its empire intact, but it was severely weakened. By the 1960s, the colonial empires of France and Britain faded into history. The United States assumed a role of predominance, rivaled only by the Soviet Union, which tried to match it in military might but was well behind it in terms of economic power. The term "superpower" came into vogue to refer to the pair.

The United States had intervened militarily abroad even prior to World War II, but had confined itself largely to the western hemisphere, where it enjoyed predominance from the turn of the twentieth century. World War II gave the United States predominance at the world level. Interventions would be undertaken on a broader geographical basis.

Just at that time, the United Nations was set up to control the use of military force by one state against another. The UN Charter viewed all states as sovereign in their territory. That meant that they could decide, without outside interference, on the way they would structure themselves. According to Article 2 of the UN Charter, a state was prohibited from using force to infringe upon either the "territorial integrity" or the "political independence" of another.

Moreover, the Charter set up an international body called the Security Council to ensure that this prohibition was not violated. Any state that considered itself to be under attack by another could complain to the Security Council, which would decide whether the force was justifiable as self-defense, the only basis on which states are allowed to use military force.

Beyond UN considerations, a U.S. president who goes to war must convince his own public that the use of military force is justified. A president who sends troops abroad has a public relations problem. Our soldiers must be willing to go, and Congress must be willing to provide the funds. Presidents who have sent troops into military conflict abroad have confronted this problem. In general, they have been successful in convincing both Congress and the public to go along. This success is perhaps remarkable, since the circumstances of many of the interventions were unclear at the time, and with historical hindsight it is clear that much of what the presidents have told the public was untrue.

Military personnel are duty bound to serve, regardless of whether they understand why they are fighting. Yet if they are disaffected, if they do not know what precipitated the hostilities, if they doubt the government's motives, they may not be effective. A president must provide a reason that makes sense to our military personnel. If the actual reason is not one that the president thinks will rally the troops, then the speechwriters are tempted to come up with something else.

Hugo Black viewed the media as a critical actor in protecting the public. In principle, one should not need to rely on the media. Governments are elected by the people, who in turn have a right to be informed by the government about what it is doing and why. The reality of politics is otherwise, unfortunately. The government is often moved to act for reasons it prefers not to disclose, even if it is committing troops abroad.

Government—the executive branch—is also, in principle, to be checked by two other branches of government. To a degree, they *do* provide a check. However, when it comes to military hostilities, they take a back seat. Even though Congress is endowed by the Constitution with the power to make war, it cedes its authority to a considerable degree to the president, who, by the same constitution, is commander in chief of the military forces. Congress gets its information from the president, to a large degree, and thus, it is ill equipped to play a significant role, particularly if the president plans to act on short notice.

The courts may play a role from time to time, as in the case Hugo Black decided, which affirmed the role of the media. Or the courts may, on rare occasions, counteract a president in the way in which he carries out the military function. An example is the 2006 case in which the Supreme Court told President George W. Bush that he had to treat captives according to international standards.[2] Yet the courts view military matters largely as a matter of presidential discretion. Challenges to the propriety of warfare have been filed in the courts, but the courts typically defer to the executive.

The media does have a critical role. The media is better placed than Congress or the courts to ferret out facts. That is the media's basic role. As we shall see in the chapters that follow, the media has covered our military ventures. In some instances, the media's efforts have been more effective than in others. At times, the media has told the public what was actually occurring and why, even if government was being less than open. At other times, the media has merely conveyed to the public the government's misleading version of a military conflict. We shall examine the media's role in a later chapter. We proceed first to examine how successive presidents have dealt with the public as they embarked upon military conflict.

NOTES

1. *New York Times v. United States*, 403 U.S. 713 (1971).
2. *Hamdan v. Rumsfeld*, 126 S. Ct. 2749 (2006).

2. HOW IT BEGAN

The United States has fashioned a set of interests for itself around the globe, which are largely related to commercial activity. Our companies are everywhere, buying and selling, making investments, digging mines, cultivating cash crops, and setting up assembly lines to manufacture consumables. By the early twentieth century, we needed raw materials unavailable at home to fuel the production system we had mastered. Our industry, which rapidly became the most robust in the world, needed markets for its expanding products.

We spread first through regions close to home, as our companies set up shop in Latin America. Our banana plantations were the most visible. In the nineteenth century, with the decline of Spain and Portugal in Latin America, the United States declared, through the Monroe Doctrine, that Europe was not to recolonize in our hemisphere. Our business activity in Latin America grew, with our government intervening militarily to protect our companies. By 1895, Secretary of State Richard Olney could assert that the United States was "practically sovereign" in the western hemisphere, because "its infinite resources combined with its isolated position render it master of the situation."[1] Many Latins doubtless agreed with Olney's assessment, although they may not have viewed the U.S. role so benignly.

Exercising our role of "master of the situation," President Theodore

Roosevelt claimed a right to intervene in any Latin country that defaulted on its public debt. To put a country's finances in order, we would operate its customs houses and put its finances back on a proper footing. Roosevelt first used this rationale, which became known as the Roosevelt corollary to the Monroe Doctrine,[2] to intervene in the Dominican Republic in 1905.

When Colombia balked at giving us Panama to build a canal, we fomented a rebellion in Panama and sent ships to stop Colombia from putting it down. In the early decades of the twentieth century, we intervened over and over in Latin America, anxious to see at the helm governments that let our companies operate without restrictions. In U.S. strategic thinking, security and economic considerations became so intertwined as to be inseparable.[3]

In 1916, President Woodrow Wilson sent the Marines to occupy the Dominican Republic, arguing that Germany, which was conducting naval operations in the Atlantic Ocean, might take it over if we stayed out. There was little evidence of any such possibility. Our real aim was greater control over the Dominican Republic. The Marines remained for eight years, leaving only in 1924. By then, our military administration had let U.S. sugar companies gain title to much of the sugar-growing land in the Dominican Republic, driving off Dominican peasants and burning their villages in the process.[4]

Intervention in Latin America subsided in the 1930s, when President Franklin Roosevelt declared a "good neighbor" policy in the hemisphere, implicitly acknowledging that we had been less than good. After World War II, we resumed interventionism in Latin America, as will be recounted in several of the chapters that follow.

At the same time, we began to spread our influence to the rest of the world. As Europe's colonial empires declined, our companies became the main outside financial force in Asia and Africa. Since the economies of these areas were weak, outside capital could play a vital role. As with Latin America, we wanted friendly governments in power, to let us extract their minerals, employ their labor force, and sell our products.

Once more, as in Latin America, we sent our military forces out to make sure the right kinds of governments were in power. We set up a worldwide military apparatus, sending naval fleets to all the world's oceans and stationing ground troops in far-flung sites. We tried to preserve friendly governments and displace the unfriendly, giving the Monroe Doctrine and its Roosevelt corollary a global reach.[5]

In Third World areas once dominated by Europe, we came into a power broker role, taking Indochina from France and the Middle East from Great Britain and France. Our companies saw nothing wrong in what they were doing, and, in some ways, their presence benefited the countries where they operated. The companies were simply doing good business, looking for the cheapest raw materials and labor as well as new markets.

Our rising preeminence in the financial life of weaker countries was accompanied by a similarly influential role in their politics. Our companies, whose assets often exceeded those of the countries where they operated, could control events. Politicians, in return for payoffs, disguised or open, let the companies operate as they liked. In reaction to this practice, opposition to our role developed in Asia and Africa, as it already had in Latin America. Often, leftist parties on close terms with the Soviet Union or China led this opposition.

When they sent troops overseas, U.S. administrations were not models of candor. It would hardly sound good to say that we were installing a government that would allow larger profits to be returned to the United States. When the Senate was debating whether to enter World War I, Senator Hiram Johnson of Texas warned, "The first casualty when war comes is truth." Administrations had been bending the truth to gain public support for interventions abroad well before World War I.

The United States' westward and southward expansion provided the context for our first major intervention. In 1846, President James Polk asked Congress to declare war on Mexico, telling it that Mexico had invaded U.S. territory and "shed American blood on the American Soil."[6] Polk's claim of a Mexican invasion was based on a skirmish between U.S. and Mexican forces in the area between the Nueces River and the Rio Grande.[7] The Nueces, which parallels the Rio Grande 150 miles northeast of it, had long been the recognized border between Texas and Mexico, and at the time was governed by Mexico.[8] So Polk's assertion that the skirmish occurred on "the American Soil" was more than a little dubious.

But Congress accepted Polk's argument, reciting in its war declaration that "by the act of the Republic of Mexico, a state of war exists between that Government and the United States."[9] This "act" by Mexico was the skirmish between the Rio Grande and the Nueces. Ulysses Grant, who as an army officer fought in the Mexican war, was on target when he wrote that the United States had initiated the war with Mexico "to acquire additional territory." Grant called the Mexican war "one of the most unjust ever waged by a stronger against a weaker nation."[10]

In 1898, we went to war with Spain under the slogan "Remember the *Maine*." Early that year, the USS *Maine* had exploded and sunk in the harbor at Havana, in Spain's colony of Cuba, with a loss of two hundred sixty-six crew members. President William McKinley ordered the Navy to conduct an inquiry, and the naval panel focused its attention on a section of the *Maine's* hull, which was dented inward after the explosion. The panel decided that this indentation was caused by an external explosion, so it concluded that the *Maine* had been destroyed by an underwater mine. Although the panel could not determine who might have laid such a mine, the surmise was that it was the Spanish, either private individuals or the government, who were afraid that the United States might encourage Cuba to revolt against Spain.[11]

The Spanish government, seeing that political hay was being made of the incident, conducted its own inquiry. There were many eyewitnesses to the event, and none noticed any disturbance of the water, which would have been visible if a mine exploded in the water. Havana harbor was home to abundant fish life, but no dead fish were reported, as would be expected from a mine exploding there.[12] The Spanish inquiry board concluded that there was no external source, but that the explosion resulted from an event inside the ship, probably the spontaneous combustion of materials on the ship. It said that the hull collapsed inward from the action of the water following an internal explosion.

Understanding that the United States was not likely to accept this conclusion, Spain proposed that the two countries hold a joint investigation, and also offered to submit the question of its liability to binding arbitration by an impartial international panel.

President William McKinley told Congress of Spain's proposal but informed it that he did not plan to reply. Instead, he asked Congress to declare war on Spain, explaining that "the destruction of the *Maine*, by whatever exterior cause, is a patent and impressive proof of a state of things in Cuba that is intolerable." Spain, he said, was unable to "assure safety and security to a vessel of the American Navy."[13] Congress authorized McKinley to go to war to drive Spain out of Cuba, giving as one reason "the destruction of a United States battle ship, with two hundred and sixty-six of its officers and crew, while on a friendly visit in the harbor of Havana."[14] We won the war with Spain, forcing it to set Cuba free. In the process, we also took from Spain its colonies of the Philippines and Puerto Rico. In all three territories we established our own control.

The U.S. Navy preserved the documentary evidence relating to the *Maine* explosion, and in 1976, Admiral Hyman Rickover did a re-examination. Rickover arrived at the same conclusion as the Spanish inquiry panel. He found no evidence of an external explosion. Like the Spanish panel, Rickover concluded that the explosion was internal, and that the hull collapsed inward from the action of the water.[15]

Another major U.S. intervention occurred in the wake of World War I, far from Latin America, and again the reasons the White House stated did not tell the whole story. In Russia, the Bolshevik party had come to power. Western governments worried that the Soviet ideas of collectivization and state property would limit foreign entrepreneurs, and that other countries might be taken over by governments that rejected free enterprise.[16]

The military attachés of Italy, France, England, and the United States met in Moscow on May 27, 1918, and decided to propose military intervention to their governments.[17]

United States ambassador David Francis issued statements calling on the Russian people to overthrow the Bolsheviks.[18] In the northern port of Archangelsk, British agents, working with anti-Bolshevik (White Russian) elements, organized an armed uprising against the local Soviet administration. On August 2, 1918, British and French warships occupied

Archangelsk, and anti-Bolshevik political parties overthrew the Soviet administration, setting up a Russian government under British and French tutelage. British, French, and U.S. troops occupied Archangelsk and became the effective controllers of the area.[19]

As the allied force landed at Archangeisk, the Soviet troops retreated south with their supplies.[20] U.S. and other allied forces, along with White Russian troops, pursued the retreating Soviet forces.[21] The U.S. forces were put under British command, so that the British determined events on the ground.[22] The allied forces took up positions in towns to the south of Archangeisk and from there fought Soviet troops. George Chicherin, the Soviet commissar for foreign affairs, sent President Wilson a note offering an armistice and asking for a withdrawal of U.S. forces, but Wilson did not reply.[23] The All-Russian Congress of Soviets then issued a public proposal to the allies to enter peace negotiations, but again got no response.[24]

For the United States, the avowed purpose of the continuation of hostilities was to prevent allied supplies from being given to Germany, with which we were still at war.[25] The *Chicago Tribune* labeled this assertion "propaganda,"[26] and in later years a leading Western historian called it a pretext.[27]

The Wilson administration, in post-war meetings with other allied governments at Versailles, spoke for nonintervention in Russia, but on the ground, U.S. troops under British command continued fighting the Bolsheviks. In a proclamation to the troops, the British commander in north Russia stated, "We are up against Bolshevism," and "the power is in the hands of a few men, mostly Jews, who have succeeded in bringing the country to such a state that order is nonexistent. Bolshevism has grown upon the uneducated masses to such an extent that Russia is disintegrated and helpless, and therefore we have come to help her get rid of the disease that is eating her up." The proclamation declared that the aim was "the restoration of Russia," by which was meant a non-Soviet Russia.[28]

In November 1918, when the armistice ending the war was signed with Germany, the allied troops in Russia thought they would be able to go home.[29] But Wilson left them there to fight the Soviet troops. This continuation of the battle even after the armistice had been signed showed that defeating Germany was not the true purpose of the allied military presence in Russia.[30] Following the armistice, a British commander explained to the troops that "there will be no faltering in our purpose to remove the stain of Bolshevism."[31] Even though the formerly stated purpose of intercepting supplies bound for Germany no longer applied, the Wilson administration refused to divulge the reason for the continued hostilities. Disaffection grew among the allied troops, who did not understand why they were still fighting.[32] Hunger and disease were widespread because of the privations brought about by the northern winter, and some mutinies occurred.[33]

Secretary of State Robert Lansing reported that troop morale was "not good and further weakened by considerable friction with [the] British."[34] According to Wilson's special envoy to Moscow, William C. Bullitt, the "American, British, and French troops at Archangelsk are no longer serving any useful purpose. Only 3,000 Russians have rallied around this force."[35]

By early 1919, we had 5,000 troops in the northern Russian theater.[36] A U.S. sergeant wrote a letter home that "we are absolutely ignorant of any cause for being here, and we appeal to the folks at home to enlighten us. If we are here to improve conditions of the Russians and to destroy bolshevism, which we must admit is a dangerous institution, does it not seem right the [R]ussians should assist us? But they refuse to go to the front and fight with us."[37]

Only in January 1919, six months after the intervention began, did Wilson publicly acknowledge that the aim was to overthrow the Bolsheviks. The allies were repelled by Bolshevism, he told the Paris Peace Conference, and for that reason had put troops into Russia.[38] In Washington, the intervention drew fire from Congress. Senator Hiram Johnson said that U.S. soldiers "without warrant of law and in violation of the Constitution of the United States are killing and being killed in Russia today."[39] Johnson complained that "there is not a representative of the Government of the United States of America, there is not anybody in power or in position who has said to the American people or said to the American Congress what is the policy of this Government toward Russia or defined it in any degree or in any aspect."[40]

The administration, Johnson continued, had insisted that "we entered

Russia not to take any territory" or to interfere in local government, but these statements "were false in fact and were given to lull not only the Russian people into a false security but to lull the American people as well."[41] Johnson quoted from the *Chicago Tribune*, which had written that the aim of the military expedition might have been to help Europe collect Russia's debt.[42] French and British citizens had loaned large sums to the czarist government, and the Bolsheviks had repudiated the debt.

The U.S. Senate passed a resolution in June 1919, asking Wilson to explain "the reasons for sending United States soldiers to Siberia."[43] Senator William Borah said that "while Congress has not declared war, we are carrying on war with the Russian people. We have an army in Russia; we are furnishing munitions and supplies." In Borah's estimation, the United States was engaged in a "military intervention to put down a certain force in Russia and establish a government satisfactory to the allied powers." He said that "every boy who dies in Russia is a sacrifice to the unlawful and intolerable scheme." While expressing no sympathy to Bolshevism, Borah thought, "if they see fit to have a soviet government, it is their business." Borah demanded the withdrawal of U.S. troops from Russia.[44] In June 1919, President Wilson withdrew them.[45]

These early examples show that lack of candor in military interventions is not a new phenomenon for the United States. We turn now to the main topic of this book, the interventions that began after World War II. The first took place in an unlikely setting.

NOTES

1. "Mr. Olney to Mr. Bayard," July 20, 1895, FRUS 1895, p. 558.
2. "Message from the President of the United States, Transmitting a Protocol of an Agreement between the United States and the Dominican Republic, Providing for the Collection and Disbursement by the United States of the Customs Revenues of the Dominican Republic, Signed on February 7, 1905," February 15, 1905, FRUS 1905, pp. 334–42.
3. Piero Gleijeses, *The Dominican Crisis: The 1965 Constitutionalist Revolt and American Intervention* (1978), p. 15.

4. Ibid., pp. 17–18.

5. Thomas J. McCormick, *America's Half-Century: United States Foreign Policy in the Cold War* (1989), p.75.

6. John H. Schroeder, *Mr. Polk's War: American Opposition and Dissent, 1846–1848* (1973), pp. 3, 11; Alfred Hoyt Bill, *Rehearsal for Conflict: The War with Mexico 1846–1848* (1947), p. 102.

7. David Wise, *The Politics of Lying: Government Deception, Secrecy, and Power* (1973), p. 25; Bill, *Rehearsal for Conflict*, p. 92.

8. Schroeder, *Mr. Polk's War*, pp. 8–11.

9. An Act Providing for the Prosecution of the Existing War between the United States and the Republic of Mexico, May 13, 1846, U.S. Congress, *Statutes at Large*, vol. 9, p. 9 (1846).

10. *Personal Memoirs of U. S. Grant* (1894), p. 37.

11. G. J. A. O'Toole, *The Spanish War: An American Epic—1898* (1984), pp. 138, 150.

12. John Edward Weems, *The Fate of the Maine* (1958), pp. 126–27.

13. William McKinley, "Message to the Congress of the United States," April 11, 1898, in *Papers Relating to the Foreign Relations of the United States. 1898* (1901), p. 758.

14. Joint Resolution: For the recognition of the independence of the people of Cuba, demanding that the government of Spain relinquish its authority and government in the Island of Cuba, and to withdraw its land and naval forces from Cuba and Cuban waters, and directing the President of the United States to use the land and naval forces of the United States to carry these resolutions into effect. U.S. Congress, *Statutes at Large*, vol. 30, p. 738 (1898).

15. H. G. Rickover, *How the Battleship Maine was Destroyed* (1976), p. 91.

16. Robert Murray, *Red Scare: A Study of National Hysteria, 1919–1920* (1964), p. 15.

17. John Cudahy, *Archangel: The American War with Russia* (1924), p. 27.

18. Michael Sayers and Albert E. Kahn, *The Great Conspiracy Against Russia* (1946), p. 11.

19. Cudahy, *Archangel: The American War with Russia*, pp. 47, 72.

20. *Foreign Relations of the United States: The Paris Peace Conference 1919*, vol. 3, p. 625 (1943) (statement of M. Noulens, former French ambassador to Russia); Cudahy, *Archangel: The American War with Russia*, pp. 47–48, 131.

21. Sayers and Kahn, *The Great Conspiracy Against Russia*, p. 28.

22. Cudahy, *Archangel: The American War with Russia*, p. 75.

23. Ibid., p. 30; E. H. Carr, *The Bolshevik Revolution 1917–1923* (1966), 3: 117.

24. Carr, *The Bolshevik Revolution* 1917-1923, 3: 117.

25. Adam Ulam, *A History of Soviet Russia* (1976), pp. 34–36; Georg von Rauch, *A History of Soviet Russia* (1959), p. 92; George Kennan, *The Decision to Intervene* (1967), p. 21; Cudahy, *Archangel: The American War with Russia*, p. 28.

26. *Congressional Record*, vol. 57, pt. 4, p. 3261 (February 13, 1919).

27. Carr, *The Bolshevik Revolution 1917–1923*, 3: 117.

28. Cudahy, *Archangel: The American War with Russia*, pp. 31–32.

29. *Congressional Record*, vol. 57, pt. 4, p. 3261 (February 13, 1919).

30. Ralph Albertson, *Fighting without a War: An Account of Military Intervention in North Russia* (1920), pp. 112–20.

31. Cudahy, *Archangel: The American War with Russia*, p. 37.

32. Albertson, *Fighting without a War*, pp. 74–75; Cudahy, *Archangel: The American War with Russia*, pp. 2–4, 71, 99–100, 159.

33. Cudahy, *Archangel: The American War with Russia*, pp. 161–62.

34. The Secretary of State to Colonel E. M. House, December 2, 1918, *Foreign Relations of the United States: The Paris Peace Conference 1919*, vol. 2, p. 465 (1943).

35. Memorandum for Colonel House, Withdrawal of American Troops from Archangel, January 30, 1919, Cudahy, *Archangel: The American War with Russia*, p. 120.

36. Albertson, *Fighting without a War*, p.57; Sayers and Kahn, *The Great Conspiracy Against Russia*, p. 28; Cudahy, *Archangel: The American War with Russia*, p. 49.

37. *Congressional Record*, vol. 57, pt. 4, p. 3261 (February 13, 1919).

38. *Foreign Relations of the United States: the Paris Peace Conference 1919* (1943), 3: 648–49.

39. *Congressional Record*, vol. 57, pt. 4, p. 3259 (February 13, 1919).

40. Ibid., p. 3260.

41. Ibid., p.3261.

42. Ibid., p. 3260.

43. Ibid., vol. 58, pt. 2, p. 1864 (June 27, 1919).

44. Ibid., pt. 5, p. 4897 (September 5, 1919).

45. Albertson, *Fighting without a War*, p. 57; Cudahy, *Archangel: The American War with Russia*, p. 169, 210–11.

3. KOREA: WHOSE WAR?

Korea after World War II was divided north and south at the 38th parallel. The southern administration, with its capital at Seoul, had skirmished frequently across the parallel with the northern administration, based at Pyongyang. On June 25, 1950, the south reported an attack by the north and said fighting continued all across Korea along the parallel.[1] The north claimed just the opposite. Pyongyang Radio announced that the south "started a surprise invasion of the north along the whole front of the 38th parallel line at dawn on the 25th."[2] First reports from U.S. military intelligence in Korea also said that the south attacked first.[3] Our Korean Military Assistance Group (KMAG), which advised the southern army, had no reports on June 25 of northern troop movements or concentration of supplies near the 38th parallel.[4]

The U.S. ambassador's first cable to Washington reported that the initial fighting was not in fact taking place all along the 38th parallel, but only at its western end, on Korea's west coast, in an area called the Ongjin peninsula.[5] Despite their public initial claims, both north and south, in their statements, agreed with the ambassador that the fighting had begun in the west. However, if the north was indeed assaulting the south, this was a strange location to choose. Moving south across the 38th parallel on the Ongjin peninsula, one goes only a few miles before dead-ending at the sea, with no access by land to Seoul or to the rest of Korea south of the 38th parallel. If, however, the south were assaulting the north, the Ongjin peninsula was a logical starting point, because Pyongyang, lying on the west coast, would be a prime objective for the south.[6]

One piece of evidence that suggests that the south made the first move is that, as announced June 25 by both the northern and southern administrations, the southern army captured the northern city of Haeju, five miles above the 38th parallel on the Ongjin peninsula.[7] The south set the first fighting at 4:00 A.M., while Pyongyang Radio broadcast at 11:00 A.M. that the south attacked in the Haeju area "at dawn."[8] U.S. military advisors who worked with the southern army confirmed this.[9] U.S. military intelligence confirmed the south's capture of Haeju, identifying the southern army unit responsible as its 17th regiment, a crack unit.[10]

The south's assault on Haeju, it appears, started well before dawn of June 25. The northern army reported that the south had moved against Haeju on the night of June 23, a report that was later confirmed by Young Woon Lee, an admiral in the south's navy. The admiral recounted that on June 23, he led an assault by sea on Haeju, which is only one mile from the ocean; on that day the south's chief of staff issued a combat order directing commanders to "go into action at 5, June 25." The admiral said that to divert attention from the planned "full-force invasion of the North," the southern army started partial attacks beginning at 10 P.M. on June 23.[11] An early cable from the U.S. ambassador confirmed a southern advance. He reported on June 26 that "North Korean armor and artillery are withdrawing all along the line," meaning the 38th parallel.[12] By then the fighting had spread eastward.

Although the facts behind the Korean fighting were unclear, and despite the indication that an invasion had been initiated by the south, officials in Washington immediately said that the north had made the first move. Two hours after receiving the first cable about the Korean fighting, the State Department approached the United Nations and arranged for an emergency meeting in the Security Council. Wasting no time, the Department drew up a resolution to submit to the Council, declaring that the north had committed an "act of aggression." Just before the Council met,

Charles Noyes, the U.S. delegate, showed the draft resolution to the Security Council representatives of Great Britain, France, India, Egypt, and Norway. All five indicated "considerable hesitancy to take a position on which party was responsible for the invasion," Noyes reported. Egypt and Norway said there was not enough information to condemn the north, and, in any event, the fighting was between Koreans, and was therefore a civil war. Moreover, they objected to the term "aggression," because it implied an invasion of one country by another.[13]

Worried that the resolution might fail, Noyes changed "act of aggression" to read "armed invasion."[14] Although this revised phraseology still implied an attack by one country against another, Noyes hoped the change might bring the doubters along. Indonesia's delegate, however, was not satisfied. He told Noyes privately that the Security Council did not have enough information to confirm which side started the fighting.[15]

The Security Council did have some information, but it was far from conclusive. The Council had in hand a cable from the UN mission in Korea, which reported,

> South Korean troops apparently withdrawing to prearranged main line of resistance which runs along Imjin River 27 miles northwest of Seoul where crossing by northern forces has been reported at one point. Attack completely unexpected to both Korean Army and KMAG. Early fragmentary reports indicating complete surprise and withdrawals everywhere now being replaced by more confident statements. Situation reported being stabilized along main line of resistance.[16]

The mission's cable was apparently considered too sensitive to be published in UN documents, but it was read orally to Security Council members.[17] The cable suggested that the north attacked first, although it reported the north crossing the 38th parallel at only one point.

The mission, curiously, did not mention the south's capture of Haeju, although the world press had reported it. The omission was probably a result of the fact that the UN mission had no observers in the field and thus had received no firsthand information on the fighting. The mission had not had an easy time in Korea, getting no cooperation from the north, which viewed the UN as partial to the south. Because the north did not cooperate, the mission did little by way of field operations, relying instead for its information on the southern army. Its report to the Security Council was based largely on official southern sources.[18]

When the Security Council convened, the doubts had not been quelled. Yugoslavia announced, "we do not feel that the picture we have been able to obtain so far from the various dispatches that have come in, some of which are contradictory, and from the statements we have heard here, is sufficiently complete and balanced, nor one which would enable us to pass judgment on the merits of the case or assess the final and definite responsibility and guilt of either of the parties involved." Before adopting any resolution, the Council should "acquire all the factual knowledge which would make that final judgment and the action taken in pursuance of it incontrovertible," and, in particular, invite the north to tell the Council its side of the story. "We have heard the representative of South Korea," said Yugoslavia's delegate; "we should grant an opportunity for a representative of the Government of North Korea, which has now been accused of aggression, to receive a hearing."[19]

By this point, however, the U.S. delegation had managed to mollify most of the other Council members, and so the Council did not take up Yugoslavia's suggestion to hear the north's view. The U.S. delegation softened the wording of the resolution once more, from "armed invasion" to "armed attack." But the resolution still called the attack a "breach of the peace," which implied the international peace. Nevertheless, with the exception of Yugoslavia, those Council members who had insisted that whatever fighting was occurring was internal to Korea began to give ground.

During an adjournment in the Council's proceedings, a curious new piece of information surfaced. The UN Secretariat told Council members confidentially that tanks just captured by the southern army were manned by Russians. This information had not been included in any official record, but Australia's delegate mentioned it in a cable to the Australian government, adding that France and Egypt changed their view and voted for the U.S. resolution because of it.[20] The information, however, was erroneous. Whether the information was deliberately planted or an honest error would never be determined.

The Soviet Union could not refute the U.S. information, because it was boycotting Council meetings over the Council's refusal to give mainland China the Chinese seat on the Council. If it had participated, it would likely have vetoed the U.S. resolution. But with the Soviet delegate absent, the U.S. resolution was put to a vote and, despite the initial doubts, it carried, with no negative votes and only Yugoslavia abstaining.[21]

Great Britain made a curious statement explaining its vote; it essentially cautioned the Council against any "action which might go beyond the bounds of the evidence which has been placed at its disposal by its own Commission in Korea." Britain said that the resolution "goes as far as the Security Council properly can go at this stage."[22] Britain was not fully convinced who had initiated the fighting but voted for the U.S. resolution anyway. Despite the softening of its language, the resolution charged the northern administration with international aggression,[23] as it had been initially construed by the U.S. delegation.[24]

This Security Council resolution, as well as another passed a few days later, provided the basis for the Truman administration to send troops to Korea. Although the administration consulted the Security Council, it did not ask Congress for a declaration of war. Secretary of State Dean Acheson explained later that Congress "might have completely muddied up the situation which seemed to be very clear."[25] While in Congress there was not substantial dissent, Senator Robert Taft of Ohio objected that there was "no legal authority" for Truman's action, and that Truman had made "no pretense of consulting the Congress." Taft called Truman's decision to send troops to Korea "a complete usurpation by the President of authority to use the Armed Forces of this country."[26]

One factor clouding the issue of responsibility for initiating the Korean conflict was that the June 25 fighting was not the first in Korea. Intermittent hostilities had raged across the 38th parallel over the previous year.[27] The summer of 1949 had seen major fighting, most of it started by the south.[28] In April 1950, Philip Jessup, a U.S. ambassador at large, reported from Korea that the 38th parallel was "a real front line," and that there was "constant fighting," with "very real battles, involving perhaps one or two thousand men."[29] In May and June 1950, cross-parallel incidents picked up.[30] Our ambassador characterized this fighting as continuous probing along the parallel by both sides, which he said made it difficult to determine what was happening on that crucial morning of June 25.[31] Despite the cross-parallel fighting, U.S. military intelligence did not anticipate a northern invasion in the summer of 1950.[32] One reason was that the northern army had a mobilization plan for an invasion of the south that called for fifteen divisions, but by June 1950 it had only six.[33] This left the north with fewer troops than the south.[34]

Another reason for doubting a northern invasion was that the north had decent prospects of achieving reunification without a war, because of the political vulnerability of the southern administration.[35] In elections held on May 30, 1950, the southern administration of President Syngman Rhee was dealt a severe blow when voters chose a parliament with a large anti-Rhee majority.[36] This defeat sapped Rhee's continued ability to convince the south to remain separate from the north and thus increased the prospects that unification could be achieved by political means.[37] For these reasons, both British intelligence and the CIA thought that the north had such a good chance of undermining Rhee from within that it would not need to invade.[38]

Rhee, on the other hand, had ample motive to provoke hostilities. The loss of support in parliament following the May 30 election threatened his hold on power, and his economy was collapsing. Beyond that, Rhee faced a serious guerrilla war in the south led by leftist elements and aimed at unification with the north.[39] A war against the north, while risky, might rally his opponents and bring military support from outside, particularly from the United States.[40] This explains why Rhee conducted raids across the 38th parallel in the summer of 1949, namely, to try to keep the United States in the picture. In the spring of 1950, in fact, Rhee announced his intention to invade the north and made actual war preparations, moving most of his troops and equipment up to the 38th parallel.[41] To General Douglas MacArthur, who would lead U.S. troops in Korea, that deployment suggested an offensive posture.[42] In the north, by contrast, only one-third of the available troops were close to the 38th parallel.[43]

Another circumstance suggesting that Rhee may have started the hostilities is that he thought he could draw the United States in on his side. On June 18, John Foster Dulles, a consultant to the State Department, addressed Korea's National Assembly and said that if the north attacked, we would respond. Rhee, who could barely contain his delight with the speech, pressed Dulles for details on our commitment. Although Dulles did not say exactly what we would do, the speech may have convinced Rhee that the best way to save his faltering government was to provoke an attack by the north.[44] As the first reports of fighting filtered into Seoul, our ambassador, who was with Rhee, reported that Rhee seemed unconcerned about the fighting. According to Rhee, doing battle "presented the best opportunity for settling the Korean problem once and for all"—an odd reaction for someone putatively caught off guard.[45]

Evidence for the possibility that the north began the fighting came years later when Soviet leader Nikita Khrushchev reported in his memoirs on a visit made to Moscow in December 1949 by Kim Il-sung, North Korea's leader. "The North Koreans," Khrushchev said, "wanted to give a helping hand to their brethren who were under the heel of Syngman Rhee."[46] Kim, reported Khrushchev, anticipated that if he attacked, the southerners would rise up against the unpopular Rhee.[47]

The leader in the north, Kim Il-Sung, had, to be sure, considered invading the south to re-unify Korea. He visited Joseph Stalin in Moscow to discuss the possibility, as reported not only by Khrushchev, but as appears from cable traffic that became available after the collapse of the Soviet Union.

One possibility is that Kim Il-sung was waiting for a southern attack to which he would mount a major counterattack. According to one cable, this option had been raised by Stalin, as Stalin was apparently advising Kim not to strike first. Stalin reportedly said, "In case of attack on the north of the country by the army of Rhee Syngman, then it is possible to go on the counteroffensive to the south of Korea."[48]

As soon as the Korean hostilities started, President Truman dispatched our Eighth Army to fight for the southern administration. He sent the State Department rushing back to the Security Council to obtain an authorization for military action on a multilateral basis.[49] On June 27, the Council obliged by asking member states to assist South Korea "to repel the armed attack."[50] As before, the Council avoided the question of who started the hostilities. By this time the UN mission in Korea had given it no new information, other than a report based on the situation at the 38th parallel two days before the hostilities started.[51]

In the initial fighting, as it spread east across the 38th parallel, neither side got the better of it. For three days the two armies fought to a standstill, at which time the southern army withdrew southward. Its 17th regiment withdrew south from Haeju, even though it was not being pressed.[52] The northern army made its first major advance in the central area, where it took the southern town of Uijongbu, opening the road to Seoul, which it then took quickly. The north's speedy advance to Seoul is offered by some historians as proof that the northern army started the war. But one historian states that the southern army put up "suspiciously token resistance" at Uijongbu.[53] The south abandoned Seoul even before the northern army could catch up.

The southern army's rapid retreat is puzzling, because its forces outnumbered the north's. The retreat surprised the northern army, which anticipated heavier fighting. U.S. military actions as well are difficult to read. When our Eighth Army, commanded by General Douglas MacArthur, came in on the southern side, it did not attack the northern army but joined the southern retreat. One possible explanation is that Rhee and MacArthur wanted to make their situation appear desperate, so that President Truman would commit enough troops not only to halt the northern advance (Truman's stated objective), but also to bring down the northern administration.[54] In a memorandum to MacArthur in August, Rhee said, "We have been withdrawing from city to city in the hope that American reinforcements would arrive soon enough to launch an offensive."[55] Even though the U.S. and southern forces outnumbered those of the north, MacArthur continued the retreat, telling Truman that we were outnumbered by the north two or three to one.[56]

The retreat, on the other hand, may have been part of the Eighth Army's purpose all along. A contingency plan drafted by Colonel Donald McB. Curtis a few days before the hostilities had anticipated not only our intervention but also a strategy to retreat south to a defensive perimeter around Pusan, to be followed by an amphibious landing at Inchon, a port city near Seoul. As the war began, MacArthur urgently requested fifty copies of the plan, and during the summer and fall of 1950 he appeared to follow it to the letter.[57]

The northern army, unprepared for an extended campaign in the south, needed a full week to regroup after taking Seoul, before it continued southward.[58] If the north had planned the attack for June 25, it had apparently not intended to go very far.[59] As the northern army moved south, it took 50,000 casualties and ran short on supplies.[60] When in September, the Eighth Army and the southern forces counterattacked, the northern army disintegrated and fled.[61] This lack of preparation for a sustained offensive casts doubt on whether the northern army initiated the fighting. On the other hand, if Khrushchev's assessment was accurate, the north may have launched an offensive it could not sustain, in the expectation of an imminent southern collapse.

In 1951, the Truman administration released captured northern documents that, it said, proved that the north had launched an unprovoked attack on June 25, 1950. But the documents did not stand the test of scrutiny.[62] One historian wrote that "what actually happened in those early hours of the war was never properly established."[63] Bruce Cumings, a leading historian of the Korean war, agrees that even with the evidence made available long after the events, it is hazardous to pin blame on either side.

Beyond the question of who started the hostilities was that of whether they were international, so that other countries might legitimately get involved. As we saw, the Truman administration got the Security Council to agree that the hostilities were international, despite the misgivings of some Council delegates.[64] But Korea had long been a single country, and at the time of World War II, it was held by Japan, which had invaded Korea early in the twentieth century. As we fought Japan, one of our war aims, as stated in the Allies' 1943 Cairo Declaration, was to set Korea free, as a single country.[65]

When World War II was nearing an end, we encouraged the Soviet Union to undertake the task of seizing Korea from Japan.[66] But as Soviet troops entered Korea, we became skittish about a Soviet occupation and offered to take the southern part ourselves, proposing the 38th parallel as a dividing line.[67] The USSR agreed, although we had no troops in Korea and the Soviet army could easily have occupied the entire country. The fact that it did not suggests that the Soviet Union had no plan to control Korea.[68]

Soon, separate administrations were established above and below the 38th parallel, each viewing Korea as a single country that would eventually be reunited.[69] In the late 1940s, the UN tried to reunify Korea but confronted a difference in political persuasion between the southern and northern administrations. Korean leftists had been prominent in the anti-Japan resistance, and, as a result, they were the most powerful political force in Korea at war's end.[70] They had local administrations, called people's committees, throughout the country, and they had begun to assume control from the Japanese administration.[71]

After the Soviet Union took control above the 38th parallel, the people's committees there formed an administration for that territory, which became the Kim Il-sung government.[72] South of the 38th parallel, too, the people's committees tried to form an administration, but U.S. occupation authorities did not want a left-leaning government. General John R. Hodge, who ran our military government in Korea, said that the country was headed for "a political-economic abyss" and that we had to "stop this drift."[73] Hodge's main aim in governing the southern ha

If of Korea—an aim he did not conceal—was to keep the people's committees from consolidating power.[74] Hodge said he wanted to "break down" what he called "this Communist government" in the south of Korea.[75]

In the south, as in the north, the people's committees called their overall administration the Korean People's Republic. When the Korean People's Republic called a convention in Seoul, Hodge made, as he termed it, a "declaration of war" against the People's Republic, even though, he admitted, this strong response "may result in temporary disorders" and "bring charges of political discrimination" from what he called the Korean "pinko press."[76]

To suppress the Korean People's Republic, Hodge formally outlawed it,[77] rounding up leftists and putting them behind bars.[78] He also suppressed the people's committees in the various localities,[79] jailing their members and replacing them with conservatives drawn from the business community.[80] To protest Hodge's suppression, southern workers went on strike in 1946, calling for a restoration of the people's committees. To put down the strike as well as the committees, Hodge arrested over a thousand workers,[81] banned leftist political parties, and formed a consultative council composed of conservatives. He excluded from official positions many Koreans who had been active in the anti-Japan resistance, out of concern that they were leftists.[82] The Korean police force that Hodge had set up was unable to put down the people's committees, however, so he created an army of Koreans, well before a Korean army was established under the Soviet occupation in the north.[83] To suppress the guerrillas who supported the people's committees, our KMAG helped the new southern army plan an anti-guerrilla strategy.[84]

As a military occupier, the United States should have remained neutral in Korea's internal politics. But Hodge's suppression of the leftists and his promotion of the conservatives made the leftists, on both sides of the 38th parallel, feel that the United States had cheated them of a political victory that was rightfully theirs. Acknowledging this perception, Hodge said that the general view in the south was to blame the United States for the partition of Korea.[85] To make matters worse, many of the conservatives Hodge promoted had been collaborators of the Japanese colonial administration and thus were disliked by other Koreans.[86] In short, General Hodge sowed the seeds of a conflict that pitted an upper class that had collaborated with Japan against a lower class that resisted it. Hodge's policies were arguably responsible for the outbreak of war in Korea in 1950.

General Hodge particularly promoted Syngman Rhee, an expatriate Korean who had long lived in the United States and who had little following in Korea.[87] The administration Rhee came to head acquired a reputation for brutality and corruption, starting with the run-up to the 1948 parliamentary elections, when Rhee used "goon squads" to terrorize opponents. Leftists boycotted the elections, thus allowing the conservatives to win a majority.[88]

The U.S. military government, by promoting the conservatives, interfered with Korea's political process and kept it from being unified under a single administration. The hostilities that began in 1950, irrespective of who started them, were internal and were aimed at reuniting Korea.[89]

The Truman administration characterized the conflict as international to give itself a reason to intervene, but that still leaves the question of why Truman was anxious to fight in Korea. To answer that question, we must look to the cold war, which formed the backdrop for the Korean hostilities.

NOTES

1. "Telegram: The Ambassador in Korea (Muccio) to the Secretary of State," June 25, 1950, 10 A.M., FRUS 1950, vol. 7, p. 125.

2. Ibid., p. 132.

3. John Gunther, *The Riddle of MacArthur* (1950), p. 165.

4. "War Is Declared by North Koreans; Fighting on Border," *New York Times*, June 25, 1950, p. Al, col. 1.

5. "Telegram: The Ambassador in Korea (Muccio) to the Secretary of State," p. 125.

6. Bruce Cumings, *The Roaring of the Cataract, 1945–1950*, vol. 2 of *The Origins of the Korean War* (1990), pp. 568–72, 584–85.

7. "North Korean Communiques," *New York Times*, June 26, 1950, p. A3, col. 3; "U.N. Calls for Ceasefire in Korea," *New York Times*, June 26, 1950, p. Al, col. 4 (South Korean announcement).

8. "Telegram: The Ambassador in Korea (Muccio) to the Secretary of State," p. 132.

9. "Threefold Advance towards Seoul," *Guardian* (Manchester), June 26, 1950, p.7, col. 1; "Defenders Launch Counterattack, Regain 5 Miles North of

Capital," *Chicago Tribune*, June 26, 1950, p. Al, col. 8; Glenn D. Paige, *The Korean Decision June 24–30, 1950* (1968), p. 130.

10. Cumings, *The Origins of the Korean War*, 2: 572–73, 578–79.

11. Committee for a New Direction for U.S. Korea Policy, *Conference for a New Direction in U.S. Korea Policy* (1977), p. 100.

12. "Telegram: The Ambassador in Korea (Muccio) to the Secretary of State," p. 165.

13. "Memorandum of Conversations, by Mr. Charles P. Noyes, Adviser on Security Council Affairs, United States Mission at the United Nations," June 25, 1950, FRUS 1950, vol. 7, pp. 144–45.

14. SCOR, 5th yr., 473rd mtg., p. 7, UN Doc. 5/ PV.473 (1950).

15. "Memorandum of Conversations, by Mr. Charles P. Noyes, Adviser on Security Council Affairs, United States Mission at the United Nations," June 25, 1950, FRUS 1950, vol. 7, pp. 144, 145.

16. "The United States Representative at the United Nations (Austin) to the Secretary of State," June 26, 1950, FRUS 1950, vol. 7, p. 172.

17. "Cablegram dated 25 June 1950 from the United Nations Commission on Korea addressed to the Secretary General concerning aggression upon the Republic of Korea," UN Doc. S/1496, text in SCOR, 5th yr., 473rd mtg., p. 2 n. 2, UN Doc. S/PV.473 (1950).

18. Cumings, *The Origins of the Korean War*, 2: 548, 635.

19. SCOR, 5th yr., 473rd mtg., pp. 14–15, UN Doc. S/PV.473 (1950).

20. Gavan McCormack, *Cold War Hot War: An Australian Perspective on the Korean War* (1983), p. 75.

21. SCOR, 5th yr., 473rd mtg., p. 16, UN Doc. S/PV.473 (1950).

22. SCOR, 5th yr., 473rd mtg., p. 9, UN Doc. S/PV.473 (1950).

23. Res. 82, June 25, 1950, SCOR, 5th yr., *Resolutions and Decisions*, p. 4, UN Doc. S/INF/5/Rev. 1 (1950).

24. SCOR, 5th yr., 474th mtg., p. 3, UN Doc. SI PV.474 (1950).

25. Cumings, *The Origins of the Korean War*, 2: 629.

26. *Congressional Record*, vol. 96, pp. 9320, 9323, June 28, 1950.

27. "Threefold Advance towards Seoul," *Guardian* (Manchester), June 26, 1950, p. 7, col. 1.

28. Cumings, *The Origins of the Korean War*, 2: 383, 388-90, 570–71.

29. Philip Jessup, "Report to the American People on the Far East," April 13, 1950, DSB, vol. 22, p. 627 (1950).

30. Cumings, *The Origins of the Korean War*, 2: 448–49,575–76.

31. Ibid., p. 580.

32. Max Hastings, *The Korean War* (1987), p. 52.

33. Walter Sullivan, "Red Mobilization Termed 'Feverish,'" *New York Times*, July 31, 1950, p. Al, col. 7; Cumings, *The Origins of the Korean War*, 2: 452, 584, 597.

34. Joyce and Gabriel Kolko, *The Limits of Power: The World and United States Foreign Policy, 1945–1954* (1972), pp. 573–74; Cumings, *The Origins of the Korean War*, 2: 452–53.

35. "Cablegram dated 26 June 1950 to the Secretary General from the United Nations Commission on Korea, transmitting a summary report on background events preceding the outbreak of hostilities on 25 June 1950," UN Doc. S/1505/ Rev. I, SCOR, 5th yr., Supplement for June, July and August 1950, p. 24; 1. F. Stone, *The Hidden History of the Korean War* (1952), p. 18; Kolko, *The Limits of Power*, p. 575.

36. Burton Crane, "Rhee's Slate's Rout Indicated in Korea," *New York Times*, May 31, 1950, p. A8, col. 3; Hastings, *The Korean War*, p. 43.

37. Hastings, *The Korean War*, p. 57; Stone, *The Hidden History of the Korean War*, p. 65.

38. Cumings, *The Origins of the Korean War*, 2: 450.

39. Ibid., p. 441.

40. McCormack, *Cold War Hot War*, pp. 90–91.

41. Kolko, *The Limits of Power*, pp. 567-75; Cumings, *The Origins of the Korean War*, 2: 437.

42. *Military Situation in the Far East*, Hearings before the Armed Services and the Committee on Foreign Relations, U.S. Senate, 82d Cong., 1st sess., Part 1, p. 231 (1951) (statement of Gen. Douglas MacArthur); Cumings, *The Origins of the Korean War*, 2: 452, 476–77, 581.

43. Cumings, *The Origins of the Korean War*, 2: 452.

44. Kolko, *The Limits of Power*, p. 577; Cumings, *The Origins of the Korean War*, 2: 503, 505.

45. Cumings, *The Origins of the Korean War*, 2: 585.

46. *Khrushchev Remembers*, Strobe Talbott, ed. (1970), p.368.

47. Ibid., p. 369.

48. Cold War International History Project: Telegram, Shtykov to Vyshinsky, January 19, 1950, Archive of Foreign Relations of the Russian Federation, Fund 059a, Opis 5a, Case 3, Packet 11, pp. 87–91.

49. SCOR, 5th yr., 474th mtg., p. 4, UN Doc. S/PV.474 (1950).

50. Res. 83, June 27, 1950, SCOR, 5th yr., *Resolutions and Decisions*, p. 5, UN Doc. S/INF/5/Rev. 1 (1950).

51. SCOR, 5th yr., 474th mtg., p. 2, UN Doc. S/ PV.474 (1950).

52. Cumings, *The Origins of the Korean War*, 2: 579.

53. Ibid., pp. 584–85.

54. McCormack, *Cold War Hot War*, p. 94.

55. Kolko, *The Limits of Power*, p. 591.

56. Cumings, *The Origins of the Korean War*, 2: 659.

57. Col. Donald McB. Curtis, "Inchon Insight," *Army: The Magazine of Landpower* (Ass'n. of the U.S. Army), July 1985, p. 5.

58. Hastings, *The Korean War*, p. 76.

59. Cumings, *The Origins of the Korean War*, 2: 617.

60. Hastings, *The Korean War*, pp. 82, 85. Roy E. Appleman, *United States Army in the Korean War: South to the Naktong, North to the Yalu* (June–November 1950) (Office of the Chief of Military History, Department of the Army, 1961), p. 263.

61. Hastings, *The Korean War*, p. 112.

62. Cumings, *The Origins of the Korean War*, 2: 588–93.

63. Philip Knightley, *The First Casualty: From the Crimea to Vietnam: The War Correspondent as Hero, Propagandist, and Myth Maker* (1975), p. 336.

64. Res. 82, June 25, 1950, SCOR, 5th yr., *Resolutions and Decisions*, p. 4, UN Doe. S/INF/5/Rev.l (1950).

65. "Report by the State-War-Navy Coordinating Subcommittee for the Far East," Appendix B, FRUS 1945, vol. 6, P. 1098.

66. Bruce Cumings, *Liberation and the Emergence of Separate Regimes, 1945–1947*, vol. 1 of *The Origins of the Korean War* (1981), p. 118.

67. "Draft Memorandum to the Joint Chiefs of Staff," FRUS 1945, vol. 6, p. 1039.

68. Cumings, *The Origins of the Korean War*, 1: 121, 125.

69. Ibid., 2: 458, 619.

70. Ibid., 1: 32–33, 80, 100.

71. Ibid., pp. 193, 267–68.

72. Ibid., p. 196.

73. "General of the Army Douglas MacArthur to the Joint Chiefs of Staff," FRUS 1945, vol. 6, p. 1147 (quoting Gen. Hodge).

74. Cumings, *The Origins of the Korean War*, 1: 135.

75. Ibid., p. 194.

76. "Lt. Gen. John R. Hodge to General of the Army Douglas MacArthur, at Tokyo," FRUS 1945, vol. 6, p. 1134.

77. Cumings, *The Origins of the Korean War*, 1: 197.

78. Ibid., pp. 249, 252.

79. Ibid., p. 287.

80. Kolko, *The Limits of Power*, p. 285; Cumi ngs, *The Origins of the Korean War*, 1: 148, 164, 263.

81. Kolko, *The Limits of Power*, p. 291; Cum ings, *The Origins of the Korean War*, 1: 354–55.

82. Cumings, *The Origins of the Korean War*, 1: 127–30.

83. Ibid., pp. 169–72.

84. Ibid., 2: 399,404–405.

85. "General of the Army Douglas MacArthur to the Joint Chiefs of Staff," FRUS 1945, vol. 6, p. 1145 (quoting Gen. Hodge).

86. Hastings, *The Korean War*, pp. 34–38; Cumings, *The Origins of the Korean War*, 1: 149–59, 263.

87. Cumings, *The Origins of the Korean War*, 1: 179–92.

88. Hastings, *The Korean War*, pp. 40–42.

89. Kolko, *The Limits of Power*, pp. 578–85; Cumings, *The Origins of the Korean War*, 2: 598.

4. KOREA: THE RUSSIANS ARE COMING

As viewed from Washington, the attack in Korea was initiated only nominally by the northern army, because behind the northern administration stood the Soviet Union. According to the State Department's intelligence office, "the North Korean Government is completely under Kremlin control and there is no possibility that the North Koreans acted without prior instruction from Moscow. The move against South Korea must therefore be considered a Soviet move."[1] Dean Rusk, assistant secretary of state for the Far East, declared that the "cold, cynical, flagrant aggression" had been "unleashed by the international Communist conspiracy."[2] According to President Truman, the attack showed "that the international Communist movement is prepared to use armed invasion to conquer independent nations."[3]

Not only was the Kremlin behind the Korea attack, but it made the move in Korea as part of a global plan to bring the capitalist world to its knees by force of arms. John Foster Dulles, just back from Korea, said, "Presumably the Soviet policy represented by the attack has its origin in planning of a global nature."[4] The invasion of the south, Dulles continued, showed that "international communism is prepared to use, in open warfare, the armed forces of puppet and satellite Communist states which are equipped with armament of Russian manufacture." Dulles reasoned that "Stalin long ago calculated that the best way to conquer the West was to involve it in fighting the anticolonial aspirations of Asia and the Pacific. . . . No doubt the Korean venture is designed in part to draw the Western world back into that trap."[5]

Warren Austin, our UN representative asked, "Can there be any doubt that the armed attack upon the Republic of Korea is part of a Soviet Communist plan of world domination?" The "significance of the aggression upon the Republic of Korea," he said," lies in the fact that the Communist masters of the North Korean puppets revealed by the attack their willingness to resort to armed force . . . to achieve imperialistic aims of world domination."[6]

The Central Intelligence Agency stated that the north attacked "at Soviet direction" and that "the Soviet objective is the elimination of the last remaining anti-Communist bridgehead on the mainland of northern Asia, thereby undermining the position of the United States and the Western Powers throughout the Far East."[7] So the scenario developed: the attack in Korea was a move on a global chessboard, and Washington awaited the next move.

President Truman even thought that the Korea attack was the first of a planned series of Soviet-backed invasions in Asia.[8] To stem the tide, Truman rushed to plug other potential holes in the dike of anti-Communism. Earlier he had said we would not defend Taiwan (Formosa) if China attacked it, but Korea made him revise his thinking. "The attack upon Korea," Truman declared, "makes it plain beyond all doubt that communism has passed beyond the use of subversion to conquer independent nations and will now use armed invasion and war. . . .. In these circumstances, the occupation of Formosa by Communist forces would be a direct threat to the security of the Pacific area and to United States forces performing their lawful and necessary functions in that area. Accordingly, I have ordered the Seventh Fleet to prevent any attack on Formosa."[9]

At the same time, Truman moved to shore up the French colonialists in Indochina, where they were under pressure from a nationalist insurgency in Vietnam. In May 1950, he began sending financial aid to France for Indochina,[10] and when hostilities began in Korea, he ordered an "acceleration in the furnishing of military assistance to the forces of France and the Associated States in Indo-China and the dispatch of a military mission to provide close working relations with those forces."[11]

Despite these statements of foreboding from the Truman administration, there was no evidence that the Soviet government had instigated a hostile advance by the northern army, or that the Korean hostilities were part of a Communist master plan.[12] From what can be determined of Soviet intentions, the Kremlin did not want a confrontation with us in Korea.[13] In 1945, as we saw, it had agreed to let the United States occupy Korea south of the 38th parallel, even though it could easily have taken the whole peninsula before we got there.[14] In 1948, the Soviet Union withdrew its occupation forces from Korea, well before we withdrew ours.[15] After withdrawing, the Soviets gave the northern administration arms and airplanes, but not the latest models (the planes it sent were props, not jets), and they charged the Koreans for every item.[16]

As for military advisors, the Soviet Union had only a handful in Korea, many fewer than we retained in the south.[17] Whereas our military advisors controlled the main airport in the south, the Soviet Union turned the northern airports over to the Koreans.[18] Khrushchev, although he may not be an unbiased source, said on the basis of Kim Il-sung's meeting with Stalin the previous winter, "the war wasn't Stalin's idea."[19] There is no indication that the Soviet government knew that hostilities would commence when they did in Korea.[20] The CIA had nothing to show that the Soviet Union was giving the north equipment for a major assault on the south in early 1950.[21] Three days into the fighting, CIA Director Roscoe Hillenkoetter admitted to the National Security Council that he had no evidence that the Soviet Union would support the north's war effort. Beyond Korea, he said there was little Soviet military activity anywhere in the far east.[22] In private comments, the Truman administration was less sure of the Soviet role than in its bombastic public declarations.[23]

Nor is there indication that the Soviets helped the northern administration plan military tactics as the fighting unfolded.[24] The Soviet government even took tentative steps to assume the role of peacemaker in the

Korean fighting. On July 6, Deputy Foreign Minister Andrei Gromyko informed the British ambassador in Moscow that his government wanted a peaceful settlement in Korea.[25] Our ambassador in Moscow thought the Soviet effort was "genuine," telling Secretary Acheson in a top-secret cable that the Soviet Union was "not disposed to enlarge the conflict into a general Asian or world conflagration."[26] The ambassador's analysis contradicted the thesis that the Korean attack was part of a Soviet plan to take over the world.

One other inconvenient fact cast doubt on Washington's analysis. If the Soviet Union was responsible, it was strange that it absented itself from the UN Security Council, where the war would surely be discussed. But, as we saw, in June 1950, the Soviet Union was boycotting Security Council meetings because the Council had refused to give China's seat to the mainland China government.[27] Under Security Council procedures, the Soviet Union enjoyed veto power over Council decisions. Its absence allowed the Council to condemn the north and to set up a UN command to fight for the south. Had the Soviet Union orchestrated the Korean attack, staying away from the Council made no sense.[28]

Yet, despite this lack of evidence of a direct Soviet hand in Korea, Truman had little difficulty, given the cold war atmosphere of the time, in convincing the public that the Kremlin was behind the Korean fighting. Polls conducted in August 1950 showed a 75 percent approval rating for Truman's decision to send troops to Korea, and of this 75 percent, more than half said their reason was to stop the Soviet Union.[29]

To the extent our policy makers actually thought that the Soviet Union was pulling the strings in Korea—and some doubtless did—that belief was based on assumptions about Soviet ideology, not on hard facts. In the cold war thinking of the time, the West needed to confront communism sooner or later, and better sooner than later. Knowing little about Korea, administration officials interpreted the Korean hostilities based upon what they knew about Europe, where we were in a push-pull with the Soviet Union for control of the continent. The same must be happening, they thought, in Korea.[30]

The key to Truman's strong reaction to the ambiguous hostilities in

Korea may be found in the plans he had already inaugurated for dealing with the Soviet Union. Through the early months of 1950, administration staffers prepared a policy paper titled "United States Objectives and Programs for National Security." Designated by the National Security Council as NSC 68, and dated April 7, 1950, the paper called for permanent militarization to confront communism. In a major shift away from the massive U.S. demilitarization that followed World War II, NSC 68 affirmed that we should "develop a level of military readiness which can be maintained as long as necessary as a deterrent to Soviet aggression."[31] The outbreak of war in Korea gave Truman an opportunity to begin permanent militarization.[32]

While Truman embraced the NSC 68 philosophy, his primary concern was Europe, not Asia. He wanted Congress to build up our forces in Europe to oppose the Soviet Union, but he was having trouble convincing Congress of the need. From Truman's perspective, a conflict in Korea might help pry open the federal coffers for a European buildup.[33]

In addition to Truman, there was one other major player in U.S. policy on Korea. General Douglas MacArthur took Truman's confrontation with communism even more seriously than Truman himself. In MacArthur's thinking, the United States had to face down China, and soon, before it became too strong.[34]

NOTES

1. "Intelligence Estimate Prepared by the Estimates Group, Office of Intelligence Research, Department of State: Korea," June 25, 1950, FRUS 1950, vol. 7, p. 149.

2. Dean Rusk, "Fundamentals of Far Eastern Foreign Policy," September 9, 1950, DSB, vol. 23, p. 466 (1950).

3. Harry S. Truman, "The Korean Situation: Its Significance to the People of the United States," July 19, 1950, DSB, vol. 23, p. 165 (1950).

4. "Memorandum by Mr. John Foster Dulles, Consultant to the Secretary of State," June 29, 1950, FRUS 1950, vol. 7, p. 238.

5. John Foster Dulles, "U.S. Military Actions in Korea," July 7, 1950, DSB, vol. 23, pp. 89–90 (1950).

6. John C. Ross, U.S. Deputy Representative in the Security Council, "The Threat of Communist Imperialism," August 23, 1950, DSB, vol. 23, p. 380 (1950).

7. Truman Papers, President's Secretary Files, June 28, 1950, in Rosemary Foot, *The Wrong War: American Policy and the Dimensions of the Korean Conflict, 1950-1953* (1985), p.59.

8. Max Hastings, *The Korean War* (1987), p.59.

9. "Statement by President Truman," June 27, 1950, DSB, vol. 23, p. 5 (1950).

10. Robert J. Donovan, *Tumultuous Years: The Presidency of Harry S. Truman 1949-1953* (1982), p. 146.

11. "Statement Issued by the President," June 27, 1950, FRUS 1950, vol. 7, p. 203.

12. Hastings, *The Korean War*, p. 51; Bruce Cumings, *The Roaring of the Cataract 1945–1950*, vol. 2 of *The Origins of the Korean War* (1990), p. 453.

13. I. F. Stone, *The Hidden History of the Korean War* (1952), p. 63.

14. Cumings, *The Origins of the Korean War*, 2: 631–32.

15. Harry S. Truman, "The Korean Situation: Its Significance to the People of the United States," July 19, 1950, DSB, vol. 23, p. 163 (1950); Hastings, *The Korean War*, p. 42.

16. Cumings, *The Origins of the Korean War*, 2: 446, 616.

17. *Khrushchev Remembers*, Strobe Talbott, ed. (1970), pp. 369–71; Cumings, *The Origins of the Korean War*, 2: 444.

18. Cumings, *The Origins of the Korean War*, 2: 444.

19. *Khrushchev Remembers*, p. 368.

20. Wilbur Hitchcock, "North Korea Jumps the Gun," *Current History*, March 1951, pp. 142–43.

21. Cumings, *The Origins of the Korean War*, 2: 447.

22. "Memorandum of National Security Council Consultants' Meeting," June 29, 1950, FRUS 1950, vol. 1, p.329.

23. Joyce Kolko and Gabriel Kolko, *The Limits of Power: The World and United States Foreign Policy, 1945-1954* (1972), p. 586.

24. Hastings, *The Korean War*, pp. 116, 121.

25. "The Ambassador in the Soviet Union (Kirk) to the Secretary of State," July 6, 1950, 8:00 P.M., FRUS 1950, vol. 7, p. 312.

26. "The Ambassador in the Soviet Union (Kirk) to the Secretary of State," July 6, 1950, 9:00 P.M., FRUS 1950, vol. 7, pp. 315–16.

27. SCOR, 5th yr., 473rd mtg., pp. I, 16-18, UN Doe. S/PV.473 (1950).

28. Stone, *The Hidden History of the Korean War*, p. 66; Cumings, *The Origins of the Korean War*, 2: 637.

29. John E. Mueller, *War, Presidents and Public Opinion* (1973), p. 48.

30. Bruce Cumings, *Liberation and the Emergence of Separate Regimes, 1945-1947*, vol. 1 of *The Origins of the Korean War* (1981), pp. 226–27.

31. "A Report to the President Pursuant to the President's Directive of January 31, 1950," April 7, 1950, FRUS 1950, vol. 1, p. 289.

32. Donovan, *Tumultuous Years*, pp. 241–47; Cumings, *The Origins of the Korean War*, 2: 627–28.

33. Kolko, *The Limits of Power*, p. 598.

34. Ibid., pp. 592–93.

5. KOREA: THE CHINESE HORDES

The Truman administration did not blame China for the outbreak of hostilities in Korea, and no evidence ever surfaced to suggest it played a role.[1] In the early phases of the war, China did not strategize with the northern leadership, although China was wary of our intentions toward it, mainly because of President Truman's statement that we would defend Taiwan. Considering Taiwan to be a part of China, the Chinese leadership called Truman's declaration about Taiwan "criminal aggression against the territory of China."[2]

By August 1950, MacArthur's Eighth Army held only a small area around Pusan, but the northern army, try though it did, was unable to dislodge MacArthur from Korea. At that point a helping hand from China might have let the northern army succeed, but China stayed out. Had China been planning to enter the Korean war to help the north, that would have been the time; China's inaction at that juncture suggests that it was planning to sit the war out.[3]

In September, deciding he had withdrawn far enough to the south, MacArthur staged an amphibious landing at Inchon, just west of Seoul, where he met little resistance because the northern forces were thin there. Simultaneously, MacArthur pushed northward from the area around Pusan, driving the northern army back to the 38th parallel. By that time

MacArthur's forces outnumbered the northern army ten to one, and the northern army could do little but retreat.[4]

When MacArthur reached the 38th parallel, he did not conceal his aim to go further, to reunite Korea under the southern administration. While others in the administration were of the same mind, they nonetheless asked themselves whether we would be invading another country if we pushed north. Secretary of State Acheson put the concern to rest, calling the 38th parallel only "a surveyor's line," meaning that Korea was a single country.[5] Warren Austin, our UN delegate, called the 38th parallel an "artificial barrier" that "has no basis for existence either in law or in reason," and one that was recognized by neither side. "An ancient people," Austin said, "has waited long and suffered much for freedom, independence, and unity."[6]

In taking this position, Acheson and Austin seemed untroubled by the UN's rationale for action in Korea, namely, that North Korea had committed aggression against South Korea. Once the administration decided it had a chance to take Communist territory, what in June had been an international border quickly became only an imaginary line.[7]

On October 7, MacArthur sent his troops north across the 38th parallel, which brought a reaction from China and a threat to enter the war. With the Truman administration viewing the Korean hostilities as a deliberate attack by world communism, China could not be sure that MacArthur would stop at the Korea-China border. Truman's announcement in June that we would defend Taiwan suggested to China that we were assuming a major military role in Asia, and that we might invade China itself.[8]

Although the administration had not in fact laid plans to invade China, the concern of the Chinese leadership was far from irrational. MacArthur, in fact, was hoping for a chance to invade China. In his memoirs on the Korean war, General Matthew Ridgway, the army's deputy chief of staff, reported that in August 1950, he discussed with MacArthur the possibility that China might intervene in Korea or in Taiwan. MacArthur responded to Ridgway, "I pray nightly that they will."[9] China's fears of a U.S. invasion were shared by Great Britain, whose foreign minister, Ernest Bevin, cautioned the administration against military action in Chinese territory, asking Truman to tell MacArthur not to "take reprisals" inside China.[10]

Chinese fears were enhanced when MacArthur quickly pushed north against the collapsing northern army, occupying Pyongyang and moving up to the Yalu River, which separates Korea from China's province of Manchuria. On October 29, Peking radio called MacArthur's rapid advance a threat to China.[11] The Chinese government was concerned not only about an invasion of its own territory, but also about generating stations in Korea, just south of the Yalu River, that supplied electrical power to China. That concern brought China's first military involvement in Korea, when in late October, it sent troops across the Yalu to the area of the power installations.[12]

Analyzing China's move, the CIA said that its "main motivation" was "to establish a 'cordon sanitaire' south of the Yalu River" to "guarantee security of the Manchurian border from UN forces" and to "insure continued flow of electric power from the vital Suiho hydroelectric system to the industries of Manchuria." The CIA noted that "the UN has made no statement regarding the distribution of Suiho power after UN forces take possession, and Chinese Communist apprehension may have been increased by the recent statement of a South Korean general that all power to Manchuria would be cut off."[13] Thus, the insertion of Chinese troops into the area south of the Yalu River was the result of concern about protecting China and its power supply; it did not presage any general Chinese involvement in the Korean war.[14]

MacArthur's push to the Yalu was the more threatening to China because of his close relation with General Chiang Kal-shek, the ruler of Taiwan, who harbored aspirations to retake the Chinese mainland, from which he had been driven in 1949. According to an October 25 report from Canada's consul in Nanking, MacArthur's connection with Chiang was a major source of China's apprehension about U.S. intentions.[15]

Despite the CIA assessment of China's motives, MacArthur denounced China's troop entry into Korea as an act of deliberate aggression, calling it "one of the most offensive acts of international lawlessness of historic record."[16] But our allies were concerned more about MacArthur than about China. Typical was the reaction of Hume Wrong, Canada's ambassador to the United States, who told Washington he worried that MacArthur "might go ahead too rapidly in its reaction to Chinese intervention."[17] Although MacArthur was claiming a massive Chinese intervention, few Chinese soldiers were to be found in Korea.[18]

To make matters worse, MacArthur ordered attacks in Korea that seemed directed against China. On November 3, the Marines' Tenth Corps attacked the Changjin reservoir, site of a major hydroelectric complex near the Yalu River that produced power for China. One journalist called the attack "a deliberate invitation to a fight" with China, because holding the border area was unnecessary for effective control of the northern half of Korea.[19]

MacArthur's recklessness caused alarm even within the administration, when a report reached Washington that the U.S. Air Force planned to bomb a Yalu River bridge at Sinuiju, an important Korean border city. Secretary of State Acheson, Deputy Under Secretary of Defense Robert Lovett, and Assistant Secretary Rusk recommended against the bombing, because the Chinese might see it as a preface to a full-scale invasion of their country.[20] Reacting to the same report, the Joint Chiefs of Staff instructed MacArthur not to attack any target within five miles of the Yalu River.[21] But almost immediately, for reasons that remain unclear, the Joint Chiefs relented and told MacArthur he could bomb the "Korean end" of the Yalu River bridge at Sinuiju.[22]

MacArthur, quick to seize the opportunity, bombed Sinuiju on November 7, destroying 90 percent of the city.[23] From there he proceeded to bomb Uiju, another major Yalu River city,[24] as well as a number of other Yalu River bridges.[25] This bombing brought a reaction from Great Britain, which pushed the administration to set up a demilitarized buffer zone south of the Yalu for the purpose of keeping MacArthur off China's doorstep.[26] MacArthur, however, rejected the idea, and the administration did not press him on the point.[27]

At the UN, delegates were frantic that MacArthur might provoke China into sending more troops into Korea, thereby escalating the war.

France, Yugoslavia, and Australia all told our delegate that if MacArthur insisted on taking all Korea up to the Yalu River, the administration should at least assure China that its electric power would not be cut off and promise that the hydroelectric facilities would not be damaged.[28] However, for reasons that again are unclear, the administration refused to give China any such assurances.[29]

MacArthur was anxious to carry the war into China, and China got the message. Our consul general in Hong Kong reported in a cable that "non-Communist Chinese" told him that the "Chinese Communists actually fear U.S. intends [to] invade Manchuria and that this is [an] important reason for their intervention in Korea."[30] According to the State Department's top China expert, Chinese government publications showed "that the Chinese Communist leaders view those UN actions as reflecting aggressive American intentions against China."[31] Our ambassador in the Netherlands passed along a cable from the Dutch chargé in Peking, expressing the chargé's view that the Chinese intervention in Korea was "primarily influenced by fear [of] U.S. aggression, particularly U.S. aims re Manchuria." The chargé said that China's expressed fear of our aggression against Manchuria was "real."[32]

MacArthur was not alone in sounding belligerent. Other U.S. commanders threatened to invade China. These comments worried a top State Department official, who complained of "irresponsible and provocative statements attributed to high American officers. Undoubtedly they have served to arouse further the suspicions of the Chinese as to our intentions."[33]

As MacArthur bombed along the Yalu River, he claimed that his purpose was to stop a Chinese invasion, but, according to a U.S. military communique, the Chinese forces were by then retreating.[34] On November 9, our chargé d'affaires in Korea reported, in truncated cable language, "considerable decrease late yesterday and last night in number vehicles moving southward across Yalu; Chinese forces have withdrawn northward; Chinese intervention thus far cannot be regarded as of direct, open nature. "[35] Despite MacArthur's claim that there were 60,000 Chinese troops in Korea,[36] the CIA on November 1 had estimated only 15,000 to

20,000,[37] and by November 8, 30,000 to 40,000.[38] On November 17, MacArthur reduced his own estimate to 25,000 to 30,000.[39]

MacArthur's apparently exaggerated and fluctuating estimates of Chinese troop strength were a further source of concern to U.S. allies.[40] Sir William Slim, chief of Britain's general staff, accused MacArthur of "colouring both intelligence and operational reports" during this period "to suit his own ends," which, Slim said, were to promote his aim of invading China.[41]

If Chinese troops were in Korea in large numbers, they were not doing much. Belying MacArthur's claims of massive Chinese action, our chargé d'affaires reported on November 14 that "no enemy aircraft were observed over northwestern Korea yesterday";[42] on November 18, "Contact with Chinese Communist forces in Eighth Army and Tenth Corps [in] areas [of] North Korea continued negligible yesterday";[43] and on November 19, "There continued yesterday to be virtually no contact between UN and CCF [Chinese Communist forces] forces in North Korea."[44] On November 23, our ambassador reported, "contact with Chinese both on ground and in air has been virtually negligible last three days."[45]

Far from starting an all-out assault on U.S. forces, the Chinese appeared content to protect the few positions they held just south of the Yalu River. The chargé reported, "Chinese Communist forces continue [to] remain strictly on defensive giving ground invariably in face [of] U.S. units moving northward; supplies and equipment are not coming from Manchuria in any substantial quantities." He concluded that Chinese forces were "not committed to all-out intervention."[46] While concerned about its own electricity supply as well as its own territory, China was apparently not anxious to engage MacArthur any more than necessary.[47]

As MacArthur engaged the vanishing Chinese, our allies continued to worry that he was provoking war with China. Acheson and Rusk reported "anxiety" among "friendly members of the UN" about "our becoming more deeply involved perhaps finally in war with Communist China."[48] Still, the administration said nothing to allay China's concern.

Instead of backing off, MacArthur planned a new offensive to take all the hydroelectric installations and to seize the small area south of the Yalu River that remained in Korean hands.[49] He launched his attack on November 24, but could not find Chinese forces to engage.[50] Our ambassador informed Washington, "Few if any Chinese troops were encountered," and that MacArthur met "little enemy resistance."[51]

On November 28, however, the Chinese and the northern army began a counteroffensive, in an apparent effort to push MacArthur away from the border area. Our ambassador reported a "general offensive" against our Eighth Army in western Korea by 48,000 Koreans and 101,000 Chinese.[52] His next report stated, "Enemy forces, composed mainly of Chinese, continued [to] exert heavy pressure yesterday in 8th Army sector. . . . There was no reported enemy air activity yesterday."[53] The Chinese were attacking on the ground, but without air support, as they were no match for U.S. forces in the air. MacArthur greeted the Chinese action as a full-scale offensive, telling the Joint Chiefs of Staff, "The Chinese military forces are committed in North Korea in great and ever increasing strength. No pretext of minor support under the guise of volunteerism or other subterfuge now has the slightest validity. We face an entirely new war."[54]

President Truman, too, said that China was launching an all-out invasion. He said we might have to use the atomic bomb against China, a statement that caused panic among our allies.[55] Our embassy in London reported "anxiety" in Britain over the "possibility that [the] atom bomb might be used in Korea thus setting off general atomic war."[56] Truman refused to retract his nuclear threat, and the army drew up contingency plans to use atomic weapons in Korea.[57]

Shortly before Christmas 1950, Truman appealed to Congress, arguing that because of the Chinese invasion, he needed an extra $16.8 billion for the military budget.[58] That represented more than a doubling of the budget, which at the time stood at $13 billion a year. Congress, convinced by Truman that we were being attacked by world communism, approved the funds.[59] Thus, Truman was well on his way to carrying out the NSC 68 policy of putting the U.S. military on a permanent war footing.

Our policy makers, in a fit of cold war hyperbole, read the Chinese counteroffensive as part of a combined Sino-Soviet plan to attack the Western powers.[60] The CIA, despite the fact that there was no hint of a Soviet role, saw a Soviet hand behind the Chinese counteroffensive: "The Soviet rulers have resolved to pursue aggressively their world-wide attack on the power position of the United States and its allies."[61] Secretary Acheson concurred in this doomsday analysis: "the central enemy is not the Chinese but the Soviet Union."[62] Acheson cabled our ambassador in India to warn him that India might be next on China's hit list: "invasion Korea by Chi Commies is part of plan to over-run all countries of E. and S. Asia."[63] Even the State Department's China expert, who should have known better, declared that "the free world is now in the preliminary stage of World War III."[64]

In response to the Chinese counteroffensive, MacArthur ordered a retreat southward. On the eastern side of the peninsula, "The X [Tenth] Corps is being withdrawn into the Hamhung area as rapidly as possible," MacArthur notified the Joint Chiefs of Staff.[65] As for the western side, our ambassador reported, "UN forces in Eighth Army sector continued withdrawal and regrouping actions yesterday and day before. CCF forces moved southward, but there only light contact and that mainly in eastern sector of front."[66]

As the ambassador's cable suggested, the retreat was not required by hostile action on the part of the Chinese forces. MacArthur said as much, stating that he retreated because of the overwhelming numbers of the Chinese forces, which he put at 200,000.[67] The Chinese and north Korean forces followed our retreat but did not attack.[68] The *Times* of London reported that the Chinese had "made not the slightest attempt" to approach the rear of the Eighth Army, and that there was "no clear evidence that they strove to bar its road."[69] As the Eighth Army and Tenth Corps withdrew, the Chinese forces harassed,[70] but they did not seriously engage them.[71]

Reports from the field confirmed the lack of military action. General Omar Bradley, chairman of the Joint Chiefs of Staff, said on December 4 that "there had not been very much pressure on the western front during the last 24 hours; [t]he Tenth Corps is being concentrated in the Hamhung-Hungnam beachhead. . . . The Seventh Division was proceeding with its withdrawal without too much opposition," Bradley stated. "There has been very little enemy air lately."[72]

Similarly, our ambassador reported, "Contact between CCF [Chinese Communist Forces] and UN forces in Eighth Army sector remained light yesterday as latter forces continued withdrawal."[73] And two days later, "Contact between UN and CCF forces in Eighth Army sector remained virtually nil yesterday."[74] On December 12, the American ambassador said that during the previous three days there had been almost no hostile contact in the Eighth Army sector.[75]

MacArthur continued to withdraw, but still the Chinese, who were supposed to be starting World War III, did not attack. On December 15, the ambassador reported, "Past 3 days have seen no contact between 8th Army units and CCF. In X [Tenth] Corps area UN units continue withdrawal without any noteworthy CCF pressure."[76] And on December 18, "Eighth Army. . .remain[s] out of contact with Chinese Communist forces. Tenth corps continues withdrawal from Hungnam with increasing CCF pressure reported."[77] Finally, on December 21, "During past 3 days UN forces in Eighth Army sector continued out of contact with CCF. Light contact was maintained, however, with North Korean forces in 38th parallel area."[78]

The speed of our retreat and the low level of hostile contact suggested that MacArthur was doing the same thing he had done in July—withdrawing to make the enemy look stronger and to gain political support for an all-out attack, this time on China.[79] The specter of a Chinese menace might move Truman to order an attack on that country. India's ambassador in Peking said that China's intervention in Korea "is what the Americans. . .want" for "a showdown with China. In any case MacArthur's dream has come true."[80]

MacArthur apparently saw in China's entry, which he had provoked, an opportunity to fight the inevitable war against communism.[81] As he withdrew southward, MacArthur called for air raids into China, telling the Joint Chiefs of Staff that our air power could destroy "China's industrial capacity to wage war."[82] MacArthur asked the Joint Chiefs of Staff for permission for "naval and air attacks on objectives in Communist China," but the Joint Chiefs turned him down.[83]

By the end of 1950, Chinese forces had come as far south as the 38th parallel, and on New Years Day 1951, MacArthur announced that they had commenced a new offensive to go even farther.[84] MacArthur continued his retreat, evacuating Seoul and pulling his troops farther south.[85]

Again, however, the Chinese failed to appear for the attack MacArthur announced they had made. They followed at a distance but did not engage U.S. troops. It was MacArthur, in fact, who initiated the first significant contact, when in mid-January 1951 he stopped and attacked, and the Chinese forces fell back without serious resistance.[86] By March 1951, MacArthur stood once again on the 38th parallel.

As for the Soviet Union, it did little to justify the CIA charge that it was behind China's move into Korea. After Chinese troops entered Korea, the Soviet Union remained firmly on the sidelines. It provided China with arms but demanded cash payment for them.[87]

Despite his best efforts, MacArthur did not get his wish of invading China. In April 1951, even Truman became frightened at MacArthur's aspirations and fired him. After that, the Korean war continued for two more costly years, with desultory fighting around the 38th parallel, and as the stalemate dragged on, both Congress and the public lost their enthusiasm for the war. By the time the Korean war ended, we had lost 34,000 of our soldiers, while Korea had sustained over two million civilian dead.[88]

The war cost Korea more than lives. It left the country in ruins: "in the capital at Seoul, hollow buildings stood like skeletons alongside streets paved with weird mixtures of concrete and shrapnel." In the north, "Pyongyang and other cities were heaps of bricks and ashes, factories stood empty, massive dams no longer held their water," As the war ended, "people emerged from a mole-like existence in caves and tunnels to find a nightmare in the bright of day."[89]

President Truman had convinced the public to support his intervention in Korea by painting a picture of the conflict that bore little relation to reality. He portrayed a civil war as international. The public, unaware of General Hodge's harsh occupation policy, and receptive to cold war claims, accepted Truman's analysis. Congress and the public thought we were responding to a major global challenge, when in fact it was we who turned a civil war in a small country into a global confrontation.

NOTES

1. Max Hastings, *The Korean War* (1987), p. 133.

2. Rosemary Foot, *The Wrong War: American Policy and the Dimensions of the Korean Conflict, 1950-1953* (1985), p. 65.

3. Wilbur Hitchcock, "North Korea Jumps the Gun," *Current History*, March 1951, p. 139.

4. Joyce and Gabriel Kolko, *The Limits of Power: The World and United States Foreign Policy,1945–1954* (1972), p. 595.

5. Hastings, *The Korean War*, p. 116.

6. "Statement by Austin to U.N. Committee on the Future of Korea," *New York Times*, October 1, 1950, p. A3, col. 1.

7. Bruce Cumings, *The Roaring of the Cataract, 1945–1950*, vol. 2 of *The Origins of the Korean War* (1990), pp. 710–11.

8. Hastings, *The Korean War*, p. 133.

9. Matthew Ridgway, *The Korean War* (1967), pp. 37–38.

10. "Memorandum of Conversation, by the Ambassador at Large (Jessup)," October 12, 1950, FRUS 1950, vol. 7, p. 932.

11. I. F. Stone, *The Hidden History of the Korean War* (1952), p. 161.

12. "Memorandum by the Director of the Central Intelligence Agency (Smith) to the President," November 1, 1950, FRUS 1950, vol. 7, p. 1025.

13. Ibid., pp. 1025–26.

14. Hastings, *The Korean War*, p. 341.

15. "Memorandum of Conversation, by the Deputy Director of the Office of Chinese Affairs (Perkins)," November 3, 1950, FRUS 1950, vol. 7, p. 1032.

16. "Text of MacArthur Statement," *New York Times*, November 6, 1950, p. A5, col. 1.

17. "Memorandum of Conversation, by the Acting Officer in Charge of Korean Affairs (Emmons)," November 6, 1950, FRUS 1950, vol. 7, p. 1065.

18. Walter Sullivan, "U.S. Bids U.N. Act on Chinese in Korea After M'Arthur Identifies Red Units; Foe Withdraws in Surprise Maneuver," *New York Times*, November 7, 1950, p. Al, col. 8.

19. Stone, *The Hidden History of the Korean War*, pp. 164–65.

20. "Memorandum of Conference Between Secretary Acheson, [Deputy] Under Secretary of Defense Lovett, and Mr. Dean Rusk," November 6, 1950, FRUS 1950, vol. 7, p. 1055.

21. "The Joint Chiefs of Staff to the Commander in Chief, Far East (MacArthur)," November 6, 1950,11:47 A.M., FRUS 1950, vol. 7, p. 1057.

22. "The Joint Chiefs of Staff to the Commander in Chief, Far East (MacArthur)," November 6, 1950, 11:57 P.M., FRUS 1950, vol. 7, p. 1076.

23. Lindesay Parrott, "379 Planes Rip Foe's New Capital Below Manchuria," *New York Times*, November 9, 1950, p. Al, col. 1.

24. Lindesay Parrott, "Chinese Continue March into Korea Despite Air Blows," *New York Times*, November 11, 1950, p. Al, col. 8.

25. Lindesay Parrott, "60,000 Chinese Reds in War, More Ready, M'Arthur Says; West Asks U.N. Debate Now," *New York Times*, November 10, 1950, p. Al, col. 8; "The Chargé in Korea (Drumright) to the Secretary of State," November 12, 1950, FRUS 1950, vol. 7, p. 1135; "The Chargé in Korea (Drumright) to the Secretary of State," November 14, 1950, FRUS 1950, vol. 7, p. 1147.

26. Foot, *The Wrong War*, p. 92.

27. "The Commander in Chief, Far East (MacArthur) to the Joint Chiefs of Staff," November 9, 1950, FRUS 1950, vol. 7, pp. 1108–1109.

28. "The United States Representative at the United Nations (Austin) to the Secretary of State," November 6, 1950, FRUS 1950, vol. 7, p. 1074.

29. Foot, *The Wrong War*, p. 95.

30. "The Consul General at Hong Kong (Wilkinson) to the Secretary of State," November 9, 1950, FRUS 1950, vol. 7, p. 1123.

31. "Memorandum by the Director of the Office of Chinese Affairs (Clubb) to the Assistant Secretary of State for Far Eastern Affairs (Rusk)," November 10, 1950, FRUS 1950, vol. 7, p. 1124.

32. "The Ambassador in the Netherlands (Chapin) to the Secretary of State," November 14, 1950, FRUS 1950, vol. 7, p. 1152.

33. "Memorandum by the Deputy Assistant Secretary of State for Far Eastern Affairs (Merchant) to the Assistant Secretary of State for Far Eastern Affairs (Rusk)," November 16, 1950, FRUS 1950, vol. 7, p. 1164.

34. Parrott, "379 U.S. Planes Rip Foe's New Capital Below Manchuria."

35. "The Chargé in Korea (Drumright) to the Secretary of State," November 9, 1950, FRUS 1950, vol. 7, p. 1116.

36. Parrott, "60,000 Chinese Reds in War, More Ready, M'Arthur Says; West Asks U.N. Debate Now."

37. "Memorandum by the Director of the Central Intelligence Agency (Smith) to the President," November 1, 1950.

38. "Memorandum by the Central Intelligence Agency: Chinese Communist Intervention in Korea," November 8, 1950, FRUS 1950, vol. 7, p. 1101.

39. "Memorandum of Conversation, by the Ambassador in Korea (Muccio)," November 17, 1950, FRUS 1950, vol. 7, p. 1175.

40. Hastings, *The Korean War*, p. 192.

41. Ibid., p. 200.

42. "The Chargé in Korea (Drumright) to the Secretary of State," November 14, 1950, FRUS 1950, vol. 7, p. 1147.

43. "The Chargé in Korea (Drumright) to the Secretary of State," November 18, 1950, FRUS 1950, vol. 7, p. 1184.

44. "The Chargé in Korea (Drumright) to the Secretary of State," November 19, 1950, FRUS 1950, vol. 7, p. 1190.

45. "The Ambassador in Korea (Muccio) to the Secretary of State," November 23, 1950, FRUS 1950, vol. 7, p. 1216.

46. "The Chargé in Korea (Drumright) to the Secretary of State," November 18, 1950.

47. Hastings, *The Korean War*, p. 132.

48. "Memorandum of Conversation, by the Ambassador at Large (Jessup)," November 21, 1950, FRUS 1950, vol. 7, p. 1205.

49. "Memorandum of Conversation, by the Political Adviser in Japan (Sebald)," November 14, 1950, FRUS 1950, vol. 7, pp. 1148–49.

50. Lindesay Parrott, "Allies Sweep Ahead on Korean Front," *New York Times*, November 25, 1950, p. A1, col. 8.

51. "The Ambassador in Korea (Muccio) to the Secretary of State," November 25, 1950, FRUS 1950, vol. 7, p. 1233.

52. "The Ambassador in Korea (Muccio) to the Secretary of State," November 28, 1950, FRUS 1950, vol. 7, p. 1238.

53. "The Ambassador in Korea (Muccio) to the Secretary of State," November 29, 1950, FRUS 1950, vol. 7, p. 1251.

54. "The Commander in Chief, Far East (MacArthur) to the Joint Chiefs of Staff," November 28, 1950, FRUS 1950, vol. 7, p. 1237.

55. "Statement by the President," November 30, 1950, and "President Clarifies Position on Use of Atom Bomb in Warfare," November 30, 1950, DSB, vol. 23, p. 925 (1950).

56. "The Chargé in the United Kingdom (Holmes) to the Secretary of State," December I, 1950, FRUS 1950, vol. 7, p. 1296.

57. Hastings, *The Korean War*, p. 183.

58. "Special Message to the Congress Requesting Additional Appropriations for Defense," December 1, 1950, *Public Papers of the Presidents of the United States: Harry S. Truman, 1950* (1965), pp. 728–31.

59. Second Supplemental Appropriations Act, January 6, 1951, U.S. Congress, Statutes at Large, vol. 64, p. 1223 (1951).

60. Hastings, *The Korean War*, p. 177; Foot, *The Wrong War*, pp. 101–105.

61. "Memorandum by the Central Intelligence Agency," December 2, 1950, FRUS. 1950, vol. 7, pp. 1309–10.

62. "United States Delegation Minutes of the First Meeting of President Truman and Prime Minister Attlee," FRUS 1950, vol. 7, p. 1366.

63. "The Secretary of State to the Embassy in India," December 4, 1950, FRUS) 1950, vol. 7, p. 1377.

64. "Memorandum by the Director of the Office of Chinese Affairs (Clubb) to the Assistant Secretary of State for Far Eastern Affairs (Rusk)," December 7, 1950, FRUS 1950, vol. 7, p. 1444.

65. "The Commander in Chief, United Nations Command (MacArthur) to the Joint Chiefs of Staff," December 3, 1950, FRUS 1950, vol. 7, p. 1320.

66. "The Ambassador in Korea (Muccio) to the Secretary of State," December 4, 1950, FRUS 1950, vol. 7, p. 1346.

67. "The Commander in Chief, Far East (MacArthur) to the Joint Chiefs of Staff," November 28, 1950.

68. Hastings, *The Korean War*, pp. 187, 341.

69. "The Retreat in Korea," *Times* (London), December 18, 1950, p. 6, col. 3.

70. Hastings, *The Korean War*, pp. 157–59.

71. Ibid., pp. 137–38, 167.

72. "United States Delegation Minutes of the First Meeting of President Truman and Prime Minister Attlee," December 4, 1950, FRUS 1950, vol. 7, p. 1362.

73. "The Ambassador in Korea (Muccio) to the Secretary of State," December 5, 1950, FRUS 1950, vol. 7, p. 1381.

74. "The Ambassador in Korea (Muccio) to the Secretary of State," December 7, 1950, FRUS 1950, vol. 7, p. 1435.

75. "The Ambassador in Korea (Muccio) to the Secretary of State," December 15, 1950, FRUS 1950, vol. 7, p. 1548.

76. "The Ambassador in Korea (Muccio) to the Secretary of State," December 15, 1950, FRUS 1950, vol. 7, p. 1548.

77. "The Ambassador in Korea (Muccio) to the Secretary of State," December 18, 1950, FRUS 1950, vol. 7, p. 1565.

78. "The Ambassador in Korea (Muccio) to the Secretary of State," December 21, 1950, FRUS 1950, vol. 7, p. 1585.

79. Kolko, *The Limits of Power*, p. 605.

80. K. M. Panikkar, *In Two Chinas: Memoirs of a Diplomat* (1955), p. 111.

81. Hastings, *The Korean War*, p. 64.

82. "The Commander in Chief, Far East (MacArthur) to the Department of the Army," December 30, 1950, FRUS 1950, vol. 7, p. 1631; Hastings, *The Korean War*, p. 193.

83. "The Joint Chiefs of Staff to the Commander in Chief, Far East (MacArthur)," January 9, 1951, FRUS 1951, vol. 7, p. 42.

84. Lindesay Parrott, "Allies Fall Back to Fixed Line," *New York Times*, January 2, 1951, p. A1, col. 8.

85. "The Ambassador in Korea (Muccio) to the Secretary of State," January 6, 1951, FRUS 1951, vol. 7, p. 30; Lindesay Parrott, "Seoul Abandoned to Red Army, *New York Times*, January 4, 1951, p. A1, col. 8.

86. Hastings, *The Korean War*, pp. 195–98.

87. Ibid., pp. 230, 340.

88. Kolko, *The Limits of Power*, p. 615.

89. Bruce Cumings, *Liberation and the Emergence of Separate Regimes, 1945–1947*, vol. 1 of *The Origins of the Korean War* (1981), p. xix.

6. GUATEMALA: DECEPTION AND TIMING

When I visited Guatemala City in 1963, soldiers patrolled the streets in pairs, with machine guns at the ready. Guatemala was in a state of seemingly permanent tension following a 1954 coup that overthrew its elected president. When that coup occurred, the administration of President Dwight Eisenhower portrayed it as one more incident in the long history of political instability south of the border, and that is how the press reported it. The reality was somewhat different.

Guatemala's president in 1954, Jacobo Arbenz, had come to office in 1950 by a free election and was peacefully in control of the country. With thousands of peasants unable to make a living, Arbenz nationalized uncultivated fields belonging to the U.S.-owned United Fruit Company, a major landowner and banana producer in Guatemala. Although the nationalization did not affect United Fruit's current operations, it did take two-thirds of the land it owned in Guatemala. Arbenz offered compensation at the value United Fruit had declared its land worth for tax purposes, but the Eisenhower administration, which quickly rose to take up United Fruit's cause, demanded twenty-five times that amount.

Beyond making a financial claim on United Fruit's behalf, the Eisenhower administration denounced Arbenz as a Communist and a danger to Guatemala and the hemisphere. The United States Information Service

(USIS), working with the CIA, placed unattributed articles in Latin American newspapers "labelling certain Guatemalan officials as Communists, and also labelling certain actions of the Guatemalan government as Communist-inspired."[1] These articles were reportedly "well received by both metropolitan and provincial papers as timely and effective and were widely printed, frequently without attribution to USIS."[2] The press followed the administration's lead, depicting Arbenz as a Communist threat.[3]

If the Arbenz government was in the Soviet camp, it did not act the part. It had no diplomatic relations with the Soviet Union, and at the United Nations it generally supported our view, not the Soviets'. Arbenz, while he himself had no affiliation with Guatemala's Communist party, had appointed Communists to posts in his bureaucracy, especially in his land reform agency. But of the fifty-two members of the Guatemalan congress, only four were Communists, and none served in Arbenz's cabinet.

When Arbenz refused to change his stand on the United Fruit land, President Eisenhower secretly instructed the CIA to overthrow him.[4] The CIA plotted psychological warfare and organized a military force, recruiting Guatemalans living abroad and putting at their head a former colonel in the Guatemalan army, Carlos Castillo Armas.[5] The CIA trained this paramilitary force at a secret location near Miami, set it up at secret bases in Honduras and Nicaragua, and gave it weapons and bomber aircraft.[6]

In January 1954, a hitch developed in the coup plotting. One plot supporter betrayed the plot. He gave Arbenz incriminating letters between two conspirators, the CIA-recruited Castillo Armas and Miguel Ydígoras Fuentes, a military officer and politician who had lost the 1950 presidential election to Arbenz. The latter now saw a chance to gain by coup what he had lost at the polls. Arbenz publicized the letters and charged publicly that the United States was colluding to overthrow him.[7]

The State Department denied any role, calling Arbenz's charge "ridiculous and untrue." The State Department affirmed, "It is the policy of the United States not to intervene in the internal affairs of other nations."[8] This false denial notwithstanding, our plotting continued and intensified. The CIA set up a secret radio station to influence public opinion against Arbenz and to cow the military into submission.[9] By June 1954, the groundwork had been laid, and the CIA set the coup in motion. Castillo Armas's force, which numbered only 150, entered Guatemala from Honduras on June 18 to take up positions just inside the border. The CIA radio station, inflating the number of troops to 5,000, "reported" a nonexistent battle with government troops.[10] At the same time, CIA airplanes, some piloted by Guatemalans, some by CIA mercenaries, bombed Guatemala City."[11]

Following the Republican presidential victory in 1952, top posts in Washington had been reshuffled, and John Foster Dulles, whom we saw as a consultant in the State Department under Truman, became secretary of state. President Eisenhower appointed Dulles's brother Allen to head the CIA. Allen Dulles ran the Guatemala coup operation. In a secret communication to Eisenhower, Allen Dulles explained the CIA strategy: "The use of a small number of airplanes and the massive use of radio broadcasting are designed to build up and give main support to the impression of Castillo Armas' strength as well as to spread the impression of the regime's weakness. . ... From the foregoing description of the effort," Dulles continued, "it will be seen how important are the aspects of deception and timing."[12]

President Arbenz saw what was happening and complained to the United Nations Security Council. Arbenz told the UN that outside forces were responsible, although at that stage he was unsure about our exact role. Arbenz's main charge was not against the United States, but against Honduras and Nicaragua, where the rebel forces had massed. But Soviet delegate Semyon Tsarapkin fingered the Americans as the perpetrators. "The United States," he said, "has prepared an armed intervention against this minute Central American country of 3,000,000 inhabitants"; Tsarapkin charged that Guatemala "has been subjected to an armed attack provoked, organized, and carried out by the United States of America."[13]

Publicly we denied any role. Our UN delegate, Henry Cabot Lodge, replied to Tsarapkin, "the situation does not involve aggression but is a revolt of Guatemalans against Guatemalans." Furthermore, Lodge protested that Tsarapkin's charge was "flatly untrue; I challenge him to prove it. He cannot do so."[14] Tsarapkin had no "smoking gun" and got little support at the UN for his charge.

In Washington, the State Department kept up the pretense of non-involvement, issuing a statement that it had "no evidence that indicates that this is anything other than a revolt of Guatemalans against the Government."[15] After Castillo Armas entered Guatemala, U.S. Ambassador John Peurifoy negotiated with top-level Guatemalan military officers to urge them to move against President Arbenz. President Eisenhower had hand-picked Peurifoy for this role, firing our previous ambassador, whom he found too soft on communism. Peurifoy brought strong anti-Communist credentials to the job and enthusiastically promoted the coup.

The officers whom Peurifoy approached quickly understood that we controlled the insurgency. To gain their participation, Peurifoy told the officers that if the Communist party was suppressed, and Arbenz removed as president, the United States would "recommend" that the invading force call off its efforts. By giving that promise, Peurifoy got Colonel Carlos Díaz to pressure Arbenz to resign. "Throughout discussion [with Díaz]," Peurifoy reported to Washington, "I emphasized [the] necessity of acting quickly to round up leading Communists before they could mobilize forces."[16] As the air raids and radio broadcasts made Guatemalan military officials think they would be overwhelmed, President Arbenz resigned, viewing his situation as hopeless, and so Díaz assumed power.

That was not the end of the machinations, however, because Peurifoy was not satisfied with Díaz, either. As part of the takeover, Díaz let Arbenz make a resignation speech on radio, in which he laid out the U.S. role in ousting him, at least as much of it as he knew. Arbenz said on the broadcast that we had supplied pilots for the air raids over Guatemala City—which was true—and charged that we had used communism merely as a pretext to commit aggression against Guatemala.

Upset with the speech, Peurifoy told Díaz to bring another officer, Colonel Elfego Monzón, into the ruling group,[17] and he urged both Díaz and Monzón to negotiate with Castillo Armas.[18] Monzón, who replaced Díaz as president,[19] agreed to negotiate with Castillo Armas.[20] With the power change moving in a favorable direction, Peurifoy called the State Department to point out that the bombing of Guatemala City was still going on and to ask "if there wasn't some way to get word to Armas to stop it."[21] We had won, so it was time to call the CIA's army off.

Peurifoy convinced Monzón to take Castillo Armas into the new ruling junta and to elect him its president, and the junta complied.[22] Next, the junta, canceling the Arbenz nationalization decrees, returned United Fruit's land. At the White House, President Eisenhower and his vice-president, Richard Nixon, held a secret celebration with the CIA operatives.[23]

For public consumption, John Foster Dulles gave a version of the coup that showed us squarely on the sidelines. "Led by Castillo Armas," he said, "patriots arose in Guatemala to challenge the Communist leadership—and to change it. Thus, the situation is being cured by the Guatemalans themselves."[24] For John Foster Dulles, Guatemala and its banana plantations were not unfamiliar territory. In 1936, as United Fruit's attorney, Dulles had drafted the concession agreements for the land Arbenz nationalized in the 1950s.

Peurifoy, too, maintained the pretense that we were not involved. Concealing his own role, Peurifoy declared, "The Guatemalan people themselves rose up and gave their support to a courageous leader, Col. Carlos Castillo Armas, in a brief encounter which pushed Arbenz' Communist clique from the seats of power." Said Peurifoy, "The task of liberation of Guatemala from communism was carried out by the Guatemalan people themselves."[25] When he received Guatemala's new postcoup ambassador in Washington, President Eisenhower also covered up our role, saying that "the people of Guatemala, in a magnificent effort, have liberated themselves from the shackles of international Communist direction."[26]

For years, little information surfaced on the CIA role in the Guatemala coup. A magazine article later in 1954 indicated that the CIA had sent guns and ammunition to Castillo Armas in Honduras. This information was apparently "leaked" by the CIA itself, torn between keeping the operation secret and taking credit for it.[27] In his memoirs, President Eisenhower acknowledged that he had authorized the CIA to fly bombing missions over Guatemala City while the coup was in progress, at a time when success was in doubt, but that made it look only as if we were helping at the last moment, when the coup makers ran into trouble.[28] Eisenhower never acknowledged that he authorized the entire operation.

Several of those involved later wrote memoirs detailing the CIA role. David Atlee Phillips, a CIA principal in the affair, gave an extensive account.[29] John Moors Cabot, who at the time had been assistant secretary of state for western hemisphere affairs, wrote that the CIA "staged" the coup.[30] Cabot had appointed a subordinate to coordinate planning for the coup between the State Department and CIA. Cabot wrote that his "principal concern" was "to keep secret any United States involvement in the projected coup."[31] Some years later, Congress looked into the Guatemala coup. The Senate select committee on intelligence called it one of "the Agency's boldest, most spectacular covert operations."[32] A major policy initiative, it had lasting consequences for our Latin America policy. To this day, it is cited by Latin nationalists as evidence that the "Colossus of the North" cannot be trusted.

Even at the time, the CIA role was widely suspected abroad, as reflected in Tsarapkin's charges. Speculation about the CIA role was so rife that Cabot was concerned that American prestige abroad had been hurt by the episode.[33] But in the United States the matter was quickly forgotten by both the press and the public. The Eisenhower administration considered the Guatemala operation a resounding success, for it had overthrown a government that had dared to counter the interests of a major American company, and no one was the wiser. This success led us to try the same tactic again elsewhere.

NOTES

1. "Report Prepared in the United States Information Agency," July 27, 1954, FRUS 1952–1954, vol. 4, pp. 1212–13.

2. Ibid., p. 1216.

3. Richard H. Immerman, *The CIA in Guatemala: The Foreign Policy of*

Intervention (1982), pp. 112–14; Jim Handy, *Gift of the Devil: A History of Guatemala* (1984), pp. 140–41.

4. John Moors Cabot, *First Line of Defense* (1979), p. 90.

5. William Colby, *Honorable Men: My Life in the CIA* (1978), p. 181; Edwin C. Hoyt, *Law and Force in American Foreign Policy* (1985), p. 104; David Wise and Thomas B. Ross, *The Invisible Government* (1964), p. 166.

6. Andrew Tully, *CIA: The Inside Story* (1962), p. 66.

7. "Guatemala Says Neighbors and U.S. Plot an Invasion," *New York Times*, January 30, 1954, p. A1, col. 4.

8. "Charges of Intervention in Guatemala Denied," DSB, vol. 30, p. 251 (1954).

9. David Atlee Phillips, *Night Watch* (1977), pp. 38–48.

10. Ibid., p. 46.

11. Hoyt, *Law and Force in American Foreign Policy*, p. 104.

12. "Memorandum by the Director of Central Intelligence (Dulles) to the President," June 20, 1954, FRUS 1952–1954, vol. 4, p. 1176.

13. SCOR, 9th yr., 675th mtg., pp. 23, 33, UN Doc. S/PV.675 (1954).

14. SCOR, 9th yr., 675th mtg., pp. 29, 31, UN Doc. S/ PV.675 (1954).

15. "Guatemalan Situation: Department Statement, June 19," DSB, vol. 30, p. 982 (1954).

16. "The Ambassador in Guatemala (Peurifoy) to the Department of State," June 27, 1954, 11 P.M., FRUS 1952–1954, vol. 4, pp. 1189–91.

17. "The Ambassador in Guatemala (Peurifoy) to the Department of State," June 28, 1954, 12 noon, FRUS 1952–1954, vol. 4, p. 1192.

18. "The Ambassador in Guatemala (Peurifoy) to the Department of State," June 28, 1954, 5 P.M., FRUS 1952–1954, vol. 4, p. 1193.

19. Immerman, *The CIA in Guatemala*, p. 175.

20. "The Ambassador in Guatemala (Peurifoy) to the Department of State," June 28, 1954, 8 P.M., FRUS 1952–1954, vol. 4, p. 1194.

21. "Memorandum of Telephone Conversation, by the Assistant Secretary of State for Inter-American Affairs (Holland)," June 29, 1954, FRUS 1952–1954, vol. 4, p. 1195.

22. "The Ambassador in Guatemala (Peurifoy) to the Department of State," July 7, 1954, FRUS 1952–1954, vol. 4, p. 1205; Immerman, *The CIA in Guatemala*, p. 177.

23. Phillips, *Night Watch*, pp. 49–51.

24. John Foster Dulles, "International Communism in Guatemala," June 30, 1954, DSB, vol. 31, p. 44 (1954).

25. "Meeting the Communist Challenge in the Western Hemisphere," August 28, 1954, DSB, vol. 31, pp. 335–36 (1954).

26. Immerman, *The CIA in Guatemala*, p. 178.

27. Richard and Gladys Harkness, "The Mysterious Doings of CIA," *Saturday Evening Post*, October 30, 1954, p. 20.

28. Dwight D. Eisenhower, *Mandate for Change 19531956* (1963), pp. 425––26.

29. Phillips, *Night Watch*, pp. 30-54.

30. Cabot, *First Line of Defense*, p. 94.

31. Ibid., pp. 90–91.

32. U.S. Senate, Select Committee to Study Governmental Operations with Respect to Intelligence Activities, *Final Report: Foreign and Military Intelligence*, Book I, 94th Cong., 2d sess., April 26, 1976, p. 111.

33. Cabot, *First Line of Defense*, p. 94.

7. INDONESIA: CAUGHT IN A COCONUT TREE

The next opportunity came on the other side of the globe. Ahmed Sukarno, who headed Indonesia's government in the 1950s, had helped free Indonesia from Dutch colonial rule in the 1940s, and he was a popular leader. A neutralist, Sukarno befriended both the Soviet Union and China. He made overtures to the Eisenhower administration; but Eisenhower kept Sukarno at arm's length. Sukarno promoted what he called "guided democracy" in Indonesia, which the State Department took as a code word for communism.[1]

In early 1958, a group of Indonesian colonels based on the Indonesian island of Sumatra withdrew their allegiance from Sukarno. They demanded local autonomy for Sumatra, were more pro-Western than Sukarno, and criticized his government as being Communist-influenced.[2] Sukarno himself did not espouse communism; in fact, the Indonesian Communist party, which had a strong local organization, was a formidable rival to Sukarno. The Communist party was popular because in the 1940s, it led the move to force the Dutch to withdraw—a move so popular that Sukarno felt he could not govern without the Communists' cooperation.[3] So he drew Communists into his government, although not into key posts.[4]

As the colonels conspired, Secretary of State Dulles removed John

Allison, our ambassador in Jakarta, calling the transfer a routine re-assignment. When reporters asked Dulles about the activity of the colonels on Sumatra, he replied, "The working out of these problems is primarily an internal problem for the Indonesian people and their Government. Actually, we observe what has gone on with interest, but we don't take any part in or interfere with these internal governmental problems."[5]

When the colonels soon after delivered an ultimatum to Sukarno, Dulles again had to comment, saying that we wanted in Indonesia a government that reflected "the real interest and desires of the people." Some reporters thought Dulles's statement implied that Sukarno's government did not fit the bill, and that we might be trying to remove it, but Dulles repeated that the conflict was "an internal problem for the Indonesian people."[6]

In February 1958, the colonels proclaimed themselves as the government of Indonesia, although they were far from being in control of the country. They controlled a healthy chunk of Sumatra, but no territory elsewhere in Indonesia. They had over 200,000 troops at their command, but no heavy weapons and no aircraft.[7] At an April 1 news conference, reporters again asked Dulles about U.S. policy. "The United States views this trouble in Sumatra as an internal matter," Dulles replied, reiterating his earlier stance. "We try to be absolutely correct in our international proceedings and attitude toward it."[8]

The Sukarno government, however, began to level public charges that American pilots were flying bombing runs for the rebels. At an April 30 news conference, President Eisenhower was asked about the charge. Like Dulles, he declared we were not involved. "When it comes to an intrastate difficulty anywhere, our policy is one of careful neutrality all the way through so as not to be taking sides where it is none of our business," Eisenhower said. "As for any United States pilots, "every rebellion that I have ever heard of has its soldiers of fortune."[9] By "soldiers of fortune," Eisenhower meant freelance fighters who sold their services. By using the term he was implicitly denying any involvement by military personnel at the behest of the U.S. government. The next day, when a reporter asked Dulles about Eisenhower's statement, Dulles denied knowing whether any Americans were active as soldiers of fortune in Indonesia, but, he added, "we have no legal obligation to control the activities of Americans of this character."[10]

By this time, the Soviet Union, too, was accusing us of having a hand in the Indonesian rebellion. Deputy Undersecretary of State Robert Murphy, testifying in Congress on Soviet anti-American actions around the world, responded to the charge by "Soviet propaganda" that we were "the major inspirer" of the Indonesia rebels and were giving them military aid. Murphy dismissed the charge as untrue.[11]

In May 1958, a rebel B-26 bomber targeting a government airfield mistakenly hit a crowded village marketplace, killing a number of residents who were on their way to church.[12] Although the B-26 was shot down over the airfield and caught fire, the crew managed to bail out. Indonesian authorities caught and arrested one pilot whose parachute got tangled in a coconut tree. They identified the pilot as Allen Lawrence Pope, an American, by documents he was carrying.

The day after this incident, Dulles was asked again by reporters whether the United States was involved with the rebels. Again Dulles replied that the rebellion was "an Indonesian matter" that should be handled "without intrusion from without."[13] But the following week Indonesian authorities brought Pope before the press in Jakarta, where they displayed his U.S. Air Force identification card, his post exchange-privilege card from our Clark Air Force base in the Philippines, and a document connecting him to Civil Air Transport, a CIA-owned airline.[14] Relying on these documents, the Indonesian government charged that Pope was not a "soldier of fortune" but a CIA operative.

As CIA insiders later revealed, the Indonesian government was correct in its charge that the CIA was supplying both planes and pilots to the rebel colonels.[15] Pope, it turned out, had been contracted for the job by the CIA, which for several years had been plotting Sukarno's fall from power.[16] The CIA had spent a million dollars in the parliamentary elections of 1955 to back a Muslim party opposed to Sukarno, but the party did badly.[17]

The Communist party, on the other hand, did well in those elections, giving them a commanding role in the Indonesian government. That concerned Secretary Dulles and the CIA, who took the view that whenever a Communist party gained a role in government it would inevitably push out the other parties. The Americans thought they saw Moscow's hand in Indonesia and feared that the country would fall under Soviet influence, with the smaller countries of southeast Asia soon to follow.[18]

Within the State Department, Ambassador Allison disputed this analysis of Indonesian politics. Unlike Dulles and the CIA, Allison saw little connection to superpower rivalry in the wrangling among the Indonesian political parties. In his memoirs, Allison wrote that Al Ulmer, the CIA chief for the far east, had been "brainwashed" about a non-existent "imminent Communist danger in Asia."[19]

The CIA's paramilitary operation against Sukarno was directed by CIA operative Joseph Burkholder Smith, who wrote in his memoirs that already by 1956 the CIA was exploring ways to counter Sukarno.[20] In order to discredit Sukarno, the CIA had planted a false press story that he was having an affair with a Soviet female intelligence agent, and that the Soviet government was blackmailing Sukarno over this.[21] The CIA hoped that the story would shatter Sukarno's credibility, but the public in Indonesia paid little notice.

In 1957, the Sumatra-based colonels asked the CIA station in Indonesia for help, and it encouraged the colonels to make demands on the government.[22] To CIA headquarters in Washington, the Indonesian station fed information designed to get approval for a major operation in support of the colonels.[23] CIA headquarters agreed to send arms, and instructors to teach the rebels how to to use them.[24] The CIA enlisted all three branches of the U.S. military in the venture: the army trained rebel troops, the navy provided offshore backup, and the air force created and operated a rebel air force.[25]

The CIA hired 350 Americans, Chinese, and Filipinos to service and fly transport aircraft and B-26 bombers for rebel operations.[26] Using Singapore and the Philippines for planning and staging, the CIA airdropped supplies to the rebels.

CIA Director Allen Dulles ran the Indonesia operation, and his brother John Foster Dulles was the moving force behind it.[27] Even after Pope had been caught, the Eisenhower administration denied American involvement, because the CIA had taken elaborate precautions to protect the secrecy of the operation. It had stripped the B-26s of markings that would identify them as ours and was counting on Pope not to disclose that he was CIA. Like all the CIA pilots, Pope had been instructed to say, if captured, that he was a soldier of fortune and unconnected with the U.S. government. To conceal the pilots' affiliation, CIA officers had instructed them not to carry U.S.-related identification documents.

Contrary to these orders, many of the CIA pilots in the Indonesia operation carried identification documents, figuring that they were less likely to be executed upon capture if they were connected to the U.S. government. Pope was captured with identification cards. When the Indonesians displayed them to the press, Pope's governmental affiliation was obvious.[28] Still, Pope maintained that he was only a mercenary, while the American administration refused to acknowledge him or admit that it had promoted the rebellion.[29] Pope was court-martialed in an Indonesian court and sentenced to death, but was pardoned and released a few years later.[30]

John Allison, whom Secretary of State Dulles fired as U.S. ambassador to Indonesia, had opposed the CIA operation all along and had tried to get the administration to work with Sukarno. That was why Dulles removed him and sent a new ambassador who would cooperate.[31]

Although it did not admit its role after Pope's capture, the administration called off the Indonesia operation.[32] Even with our aid, the rebels had made little progress against Sukarno,[33] and after we pulled out, the rebel colonels lost heart.[34] By the time they gave up, several thousand Indonesians had been killed in the fighting.[35]

The Indonesia operation caused little immediate harm for the United States. The Indonesian government did not raise the matter at the United Nations. The American press, despite the evidence of the documents, accepted the story that Pope had been a soldier of fortune. In 1965, the CIA got its revenge in Indonesia when conservative military officers forced Sukarno out of office. Once in power, the officers decided to kill

Communist activists, but they did not know who all the Communists were. Our embassy and the CIA station had compiled lists of local Communist party officials that included 5,000 names. As embassy and CIA officials revealed for the first time only in 1990, our ambassador, Marshall Green, allowed the lists to be turned over to an Indonesian official so that the army could track the Communists down.

"It really was a big help to the army," said Robert J. Martens, who served in our embassy's political section in Indonesia in 1965. "No one cared, so long as they were Communists, that they were being butchered," said Howard Federspiel, the Indonesia expert in the State Department's bureau of intelligence and research. The Indonesian military found many other alleged Communists on its own, killing several hundred thousand Communists during this purge. It was one of the largest political bloodlettings in history.

As the Indonesian army killed the Communists, our embassy kept tabs on its success. The army would report which people on the lists it had killed, while the embassy and CIA checked the names off to see if the Communist party was being effectively eradicated. They concluded it was, and after 1965, the Communist party in Indonesia remained dormant.[36]

NOTES

1. John M. Allison, *Ambassador from the Prairie: or Allison Wonderland* (1973), p. 305.

2. Tillman Durdin, Indonesia Rebels Proclaim Regime, Defying Jakarta," *New York Times*, February 16, 1958, p. Al, col. 8.

3. James Mossman, *Rebels in Paradise: Indonesia's Civil War* (1961), pp. 23–27.

4. Ibid., p. 37.

5. "Secretary Dulles' News Conference of February 11," DSB, vol. 38, p. 334 (1958).

6. "Doubt on Sukarno Voiced by Dulles," *New York Times*, February 12, 1958, p. Al, col. 2.

7. Tillman Durdin, "Indonesia Rebels Proclaim Regime, Defying Jakarta," *NewYork Times*, February 16, 1958, p. Al, col. 8; Mossman, *Rebels in Paradise*, pp. 104–`111.

8. "Secretary Dulles' News Conference of April 1," DSB, vol. 38, p. 644 (1958).

9. "Transcript of the President's News Conference on Domestic and Foreign Matters," *New York Times*, May 1, 1958, p. A14, col. 1.

10. "Secretary Dulles' News Conference of May 1," DSB, vol. 38, P. 808 (1958).

11. Robert Murphy, "Review of Recent Anti-American Demonstrations," DSB, vol. 38, p. 960 (1958).

12. Joseph Burkholder Smith, *Portrait of a Cold Warrior* (1976), p. 247.

13. "Secretary Dulles' News Conference of May 20," DSB, vol. 38, p. 946 (1958).

14. Tillman Durdin, "Jakarta Reports U.S. Flier Downed," *New York Times*, May 28, 1958, p. A9, col. 1.

15. Leonard Mosley, *Dulles: A Biography of Eleanor, Allen, and John Foster Duties and Their Family Network* (1978), p. 437.

16. Victor Marchetti and John Marks, *The CIA and the Cult of Intelligence* (1974), p. 29; Thomas Powers, *The Man Who Kept Secrets: Richard Helms and the CIA* (1979), p. 90; Richard Barnet, *Intervention and Revolution: The United States in the Third World* (1968), p. 236.

17. Smith, *Portrait of a Cold Warrior*, pp. 210–16.

18. Ibid., p. 214.

19. Allison, *Ambassador from the Prairie*, p.307.

20. Smith, *Portrait of a Cold Warrior*, pp. 216–17.

21. Ibid., pp. 238–39.

22. Ibid., pp. 225–27, 233; Mossman, *Rebels in Paradise*, p. 174; Col. L. Fletcher Prouty, U.S. Air Force, Ret., *The Secret Team: The CIA and Its Allies in Control of the United States and the World* (1973), p. 323; Brian May, *The Indonesian Tragedy* (1978), p. 79.

23. Smith, *Portrait of a Cold Warrior*, p. 229.

24. Ibid., p. 242; Powers, *The Man Who Kept Secrets*, p. 90; Mosley, *Dulles: A Biography of Eleanor, Allen, and John Foster Dulles and Their Family Network*, p. 437.

25. Prouty, *The Secret Team*, pp. 323–24.

26. John Prados, *Presidents' Secret Wars: CIA and Pentagon Covert Opera-*

tions Since World War II (1986), pp. 140–42; Smith, *Portrait of a Cold Warrior*, p. 247. Powers, *The Man Who Kept Secrets*, p. 90; Prouty, *The Secret Team*, pp. 323–24.

27. Prados, *Presidents' Secret Wars*, p. 135.

28. Prouty, *The Secret Team*, pp. 325–26.

29. "U.S. Aide Sees Captive," *New York Times*, June 5, 1958, p. Al2, col. 4; Mosley, *Dulles: A Biography of Eleanor, Allen, and John Foster Dulles and Their Family Network*, p. 438.

30. "Indonesia Sentences U.S. Flier to Death," *New York Times*, April 29, 1960, p. A4, col. 8; Robert F. Whitney, "Indonesia Frees American Flier," *New York Times*, August 23, 1965, p. A3, col. 4.

31. Allison, *Ambassador from the Prairie*, pp. 338–39; Smith, *Portrait of a Cold Warrior*, pp. 229–30, 240, 246.

32. Powers, *The Man Who Kept Secrets*, pp. 90–91.

33. Smith, *Portrait of a Cold Warrior*, p. 248; Mossman, *Rebels in Paradise*, pp. 135–87; Prouty, *The Secret Team*, p. 324.

34. Mossman, *Rebels in Paradise*, p. 225.

35. Smith, *Portrait of a Cold Warrior*, pp. 247–48.

36. Kathy Kadane, "U.S. Officials' Lists Aided Indonesian Bloodbath in '60s," *Washington Post*, May 21, 1990, p. A5, col. 1; Ralph McGehee, "The Indonesia File," *Nation*, September 24, 1990, p. 296.

8. LEBANON, IRAQ, AND JORDAN: COKES ON THE BEACH

"**I**nternational communism," as seen by Washington, was a particular threat in the Middle East. The Eisenhower administration decided that if Communists tried to take any country in the Middle East, we would stop them. Enshrined in a 1957 joint resolution of Congress, the policy, which came to be known as the Eisenhower Doctrine, was that

> the United States regards as vital to the national interest and world peace the preservation of the independence and integrity of the nations of the Middle East. To this end, if the President determines the necessity thereof, the United States is prepared to use armed forces to assist any such nation. . .requesting assistance against armed aggression from any country controlled by international communism.[1]

After Congress adopted the resolution, the Eisenhower administration approached Lebanon's president, Camille Chamoun, and asked him to "accept" the Eisenhower Doctrine, meaning that he would agree to military intervention if Lebanon were threatened by "international communism."

For better or worse, Chamoun conceded.[2] In a country sharply divided between Muslim and Christian communities, Chamoun's government was Christian-dominated. Lebanon's Christian population had close ties to the

West, both culturally and politically.[3] But Lebanon's opposition, united as the National Front, was based in the Muslim community, which constituted a majority of Lebanon's population. The National Front reflected Arab nationalism as espoused by Egyptian President Gamal Abdul Nasser.[4]

In 1956, Nasser had shocked the West by nationalizing the British- and French-owned Suez Canal. Then Syria, which shared Egypt's Arab nationalist attitude, merged with Egypt to form the United Arab Republic (UAR). The Eisenhower administration feared the spread in the region of anti-Western sentiment, which might attract Soviet support.

This anti-Western attitude, which rejected Western control of the economies and politics of the region, was understandable in light of the history of European involvement there. After defeating the Ottoman Empire in World War I, Britain and France took control, much to the cha- grin of the Arabs, who had expected independence. Britain and France gave most of the region independence in the 1930s and 1940s, but they continued in a strong financial role. After World War II, the United States began to compete for influence, as reflected in the Eisenhower Doctrine.

Chamoun's acceptance of the Eisenhower Doctrine put him at odds with both Egypt and Syria, as well as with Lebanon's own Nationalist Front, which immediately demanded that he renounce it.[5] Chamoun refused, and to reward him, the CIA secretly funded pro-Chamoun candi- dates in parliamentary elections scheduled for 1957, resulting in a pro- Chamoun parliamentary majority.[6] Deprived of control of the parliament, the National Front was furious.[7] The most serious consequence of this defeat, from its standpoint, was that the new parliament would be selecting a president in July 1958, and Chamoun was seeking reelection. As Wilbur Crane Eveland, the CIA station chief in Beirut at the time, explained, Chamoun was a shoo-in for the presidency, because the parlia- ment had been "bought" for him by the CIA.[8]

Its frustration with U.S.-bought control, which did not remain wholly secret, led the National Front to move against Chamoun two months before the scheduled election. In May 1958, the Front mounted a military campaign against Chamoun and quickly gained control of most of Lebanon's territory.[9] Chamoun responded by seeking the aid of the

United Nations Security Council. Chamoun complained that the Front was being supplied and trained by the UAR.[10] After the UAR denied the charge,[11] the Council sent an observation mission "to ensure that there is no illegal infiltration of personnel or supply or arms or other materiel across the Lebanese borders."[12] The mission reported "substantial movements of armed men" in Lebanon, but said it could not determine whether they "had infiltrated from outside," or where they had obtained their arms. It said that of those involved against Chamoun in Lebanon, "the vast majority were in any case Lebanese."[13] Rejecting the UN mission's report, Chamoun and the Eisenhower administration said that since the mission had not established good access to border areas, it might have missed acts of infiltration.[14]

Just at this point a new political development took place nearby. On July 14, the solidly pro-Western government of Iraq was overthrown in a coup. The political complexion of the Iraqi coup makers was unclear, but because of the nationalist activity in Lebanon and the UAR, the Eisenhower administration feared that the Iraqi coup might be nationalist as well. Apart from what the Iraqi coup might portend for Iraq, President Eisenhower was concerned that this new development might encourage the Lebanese National Front to mount a final offensive against Chamoun.

Concerned over both Iraq and Lebanon, Eisenhower decided to send troops into Lebanon. Quickly he landed a force of 10,000 Marines and airborne units, backed up by the 35,000-man Sixth Fleet offshore in the eastern Mediterranean.[15] Eisenhower's purpose was twofold: to keep the National Front from moving against Chamoun, and to have troops close to Iraq in case a similar nationalist threat might emerge there.[16]

In the UN Security Council, U.S. Ambassador Henry Cabot Lodge justified the American intervention by explaining that our purpose in Lebanon was "to stabilize the situation brought on by the threats from outside."[17] President Eisenhower said that the rebellion in Lebanon was "supported by sizable amounts of arms, ammunition, and money and by personnel infiltrated from Syria to fight against the lawful authorities."[18] To bolster its case, the White House held that Lebanon's complaint to the Security Council had charged "indirect aggression."[19]

But Lebanon had not actually charged aggression, direct or indirect. In framing his complaint against the UAR, President Chamoun made the softer complaint that the UAR was creating a situation that "is likely, if continued, to endanger the maintenance of international peace and security."[20] This language derived from the UN Charter's Chapter 6 titled "Pacific Settlement of Disputes," while aggression involves more military action and is covered under Chapter 7 of the Charter. Thus, Lodge's charge against the UAR went beyond that made by Chamoun.

Two days after our Lebanon landing, the region's situation became more complicated still. At the request of Jordan, Britain landed troops in that country.[21] Britain claimed to have intelligence information that a Syrian-backed coup would form that day in Jordan.[22] Like Lebanon, Jordan had a pro-Western government. Jordan's King Hussein received regular subsidies from the CIA.[23]

To scare off the supposed coup plotters in Jordan, Eisenhower sent fifty U.S. jet fighters to fly over Jordan as a show of force.[24] At the UN we declared that we were supporting Britain's action "in the defense of Jordan's independence and integrity," and called our overflights "a justified exercise of the inherent right of nations to call for assistance when threatened."[25] Whether Syria was actually involved in an anti-Hussein plot was never clarified.

There was a legitimate reason, though, to doubt the Eisenhower administration's good faith in making charges against the Syrian government. As in Lebanon, we were anxious to suppress Arab nationalism in Syria. In 1956 and again in 1957, we paid Syrian military officers to overthrow Syria's leaders and replace them with less nationalistic types. In the 1957 attempt, the plotters turned themselves in and named two CIA officers, whom the Syrian government then expelled from the country.[26]

As for Lebanon, Ambassador Lodge explained that the UN mission there had "helped to reduce interference from across the border," but "with the outbreak of the revolt in Iraq, the infiltration of arms and personnel into Lebanon from the United Arab Republic in an effort to subvert the legally constituted Government has suddenly become much more alarming." The Iraqi coup, Lodge said, "coupled with persistent efforts over the past months to subvert the government of Jordan, must be a cause of grave concern to us all. They place in jeopardy both the independence of Lebanon and that of any Middle Eastern State which seeks to maintain its national integrity free from outside influences and pressures."[27]

The Iraqi coup and the supposed coup attempt in Jordan proved to Lodge that "there is, in the Middle East, a common purpose to take over everywhere, all at once. Clearly, there is a common purpose, masterminded from one source." As for the identity of that source, Lodge pinned the blame on the UAR. "You can read all about it in the Cairo newspapers," he said, "or listen to the incessant radio broadcasts from Cairo to other Arab countries."[28]

Lodge's charge of outside involvement in Lebanon had some basis in fact. Some arms may well have been smuggled to the National Front from Syria.[29] But the Eisenhower administration could not prove aggression.[30] By mid-July, the UN mission had set up an extensive network of border checkpoints to watch for infiltration of arms and personnel.[31] Observing by air and on the ground, both during the day and at night, the mission reported on July 30 that infiltration of arms into Lebanon "cannot be on anything more than a limited scale, and is largely confined to small arms and ammunition." As for personnel, it said, "in no case have United Nations observers, who have been vigilantly patrolling the opposition-held areas and have frequently observed the armed bands there, been able to detect the presence of persons who have indubitably entered from across the border for the purpose of fighting."[32]

Whatever the facts about infiltration, the Lebanese conflict was, as the UN mission stated in its first report, of Lebanese, not Syrian or Egyptian, making. The United States, as we saw, was a catalyst for that conflict, because by drawing Chamoun into our orbit, and by skewing the makeup of the Lebanese parliament in his favor, we had aroused the National Front to action.

Beyond the alleged UAR involvement, President Eisenhower gave an additional reason for the Lebanon landing, namely, that U.S. citizens in Lebanon, whom he estimated at 2,500, were endangered by the hostilities and needed to be evacuated.[33] This justification was hardly sustainable. In June the State Department had already warned U.S. citizens against travel to Lebanon,[34] and in June and July it had evacuated most dependents of official U.S. personnel there.[35] By July 15, the date of the landing, most U.S. citizens resident in Lebanon were already gone.[36] After the Marines landed, the administration seemed to have forgotten the issue, because the Marines did not organize an evacuation and the administration no longer mentioned any endangered citizens.

The Lebanon landing piqued the interest of reporters from the standpoint of U.S. Middle East policy. The Eisenhower Doctrine referred only to opposing communism, but the administration was not alleging any involvement in Lebanon by Communist countries or even by local Communists.[37] No matter, replied Secretary of State Dulles, the Eisenhower Doctrine could be expanded. The doctrine, he explained, meant "that the independence of these countries is vital to peace and the national interest of the United States," and "that is certainly a mandate to do something if we think that our peace and vital interests are endangered from any quarter."[38] With this sleight of hand, Dulles broadened our interventionist aims from opposing communism to opposing Arab nationalism.

One way in which the United States sought to curb nationalism in Lebanon was to make the Front come to terms with the government.[39] By September, a political compromise was reached, with President Chamoun stepping aside and the head of the Lebanese army assuming the presidency. In Jordan and Iraq, all went well for us, too. In Jordan, King Hussein remained in power, his relation with the CIA unimpaired, while the new Iraqi government, contrary to expectations, turned out to be pro-Western.[40]

The Eisenhower administration's stated reasons for the Lebanon intervention did not hold water. There was little to back up our claim of outside aggression.[41] The claim of a need to evacuate U.S. citizens was a pretext.*

---

*One curious aside to the Lebanon intervention was that, once in Lebanon, our forces did little but sit in positions they had established on Lebanon's lovely Mediterranean beach. This deployment proved to be enough to intimidate the National Front from moving against Chamoun, so no military action was needed. Lebanese soft drink vendors on the beach, however, carried on a lively business with the Marines.

NOTES

1. Joint Resolution to Promote Peace and Stability in the Middle East, H. J. Res. 117, U.S. Congress, *Statutes at Large*, vol. 71, p. 5 (1957), also in DSB, vol. 36, p. 481 (1957).

2. Richard Barnet, *Intervention and Revolution: The United States in the Third World* (1968), p. 142.

3. Thomas M. Franck, "Who Killed Article 2(4)? or Changing Norms Governing the Use of Force by States," *American Journal of International Law* 64 (1970): 814.

4. Helena Cobban, *The Making of Modern Lebanon* (1985), pp. 84–85.

5. Wilbur Crane Eveland, *Ropes of Sand—America's Failure in the Middle East* (1980), p. 276.

6. Ibid., pp. 248–53; Jonathan Kwitny, *Endless Enemies: The Making of an Unfriendly World* (1984), p. 316.

7. Kwitny, *Endless Enemies*, p. 316.

8. Eveland, *Ropes of Sand*, p. 266.

9. Cobban, *The Making of Modern Lebanon*, p. 88.

10. SCOR, 13th yr., 823rd mtg., pp. 4-35, UN Doc. S/PV.823 (1958).

11. SCOR, 13th yr., 824th mtg., pp. 2-13, UN Doc. S/PV.824 (1958).

12. SCOR, 13th yr., 824th mtg., p. 23, UN Doc. S/PV.824 (1958); Res. 128, SCOR, 13th yr., *Resolutions and Decisions*, p. 5, UN Doc. S/ INF/ 13/ Rev. 1 (1958).

13. "First Report of the United Nations Observation Group in Lebanon," July 3, 1958, SCOR, 13th yr., Supplement (July, August, September 1958), pp. 8–9, UN Doc. S/4040 (1958).

14. Eveland, *Ropes of Sand*, p. 279.

15. "Radio-TV Statement (White House press release dated July 15)," DSB, vol. 39, p. 183 (1958); Eveland, *Ropes of Sand*, p. 294.

16. Cobban, *The Making of Modern Lebanon*, p. 89.

17. SCOR, 13th yr., 827th mtg., p. 7, UN Doc. S/PV. 827 (1958).

18. "Message to the Congress," DSB, vol. 39, p. 182 (1958).

19. "Radio-TV Statement (White House press release dated July 15)."

20. SCOR, 13th yr., 823rd mtg., p.4, UN Doc. S/PV.823 (1958), p. 184.

21. Drew Middleton, "British Land in Jordan, Backed by U.S. Jets," *New York Times*, July 18, 1958, p. Al, col. 8.

22. "Statement by MacMillan on Jordan," *New York Times*, July 18, 1958, p. A2, col. 4.

23. "Can Anyone Keep a Secret," and "Hussein on His CIA Money," *Newsweek*, March 7, 1977, p. 16; Bob Woodward, "CIA Paid Millions to Jordan's King Hussein," *Washington Post*, February 18, 1977, p. Al, col. 1.

24. Jack Raymond, "U.S. Jets Display Power in Jordan," *New York Times*, July 18, 1958, p. Al, col. 7.

25. "First Statement of July 17 (U.S./U.N. press release 2963)," DSB, vol. 39, p. 193 (1958).

26. Eveland, *Ropes of Sand*, pp. 253–54; "Syria Expelling 3 U.S. Diplomats," *New York Times*, August 14, 1957, p. Al, col. 7.

27. SCOR, 13th yr., 827th mtg., pp. 7–8, UN Doc. S/PV.827 (1958).

28. SCOR, 13th yr., 831st mtg., p. 10, UN Doc. S/PV.831 (1958).

29. Eveland, *Ropes of Sand*, pp. 275, 279.

30. SCOR, 13th yr., 831st mtg., p. 8, UN Doc. S/PV.831 (1958); Pitman B. Potter, "Legal Aspects of the Beirut Landing," *American Journal of International Law* 52 (1958): 727–28.

31. "Interim Report of the United Nations Observation Group in Lebanon," July 15, 1958, SCOR, 13th yr. Supplement (July, August, September 1958), p. 33, UN Doc. S/4051 (1958); "Second Interim Report of the United Nations Observation Group in Lebanon," July 17, 1958, SCOR, 13th yr., Supplement (July, August, September 1958), p. 34, UN Doc. S/4052 (1958).

32. "Second Report of the United Nations Observation Group in Lebanon," July 30, 1958, SCOR, 13th yr., Supplement (July, August, September 1958), p. 93, UN Doc. S/4069 (1958).

33. "Statement by President Eisenhower," DSB, vol. 39, p. 181 (1958); "Message to the Congress," DSB, vol. 39, p. 182 (1958).

34. "U.S. Issues Alert to Americans Traveling in Lebanon," DSB, vol. 39, p. 31 (1958).

35. "U.S. Dependents Authorized to Return to Lebanon," DSB, vol. 39, p. 688 (1958); Sam Pope Brewer, "Beirut Welcomes Marines; Second Contingent Ashore," *New York Times*, July 16, 1958, p. Al, col. 6.

36. Eveland, *Ropes of Sand*, p. 276.

37. René-Jean Dupuy, "Agression indirecte et intervention sollicitée à propos de l'affaire libanaise," *Annuaire Français de Droit International* 5 (1959): 463.

38. "Secretary Dulles' News Conference of May 20," DSB, vol. 38, p. 945 (1957).

39. Mohammed Bennouna, *Le consentement à l'ingérence militaire dans les conflits internes* (1974), pp. 150, 178–79.

40. Cobban, *The Making of Modern Lebanon*, pp. 92–93.

41. Quincy Wright, "United States Intervention in the Lebanon," *American Journal of International Law* 53 (1959): 114.

9. CUBA: WE WERE NOT INVOLVED

Not long after the Lebanon intervention a situation closer to home attracted the interest of the Eisenhower administration. A revolution in Cuba had overthrown longtime ruler Fulgencio Batista. The new government was headed by Fidel Castro, whom Eisenhower considered too far to the left. Castro eventually did attach his star to the Kremlin, but it was never clear whether this resulted from Castro's rejecting us or our rejecting him. During 1960, Castro and Eisenhower traded jabs, which led to a complete trade embargo with Cuba.

Eisenhower decided to get rid of Castro's new government. The CIA set in motion a plan to infiltrate small groups of Cuban exiles, who would build up underground resistance units. Then the CIA shifted to a plan for a single major invasion, designed to spark a popular rebellion against Castro.[1] President Eisenhower approved the plan, and CIA operatives recruited Cuban exiles living in Florida to form an invasion force.[2]

The State Department, skittish about the plan, insisted that no military training be done in the United States, lest word of it leak out.[3] So the CIA approached the Guatemalan government, the one we had brought to power in 1954. Guatemala's president in 1960 was Miguel Ydígoras Fuentes, who was one of the coup plotters in 1954. Castillo Armas, whom we had engineered into the presidency, was assassinated in 1957, and

Ydígoras assumed office in his place. When approached by the CIA to provide training sites for the secret force of Cubans, Ydígoras was happy to return the favor. The CIA set up shop at a remote location in Guatemala.[4]

Ydígoras's willingness was almost his undoing. Soon after the training began, an armed rebellion broke out against him in the Guatemalan army. Word about the training of the Cubans leaked out in Guatemala, and the rebels objected, arguing that Ydígoras was needlessly involving the country in a hostile action against a nearby country. In short order the rebels put together enough troops to pose a serious threat to Ydígoras, and took over the important Guatemalan port city of Puerto Barrios, in addition to two army bases.[5]

President Eisenhower came to Ydígoras's defense, because if the Guatemala rebellion succeeded, the cover might be blown on the secret training of the Cubans. Eisenhower sent U.S. Navy ships from the Guantanamo naval base in Cuba to Guatemalan waters, announcing that the purpose was to "prevent intervention on the part of Communist-directed elements in the internal affairs of Guatemala."[6] By this Eisenhower meant to imply that Cuba was behind the Guatemala rebellion, although there was little evidence of that. The Guatemala army rebels who opposed Ydígoras were not sympathetic to Cuba, and Cuba, for its part, was not involved in their movement. The rebels merely objected to Ydígoras getting Guatemala involved in unnecessary conflicts.[7]

The U.S. Navy deployment around Guatemala was only for show, however. Eisenhower took more serious action to put down the Guatemala rebellion, permitting U.S. Air Force pilots who were training the Cubans at the CIA base to strafe the rebel headquarters. The rebels, who were no match for the U.S. Air Force, quickly surrendered.[8] The American press had discovered that planes from the training base put down the revolt and that we were financing the training, but it did not learn that our own pilots were involved. As for the purpose of the training, the press reported, although without coming to any conclusion, two contradictory stories: according to Ydígoras, it was to protect against a possible invasion by Cuba; the rebels, on the other hand, declared that the training was to prepare for an attack on Cuba.[9] After the rebellion failed, the Guatemalan government publicly thanked Eisenhower for the navy deployment, but with no mention of the strafing.[10] Eisenhower, too, kept mum about it, so once again we had intervened in Guatemalan politics and no one was the wiser.

The Cuban government found out about the training in Guatemala. In January 1961, its foreign minister protested, charging that the objective was an invasion of Cuba.[11] *Time* magazine, reporting on the training in Guatemala, wrote that planes were flying in and out of an air base in Florida.[12]

Meanwhile, despite disclosures, the training of the Cuban exile force in Guatemala continued. When John F. Kennedy became president, he continued with the operation.[13] With Kennedy's approval, the CIA made final preparations for the invasion.[14] Lyman Kirkpatrick, CIA inspector general at the time, conducted an official post mortem on the operation in a book he wrote some years later.[15] In preparation for landing on Cuba, the CIA built the Cuban exile force to a strength of 1,450 and provided all its financing and equipment.[16]

In April 1961, the CIA set the invasion plan in motion, sending Cuban pilots to bomb fighter aircraft on the ground at Cuban air bases in order to eliminate Cuba's air defense.[17] As a cover story, the CIA had the pilots land in Miami after the raids and say they were Cuban air force pilots defecting to the United States.[18] At the United Nations we repeated this story,[19] but it was full of inconsistencies and was quickly exposed by the press as a fabrication.[20]

After last-minute consultations with the Joint Chiefs of Staff and the State Department, the CIA launched the Cubans by sea from a base in Nicaragua toward the Bay of Pigs on Cuba's southern shore, under the command of their CIA trainers.[21] Meanwhile, U.S. Navy destroyers waited offshore at the Bay of Pigs to offer logistical support, while pilots from the USS *Essex* flew strafing missions for the landing force.[22] As the exiles headed ashore in landing crafts, CIA instructors led them to the beaches.[23]

Despite all this effort, the landing force made little headway. Contrary to expectations, the Cuban people did not rise up against their leader, and military resistance to the exile force was stiff. The Cuban military repelled the exiles, killing 114 of them, and taking over a thousand prisoner.

Although the U.S. role in the affair was not public knowledge, it was widely suspected.[24] One reporter wrote that it "has been an open secret in Florida and Central America for months" that "the CIA planned, coordinated, and directed the operations that ended in the defeat on a beachhead in southern Cuba."[25] In a formal protest to President Kennedy, Soviet Premier Nikita Khrushchev charged that the invasion force had been "prepared, equipped, and armed in the United States." "The planes," he said, "which bomb Cuban towns belong to the United States of America, the bombs which they drop have been put at their disposal by the American Government."[26] In response to these charges of American involvement, President Kennedy expressed admiration for the Cubans but portrayed them as having acted on their own.[27] Kennedy did not acknowledge that the CIA had organized the failed invasion.[28]

In the 1970s, the U.S. Senate investigated covert operations by the CIA, and for the first time in an official way acknowledged the CIA role in the Bay of Pigs. A Senate committee wrote that "the President authorized the CIA to secretly direct and finance the military invasion" of Cuba. The operation, the committee said, may have amounted to "an act of war."[29] By acting covertly, the committee said, Presidents Eisenhower and Kennedy frustrated "the constitutional system of checks and balances" that is supposed to apply to military operations abroad. The Cuban operation ran the risk of full-scale war with Cuba, the committee said, "on the sole authority of the President."[30]

The Bay of Pigs invasion nearly did bring war, not only with Cuba but also with the Soviet Union, which, like Cuba, was concerned that we might strike Cuba again.[31] In the months following the failed invasion, the CIA, far from backing off its efforts, fed the Cuban-Soviet fears by plotting to foment internal dissension in Cuba, and to assassinate President Fidel Castro. This CIA scheme, much like the plan that preceded the Bay of Pigs, was to send in Cuban exiles to organize underground cells. In addition, in what it dubbed "Operation Mongoose," the CIA inserted raiding parties from Florida in Cuba in the summer of 1961, to sabotage sugar refineries and oil depots.[32]

To this activity the Soviet Union responded by giving Cuba missiles with nuclear warheads, apparently to deter another invasion. "We had to establish a tangible and effective deterrent to American interference," said Khrushchev in his memoirs. The "logical answer" to this problem "was missiles," he said. "We wanted to keep the Americans from invading Cuba, and, to that end, we wanted to make them think twice by confronting them with our missiles."[33]

Having discovered that Khrushchev was installing missiles in Cuba, Kennedy sent ships to intercept Soviet vessels entering Cuban waters.[34] Calling the operation a quarantine, Kennedy declared that if a Soviet ship refused to be searched, we would stop it by force. So the action risked military confrontation with the Soviet Union, a danger that Kennedy himself acknowledged. "This is a difficult and dangerous effort on which we have set out," he said; "no one can foresee precisely what course it will take or what costs or casualties will be incurred." The Soviet army could have moved against our forces in Europe, leading to general war. Kennedy warned, "Any hostile move anywhere in the world against the safety and freedom of peoples to whom we are committed will be met by whatever action is needed."[35]

If there were a confrontation on the seas around Cuba, we might invade it. I watched Kennedy announce the missile intercept with something of a personal interest. A member of the Marine Corps reserve, I had been trained in amphibious landings. I wondered if I would be climbing down the side of a ship on a rope ladder to run up a Cuban beach.

I had followed the moves by Kennedy and Khrushchev as well from the perspective of an international relations course I had just taken at Harvard. The instructor was Henry Kissinger, who airhopped to Washington to consult at the National Security Council and the Arms Control and Disarmament Agency. Kissinger approached international relations as a chess master approaches the checkered board. Kissinger's playing surface was the globe, and the United States and the Soviet Union were the players.

When Kennedy ordered the missile interdiction, he said that we could not tolerate "offensive threats."[36] At the United Nations, Ambassador Adlai Stevenson alleged that the installation of missiles in Cuba gave clear evidence that the Soviet Union "has decided to transform Cuba into a base for Communist aggression."[37] The public, however, remained unaware that Eisenhower and Kennedy had organized the Bay of Pigs invasion, and it knew nothing of Operation Mongoose, so it viewed the Soviet action not as a defensive move but as Kennedy had portrayed it— an offensive, unprovoked act. The Bay of Pigs invasion, and the wraps under which the administration kept it, had brought the world to the brink of nuclear war. Fortunately, Khrushchev and Kennedy worked out a solution. Khrushchev removed the missiles in exchange for a promise by Kennedy not to invade Cuba.[38]

The press referred to the 1961 invasion of Cuba as a "fiasco," because it failed, and the episode makes only a footnote in our official postwar history. But in Cuba the failed invasion left a permanent stamp. On the island it is impossible to talk politics very long before someone brings up the Bay of Pigs. The threat of "Yankee invasion" left Cuba permanently militarized. Because Cuban exiles had formed the invasion force at the Bay of Pigs, the Cuban government became even more sensitive to dissent than it had already been. Successive American administrations castigated Cuba for violating human rights; however, if we had set a course of friendly relations, the internal situation in Cuba might have been far different.

NOTES

1. Lyman B. Kirkpatrick, Jr., *The Real CIA* (1968), pp. 191–93.

2. Ibid., pp. 187–89, 200; Theodore C. Sorensen, *Kennedy* (1965), p. 295.

3. Kirkpatrick, *The Real CIA*, pp. 193–94.

4. Sorensen, *Kennedy*, p. 295.

5. "Guatemala Fights Revolt; State of Siege Is Imposed," *New York Times*, November 14, 1960, p. Al, col. 3.

6. "U.S. Positions Naval Units as Aid to Guatemala and Nicaragua," State-

ment by James C. Hagerty, Press Secretary to the President, November 17, 1960, DSB, vol. 43, p. 888 (1960).

7. Richard Gott, *Rural Guerrillas in Latin America* (1973), p. 70.

8. Ibid., pp. 71–72; Col. L. Fletcher Prouty, U.S. Air Force, Ret., *The Secret Team: The CIA and Its Allies in Control of the United States and the World* (1973), p. 41.

9. Paul P. Kennedy, "U.S. Helps Train an Anti-Castro Force at Secret Guatemala Air-Ground Base," *New York Times*, January 10, 1961, p. Al, col. 5.

10. "Guatemala Thanks United States for Naval Aid," DSB, vol. 43, p. 924 (1960).

11. "Cuban Charges Recalled," *New York Times*, January 10, 1961, p. A11, col. 5.

12. "Cuba: The Underground," *Time*, January 27, 1961, p. 26.

13. Arthur B. Schlesinger, Jr., *A Thousand Days* (1965), p. 257; Sorensen, *Kennedy*, pp. 295–96.

14. *Final Report: Foreign and Military Intelligence*, U.S. Senate, Select Committee to Study Governmental Operations with Respect to Intelligence Activities, Book 1, 94th Cong., 2d sess., April 26, 1976, p. 25; William Colby, *Honorable Men: My Life in the CIA* (1978), p. 172.

15. Kirkpatrick, *The Real CIA*, p. 189.

16. Ibid., p. 193; Sorensen, *Kennedy*, p. 294; *Final Report: Foreign and Military Intelligence*, p. 35.

17. Peter Wyden, *Bay of Pigs: The Untold Story* (1979), pp. 173–79.

18. Ibid., pp. 174–76, 186–90.

19. "U.S. Delegation Press Release 3697," April 15, 1961, DSB, vol. 44, p. 667 (1961).

20. Sorensen, *Kennedy*, p. 300.

21. Kirkpatrick, *The Real CIA*, pp. 195–98; Wyden, *Bay of Pigs*, pp. 163, 217–18.

22. Wyden, *Bay of Pigs*, pp. 214, 235–40, 261.

23. Ibid., pp. 216–20, 229.

24. Sorensen, *Kennedy*, pp. 300–301.

25. Tad Szulc, "C.I.A. Is Accused by Bitter Rebels," *New York Times*, April 22, 1961, p. Al, col. 3.

26. "Mr. Khrushchev to President Kennedy," April 18, 1961, DSB, vol. 44, p. 662 (1961).

27. Ibid., p. 661.

28. John F. Kennedy, "News Conference," April 12, 1961, DSB, vol. 44, p. 661 n. 2 (1961); John F. Kennedy, "The Lesson of Cuba," April 20, 1961, DSB, vol. 44 p. 659 (1961); "Text of Address by President to U.S. Editors," *New York Times*, April 21, 1961, p. A2, col. 2; "Transcript of the President's News Conference on World and Domestic Affairs," *New York Times*, April 22, 1961, p. A8, col. 1; "President's Remarks to Patriots of Cuba," *Washington Post*, December 30, 1962, p. A9, col. 1.

29. *Final Report: Foreign and Military Intelligence*, pp. 37–38; Richard A. Falk, "American Intervention in Cuba and the Rule of Law," *Ohio State Law Journal* 22 (1961): 568; Edwin C. Hoyt, *Law and Force in American Foreign Policy* (1985), p. 123.

30. *Final Report: Foreign and Military Intelligence*, pp. 37–38.

31. *Khrushchev Remembers*, Strobe Talbott, ed. (1970), p. 492.

32. *Alleged Assassination Plots Involving Foreign Leaders: An Interim Report of the Select Committee to Study Governmental Operations with Respect to Intelligence Activities*, U.S. Senate, 94th Cong., 1st sess., Report no. 94-465, November 20, 1975, pp. 139–70; Colby, *Honorable Men*, p. 190; Hoyt, *Law and Force in American Foreign Policy*, p. 123; Thomas Powers, *The Man Who Kept Secrets: Richard Helms & the CIA* (1979), p. 139.

33. *Khrushchev Remembers*, pp. 493-96.

34. "Interdiction of the Delivery of Offensive Weapons to Cuba, Presidential Proclamation," October 23, 1962, DSB, vol. 47, p. 717 (1962).

35. John F. Kennedy, "The Soviet Threat to the Americas," October 22, 1962, DSB, vol. 47, pp. 718-19 (1962).

36. Ibid., p. 716 (1962).

37. "U.N. Security Council Hears U.S. Charges of Soviet Military Buildup in Cuba," DSB, vol. 47, p. 733 (1962).

38. "President Kennedy's Message of October 27," DSB, vol. 47, p. 743 (1962); *Khrushchev Remembers*, pp. 498–99.

10. LAOS: A FREE-FIRE ZONE

When I passed through Laos in 1978, it was enjoying its first peace in decades. From the time France packed up its colonial bags and left the country in 1954, civil war, with more than a little outside involvement, became Laos's fate. The troubles continued until 1973. Seeing the Lao, however, I found it hard to imagine them at war. A Melanesian people, the Lao move harmoniously in their sarongs, a picture of grace. One oft-repeated tale, perhaps apocryphal, about the Laotian civil war is that one day in Vientiane, the capital city, a battalion of government troops marched down a major thoroughfare. In the opposite direction, on a parallel street, came a battalion of opposition troops. Neither commander was anxious to engage the other, so they pretended not to notice. The moral that Laotians drew from the story was that the Lao, if left to themselves, would not fight each other too strenuously.

In 1954, France lost a major battle at Dien Bien Phu in Vietnam. It was that defeat that led to independence talks in Geneva and to French withdrawal from all Indochina. After the French pullout, the leftist Pathet Lao organization enjoyed a great following and had a military force in the northeast part of the country. But the government of Laos was neutralist and sought to accommodate the Pathet Lao. Little concerned over superpower politics, the neutralist government sought to keep the peace and to

improve the rice harvest. It was a reluctant participant in the internal conflict, content to leave the Pathet Lao alone.

The civil war in Laos might have remained a minor episode had Laos
not been "blessed" by our strong interest in it. Just as in Korea, where
leftists led the anti-Japan resistance, so in Laos did leftists lead the anti-
France resistance. To the Eisenhower administration, imbued with the
Korea mentality, however, Laos was a player on a global chessboard.[1] If
communism won in Laos, it might spread to Cambodia, or Vietnam, or
Taiwan. Secretary of State Dulles told the U.S. Senate that whether Laos
and the rest of southeast Asia "can be kept out of Communist control
depends very much on whether we build a dike around this present loss."
By "loss," Dulles meant the French defeat at Dien Bien Phu. "The only
thing we have to build that dike with is this money," he said, meaning the
foreign aid money he was asking the Senate to appropriate for Laos. "It
will be a domino business," Dulles continued, "unless we can bolster this
situation up."[2] To keep friendly governments in the region on our side,
Dulles organized them into an association called the Southeast Asia
Treaty Organization.

Walter Robertson, assistant secretary of state for Far Eastern affairs,
told the House of Representatives that our "sole reason" for being involved in Laos was "to keep this little country from being taken over by
the Communists." He said, "we are trying to keep Laos in the free world."
Robertson called Laos "a finger pointing into the heart of Southeast
Asia," which was "one of the prime objectives of the international Communists in Asia." So more than Laos was at stake: "Every time you lose
a country, Robertson warned, "they become correspondingly stronger and
the free world becomes weaker . . . . [I]t is happening all over the world,
everywhere. We are engaged in a struggle for the survival of what we call
a free civilization. The Communists probe first in Europe, then in the
Middle East, in Africa, Taiwan, in Laos." He concluded, "this is an expan-
sionist movement and they [the Communists] are dedicated to taking over
the world."[3]

Robertson's deputy, J. Graham Parsons, told the House that our aim
was "to keep Laos this side of the Bamboo Curtain." In Parsons' estimate,

the Laotian army, which we were financing, was "the principal bulwark of the country against Communist subversion."[4] Our goal in Laos thus was clear. Dulles viewed it as an advantage in the anti-Communist effort in Laos that the French were no longer in Indochina, because that put the anti-Communist fight on a higher moral plane. "We have a clean base there now, without a taint of colonialism," Dulles stated. "Dienbienphu was a blessing in disguise."[5]

The State Department's analysis of Laos bore little relation to the reality on the ground there. As they had done in Korea and Indonesia, our policy makers misread the situation because of their cold war mentality. At that juncture, China and the Soviet Union were not focused on Laos.[6] When neutralist Prime Minister Souvanna Phouma made a visit to China and the Soviet Union, however, the State Department decided he was "Communist-influenced." In fact, Phouma was trying to show his neutrality, in order to facilitate talks with the Pathet Lao. As in Indonesia, our policy makers worried that if Communists gained a role in a coalition government, they would push the other parties out.[7]

To prevent a role for the Communists, Eisenhower pressured Laotian politicians to exclude the Pathet Lao.[8] In 1956, the administration opened a military mission in Laos, to advise the Laotian army on how to defeat the Pathet Lao. In good bureaucratese, it named the mission the Program Evaluation Office, to disguise its military role.[9] We gave generous aid, funding the entire budget of Laos' army.[10] After National Assembly elections were scheduled in 1958, we became more generous still, in an effort to secure victory for anti-communist candidates. The Pathet Lao was strong in rural areas, but Souvanna Phouma's government paid little attention to rural development. So we mounted Operation Booster Shot to get economic aid to rural areas, to win hearts and minds for the government in time for the 1958 election.[11] To favored candidates we gave money, which they then distributed for high-visibility development projects.[12]

The booster shot did not take, however. Our candidates did poorly, while the Pathet Lao and one allied party won a majority in the National Assembly.[13] Despite the leftist victory, however, the executive branch of the Laotian government remained neutralist. But President Eisenhower continued to worry that the Laotians were not serious about putting down the Pathet Lao. If the Laotian army was not willing to fight the communists, the Eisenhower administration concluded, it must do the job itself. So under the code name Operation White Star, the CIA organized its own army, separate from the government's.[14]

CIA operatives covertly approached leaders of the Hmong, an ethnic minority in the mountains of northeast Laos, and asked them to fight the Pathet Lao. The Hmong, also known as the Meo, had fought on the side of France against the Lao, so they found it an easy transition to fight for the United States.[15]

The logistics were simple: the CIA had an airline called Air America, nominally a private cargo operation.[16] Air America was affiliated with Civil Air Transport, the CIA airline that operated in Indonesia during the 1958 rebellion. In Air America planes, the CIA men flew from one mountain village to another.[17] If the village would provide a few recruits, the CIA gave it money, guns, and rice. To the Hmong, whose livelihood was marginal at best, the offer was one they found hard to refuse. Moreover, if a village declined to contribute recruits, the CIA considered it pro-Pathet Lao, and made life difficult for it.[18] So most Hmong villages cooperated, for reasons either of gain or coercion, and the Hmong army began to attack Pathet Lao positions.

The CIA had one other economic lever to maintain Hmong loyalty. The area inhabited by the Hmong formed part of what was known as the Golden Triangle, famous for its opium. For the Hmong, opium was their major cash crop. But living in remote areas, the Hmong had difficulty getting opium to market. Air America's supply flights into their villages provided the perfect solution.[19] The Hmong got their opium out of their villages as transport cargo onto Air America planes.[20] The CIA acknowledged that it knew the Hmong transported opium on Air America, but it claimed it tried to stop them.[21]

Challenging that claim, a number of CIA pilots reported that they were under orders from their superiors not to interfere with the opium shipments. The CIA was apparently concerned that opium might be detected on Air America flights landing outside Laos, so to help the Hmong get their opium out more quietly, the CIA set up a special airline for the Hmong army, called the Xieng Khouang airline. Xieng Khouang took opium to Vietnam, where some was used by our soldiers, and the rest went into the international opium market. Some of the proceeds were used by the CIA and Hmong army leadership to pay Hmong soldiers. We were running a secret war on opium profits.[22]

The press did not learn about Operation White Star and the Hmong army until some years later. When Kennedy assumed office, he stepped up operations in Laos, sending additional advisors to the Laotian army.[23] In March 1961, just at the time of the Bay of Pigs landing, the Pathet Lao seemed to be gaining the upper hand. Kennedy became so concerned about a Pathet Lao victory that he put Marines in Okinawa on alert and sent helicopters to Thailand for possible deployment in Laos.[24] Kennedy came close to sending the Marines in and reportedly would have done so except for the failure at the Bay of Pigs, which gave him pause concerning another landing. Kennedy later had second thoughts about whether a landing in Laos would have worked. He told an advisor, "Thank God the Bay of Pigs happened when it did. Otherwise we'd be in Laos by now, and that would be a hundred times worse."[25]

Kennedy built up the ranks of the Hmong army. In a confidential report, Brigadier General Edward G. Lansdale stated that 9,000 Hmong had been trained and were operating "with considerable effectiveness in Communist-dominated territory in Laos." The Hmong army was commanded by the CIA station chief in Vientiane, while the Chief of our Military Assistance Advisory Group, which advised the Laotian army, played a consulting role.[26] Kennedy thought the Hmong army so effective that he ordered that 2,000 more Hmong be recruited.[27]

In 1962, when the Laotian political parties agreed at a Geneva meeting on the formation of a new government that would be free from foreign control and intervention, Kennedy was forced to withdraw American military advisors from the Laotian army. However, Kennedy continued secretly to fund the Hmong army, which let us keep pressure on the Pathet Lao without appearing to be involved.[28] In short order Kennedy built the Hmong army up to 30,000.[29] To augment it further, the CIA hired 20,000 members of the Thai army and brought them into Laos to fight the Pathet Lao. Because of the operation's size, the CIA had to inform a congressional committee, so that funds could be allocated. The CIA's chief for the Far East, William Colby, urged the committee to let him recruit even more Hmong.[30]

The secret war dragged on inconclusively, because the Hmong could not defeat the Pathet Lao. Soon after Lyndon Johnson assumed office, the CIA devised a new tactic, which was to send U.S. Air Force planes to bomb the Pathet Lao stronghold in northeast Laos, on the Plain of Jars, a region that derived its name from ancient jar-like structures that archaeologists had found there. Johnson sent the first raids in May 1964,[31] and the air force started bombing in earnest in December.[32] The National Security Council oversaw the bombing operation, making sure to keep it secret. At a December 12, 1964, meeting, the Council decided not to make public statements about the bombing of the Plain of Jars, "unless a plane were lost." If that happened, the administration would claim that "we were merely escorting reconnaissance flights as requested by the Laotian government."[33]

In 1965, the U.S. Air Force built a secret radar station in northeast Laos to guide its planes bombing northern Vietnam.[34] North Vietnamese forces by then were operating in northeast Laos to support the Pathet Lao, and they overran the station, killing the dozen air force personnel who staffed it.[35]

Also in 1965, the air force and army began air and ground attacks in southeast Laos, an area it called the Ho Chi Minh trail, which was used by the Vietnamese to ferry supplies and personnel from the northern to the southern part of Vietnam.[36] To aid this bombing, the air force installed high-tech sensors that could detect movement on the ground. The sensors sent signals to airplanes, which then bombed the area of movement.[37] Since the sensors could not distinguish the type of movement, the targets might be combatants, but they might just as easily be civilians or farm animals. Like the bombing in northeast Laos, this operation was kept secret.

In 1966, the Johnson administration stepped up the bombing on the Plain of Jars, still keeping it quiet, even though by this time whole villages had been destroyed and thousands of inhabitants had been displaced.[38] George Chapelier, a Belgian UN official in Laos, reported that the bombing was so intense "that no organized life was possible in the villages."[39]

In November 1968, our bombing raids over North Vietnam stopped, as President Johnson came under heavy international pressure against them. But the Laos bombing campaign remained unpublicized, so Johnson decided to divert our bombers to the Plain of Jars.[40] The air force ran up to 800 bombing sorties a day, turning the plain, in military parlance, into a "free-fire" zone, to break the Pathet Lao's hold by making the Plain uninhabitable.[41] Chapelier described the impact: "The villagers moved to the outskirts and then deeper and deeper into the forest as the bombing climax reached its peak in 1969 when jet planes came daily and destroyed all stationary structures. Nothing was left standing. The villagers lived in trenches and holes or in caves. They only farmed at night."[42] In February 1970, the air force began using its giant B-52s, which obliterate a large area through so-called "carpet bombing."[43]

A thirteen-year-old Laotian boy described the bombing of his village on the Plain of Jars. "The airplanes came bombing my ricefield until the bomb craters made farming impossible. And the village was hit and burned," he said. "And some relatives working in the fields came running out to the road to return to the village but the airplanes saw and shot them . . .. [W]e heard their screams, but could not go to help them. When the airplanes left, we went out to help them, but they were already dead."[44]

The Pathet Lao protested the bombing and the press reported the protests;[45] but the air force, in accordance with the 1964 National Security Council (NSC) decision, claimed it was only flying "armed reconnaissance" and kept the press from speaking to its Thailand-based pilots.[46] So the bombing still remained secret, even as it drove the Pathet Lao off the Plain of Jars, turning its towns to rubble and sending its inhabitants to refugee camps near Vientiane.[47]

When Richard Nixon became president in 1969, he continued the bombing of the Plain of Jars, but by then the curtain of secrecy over the operation was crumbling. Reporters got wind of the devastation.[48] "The rebel economy and social fabric," wrote one, had become "the main United States targets."[49] Senator Stuart Symington of Missouri held hearings on the Laos bombing and uncovered its scope. "We are fighting a big war in Laos," he concluded, yet "we are still trying to hide it not only from the people but also from the Congress." Said Symington, "we are telling Americans they must fight and die to maintain an open society, but not telling our people what we are doing."[50] With the Indochina war controversial and divisive at home, the administration feared that if the public knew we were waging another war in Laos, it might force an end to the whole Indochina project.

In 1970, with the Laos war in its fourth presidential administration, reporters finally discovered the CIA's Hmong army and blew the lid off that aspect of the secret war. This revelation forced President Nixon to make the Laos war public, with expenditures on Laos entering the official Pentagon budget.[51] Despite the press disclosures about the bombing on the Plain of Jars, Nixon still tried to conceal the true purpose, arguing that the air force was running only "combat-support missions for Laotian forces."[52]

Senator Edward Kennedy of Massachusetts took testimony from ranking officials and accused the administration of "saturation bombing" and "the forced evacuation of population from enemy held or threatened areas."[53] Kennedy found that the Plain of Jars was "almost completely depopulated" of its previous 150,000 inhabitants[54] and berated the administration for doing all this secretly, "to cover the expanding American involvement in Laos from the American people."[55]

In 1973, when peace talks were held for Indochina, Nixon ended operations in Laos. By then the Air Force had dropped 1.5 million tons of bombs in Laos, more than we used in all of World War II.[56] The CIA disbanded the Hmong army, and a new neutralist government took power in Vientiane. Two years later it was replaced by a leftist government allied to North Vietnam. Our money, secret army, and bombing were not enough to keep Laos on our side of the "bamboo curtain." We had achieved, said

Senator Frank Church of Idaho, "a hostile Laos," a country "that preferred the indigenous forces of communism to control imposed by Westerners."[57]

NOTES

1. Charles A. Stevenson, *The End of Nowhere: American Policy Toward Laos since 1954* (1972), p. 37.

2. *Mutual Security Appropriations for 1955*, Hearings on H. R. 10051, an Act Making Appropriations for Mutual Security for the Fiscal Year Ending June 30, 1955, and For Other Purposes, Committee on Appropriations, U.S. Senate, 83rd Cong., 2d sess., p. 306 (1954).

3. *United States Aid Operations in Laos*, Hearings before a Subcommittee of the Committee on Government Operations, U.S. House of Representatives, 86th Cong., 1st sess., 1959, pp. 184–85.

4. *Mutual Security Appropriations for 1959*, Hearings before the Subcommittee of the Committee on Appropriations, U.S. House of Representatives, 85th Cong., 2d sess., 1958, p. 972 (testimony of J. Graham Parsons).

5. Quoted in Emmet John Hughes, *The Ordeal of Power: A Political Memoir of the Eisenhower Years* (1963), p. 208.

6. Stevenson, *The End of Nowhere*, p. 10.

7. Ibid., p. 41.

8. Ibid., pp. 44–45.

9. Walt Haney, "The Pentagon Papers and the United States Involvement in Laos," in Noam Chomsky and Howard Zinn, eds., *The Pentagon Papers: The Defense Department History of United States Decisionmaking on Vietnam* (Senator Gravel ed., 1972), 5: 248, 251–52.

10. *U.S. Aid Operations in Laos*, Seventh Report by the Committee on Government Operations, U.S. House of Representatives, House Report 546, 86th Cong., 1st sess., 1959, p. 8; Stevenson, *The End of Nowhere*, pp. 26–27, 35–38. Andrew Tully, *CIA: The Inside Story* (1962), p. 217.

11. Haney, "The Pentagon Papers and the United States Involvement in Laos," in *The Pentagon Papers*, 5: 253.

12. Stevenson, *The End of Nowhere*, p. 47.

13. Tillman Durdin, "Leftists in Laos Prevail at Polls," *New York Times*, May 13, 1958, p. A7, col. 4.

14. James William Gibson, *The Perfect War: Technowar in Vietnam* (1986), p. 386; Stevenson, *The End of Nowhere*, p. 125.

15. John Prados, *Presidents' Secret Wars: CIA and Pentagon Covert Operations Since World War II* (1986), p. 269.

16. *Final Report: Foreign and Military Intelligence*, U.S. Senate, Select Committee to Study Governmental Operations with Respect to Intelligence Activities, Book I, 94th Cong., 2d sess., April 26, 1976, pp. 208–209, 219–27; William Colby, *Honorable Men: My Life in the CIA* (1978), p. 198.

17. Colby, *Honorable Men*, p. 195.

18. Gibson, *The Perfect War*, pp. 386–87.

19. Prados, *Presidents' Secret Wars*, p. 285.

20. Gibson, *The Perfect War*, p. 387; Alfred W. McCoy, *The Politics of Heroin in Southeast Asia* (1972), pp. 274–77.

21. *Final Report: Foreign and Military Intelligence*, pp. 228–30.

22. Transcript, "Frontline" Special, "Guns, Drugs and the CIA," WGBH, Public Broadcasting System (1988), pp. 4–18.

23. "National Security Action Memorandum No. 80," August 29, 1961, *United States-Vietnam Relations 1945–1967: Study Prepared by the Department of Defense* (1971), 11: 247–48; Haney, "The Pentagon Papers and the United States Involvement in Laos," in *The Pentagon Papers*, 5: 260, 263.

24. Haney, "The Pentagon Papers and the United States Involvement in Laos," in *The Pentagon Papers*, 5: 261; Stevenson, *The End of Nowhere*, pp. 146–53.

25. Theodore C. Sorensen, *Kennedy* (1965), p. 644.

26. Brig Gen. Edward G. Lansdale, "Resources for Unconventional Warfare, S.E. Asia," July, 1961, in *The Pentagon Papers: The Defense Department History of United States Decisionmaking on Vietnam* (Senator Gravel ed., 1971), 2: 646.

27. "National Security Action Memorandum No. 80," August 29, 1961, *United States-Vietnam Relations 1945–1967: Study Prepared by the Department of Defense* (1971), 11: 247-48.

28. Haney, "The Pentagon Papers and the United States Involvement in Laos," in *The Pentagon Papers*, 5: 265–66.

29. Prados, *Presidents' Secret Wars*, p. 272; Stevenson, *The End of Nowhere*, p. 212; Victor Marchetti and John Marks, *The CIA and the Cult of Intelligence* (1974), pp. 31–32.

30. Ralph McGehee, *Deadly Deceits: My 25 Years in the CIA* (1983), p. 83.

31. Charles W. Corddry, "Communist Antiaircraft Batteries in Laos Attacked by U.S. Planes," *Washington Post*, June 14, 1964, p. Al, col. 1; Stevenson, *The End of Nowhere*, pp. 201–203; Haney, "The Pentagon Papers and the United States Involvement in Laos," in *The Pentagon Papers*, 5: 268; *Refugee and Civilian War Casualty Problems in Indochina*, A Staff Report Prepared for the Use of the Subcommittee to Investigate Problems Connected with Refugees and Escapees of the Committee on the Judiciary, U.S. Senate, 91st Cong., 2d sess., September 28, 1970, p. 29.

32. Stevenson, *The End of Nowhere*, p. 207.

33. "Military Pressures Against North Vietnam, February 1964–January 1965," in *The Pentagon Papers*, 3: 253–54.

34. *Refugee and Civilian War Casualty Problems in Indochina*, pp. 21–22. Prados, *Presidents' Secret Wars*, pp. 281–82.

35. T. D. Allman, "12 Americans Died in Loss of Secret Laotian Outpost," *Washington Post*, March 16, 1970, p. Al, col. 1.

36. "The Air War in North Vietnam: Rolling Thunder Begins, February–June, 1965," in *The Pentagon Papers*, 3: 341–42; Colby, *Honorable Men*, p. 198; *Bombing in Cambodia*, Hearings before the Committee on Armed Services, U.S. Senate, 93rd Cong., 1st sess. (1973), pp. 492–93.

37. Gibson, *The Perfect War*, pp. 396–97.

38. *Refugee and Civilian War Casualty Problems in Indochina*, p. 29.

39. George Chapelier, "Plain of Jars: Social Changes Under Five Years of Pathet Lao Administration," excerpted in *War-Related Civilian Problems in Indochina. Part II: Laos and Cambodia*. Hearings before the Subcommittee to Investigate Problems Connected with Refugees and Escapees of the Committee on the Judiciary, U.S. Senate, 91st Cong., 1st sess., April 21–22, 1971, p. 92.

40. Stevenson, *The End of Nowhere*, p. 218.

41. *Refugee and Civilian War Casualty Problems in Indochina*, pp. 29–30; Jacques Decornoy, "Guerre oubliée au Laos," *Le Monde*, July 4, 1968, p. 2, col. 1; also in *War-Related Civilian Problems in Indochina. Part II*, p. 93.

42. Chapelier, "Plain of Jars," in *War-Related Civilian Problems in Indochina. Part II*, p. 93.

43. Gibson, *The Perfect War*, p. 395. William Shawcross, *Sideshow: Kissinger, Nixon and the Destruction of Cambodia* (1979), p. 211; John W. Finney, "U.S. Discloses Use of B-52's over Northern Laos," *New York Times*, May 4, 1971, p. A10, col. 4; *Bombing in Cambodia*, p. 489.

44. Fred Branfman, *Voices from the Plain of Jars* (1972), p. 45.

45. "Pathet Lao Cites U.S. Losses," *New York Times*, December 22, 1968, p. A3, col. 2; "Pathet Lao Complains U.S. Is Intensifying Its Bombing," *New York Tines*, December 31, 1968, p. A6, col. 8.

46. John W. Finney, "U.S. Discloses Use of B-52's for Raids over Northern Laos," *New York Times*, May 4, 1971, p. A10, col. 4.

47. Gibson, *The Perfect War*, p. 392; Robert Shaplen, "Our Involvement in Laos," *Foreign Affairs 48* (April 1970): 489; Branfman, *Voices from the Plain of Jars*, p. 23; *Refugee and Civilian War Casualty Problems in Indochina*, p. 24.

48. Daniel Southerland, "What U.S. Bombing Feels like to Laotians," *Christian Science Monitor*, March 14, 1970, p. 1, col. 2.

49. Timothy D. Allman, "Support by U.S. Alters Laos War," *New York Times*, October 1, 1969, p. A9, col. 1.

50. *United States Security Agreements and Commitments Abroad: Kingdom of Laos*, Hearings before the Subcommittee on United States Security Agreements and Commitments Abroad, Comm. on Foreign Relations, U.S. Senate, 91st Cong., 1st sess., Part 2, October 20–28,1969, p.543.

51. Prados, *Presidents' Secret Wars*, pp. 290–94.

52. "Text of Statement Issued by President Nixon on U.S. Policy and Activity in Laos," *New York Times*, March 7, 1970, p. A10, col. 1.

53. *Refugee and Civilian War Casualty Problems in Indochina*, p. 19.

54. Ibid., p. 24.

55. Ibid., p. 19.

56. William S. Turley, *The Second Indochina War: A Short Political and Military History, 1954–1975* (1986), p. 87.

57. Frank Church, "Covert Action: Swampland of American Foreign Policy," *Bulletin of the Atomic Scientists*, February 1976, p. 11.

11. VIETNAM: WHAT WERE THOSE BLEEPS?

Our interest in Indochina was not limited to Laos. The Truman administration, as we saw earlier, used the Korean hostilities in 1950 as an occasion to start paying France's expenses to fight the Vietnamese insurgency. By the time France pulled out in 1954, following negotiations in Geneva, we were paying most of the bill for its war, and then it became our war. As in Laos, the leftists in Vietnam had been strong in fighting France, so their popularity was high.

The leftists set up an administration in Hanoi, while those Vietnamese who had not opposed France set up their own administration in Saigon. Under the agreement reached in Geneva, the two governments were separated by an imaginary line drawn at the 17th parallel. Important to note, however, is that the Geneva agreement called for national elections in 1956 to pick a single government for all Vietnam.

President Eisenhower, suspicious of the leftist administration in Hanoi, took the Saigon administration under his wing. Worried that if national elections were held, the popular president of the Hanoi administration, Ho Chi Minh, would win, Eisenhower told the Saigon administration it needn't go through with the elections scheduled for 1956, and, as a result, those elections were not held. This led to an exploration of other options to reunite the country, both by the Hanoi administration and by those Vietnamese living below the 17th parallel who viewed the Saigon administration as a foreign implant.

In 1963, the commanding officer of my Marine Corps reserve unit assigned me to give lectures to my unit on world affairs, especially on potential trouble spots. When I lectured on Vietnam, few of the Marines knew where it was, or what connection the United States had to it. I told them that Vietnam was important to the United States for strategic and economic reasons. The Communists, after all, were out to get it, I said. One Marine raised his hand to object. "I don't think we need to get in there; there's no reason to get into a war." I explained patiently that there was oil under Vietnam's continental shelf, that Vietnam's large population was an important market for our products, and that Vietnam commanded the sea route from the Middle East to the Far East.

By 1963, in fact, the Kennedy administration had military advisors in Vietnam, and in 1964, President Johnson decided on a major escalation to boost the Saigon administration's fortunes. We would bomb targets in the north to convince the Hanoi government to stop supporting the leftists in the south. Before starting the bombing raid, however, Johnson wanted to protect his political flank by securing Congress's blessing.[1] So he had his staff draft a joint resolution that Congress might pass to authorize a bombing campaign over North Vietnam.[2] At the time, however, Congress's attention was not focused on Indochina, and there was little hope it would go along.

Soon an opportunity for convincing Congress presented itself. On July 30, 1964, South Vietnamese naval forces under our direction raided two islands in the Gulf of Tonkin, which cuts into the Vietnamese coast north of the 17th parallel. At the same time, the destroyer USS *Maddox*, outfitted for electronic spying, sailed into the Gulf of Tonkin looking for intelligence information to use in bombing the north.[3] Several days later, the South Vietnamese naval forces raided again, and on August 3, North Vietnamese torpedo boats approached the *Maddox*, evidently thinking it was involved in the South Vietnamese raids. The *Maddox* frightened the torpedo boats off, and President Johnson ordered another destroyer, the USS *C. Turner Joy*, to provide protection for the *Maddox*. That same night, August 3, South Vietnamese PT boats attacked sites on the North Vietnamese shore.[4]

The next day, August 4, the *Maddox* reported being fired upon by North Vietnamese torpedo boats.[5] The report was based on sonar readings and by bleeps on the *Maddox*'s radar screen.[6] But the *C. Turner Joy*, which had more sophisticated sonar than the *Maddox*, did not detect any such firings, although it was watching the situation closely.[7] Neither of the two destroyers was hit, and their crews did not see any torpedo explosions. Navy pilot James B. Stockdale, who flew over the *Maddox* and *C. Turner Joy* that night looking for North Vietnamese action, saw no boats, no gunfire, and no torpedo wakes.[8]

The commander of the two ships quickly decided that the report of a firing on the *Maddox* had been erroneous. *Maddox* crew members had apparently mistaken sonar reflections of the *Maddox*'s own rudder for enemy torpedoes.[9] The commander immediately flashed an urgent message to Washington to withdraw the report.[10]

At the White House, the retraction message, curiously, was not accepted at face value. Instead it created "confusion over whether an attack on the destroyers had actually taken place."[11] Secretary of Defense Robert McNamara asked military commanders whether the first report might somehow have been accurate.[12] Despite the second report, the Defense Department publicly announced a "deliberate attack" on the two destroyers,[13] with President Johnson declaring that we would take reprisal strikes against North Vietnam.[14] In a televised address, Johnson said somberly, "It is my duty to the American people to report that renewed hostile actions against United States ships on the high seas in the Gulf of Tonkin have today required me to order the military forces of the United States to take action in reply." He accused the northern forces of "open aggression."[15]

Relying on the dubious intelligence he had received about the supposed attack, President Johnson redrafted his congressional authorization resolution for air strikes and submitted it for adoption.[16] In a Senate hearing on the draft resolution on August 6, Senator Wayne Morse of Oregon confronted Secretary McNamara with the information that the two destroyers had been associated with the South Vietnamese raids. McNamara denied that our commanders in Vietnam had been aware of these.

Senator Morse's misgivings notwithstanding, Congress accepted the false information about a firing on the *Maddox* and passed a joint resolution, solemnly intoning, "Whereas naval units of the Communist regime in Vietnam, in violation of the principles of the Charter of the United Nations and of international law, have deliberately and repeatedly attacked United States naval vessels lawfully present in international waters . . . ." On that basis, Congress "approved" the "determination of the President" to take "all necessary measures to repel any armed attack against the forces of the United States and to prevent further aggression." Congress said that the United States was "prepared, as the President determines, to take all necessary steps, including the use of armed force, to assist any member or protocol state of the Southeast Asia Collective Defense Treaty requesting assistance in defense of its freedom."[17] So certain was Congress of Johnson's information that the Senate passed the Gulf of Tonkin resolution 88 to 2, and the House 416 to 0.[18]

The Gulf of Tonkin incident as reported by President Johnson influenced not only Congress but the public, convincing it to back strong action against North Vietnam.[19] Whereas opinion polls before the resolution showed a 58 percent disapproval of Johnson's Vietnam policy, afterward it rose to a 72 percent approval rate, a remarkable overnight turnaround.[20] According to an administration report, the reprisal strikes that President Johnson ordered after the Gulf of Tonkin resolution "marked the crossing of an important threshold in the war, and it was accomplished with virtually no domestic criticism, indeed, with an evident increase in public support for the Administration."[21]

Undersecretary of State George Ball said later that while President Johnson knew that the information about a firing on the *Maddox* was shaky, being eager to attack North Vietnam, he used it anyway.[22] To make his case believable, President Johnson concealed from the public and from Congress the spy mission of the *Maddox*, the South Vietnamese raids in the vicinity, our support of those raids, and the commander's retraction of the initial report of a firing.[23]

Senator J. William Fulbright of Arkansas, who introduced the Gulf of Tonkin resolution in the Senate at Johnson's request, held hearings on the incident in 1968, by which time the facts were beginning to come out.

Fulbright admitted then that had he known in 1964 about the actual communications from the commander, "I certainly don't believe I would have rushed into action." "I think I did a great disservice to the Senate," Fulbright said. "The least I can do. . . is to alert. . . future Senates that these matters are not to be dealt with in this casual manner."[24]

Having received his resolution from Congress, President Johnson in 1965 stepped up the bombing in North Vietnam and brought U.S. troops into South Vietnam. But something was still lacking in Johnson's ideological armor. The phantom assault in the Gulf of Tonkin provided a pretext for retaliation, but not a rationale for an all-out war. Johnson needed such a rationale in order to ensure the public's acceptance before he could use large numbers of troops in Vietnam.

The State Department took on the task, publishing a paper it titled *Aggression From the North: The Record of North Vietnam's Campaign to Conquer South Viet-Nam.*[25] For the duration of the Vietnam war, this document, which the press called the white paper on Vietnam, would be the administration's explanation of why we were fighting.

"South Viet-Nam," the white paper began, "is fighting for its life against a brutal campaign of terror and armed attack inspired, directed, supplied, and controlled by the Communist regime in Hanoi." The paper averred that "a Communist government [i.e., that of North Vietnam] has set out deliberately to conquer a sovereign people in a neighboring state [South Vietnam]."

North Vietnam's commitment to succeed, the paper said, "is no less total than was the commitment of the regime in North Korea in 1950." North Vietnam, according to the paper, had learned from North Korea's failure and did not attack openly, beginning instead "concealed aggression" against South Vietnam, hoping to take over the south before the world realized its aim.

As with the Korean war, our policy makers found Communist expansionism a key ingredient in rationalizing our purpose. Even before he became president, John Kennedy viewed Vietnam as "the cornerstone of the Free World in Southeast Asia, the keystone to the arch, the finger in the dike." "Burma, Thailand, India, Japan, the Philippines and obviously

Laos and Cambodia," he said, would be threatened "if the Red Tide of Communism overflowed into Vietnam."[26] To stem this tide, Kennedy's staff worked out strategies for counterinsurgency efforts in "brush fire wars" in the Third World.[27]

Like Kennedy, President Johnson saw Vietnam as a cold war battleground. In 1961, while still vice president, Johnson visited Vietnam and reported back to Kennedy that "the battle against Communism" must "be joined in Southeast Asia with strength and determination to achieve success there—or the United States, inevitably, must surrender the Pacific and take up our defenses on our own shores."[28]

The white paper gave a scathing account of North Vietnam's tactics. The insurgency in South Vietnam that called itself the National Liberation Front, and which the Johnson administration called the Viet Cong, was not genuine, charged the paper, but "was formed at Hanoi's order in 1960." The "principal function" of the Viet Cong was "to create the false impression that the aggression in South Vietnam is an indigenous rebellion against the established government." The Viet Cong was "directed by the Military High Command in Hanoi," the white paper said; its "hard core" was trained in North Vietnam and was "ordered into the South by Hanoi."

As evidence that the southern insurgency was being run from North Vietnam, the white paper averred that "many of the weapons and much of the ammunition and other supplies" were sent by North Vietnam, which had obtained this equipment from "Communist China and other Communist states." South Vietnam, the white paper continued, was merely fighting in self-defense. As for our own role, "the United States has responded to the appeals of the Government of the Republic of Vietnam for help in this defense of the freedom and independence of its land and its people." The white paper's bottom line was that we were in the right because South Vietnam was being attacked by an outside state, and under the United Nations Charter, a state may ask another state to help repel an aggressor. At the political level, the white paper's thrust was that a non-Communist nation was being blatantly attacked by a Communist country.

There was, to be sure, northern involvement in developments in the south of Vietnam. The Vietnamese Communist party had not split into southern and northern divisions after 1954, so party members in the north retained a voice in the party in the south.[29] This united party had, in fact, decided at a congress in Hanoi, in September 1960, to establish the National Liberation Front (NLF) in the south.[30] In 1961, the party's political bureau, referring to the north as a "source of support and a base area of the revolution to liberate the South," directed the NLF to step up military efforts against the Saigon administration in rural areas.[31]

This directive, however, did not necessarily impose policy on the southerners, as the white paper suggested it did. On the contrary, southern elements in the party pushed for a policy of starting military action against the Saigon administration. The core of the insurgency in the south were people who had long opposed French rule, and who viewed the Saigon administration as a continuation of Western control of Vietnam.[32] In 1960–61, these southerners saw military action as urgent, because legislative elections held in the south in 1959 had gone against Ngo Dinh Diem, who headed the Saigon administration; as a result, Diem began ruthlessly to suppress his opponents. The southerners feared that if they did not take the initiative against Diem, he would get them first.[33]

Although the Communist party's directive advocated stepping up military efforts, it did not call for a major military insurgency. The Party in Hanoi was preoccupied with consolidating its rule in the north, and both the Soviet Union and China were reluctant to see armed action against the Saigon administration.[34] As at the start of the war in Korea, they were not anxious for a confrontation with the United States.

A major omission in the white paper was that it ignored the fact that the NLF had a following in the south. The NLF rose to prominence in the villages, where the Saigon administration was weak, and where Communist cadres succeeded in forcing out local Saigon officials and assuming authority themselves.[35] NLF military units, in fact, were militia that relied on the support of the villagers.[36] The NLF controlled over half the countryside,[37] collecting taxes in most of the villages of South Vietnam.[38] NLF control of the villages was so strong that the CIA initiated what it called its Phoenix Program, aimed at assassinating NLF village leaders.

The white paper exaggerated the north's role, leading the reader to think that the NLF obtained all its personnel and equipment from there; but these imports accounted for only a fraction of the NLF's strength. As for arms, some, indeed, were brought from the north, either by sea or over the Ho Chi Minh trail in Laos.[39] In 1962, the International Control Commission for Vietnam, which policed the 1954 Geneva agreement, found evidence "in specific instances" that "armed and unarmed personnel, arms, munitions and other supplies have been sent from the Zone in the North to the Zone in the South."[40] Most of the NLF's weapons, however, were manufactured in the south, or were bought or captured from the Saigon army. Adept at seizing weapons, the NLF, according to Pentagon figures for 1962–1964, captured 12,300 more weapons than it lost to the Saigon army.[41]

In an effort to demonstrate NLF dependence on the Communist world, the white paper included a statistical appendix on weapons produced in Communist countries that wound up in the NLF's hands.[42] The appendix, however, showed only one hundred weapons a year, mostly light rifles, a minuscule fraction of the total number of weapons the NLF held. When pressed by reporters, the Pentagon admitted that only 15–20 percent of the NLF's arms and equipment had come from North Vietnam.[43] Even to the extent that the NLF's weapons were Soviet or Chinese, this did not prove direct Soviet or Chinese aid, because these weapons were available on the international arms market.

As for personnel, the white paper stated in another appendix that the State Department could "confirm" 39,550 combatants who had joined the NLF from the north between 1959 and 1964, and estimated an additional 17,550 whom, it said, could not be "confirmed."[44] These figures, even if true, still could not reveal an impressive level of infiltration but, to the contrary, confirmed that most NLF recruits were local inhabitants in the south.[45] According to U.S. government figures for 1965, arrivals from the north accounted for only 10 percent of the total forces of the NLF, which was recruiting 3,500 men a month in the south.[46]

Of those who did travel south to join the NLF, most were people originally from the south, who had moved north after the demarcation line was drawn in 1954.[47] The white paper recognized this phenomenon and went to some pains to deal with it, charging that 75 percent of those coming south were actually natives of the north. But the white paper could give no firm evidence for this figure, reciting only a few case histories of individuals who went south, and most of these in fact involved Vietnamese who were natives of the south.[48] As for regular military units of native northerners entering the south, this began only after the Gulf of Tonkin resolution and President Johnson's bombing of the north; by the time of the white paper, these forces numbered only a few thousand [49]

Beyond its weaknesses in showing levels of arms and personnel moving south, the State Department's white paper had a more fundamental flaw, because it did not explain the origin of the division between north and south in Vietnam. The white paper spoke of the north and south as if they were two separate countries, so that an attack by one on the other would constitute an act of international aggression, rather than a civil war; however, as we have seen, the 1954 demarcation line was not an international boundary.

The white paper's reference to Korea was instructive, however, because it gave the same false impression about Vietnam that the Truman administration had given about Korea in 1950. Korea and Vietnam were both single countries, but we tried to make them appear divided. Indeed, in Vietnam, the only major foreign element was the military presence of the United States, whom the International Control Commission criticized for bringing in military advisors, which, it said, violated the 1954 agreements.[50]

We were intervening militarily in a domestic dispute in Vietnam; and to cover that intervention, we portrayed a civil war as an act of international aggression. In the process, we lost 50,000 of our own forces, and overall two million were killed on both sides, the bulk of them civilians.[51] Had we not interfered, the Vietnamese would probably have settled their differences with far fewer casualties.

After the war ended, I visited Vietnam and witnessed the devastation. In the south alone, the bombs dropped by B-52s left an estimated 23 million craters, turning the land into swamp, and denuding nearly half of the south's forests.[52] Thousands of our explosive mines remained in the farmland, so that Vietnamese farmers continued to be killed and maimed by them.[53]

In downtown Hanoi I saw a neighborhood we had bombed in December 1972, because President Nixon said that bombing would convince North Vietnam to negotiate. Here thousands had been killed in a short time. There was no monument to the dead, but an exhibit had been set up with photographs of victims and demolished houses. An elderly man, a survivor of the bombing, was caretaker for the exhibit. As he showed it to me, I could see he was straining to avoid putting awkward questions to a guest whose country was responsible for the bombing. Finally he asked me, as politely as he could, how America could do this to his neighborhood. I had no answer.

NOTES

1. *The Pentagon Papers As Published by the* New York Times (1971), pp. 253, 256, 259.

2. "Draft Resolution for Congress on Actions in Southeast Asia," May 25, 1964, in *The Pentagon Papers As Published by the* New York Times, p. 294.

3. *The Pentagon Papers As Published by the* New York Times, p. 267; Robert Scheer, "Tonkin—Dubious Premise for War," *Los Angeles Times*, April 29, 1985, p. Al, col. 1.

4. *The Pentagon Papers As Published by the* New York Times, pp. 267–68; Scheer, "Tonkin–Dubious Premise for War."

5. *The Pentagon Papers As Published by the* New York Times, p. 269; "The Tonkin Chronology," *Los Angeles Times*, April 29, 1985, p. A6, col. 5.

6. Scheer, "Tonkin–Dubious Premise for War."

7. Alan E. Goodman and Seth E. Tillman, "Debris from the Tonkin Resolution," *New York Times*, August 5, 1984, p. D21, col. 2.

8. Scheer, "Tonkin–Dubious Premise for War."

9. Ibid.

10. Joseph C. Goulden, *Truth Is the First Casualty: The Gulf of Tonkin Affair-Illusion and Reality* (1969), p. 152.

11. *The Pentagon Papers As Published by the* New York Times, p. 270.

12. Scheer, "Tonkin–Dubious Premise for War."

13. Arnold H. Lubasch, "Two Torpedo Vessels Believed Sunk in Gull of Tonkin," *New York Times*, August 5, 1964, p. Al, col. 4.

14. Tom Wicker, "U.S. Planes Attack North Vietnam Bases; President Orders 'Limited' Retaliation After Communists' PT Boats Renew Raids," *New York Times*, August 5, 1964, p. Al, col. 8.

15. "The President's Address," *New York Times*, August 5, 1964, p. Al, col. 6.

16. *The Pentagon Papers As Published by the* New York Times, pp. 272–73.

17. Joint Resolution to Promote the Maintenance of International Peace and Security in Southeast Asia, August 10, 1964, U.S. Congress, *Statutes at Large*, vol. 78, p. 384, §§ 1–3 (1964).

18. *The Pentagon Papers As Published by the* New York Times, pp. 273–75.

19. Ibid., p. 277.

20. Scheer, "Tonkin–Dubious Premise for War."

21. *The Pentagon Papers As Published by the* New York Times, p. 278.

22. Scheer, "Tonkin–Dubious Premise for War"; Goodman and Tillman, "Debris from the Tonkin Resolution."

23. Goulden, *Truth Is the First Casualty*, pp. 239–40.

24. Scheer, "Tonkin–Dubious Premise for War."

25. Pub. no. 7839, DSB, vol. 52, p. 404 (1965).

26. John F. Kennedy, "America's Stake in Vietnam: The Cornerstone of the Free World in Southeast Asia," *Vital Speeches of the Day*, vol. 22, p. 618 (August 1, 1956).

27. William S. Turley, *The Second Indochina War: A Short Political and Military History*, 1954–1975 (1986), p. 37.

28. *The Pentagon Papers: The Defense Department History of the United States Decisionmaking on Vietnam* (Sen. Gravel ed. 1971), 2: 57.

29. Turley, *The Second Indochina War*, pp. 19–21.

30. Ibid., p. 28; War Experiences Recapitulation Committee of the High-Level Military Institute, People's Army Publishing House, Hanoi, *The Anti-U.S. Resistance War for National Salvation 1954–1975: Military Events*, in U.S. Government, Joint Publications Research Service no. 80968, June 3, 1982, P. 43.

31. Turley, *The Second Indochina War*, p. 28; *The Anti-U.S. Resistance War for National Salvation 1954–1975: Military Events*, pp. 45–46.

32. Turley, *The Second Indochina War*, p.41.

33. Jean Lacouture, "Viet Cong. Who Are They, What Do They Want," *New Republic*, March 6, 1965, p. 21, at p. 22.

34. Turley, *The Second Indochina War*, p. 21.

35. Ibid., pp. 27, 30–31.

36. Ibid., pp. 40–41.

37. Lacouture, "Viet Cong. Who Are They, What Do They Want," p. 24.

38. Bernard B. Fall, *Viet-Nam Witness 1953–66* (1966), p. 284.

39. Turley, *The Second Indochina War*, pp. 43–45.

40. *Special Report to the Co-Chairmen of the Geneva Conference on Indo-China*, International Commission for Supervision and Control in Vietnam, Saigon, June 2, 1962, Command Paper 1755, in Great Britain, Parliamentary Papers (House of Commons and Command), Session 31 October 1961–25 October 1962, vol. 39, p.7; "U.S. Comments on Report of Control Commission for Viet-Nam," DSB, vol. 47, P. 109 (1962).

41. I. F. Stone, "A Reply to the White Paper," in Marvin E. Gettleman, *Vietnam: History, Documents, and Opinions on a Major World Crisis* (1965), pp. 317–18.

42. Gettleman, *Vietnam: History, Documents, and Opinions on a Major World Crisis*, pp. 314–16.

43. Lacouture, "Viet Cong. Who Are They, What Do They Want," p. 24.

44. Gettleman, *Vietnam: History, Documents, and Opinions on a Major World Crisis*, p. 314.

45. Fall, *Vietnam Witness 1953–66*, p. 312; Turley, *The Second Indochina War*, p. 43.

46. Fall, *Vietnam Witness 1953–66*, p. 343.

47. Turley, *The Second Indochina War*, p. 42.

48. Stone, "A Reply to the White Paper," in Gettleman, *Vietnam: History, Documents, and Opinions on a Major World Crisis*, pp. 320–21.

49. Turley, *The Second Indochina War*, p. 58.

50. *Special Report to the Co-Chairmen of the Geneva Conference on Indo-China*, p. 10.

51. Richard Dean Burns and Milton Leitenberg, *The Wars in Vietnam, Cambodia, and Laos, 1945—1982: A Bibliographic Guide* (1984), p. xxiv.

52. Charles Piller and Keith R. Yamamoto, *Gene Wars: Military Control over the New Genetic Technologies* (1988), p. 70.

53. Burns and Leitenberg, *The Wars in Vietnam, Cambodia, and Laos, 1945–1982*, p. xxiv.

12. THE CONGO: TROUBLE OUT EAST

Even as war was heating up in Indochina, the Johnson administration found reason for a more limited military action in the heart of Africa. Again there was more involved than met the public eye. The State Department announced in late 1964 that US aircraft had taken 600 Belgian paratroopers into Stanleyville, capital of the Congo's eastern province, Orientale:

> A short time ago—early in the morning of November 24 in the Congo— a unit of Belgian paratroopers carried by United States military transport planes landed at Stanleyville in the Congo. The purpose of this action is to save the lives of innocent men, women, and children, both Congolese and citizens of at least 18 foreign countries. More than 1,000 civilians have been held as hostages by the Congolese rebels. They have been threatened repeatedly with death by their captors. The decision to send in a rescue force was taken only after the most careful deliberation and when every other avenue to secure the safety of these innocent people was closed by rebel intransigence. This decision was made jointly by the United States and Belgian Governments with the full knowledge and agreement of the legal Government of the Congo. The immediate mission is the rescue of innocent civilians and the evacuation of those who wish to leave the area. When this mission is accomplished, the rescue force will be withdrawn promptly.[1]

The landing was one more episode in the troubled history of the Congo, which had been pieced together by Belgium out of a huge area in central Africa. The Congo had gained independence from Belgium in 1960. An unwieldy country, it included half a dozen major nationalities that had no reason to be united under a single flag. Various regions tried to split off, and in November 1964, Orientale province was controlled by an opposition group in rebellion against the central government, located in Leopoldville.

On the face of it, the paratrooper landing did appear to be a rescue mission, as the State Department announcement affirmed. The opposition group was holding hostage eight hundred foreigners of various nationalities, many of them Belgians and Americans. Opposition leaders had threatened to kill them. The opposition government had taken control not only of Orientale but of other parts of the Congo. At the time of the Belgian landing, however, the central government's forces were moving quickly to retake Stanleyville, and the opposition forces were no match for them. The apparent reason for the hostage-taking was that Belgium and the United States were giving military support to the central government in its efforts against the opposition group, which hoped that, by taking hostages, it could deter the expected central government attack on Stanleyville. The tactic worked for a time, as the government army held back. But then the Belgians landed, and simultaneously the central government forces moved into Stanleyville, wresting it away from the rebels.

The Organization of African Unity (OAU) condemned the landing as "an intervention in African affairs" and a threat to the peace of the African continent. In a letter to the UN Security Council, twenty-two countries, mostly African, declared that the OAU had been mediating between the two Congolese governments, and that it had kept Belgium and the United States apprised of its progress. The landing, they said, disrupted the OAU effort to resolve the situation.[2]

The American ambassador in Nairobi, Kenya, held negotiations there with the foreign minister of the opposition government, although the State Department was alleging that "the rebel representative was not concerned with the safety of the hostages."[3] The ambassador insisted on the release of the hostages as the only item for discussion, while the opposition government said it would release them if the central government army agreed not to attack. The ambassador, admitting that he was unable to speak for the Congolese army, broke off the talks.[4]

African countries charged that the purpose of the landing was not to rescue the hostages but to retake Stanleyville for the central government. "The objective of the imperialist aggressors," declared Guinea in the UN Security Council, "was none other than the fall of Stanleyville, the stronghold of popular resistance to foreign domination."[5] The saving of the hostages, alleged the other Congo, with its capital at Brazzaville, was merely a "pretext."[6] Guinea charged that the talks in Nairobi were a "travesty," whose only purpose was to provide an excuse to intervene.[7]

Whether the opposition government actually did plan to kill the hostages may never be known. It had mistreated them and had threatened them. It had killed foreigners elsewhere in its campaign against the central government—thirty-seven according to the Belgians.[8] On the other hand, the opposition had issued an order threatening to execute anyone who killed "a single white man"[9] among the hostages. It apparently feared that if hostages were killed, the central government troops would attack Stanleyville.

According to Belgium's foreign minister, Paul Henri Spaak, there was no way to prevent the central government from advancing on Stanleyville. The opposition government, however, was not impressed with Spaak's logic, because the central government had collaborated closely, it said, with the United States and Belgium. By its lights, the United States bore direct responsibility if the central government decided to attack Stanleyville. The paratrooper landing, from the perspective of the opposition, was part of the central government's assault on Stanleyville. Kenya, taking up this analysis, charged that U.S. and Belgian aid let the central government ignore calls for a cease-fire that might have resolved the civil war short of an assault on Stanleyville.[10]

Viewing the central army's assault as inevitable, Spaak told the UN Security Council that the central army "would have to start fighting as soon as it arrived outside Stanleyville. We thought that that was the time when the foreigners' lives would be in the greatest danger." "That," the foreign minister reasoned, "is why we chose that particular time for the parachute drop on the town."[11]

Viscount Étienne Davignon, of the Belgian foreign office, described what happened when the paratroopers arrived. As the U.S. troop transports approached Stanleyville airport, the opposition's commander led 250 hostages outside a hotel where they were being held, saying he intended to march them to the airfield to trade them to the paratroopers for the safe exit of the opposition army. As the entourage reached the town square, firing could be heard from the airfield; those guarding the hostages became frightened and made the hostages crouch down. An opposition officer ran up, shouting, "The paratroopers have come, shoot the whites." The hostages panicked and ran, and the guards fired, killing thirty of them.[12] In the Security Council, Ghana argued, "Was it not to be feared and foreseen that these tribesmen, faced with heavily armed soldiers dropping from the skies, would panic and, in a state of mass hysteria, would vent their wrath on the helpless hostages?"[13]

In the paratroopers' wake, the Fifth Brigade of the Congolese army entered Stanleyville and retook it.[14] A fact that provided some support for the OAU view that the central army force was beholden to Belgium and the United States was that a combined force of Congolese and outside mercenaries, called the Fifth Brigade of the Congo Army, was commanded by Major Michael Hoare, a Briton. The paratrooper landing allowed the Filth Brigade to enter Stanleyville; the paratroopers themselves were to rescue the hostages, thereby removing that obstacle to an assault on the town.[15] Together, the Fifth Brigade and the Belgian paratroopers took control of Stanleyville from the rebels[16] and then evacuated upwards of a thousand foreigners.[17]

Belgian minister Spaak insisted that the paratroopers landed only to save the hostages, not to retake Stanleyville or to assist the Fifth Brigade,[18] but Uganda countered by charging that "it was obviously an operation in support of the one led by Major Hoare."[19] As some evidence for Uganda's view, the paratroopers did take pieces of territory in Stanleyville and turn them over to the Fifth Brigade.[20] The paratroopers, however, left before the fighting ended, as Spaak was quick to point out in reply.[21] Moreover, the "number of rebels killed by the Belgian troops," Spaak said, was "very small." The paratroopers fought only to the extent necessary to get the hostages out.[22]

That disclosure alone was incriminating. Whatever their intent, the paratroopers, by attacking the opposition forces, did help the Fifth Brigade take Stanleyville.[23] President Johnson, to justify our collaboration with Belgium, backed Spaak's position. "The United States has no political goals to impose upon the Congo," he said. "We have no narrow interest. We have no economic gain to be served in the Congo."[24] In the UN Security Council, our delegate, Adlai Stevenson, reiterated that by transporting the Belgian paratroopers to Stanleyville, the United States sought only to protect the hostages. Stevenson denied that the United States was taking a military role in support of the central government.[25]

Stevenson did, however, acknowledge that earlier in 1964, "the United States provided some military material and training assistance to the Congo," but with the qualifier that many African nations got such help from abroad. "There is not one of them, I dare say, that does not obtain military equipment or training or both from outside Africa." As the year wore on, the United States gave "additional equipment and transport." But, Stevenson affirmed, the United States "was not requested to, and it did not, undertake military operations in the Congo."[26]

Stevenson's statement, while it contained an element of truth, underplayed our role in the Congo. In 1963, the CIA began a paramilitary program there, enlisting South Africa's covert action organization, the Bureau of State Security, to develop an army of mercenaries to function as part of the Congo's national army.[27] In early 1964, the CIA used this paramilitary apparatus to put down a rebellion in Kwilu, another Congolese province; at the same time, it recruited Cuban exile pilots in Miami to fly missions for the central government.[28]

The State Department gave aircraft to the central government, as Stevenson acknowledged; then, as the Department affirmed, it sent pilots to fly them "in the eastern part of the Congo."[29] When confronted by reporters with the information that the pilots were recruited and supervised by the CIA, the State Department gave "no comment."[30]

In August 1964, after the opposition took Orientale province, President Johnson sent Undersecretary of State Averell Harriman, his top troubleshooter, to Brussels to coordinate Congo strategy with the Belgian government. According to the French daily *Le Monde*, Harriman asked the Belgians to help us in providing military support to the central government, to keep the Congo in the Western camp.[31] The central government was decidedly pro-Western, while the opposition government had befriended the Soviet bloc. President Johnson did not want a leftist government in the Congo any more than he did in Vietnam.[32]

After the Brussels meeting, the Johnson administration sent 106 U.S. military personnel, including 42 paratroopers; helicopters; and four C-130 transport planes, to help the central government. This deployment led Senator John Stennis of Mississippi to worry aloud that we might be drawn into "another undeclared war such as that in Vietnam."[33]

The Johnson administration, however, went ahead with its plans. Secretary of State Dean Rusk authorized an immediate effort, in conjunction with Belgium, to help the central government raise a mercenary force to hold government strong points, and to start a rebel rollback.[34] With that assistance, the central government recruited a mercenary force of 700, primarily from Belgium, South Africa, and Rhodesia. By September, this force had become the Fifth Brigade, the spearhead of the central government's army.[35] Flying the C-130 transports, U.S. pilots ferried Congolese troops, including the mercenaries, to battle areas. Johnson sent T-28 fighter bombers piloted by Cuban exiles, some of them veterans of the Bay of Pigs operation; these pilots strafed opposition positions in the eastern Congo. He also sent counterguerrilla advisors, who worked with central army combat units in the field.[36] When the Belgian paratroopers landed in Stanleyville, a force of Cubans was nearby with the mercenaries to help out if needed.[37]

The involvement of the mercenaries on the central government's behalf was a major reason for the OAU's negative reaction to the Stanleyville landing. The OAU saw the use of mercenaries in Africa as a continuation of colonial control. Unsuccessfully, it asked the Congo central government to send them home.[38] The UN Security Council, viewing mercenaries as a destabilizing influence, had earlier asked other countries to keep their citizens from becoming mercenaries.[39] European mercenaries were fighting for colonial governments in the Portuguese colonies and in Rhodesia, and many hopscotched from one war to another. Most African countries condemned the U.S.–Belgian intervention, because they viewed the opposition government as true nationalists, while the central government had allied itself with European governments.[40]

NOTES

1. "Department Statement," November 24, 1964, DSB, vol. 51, p. 841 (1964).

2. UN Doc. S/6076, and Add. 1–5, December 1, 1964, SCOR, 19th yr., Supplement (October, November, December 1964), p. 198.

3. "Department Statement," November 24, 1964, DSB, vol. 51, p. 841 (1964).

4. SCOR, 19th yr., 1173rd mtg., p. 8, UN Doc. S/PV.1173 (1964); SCOR, 19th yr., 1174th mtg., pp. 14–15, UN Doc. S/PV.1174 (1964).

5. SCOR, 19th yr., 1171st mtg., pp. 9–10, UN Doc. S/PV.1171 (1964).

6. SCOR, 19th yr., 1170th mtg., p. 15, UN Doc. S/PV.1170(1964).

7. SCOR, 19th yr., 1171st mtg., p. 14, UN Doc. S/PV.1171 (1964).

8. SCOR, 19th yr., 1177th mtg., p. 12, UN Doc. S/PV.1177 (1964).

9. Pierre de Vos, "Les réfugiés rentrés à Bruxelles font des récits hallucinants sur les derniers jours de la capitale de la rébellion," *Le Monde*, November 28, 1964, p. 6, col. 1.

10. SCOR, 19th yr., 1175th mtg., p. 12, UN Doc. S/PV.1175 (1964).

11. SCOR, 19th yr., 1173rd mtg., p. 9, UN Doc. S/PV.1173 (1964).

12. Edward T. O'Toole, "Belgian Troops Start to Leave," *New York Times*, November 28, 1964, p. A3, col. 1.

13. SCOR, 19th yr., 1170th mtg., p.29, UN Doc. S/PV.1170 (1964).

14. "Des troupes aéportées belges procèdent a l'évacuation des otages de Stanleyville," Le Monde, November 25, 1964, p. 1, col. 2.

15. Mohammed Bennouna, *Le consentement à l'ingérence militaire dans les conflits internes* (1974), p. 180.

16. Stephen R. Weissman, *American Foreign Policy in the Congo 1960–1964* (1974), p. 247.

17. SCOR, 19th yr., 1177th mtg., p. 16, UN Doc. S/PV.1177 (1964).

18. SCOR, 19th yr., 1173rd mtg., p. 3, UN Doc. S/PV.1173 (1964).

19. SCOR, 19th yr., 1177th mtg., p.24, UN Doc. S/PV.1177 (1964).

20. Lloyd Garrison, "Refugee Airlift Halted in Congo," *New York Times*, November 29, 1964, p. Al, col. 7.

21. SCOR, 19th yr., 1173rd mtg., p. 10, UN Doc. S/PV.1173 (1964).

22. Ibid., p. 12.

23. Madeleine Kalb, *The Congo Cables* (1982), p. 378; Weissman, *American Foreign Policy in the Congo 1960–1964*, pp. 251–52.

24. "Statement by President Johnson," November 28, 1964, DSB, vol. 51, pp. 845–46 (1964).

25. SCOR, 19th yr., 1174th mtg., p. 12, UN Doc. S/PV.1174 (1964).

26. Ibid., p. 18.

27. John Stockwell, *In Search of Enemies: a CIA Story* (1978), pp. 34, 187–88.

28. Stephen R. Weissman, "CIA Covert Action in Zaire and Angola: Patterns and Consequences," *Political Science Quarterly* (Summer 1979): 271.

29. Max Frankel, "Flights in Congo Confirmed by U.S.," *New York Times*, June 17, 1964, p. Al, col. 5.

30. "U.S. Civilians Halt Congo Air Sorties," *New York Times*, June 18, 1964, p. Al, col. 7.

31. Pierre de Vos, "M. Harriman s'entretient avec M. Spaak de la situation au Congo," *Le Monde*, August 8, 1964, p. 1, col. 2.

32. "Intervention au Congo?" *Le Monde*, August 7, 1964, p. 1, col. 1.

33. M. S. Handler, "Revolt in Congo Termed 'Serious' by U.S. Officials," *New York Times*, August 15, 1964, p. Al, col. 8.

34. Weissman, "CIA Covert Action in Zaire and Angola," p. 271.

35. Ibid., p. 272. Lloyd Garrison, "20 to 30 Hostages Killed as Congo Rescue Begins; Stanleyville is Retaken," *New York Times*, November 25, 1964, p. Al, col. 8.

36. Handler, "Revolt in Congo Termed 'Serious' by U.S. Officials"; Tad Szulc, "Tide in Congo War Believed Turning in Regime's Favor," *New York Times*, October 5, 1964, p. Al, col. 1.

37. Weissman, *American Foreign Policy in the Congo 1960–1964*, p. 252.

38. SCOR, 19th yr., 1171st mtg., p. 4, UN Doc. S/PV.1171 (1964).

39. Res. 161, SCOR, 16th yr., *Resolutions and Decisions*, p. 2, UN Doc. S/INF/16/Rev. 1 (1961).

40. SCOR, 19th yr., 1178th mtg., p. 9, UN Doc. S/PV.1178 (1964).

13. THE CONGO: ANOTHER CUBA

American involvement in Congolese politics started well before 1964. It was actions of ours that, in a sense, led to the Stanleyville rebellion. The opposition government based at Stanleyville was headed by Antoine Gizenga, who in 1960 had served as deputy prime minister of the Congo under Patrice Lumumba, the Congo's first prime minister. Lumumba, a nationalist who had given the Congolese a sense of self-identity as colonial rule ended, was killed by opponents and subsequently held the status of a martyr for many Congolese.

Gaston Soumialot, another opposition leader active in the Stanleyville government, claimed Lumumba's mantle, declaring "I am the new Lumumba."[1] The political groups that paid homage to Lumumba were the most popular in the country.[2] To the opposition politicians, the deceased Lumumba was the bearer of true independence for the Congo, and those who killed him were out to feather their own nests by close ties with Belgium and the United States, which both had financial interests in the Congo. A major reason for the 1964 rebellion was that the Lumumbists chafed under the thought that they had been outmaneuvered by self-seeking political figures who were selling the country out.

Adlai Stevenson, hammering home his point that the United States had no ulterior motive in the Stanleyville landing, averred that we had never interfered in Congolese politics. "From the beginning," he said, referring to Congolese independence in 1960, "we have been opposed—and remain opposed—to foreign intervention in the internal affairs of the sovereign and independent state of the Congo."[3]

We were, however, hardly idle observers as the Congo forged a political system after independence in 1960. The Congo had no developed political parties, and our officials on the scene worried about whether the Congo might tilt toward the Soviet bloc. The CIA station chief in Leopoldville, Lawrence Devlin, cabled Washington that both he and our ambassador, Clare Timberlake, believed, "Congo experiencing classic Communist effort takeover government . . .. Whether or not Lumumba actually Commie or just playing Commie game to assist his solidifying power, anti-West forces rapidly increasing power Congo and there may be little time left in which take action to avoid another Cuba."[4]

CIA Director Allen Dulles cabled back, "In high quarters here it is the clear-cut conclusion that if [Lumumba] continues to hold high office, the inevitable result will at best be chaos and at worst pave the way to Communist takeover of the Congo . . .. Consequently we conclude that his removal must be an urgent and prime objective and that under existing conditions this should be a high priority of our covert action."[5]

Richard Bissell, director of CIA covert actions, who at the time was gearing up the Bay of Pigs operation, later told Senate investigators that when CIA Director Dulles wrote "removal," he meant that President Eisenhower wanted Lumumba assassinated. Bronson Tweedy, who ran the CIA division for covert actions in Africa, said that the Dulles cable was an "authoritative statement" of a "policy consensus in Washington" that Lumumba should be removed by any means necessary, including assassination.[6]

Although Lumumba, elected prime minister in May 1960,[7] was, in Devlin's view, firmly in the Soviet camp, he had no clear political program. Lumumba had visited Washington and Ottawa shortly after independence to ask for American and Canadian economic aid.[8] Lumumba signed a 50-year contract with a U.S. firm to develop the Congo's mining and hydroelectric resources.[9] These moves indicated that Lumumba wanted to form a compact with the West.

One other indication of Lumumba's leanings was that he was not reluctant to seek help from the United Nations, even though it was Western-dominated. When Congolese soldiers rebelled against their Belgian officers in July 1960, Belgian troops reentered the Congo and helped a secessionist movement in the mineral-rich province of Katanga. To counter them, Lumumba asked for UN intervention.[10] A few days later, Lumumba and Joseph Kasavubu, the Congo's president, sent a message to Soviet Premier Nikita Khrushchev, suggesting that they might be forced to ask for Soviet intervention if Belgium did not pull its troops out of the Congo.[11] This request drew only a noncommittal reply from Khrushchev but earned Lumumba a reputation in the Eisenhower administration of being pro-Soviet. The request was initially motivated by a fear that the UN might not act forcefully; but when the Security Council issued a strong demand to Belgium to withdraw, Lumumba said that he would no longer ask for Soviet intervention.[12]

Lumumba did, however, turn to the Soviet Union again the following month, when the issue of the secession of the province of Katanga came to the fore, and the UN refused to help the central government put it down. Lumumba asked the Soviet government for military aid and got it.[13]

Convinced by now of Lumumba's leftism, and following through on the directive from CIA Director Dulles, Devlin and Timberlake explored ways to engineer a no-confidence vote against Lumumba in the Congolese parliament and encouraged Kasavubu to dismiss Lumumba.[14] Although the Congolese constitution did not give the president that power, Kasavubu did it anyway.[15] Lumumba, who enjoyed strong support in the parliament, responded by dismissing Kasavubu, and parliament voted to annul both dismissals.[16]

Since parliament would not fire Lumumba, Devlin approached Joseph Mobutu, a colonel who headed the Congolese army, promising financial support if Mobutu sided with Kasavubu against Lumumba.[17] Mobutu, like Kasavubu, was seen by Devlin as friendly to the West. Mobutu was quick to respond: on September 14, he suspended parliament and took power from the prime minister in the name of the army. This move kept Kasavubu as president and sent Lumumba fleeing to Stanleyville, his political base.[18] Devlin, true to his promise to Mobutu, began giving him under-the-table subsidies.[19]

The next day, Mobutu arrested Lumumba, but Lumumba escaped.[20] To avoid re-arrest, Lumumba put himself in protective custody in a house guarded by UN troops. Soldiers from Mobutu's army tried to apprehend him, but the UN troops kept them out.[21]

Despite Lumumba's removal from power, the CIA still found him a threat. Devlin worried that Mobutu might let parliament meet again, and cabled to the CIA that "pressures for [Lumumba's] return will be almost irresistible."[22] To keep this from happening, Devlin worked behind the scenes to see that parliament was not re-opened.[23] Devlin suggested to a "key Congolese leader" (the cable does not name him) to arrange the "arrest or other more permanent disposal of Lumumba, Gizenga, and Mulele."[24] Pierre Mulele, along with Antoine Gizenga, led Lumumba's supporters while Lumumba was in UN custody. Mobutu took up the suggestion, arresting Gizenga and making plans to hand him over to Katanga province authorities, who hated him and would likely have killed him. Gizenga was released, however, by sympathetic UN troops from Ghana, who managed to wrest him from Mobutu's men.[25]

With Lumumba still in UN custody, the CIA covert action department took to carrying out Director Dulles's order to kill him. It enlisted a toxicology expert to prepare a poison that would produce a fatal disease, while giving the appearance, in the event of an autopsy, that Lumumba died from natural causes. CIA headquarters in Washington sent the toxicologist to Leopoldville, where he delivered the poison to Devlin with the message from Tweedy that he was to deliver the poison so that the Leopoldville station could "seriously incapacitate or eliminate Lumumba." The Leopoldville station then began looking for someone who could get Lumumba to take the poison.[26]

But it was difficult to slip anyone into the house where Lumumba lived, surrounded as he was by UN troops. After one person who had agreed to try was unable to "penetrate entourage," Tweedy cabled a more direct approach: "Possibility use commando type group for abduction [Lumumba], either via assault on house up cliff from river or, more probably, if [Lumumba] attempts another breakout into town.[27] Undersecretary of State C. Douglas Dillon said that this idea to abduct Lumumba from his UN-protected house had been approved at the highest level of the U.S. government.[28]

CIA station chief Devlin also urged Kasavubu to arrest Lumumba, cabling CIA Director Dulles: "Station has consistently urged [Congolese] leaders arrest Lumumba in belief Lumumba will continue be threat to stability Congo until removed from scene."[29] It was clear that if the other leaders arrested Lumumba, they could not leave him alive and remain sure he would not make a comeback.

On the night of November 27, 1960, Lumumba decided that he had had enough of being protected and slipped past his UN guards toward Stanleyville.[30] Kasavubu immediately sent a team to catch Lumumba, with the CIA station lending a hand. According to a CIA cable, "[Station] working with [Congolese government] to get roads blocked and troops alerted [block] possible escape route."[31]

Kasavubu's men soon found Lumumba and arrested him,[32] after which Gizenga set up an administration in Stanleyville to back Lumumba's claim to retain the prime minister's position.[33] With Lumumba in detention, Devlin pressed President Kasavubu to kill Lumumba, because he feared Lumumba might return to power. Devlin cabled Washington, "Station and embassy believe present government may fall within few days. Result would almost certainly be chaos and return [Lumumba] to power. . . . Refusal take drastic steps at this time will lead to defeat of [U.S.] policy in Congo."[34]

The next day, Kasavubu told the CIA he would send Lumumba to the town of Bakwanga, which was controlled by Lumumba opponents, in the expectation that these opponents would kill him. Three days later, Kasavubu had Lumumba put on a plane to Bakwanga, but while the plane was in the air, Kasavubu learned that UN troops were installed at the Bakwanga airfield. Since this would make it difficult for Lumumba's opponents there to seize him, Kasavubu diverted the plane to Elisabethville, capital of Katanga province, which was run by Moise Tshombe, another Lumumba opponent who could be counted on to kill him.

In Elisabethville, Lumumba was forced off the plane and quickly killed. A UN inquiry team found both the central and Katanga governments responsible for the death, concluding that Kasavubu turned Lumumba over to the Katangan authorities "knowing full well" that he was giving him over to his "bitterest political enemies."[35]

Devlin admitted that the CIA station had been in touch with the Congolese officials involved in the plan to ship Lumumba off to his death,[36] while U.S. Senate investigators found that the station was aware in advance of the plan to arrest Lumumba and to turn him over to his enemies.[37] One scholar reviewing the data concluded that the CIA was guilty of "complicity in murder."[38]

After Lumumba's death, the United States would not acknowledge the CIA role, voting in the UN Security Council in favor of a resolution that expressed "deep regret" over the killing of Lumumba and calling it a "crime" likely to have "grave repercussions." In a paragraph that must have amused Devlin, the resolution spoke of "the imperative necessity for the restoration of parliamentary institutions in the Congo."[39]

Our collusion with President Kasavubu and Colonel Mobutu against Patrice Lumumba, as well as against parliamentary rule, was widely suspected in the Congo. One reason for the on-and-off rebellion throughout 1964 was that many Congolese viewed the central government as having cooperated with the United States in killing Lumumba and in obstructing parliament. Had we let Lumumba contend with the other political forces, the 1964 rebellion leading to the Stanleyville situation might never have broken out.

Unfortunately for the Congo, the Eisenhower, Kennedy, and Johnson administrations viewed this African nation from a cold war perspective. In addition, we had business interests there that caused the three administrations concern over the Congo's political future. During the Stanleyville events, Ambassador Stevenson denied that we were motivated by financial interests, but U.S. policy makers were not unaware of the Congo's rich deposits of copper, diamonds, and cobalt. The United States bought much of the Congo's cobalt for use as an alloy in the manufacture of jet engines.[40] During World War II, the Belgian mining company,

Union Minière, had supplied us with Congolese uranium to build the atomic bomb.[41] In Katanga province, Moise Tshombe rebelled from the central government on a platform of giving free rein to foreign mining companies. One of the major foreign players was the Belgian-American billionaire Maurice Tempelsman, who had investments in Congo diamonds and copper. After retiring as Leopoldville CIA station chief, Devlin took a job as manager of Tempelsman's Congo interests.[42]

To protect the Congo government after the Stanleyville landing, the CIA kept its paramilitary operation in the Congo alive until 1967.[43] In 1965, it began to doubt Kasavubu's pro-Western credentials and helped Joseph Mobutu, from his army position, replace Kasavubu as president.[44] Mobutu retained close ties to the CIA, a fact that will be important when we get to our next African military operation.

NOTES

1. Pierre de Vos, "M. Harriman s'entretient avec M. Spaak de la situation au Congo," *Le Monde*, August 8, 1964, p. 1, col. 2.

2. Stephen R. Weissman, "CIA Covert Action in Zaire and Angola: Patterns and Consequences," *Political Science Quarterly* (Summer 1979): 275.

3. SCOR, 19th yr., 1174th mtg., p. 17, UN Doc. S/PV.1174 (1964).

4. CIA cable, Leopoldville to Director, August 18, 1960, in *Alleged Assassination Plots Involving Foreign Leaders: An Interim Report of the Select Committee to Study Governmental Operations with Respect to Intelligence Activities*, U.S. Senate, 94th Cong., 1st sess., Report no. 94-465, November 20, 1975, p. 14 (the Committee referred to Devlin by the pseudonym "Victor Hedgman"); John Stockwell, *In Search of Enemies: A CIA Story* (1978), pp. 71, 136.

5. CIA cable, Dulles to Station Officer, Leopoldville, August 26, 1960, in *Alleged Assassination Plots*, p. 15.

6. *Alleged Assassination Plots*, p. 16.

7. Madeleine Kalb, *The Congo Cables* (1982), p. xxv.

8. Ibid., pp. 36, 41.

9. Henry Tanner, "Congo Signs Pact with U.S. Concern to Tap Resources," *New York Times*, July 23, 1960, p. Al, col. 5.

10. Kalb, *The Congo Cables*, pp. 9–10.

11. Joseph Kasavubu and Patrice Lumumba, "To His Honor the Chair of the Council of Ministers of the Soviet Union," *Pravda*, July 16, 1960, p. 1, col. 5; "Text of Congolese Leaders' Appeal to Premier Khrushchev and His Reply," *New York Times*, July 16, 1960, p. 3, col. 2.

12. Res. 145, SCOR, 15th yr., *Resolutions and Decisions*, p. 6, UN Doc. S/INF/15/Rev. 1 (1960).

13. Kalb, *The Congo Cables*, pp. 56, 60.

14. *Alleged Assassination Plots*, p. 15; Andrew Tully, *CIA: The Inside Story* (1962), p. 221; Kalb, *The Congo Cables*, p. 61.

15. *Alleged Assassination Plots*, p. 16.

16. Henry Tanner, "Leopoldville's Parliament Rejects Ousters—Step Helps Lumumba," *New York Times*, September 8, 1960, p. Al, col. 8.

17. Kalb, *The Congo Cables*, p. 93; Tully, *CIA: The Inside Story*, p.222.

18. Weissman, "CIA Covert Action in Zaire and Angola," pp. 267–68; *Alleged Assassination Plots*, p. 16.

19. Kalb, *The Congo Cables*, p. 96.

20. Weissman, "CIA Covert Action in Zaire and Angola," pp. 268–69.

21. Jonathan Kwitny, *Endless Enemies: The Making of an Unfriendly World* (1984), pp. 66–67.

22. CIA cable, Leopoldville to Director, October 26, 1960, in *Alleged Assassination Plots*, p. 18.

23. *Alleged Assassination Plots*, p. 17.

24. CIA cable, Leopoldville to Director, September 20, 1960, in *Alleged Assassination Plots*, p. 18.

25. Weissman, "CIA Covert Action in Zaire and Angola," p. 268.

26. *Alleged Assassination Plots*, pp. 21–22, 23, 28.

27. Ibid., p. 32.

28. Ibid., p. 42.

29. CIA cable, Leopoldville Station Officer to Director, October 11, 1960, in *Alleged Assassination Plots*, p. 42.

30. Kalb, *The Congo Cables*, p. 157.

31. CIA cable, November 28, 1960, in *Alleged Assassination Plots*, p. 48.

32. Paul Hoffman, "Lumumba Seized in Congo," *New York Times*, December 3, 1960, p. Al, col. 8.

33. Paul Hoffman, "Pro-Red Lumumba Aide Claims Authority to Rule," *New York Times*, December 14, 1960, p. Al, col. 4.

34. CIA cable, Leopoldville CIA station to Director, January 13, 1961, in *Alleged Assassination Plots*, p. 49.

35. "Report of the Commission of Investigation established under the terms of General Assembly resolution 1601 (XV) of 15 April 1961," November 11, 1961, UN Doc. S/4976, SCOR, 16th yr., Supplement (October, November, December 1961), p. 118.

36. *Alleged Assassination Plots*, p. 51.

37. Ibid., p. 48.

38. Weissman, "CIA Covert Action in Zaire and Angola," p. 269.

39. Res. 161, SCOR, 16th yr., Resolutions and Decisions, p. 2, UN Doc. S/INF/ 16/Rev. 1 (1961).

40. Kalb, *The Congo Cables*, p. 349.

41. Ibid., p. xxii.

42. Kwitny, *Endless Enemies*, pp. 9, 58; Weissman, "CIA Covert Action in Zaire and Angola," p. 275.

43. Weissman, "CIA Covert Action in Zaire and Angola," pp. 272–73.

44. Ibid., p. 273; Kalb, *The Congo Cables*, p. 379.

14. THE DOMINICAN REPUBLIC: BULLETS IN THE EMBASSY WINDOW

In 1965, the Johnson administration intervened much closer to home, in the midst of turmoil in the Dominican Republic. When Juan Bosch was elected president of the Dominican Republic in 1963, the military reacted by staging a coup to open the way for its own ruling junta. Bosch was a left-of-center nationalist, who had not been hostile to the United States. After leaving the Dominican Republic in 1963 Bosch spent his exile living in Puerto Rico, a U.S. territory. The junta officers, however, were closer politically to the United States.

In April 1965, military and civilian elements revolted against the junta to restore Bosch to office, and, after sometimes intense street fighting, they had the junta on the run.[1] On the evening of April 28, President Johnson sent in a military force, which he built up over several days to 23,000 troops.[2] In several weeks of fighting, the pro-Bosch forces were defeated, and a new military junta friendly to the United States assumed power.

When President Johnson sent in the first contingent of troops, he said his aim was to rescue U.S. citizens. We had "been informed," Johnson explained, "by military authorities in the Dominican Republic that American lives are in danger. These authorities are no longer able to guarantee their safety and they have reported that the assistance of military personnel is now needed for that purpose."[3]

The "military authorities" to whom Johnson referred were Dominican Air Force Colonel Pedro Benoit and other air force officers, including General Elias Wessin y Wessin, who had led the 1963 overthrow of Bosch.[4] Headquartered at the San Isidro air base east of Santo Domingo, the capital city, these officers had declared themselves to be a junta, after prompting in that direction from U.S. embassy officials and the CIA.[5] The junta did not have many troops loyal to it.[6] Johnson's reference to the junta officers as "military authorities" made it sound as if they controlled the country, though they did not. So when he argued that the officers could not protect our citizens, it was not because of any overriding danger, but because the officers were out of power.

In a plea for American help, Benoit phoned U.S. Ambassador Tapley Bennett to tell him that the officers at San Isidro were weeping, and that one was hysterically urging a retreat.[7] Their only hope for gaining power against the pro-Bosch forces, Benoit pleaded, was direct U.S. intervention. Knowing which buttons to press with the Johnson administration, Benoit told Bennett that the return of Bosch would "convert the country into another Cuba."[8] Bennett immediately cabled Washington and recommended military intervention to prevent "another Cuba."[9]

The State Department denied the request. Bennett then advised Colonel Benoit that it would be more politic to ask for assistance on the grounds that he could not protect U.S. citizens, because this would provide a more publicly acceptable rationale.[10] In making a second request for intervention, Benoit duly stressed the supposed danger to Americans residing in the Dominican Republic. On that basis Johnson sent in a contingent of Marines.[11]

At the time, there were nearly 2,000 U.S. citizens in the Dominican Republic. Of these, one thousand lived in Santo Domingo, the only scene of hostilities.[12] On April 27, the day preceding the intervention, 1,172 of them were evacuated by ship and helicopter by the U.S. Navy, without the landing of troops.[13] On April 28, but before the Marines arrived, another 684 were evacuated by the same means.[14] In all, then, 1,856 Americans were evacuated before the intervention.

A few weeks later, Secretary of State Dean Rusk declared that overall we had evacuated 1,800 U.S. citizens from the Dominican Republic, counting those evacuated both before and after the intervention.[15] But with 1,856 evacuated prior to the intervention, that left none to be evacuated by the time the Marines arrived. Even more remarkably, President Johnson claimed on May 2 that 1,500 of our citizens in the Dominican Republic were still desperate to be saved, thus giving him the excuse to send in more Marines.[16]

Even if there were American citizens in the Dominican Republic desiring to leave after April 28, they could have been evacuated without a military intervention. Residential areas occupied by Americans in Santo Domingo were free of hostilities, and all the major Dominican factions had agreed to facilitate the evacuation of any foreigners who wanted to leave.[17] Nevertheless, President Johnson claimed that the Marines were fired upon as soon as they arrived: "We had 20 of our boys killed by the rebels, who fired first and who tried to keep us from evacuating these people." This was patently untrue. Johnson announced that Ambassador Bennett "had a thousand American men, women, and children assembled in the [Embajador] hotel who were pleading with their President for help to preserve their lives."[18] But U.S. citizens wanting to get out had already been evacuated.

Secretary Rusk, like President Johnson, characterized the sending of troops as a "rescue operation," in which the Marines arrived "just in time to avoid a major calamity."[19] Our citizens, Rusk said, "were actually under fire" on April 28, the date of the intervention. He elaborated the scene at the hotel described by Johnson: "[H]undreds were gathered in the Embajador Hotel, and there were people running around the hotel, shooting it up with tommyguns, and so forth. There were large numbers of people gathered on the Polo Grounds [near the hotel] who were then apparently under fire. When the Marines got there at 7 o'clock [April 28], or thereabouts, they in fact found that these people were under fire."[20]

There was little truth in Rusk's account. Although some shooting had occurred at the Embajador Hotel on April 28, no U.S. citizens were under fire when the Marines arrived. Rusk's reference may have been to an incident that occurred not on April 28 but the day before, when armed pro-

Bosch elements entered the Embajador Hotel looking for a rightist opponent. A few shots were fired, for reasons that are not clear, but no fire was directed at foreigners, and the evacuation proceeded smoothly.[21]

In another vivid but equally fallacious account, President Johnson reported a firing on the U.S. embassy building in Santo Domingo on April 28, while inside Ambassador Bennett was making frequent telephone calls to Washington: "As we talked to our ambassador to confirm the horror and tragedy and the unbelievable fact that they [the rebels] were firing on Americans and the American Embassy," Johnson said, "he was talking to us from under a desk while bullets were going through his windows."[22] Whatever may have been the source of Johnson's information, Bennett denied that he had hidden under his desk while bullets flew through the windows.[23] Nor had there been any firing on U.S. citizens, either at the embassy or anywhere else. During the entire episode, from what can be gathered, no American was harmed by a Dominican.[24] The only U.S. citizens injured during the conflict were two newsmen shot and seriously wounded by "friendly fire" from U.S. Marines.[25]

During the crisis, both Ambassador Bennett and top U.S. military officers gave press briefings vividly describing atrocities that later turned out to be untrue.[26] The distortions became so obvious to the press that one reporter called the briefings "an important part of the whole picture of misleading newsmen and, through them, public opinion about what the United States was doing or planning to do in the Dominican Republic."[27]

President Johnson kept elaborating the horrors, stating that as of May 4, "1,000 to 1,500" Dominicans were lying "dead in the street" in Santo Domingo, many of them beheaded.[28] But reporters never saw more than a few bodies in the streets.[29] Although several hundred Dominicans were killed in street fighting,[30] there were no reports of beheadings, or execution-style killings.[31] One reporter called President Johnson's public statements about the Dominican Republic "hyperbolic."[32]

A journalist covering the U.S. embassy during the Dominican crisis wrote that the decisive element in its recommendations to the State Department was "the ebb and flow of rebel fortunes, rather than the degree of danger to U.S. or other foreign nationals."[33] In Congress,

Johnson's claim of intervention to protect our citizens was questioned.[34] Senator J. William Fulbright, who conducted closed hearings into the Dominican situation, concluded that "the danger to American lives was more a pretext than a reason."[35] Senator Joseph Clark of Pennsylvania put his finger on the real reason for the intervention: "It is all very well to talk about protecting American lives," he said, "but the real reason that the Marines went in there was to prevent a Communist takeover."[36]

NOTES

1. "Dominican Coup Deposes Regime; Rebels Are Split," *New York Times*, April 26, 1965, p. Al, col. 8.

2. "Johnson Charges Red Plotters Took Over Dominican Uprising; Increases U.S. Forces to 14,000," *New York Times*, May 3, 1965, p. Al, col. 8; "U.S. Acts to Meet Threat in Dominican Republic, White House press release," April 28, 1965, DSB, vol. 52, p. 738 (1965); Abraham F. Lowenthal, *The Dominican Intervention* (1972), p. 112; Tad Szulc, *Dominican Diary* (1965), p. 149.

3. "U.S. Acts to Meet Threat in Dominican Republic, White House press release," April 28, 1965, DSB, vol. 52, p. 738 (1965).

4. Szulc, *Dominican Diary*, p. 15.

5. John Bartlow Martin, *Overtaken by Events: The Dominican Crisis from the Fall of Trujillo to the Civil War* (1966), p. 655; Szulc, *Dominican Diary*, p. 85; *Congressional Record*, vol. 111, p. 24242, September 17, 1965 (statement of Sen. Joseph Clark).

6. Theodore Draper, *The Dominican Revolt: A Case Study in American Policy* (1968), pp. 117–18.

7. Martin, *Overtaken by Events*, p. 656.

8. Ibid., p. 656; *Congressional Record*, vol. 111, p. 23857, September 15, 1965 (statement of Sen. J. William Fulbright).

9. Martin, *Overtaken by Events*, pp. 656–57.

10. *Congressional Record*, vol. 111, p. 23857, September 15, 1965 (statement of Sen. J. William Fulbright); Philip Geyelin, *Lyndon B. Johnson and the World* (1966), p. 252.

11. Draper, *The Dominican Revolt*, pp. 119–21; Philip Geyelin, "Dominican

Flashback: Behind the Scenes," *Wall Street Journal*, June 25, 1965, p. 8, col. 3.

12. Charles Mohr, "President Sends Marines to Rescue Citizens of U.S. from Dominican Fighting," *New York Times*, April 29, 1965, p. Al, col. 8; David Atlee Phillips, *The Night Watch* (1977), pp. 147–50; Piero Gleijeses, *The Dominican Crisis: The 1965 Constitutionalist Revolt and American Intervention* (1978), p. 241.

13. Captain James A. Dare, "Dominican Diary," *U.S. Naval Institute Proceedings*, December 1965, pp. 41–42; Martin, *Overtaken by Events*, p. 652; Tad Szulc, "Dominican Revolt Fails After a Day of Savage Battle," *New York Times*, April 28, 1965, p. Al, col. 3.

14. Lowenthal, *The Dominican Intervention*, p. 103; Szulc, *Dominican Diary*, p. 42; Dare, "Dominican Diary," p. 42. Gleijeses, *The Dominican Crisis*, p. 397.

15. "Secretary Rusk's News Conference of May 26," DSB, vol. 52, p. 938 (1965).

16. "Statement by President Johnson," May 2, 1965, DSB, vol. 52, p. 746 (1965), also in "Remarks by President Johnson," May 4, 1965, DSB, vol. 52, pp. 820–21 (1965).

17. Draper, *The Dominican Revolt*, p. 62; Phillips, *The Night Watch*, p. 147; Gleijeses, *The Dominican Crisis*, p. 237.

18. Lyndon B. Johnson, "An Assessment of the Situation in the Dominican Republic," DSB, vol. 53, p. 20 (1965).

19. "Secretary Discusses Situation in Dominican Republic," May 8, 1965, DSB, vol. 52, p. 842 (1965).

20. "Secretary Rusk's News Conference of May 26," DSB, vol. 52, p. 941–42 (1965).

21. Geyelin, "Dominican Flashback: Behind the Scenes"; Gleijeses, *The Dominican Crisis*, p. 397; Lowenthal, *The Dominican Intervention*, p. 204 n. 27; Szulc, *Dominican Diary*, p. 33.

22. Johnson, "An Assessment of the Situation in the Dominican Republic."

23. David Wise, *The Politics of Lying: Government Deception, Secrecy, and Power* (1973), p. 43; Draper, *The Dominican Revolt*, p. 116; Frank Cormier, *LBJ: The Way He Was* (1977), p. 188; Szulc, *Dominican Diary*, p. 45.

24. *Congressional Record*, vol. 111, p. 23855, September 15, 1965 (statement of Sen. J. William Fulbright); *Congressional Record*, vol. 111, p. 24973, September 23. 1965 (statement of Rep. Armistead Selden); Lyndon B. Johnson,

"The Search for a Durable Peace in the Dominican Republic," May 28, 1965, DSB, vol. 52, p. 990 (1965).

25. James Deakin, *Lyndon Johnson's Credibility Gap* (1968), p. 34; Szulc, *Dominican Diary*, p. 150.

26. Draper, *The Dominican Revolt*, p. 94.

27. Szulc, *Dominican Diary*, p. 102.

28. "Remarks by President Johnson," May 4, 1965, DSB, vol. 52, p. 822 (1965).

29. Draper, *The Dominican Revolt*, pp. 92–93.

30. Martin, *Overtaken by Events*, p. 655.

31. Lowenthal, *The Dominican Intervention*, p. 207, n. 50; Merle Miller, *Lyndon: An Oral Biography* (1980), p.427.

32. Geyelin, *Lyndon B. Johnson and the World*, p. 238.

33. Ibid., p. 246.

34. Mohammed Bennouna, *Le consentement a l'ingérence militaire dans les conflits internes* (1974), p. 180.

35. *Congressional Record*, vol. 111, p. 23857, September 15, 1965 (statement of Sen. J. William Fulbright).

36. Ibid., p. 24242, September 17, 1965 (statement of Sen. Joseph Clark).

15. THE DOMINICAN REPUBLIC: SEEING RED

Four days after the initial April 28, 1965 Marine landing in the Dominican Republic, President Johnson announced that he was sending in additional Marines because, as he put it, Communists were participating on Bosch's side. "Our goal," Johnson said, "is to help prevent another Communist state in this hemisphere."[1] Dean Rusk concurred that "the Communists had captured the revolution according to plan, and the danger of a Communist takeover was established beyond question."[2]

These statements seemed to repudiate the original reason of rescuing U.S. citizens, but Johnson and Rusk refused to let go of it. They explained that while they were carrying out the rescue, Communists were assuming a new and prominent government role on the pro-Bosch side. "What began as a popular democratic revolution, committed to democracy and social justice," Johnson said on May 2, was "seized and placed into the hands of a band of Communist conspirators."[3] To accept this version of the story, one would have had to believe that in a period of four days, with U.S. Marines in town, the communists came to the fore.

As we saw in the last chapter, the Dominican Air Force officers first requested intervention to prevent "another Cuba"; before sending the first units, Johnson mentioned to congressional leaders his own concern about communism in the Dominican Republic.[4] As Senator Fulbright said, from the beginning of the crisis the administration's policy "was directed against the return of Bosch and against the success of the rebel movement."[5] Johnson saw the junta as being firmly in the U.S. camp. Bosch was, for Johnson, too independent-minded. Fulbright said, doubtless correctly, that "very close to the beginning of the [pro-Bosch] revolution, U.S. policymakers decided that it should not be allowed to succeed."[6] Indeed, two days before the initial intervention, the American embassy in Santo Domingo sent the State Department a cable proposing intervention to keep Bosch out of office. "All members of the country team," the cable read, "feel Bosch's return and resumption of control of the government is against U.S. interest in view of extremists in the coup and Communist advocacy of Bosch return."[7]

By the time this embassy cable was sent, the pro-Bosch forces had already pulled off a virtually bloodless coup. Street crowds, made up largely of poor people, supported both the coup and Bosch's return to office.[8] If we had done nothing, Bosch would have been restored as the lawfully elected president.

According to a cable sent to the State Department by our chargé d'affaires in Santo Domingo, the Dominican Republic's officers asked him whether the United States would back them if they started fighting against the pro-Bosch forces. The chargé "reluctantly agreed to the de los Santos-Wessin [two Air Force officers] plan even though it could mean more bloodshed." His cable continued, "Our attachés have stressed to the three military leaders, Rivera, de los Santos and Wessin, our strong feeling everything possible should be done to prevent a Communist takeover."[9] Buoyed by the promise of U.S. support, the Dominican Air Force began to strafe the National Palace on April 25.[10] It was this strafing that resulted in the bulk of civilian casualties in the Dominican fighting."[11]

Although the administration claimed to favor neither the anti-Bosch nor pro-Bosch forces,[12] Ambassador Bennett encouraged the pro-Bosch forces to give up,[13] while our embassy's military attachés plotted military strategy with the Dominican officers,[14] urging them to take up the fight after the pro-Bosch units appeared to have won.[15]

Our embassy also provided material support, granting a request by the Dominican Air Force officers for walkie-talkies, just prior to the intervention. Ambassador Bennett gave them food and equipment.[16] To hinder the Bosch elements, U.S. military intelligence jammed radio broadcasts of the pro-Bosch forces to keep them from getting their message to the public.[17] To cover salaries for the junta's troops, the U.S. embassy gave the junta a reported $750,000.[18]

Once the Marines landed, they assisted the Dominican officers against the pro-Bosch units. Fearing that a direct U.S. attack on the Bosch partisans might backfire, Johnson secretly instructed the Joint Chiefs of Staff to ensure that the pro-Bosch forces were defeated not by outright assault but by attrition.[19] At press briefings in Santo Domingo, American military officers referred to the anti-Bosch forces as "friendlies" and to the pro-Bosch units as "unfriendlies."[20] The Marines set up a perimeter to confine the pro-Bosch forces to a small downtown area, thereby preventing them from advancing and making it easier for the junta forces to attack them.[21]

U.S. Army airborne units coordinated efforts with the Marines. Landing at the air force officers' headquarters located on the San Isidro air base, airborne units secured it for them and moved towards downtown Santo Domingo, where they seized a key bridge from the pro-Bosch forces in heavy fighting.[22] They then occupied part of the downtown area itself and, after linking up with the Marines, began to patrol downtown Santo Domingo.[23] There the combined American forces made little pretense of neutrality, setting up checkpoints jointly with the Dominican junta to inspect suspected Bosch supporters for weapons,[24] and on occasion exchanging fire with pro-Bosch forces.[25] The American military stopped the delivery of supplies, the aim being, as one of our officers later told a reporter, to starve the Bosch supporters into submission. The Marines and airborne units helped the junta forces capture the pro-Bosch radio station and do a house-by-house sweep in order to find pro-Bosch combatants.[26] Thus, U.S. units played a key role in helping the anti-Bosch forces consolidate power.[27]

While the Johnson administration was apparently motivated by anti-communism, it never made a solid case that the Dominican strife had much to do with the East-West split, or that leftists controlled the pro-Bosch forces.[28] Johnson claimed to the press that U.S. intelligence had identified fifty-eight "Communists and Castroites," whom he called "evil persons who had been trained in overthrowing governments and in seizing governments and establishing Communist control."[29] But the list contained so many factual errors that reporters quickly discredited it. The administration had no evidence that the persons listed were even active in the revolt, much less in charge of it.[30]

Leftists, in fact, played only a minor role in the Dominican conflict.[31] Of the Dominican Republic's three leftist parties, the Dominican Communist party (pro-Soviet), the Dominican Popular Movement (pro-China), and the June 14 Party (pro-Cuba), none was involved in planning the pro-Bosch coup.[32] As events unfolded, the three parties could not even agree among themselves how to react.[33]

Once fighting began, leftists did go into the streets in support of the pro-Bosch faction, but leadership remained squarely with the military figures and politicians across the political spectrum.[34] Senator Fulbright, who took evidence on this issue, found "little basis" for "the assertion that the rebels were Communist-dominated or certain to become so; on the contrary, the evidence suggests a chaotic situation in which no single faction was dominant at the outset and in which everybody, including the United States, had opportunities to influence the shape and course of the rebellion."[35]

Fulbright told the Senate that U.S. policy "throughout the whole affair" had been "characterized by a lack of candor."[36] Administration officials in both Washington and Santo Domingo operated from a cold war mindset that led them to interpret events in an East-West framework.[37] The State Department, stung by having "lost" Cuba, was perhaps predisposed to find a Cuban hand.[38] Johnson's aim from the beginning of the intervention in the Dominican Republic was ideological;[39] when he could no longer pretend to be saving U.S. citizens, he gave a public airing to what had been his true motive all along—a fear that the Dominican Republic would go Communist.[40]

Was the fight against communism worth the candle? Was it worth con-
cocting stories that kept the public and Congress from assessing what a
president was doing? I was beginning to have doubts. About that time I
got a chance to view life from the other side, after Eisenhower and
Khrushchev negotiated a university student exchange program. Each
probably thought he would get more useful information to use against the
other. I had a different idea. If the United States were to buy Soviet products, I thought, and sell them ours, perhaps we would develop a mutual
interest in the other's continued existence.

To promote this trade, I found a place for myself, in 1966, in the
Eisenhower-Khrushchev exchange program, to do research at Moscow
University. I would study the Soviet system of export and import and
write an explanation of it from the technical side, so that people at home
could understand how to buy and sell there. Then trade would flourish,
and perhaps peace would break out.

My room in Moscow was in a severe-looking skyscraper dormitory
on the city's outskirts. The view I had from my window of the Kremlin,
with the sun reflecting off the gold cupolas of its cathedrals, was so
splendid that it made getting up on below-zero mornings almost a
pleasure. The subway took me downtown, where I pored over trade laws
and yellowing documents in a reading room across the street from the
Kremlin. And all the while missiles in silos in Nebraska or Oklahoma
were pointed at my head. I knew that Soviet missiles were aimed at our
cities as well, but it seemed ironic to be living in the prime target zone of
our own missiles. Would the war start while I was there, and would I be
hit by one of our missiles?

The friends I made in Moscow were also in the prime target zone.
They were not, however, the faceless "Soviets" whose history I had studied, but were real people, with names, personalities, character flaws,
senses of humor. And they were suffering from the cold war more than we
were, because even with a smaller economy they were building a military
to match ours.

The cold war entered my life in Moscow in another way, although I
did not learn of it until later. During those years the CIA routinely opened

mail coming from the Soviet Union. As part of this mail cover, they intercepted the letters I wrote home. A few years later, after the CIA program was revealed, Congress, in legislation against government secrecy, required agencies to turn over documents they had collected about individuals. I wrote the CIA, which sent me photocopies of all my letters. I don't know if my letters yielded anything valuable. Several recounted my difficulty coping with the ancient washing machines in which I did my laundry at Moscow University. If the CIA was concerned about a "laundry gap" between the two countries, I may have provided valuable information.

NOTES

1. "Statement by President Johnson," May 2, 1965, DSB, vol. 52, pp. 744–47 (1965).

2. "Secretary Discusses Situation in Dominican Republic," May 8, 1965, DSB, vol. 52, p. 842 (1965).

3. "Statement by President Johnson," May 2, 1965, DSB, vol. 52, p. 745 (1965).

4. David Wise, *The Politics of Lying: Government Deception, Secrecy, and Power* (1973), p. 42; Tad Szulc, *Dominican Diary* (1965), pp. 50–51.

5. *Congressional Record*, vol. 111, p. 23858, September 15, 1965 (statement of Sen. J. William Fulbright).

6. Ibid., p. 23855.

7. Theodore Draper, *The Dominican Revolt: A Case Study in American Policy* (1968), pp. 60–61.

8. Piero Gleijeses, *The Dominican Crisis: The 1965 Constitutionalist Revolt and American Intervention* (1978), pp. 161, 176, 182, 185, 187, 208, 212–13, 224.

9. Draper, *The Dominican Revolt*, p. 61.

10. Ibid., pp. 60–61. Gleijeses, *The Dominican Crisis*, pp. 191–95.

11. Draper, *The Dominican Revolt*, p. 95. Abraham F. Lowenthal, *The Dominican Intervention* (1972), pp. 78, 89–90.

12. Szulc, *Dominican Diary*, p. 79.

13. John Bartlow Martin, *Overtaken by Events: The Dominican Crisis from the Fall of Trujillo to the Civil War* (1966), pp. 653–54.

14. Martin, *Overtaken by Events*, p. 658; Lowenthal, *The Dominican Intervention*, p. 119; Szulc, *Dominican Diary*, pp. 56, 243.

15. Draper, *The Dominican Revolt*, pp. 74–76.

16. *Congressional Record*, vol. 111, p. 23855, September 15, 1965 (statement of Sen. J. William Fulbright); Martin, *Overtaken by Events*, p. 655; Draper, *The Dominican Revolt*, pp. 99–102,123.

17. Lowenthal, *The Dominican Intervention*, p. 205; Szulc, *Dominican Diary*, p. 177.

18. Szulc, *Dominican Diary*, p. 200.

19. Lowenthal, *The Dominican Intervention*, pp. 116–18.

20. Szulc, *Dominican Diary*, p. 124.

21. Lowenthal, *The Dominican Intervention*, pp. 114, 131, 139; Draper, *The Dominican Revolt*, pp. 132, 185–86.

22. Lowenthal, *The Dominican Intervention*, p. 115; Szulc, *Dominican Diary*, p. 78.

23. Lowenthal, *The Dominican Intervention*, pp. 120, 127; Szulc, *Dominican Diary*, pp. 79, 109.

24. Szulc, *Dominican Diary*, pp. 104, 158; James Nelson Goodsell, "Dominican Role of U.S. Clouded," *Christian Science Monitor*, May 18, 1965, p. 1, col. 4.

25. Tad Szulc, "14 Marines Are Wounded; 4 Army Men Are Also Hit," *New York Times*, May 1, 1965, p. Al, col. 6; *Congressional Record*, vol. 111, p. 23857, September 15, 1965 (statement of Sen. J. William Fulbright); Szulc, *Dominican Diary*, pp. 80–81, 187, 195, 214; David Atlee Phillips, *The Night Watch* (1977), p. 159.

26. Barnard L. Collier, "Dominican Junta Gets U.S. Help," *Washington Post*, May 20, 1965, p. Al, col. 8.

27. Szulc, *Dominican Diary*, p. 256.

28. Robert A. Caro, *The Years of Lyndon Johnson: Means of Ascent* (1990), p. xxv; Draper, *The Dominican Revolt*, p. 65.

29. Max Frankel, "Red Role in Rising Grows," *New York Times*, May 2, 1965, p. Al, col. 5; "Remarks by President Johnson," May 4, 1965, DSB, vol. 52, pp. 82122(1965). Draper, *The Dominican Revolt*, p. 91.

30. Frank Cormier, *LBJ: The Way He Was* (1977), p. 188; Philip Geyelin, *Lyndon Johnson and the World* (1966), p. 253; Draper, *The Dominican Revolt*, pp. 141–43; Szulc, *Dominican Diary*, p. 70.

31. Szulc, *Dominican Diary*, pp. 82–83, 108; Gleijeses, *The Dominican Crisis*, p. 207; Lowenthal, *The Dominican Intervention*, p. 48.

32. Draper, *The Dominican Revolt*, pp. 66–68, 87; Lowenthal, *The Dominican Intervention*, pp. 40, 56–57; *Congressional Record*, vol. 111, p. 23857, September 15, 1965 (statement of Sen. J. William Fulbright).

33. Martin, *Overtaken by Events*, p. 651; Gleijeses, *The Dominican Crisis*, p. 211.

34. Gleijeses, *The Dominican Crisis*, pp. 224, 229–30, 251; Draper, *The Dominican Revolt*, pp. 68–71; *Congressional Record*, vol. 111, pp. 23857–58, September 15, 1965 (statement of Sen. J. William Fulbright).

35. *Congressional Record*, vol. 111, p. 23859, September 15, 1965 (statement of Sen. J. William Fulbright).

36. Ibid., p. 23855.

37. Geyelin, *Lyndon B. Johnson and the World*, p. 254.

38. Lowenthal, *The Dominican Intervention*, pp. 25–26, 31.

39. Szulc, *Dominican Diary*, p. 19.

40. Phillips, *The Night Watch*, p. 144.

16. CAMBODIA: FISH IN THE CRATERS

Flying over Cambodia in 1979, I was puzzled by what appeared to be large ponds, all perfectly circular, across the countryside. Since cultivation of fish is a major Cambodian industry, the Cambodians, I thought, must have gone to great pains to cut the ponds so precisely. But I kept seeing more. Could they have so many fish ponds?

Once in Phnom Penh, I learned that the holes were not the product of Cambodian handiwork, but craters from bombs dropped by American B-52s. From 1969 to 1975, the air force dropped half a million tons on Cambodia, not as much as in Laos or Vietnam, but still enough to alter the character of the countryside.[1] My first guess had not been completely wrong, however, because once the craters filled with water, the Cambodians did use them to cultivate fish.

Our military action in Cambodia came first as an outgrowth of the action in Vietnam. Beginning in 1967, our commanders there decided that the National Liberation Front (NLF) must have a central command post. After failing to find one in South Vietnam, they crossed the border into Cambodia to look there.[2] When that effort failed to turn up the desired command post, the commanders, beginning in 1969, asked for permission to bomb in Cambodia, both to find the command post and to destroy other suspected NLF bases. President Nixon approved but insisted that the operation remain secret, because Congress had not authorized action in Cambodia. With opposition to the Vietnam war building in the United States, Nixon could not risk public discussion of our forces operating in still another country of Indochina.

In March 1969, the air force began using B-52s for bombing raids over Cambodia.[3] The bombing was heavy, and the Cambodian government was quick to complain. Cambodian Prince Norodom Sihanouk told the press that the bombs were hitting not Communist soldiers, but "peasants, women and children in particular."[4] The American press all but ignored Sihanouk's protests, and the American public remained unaware of the Cambodia bombing.

In May 1970, Nixon sent a large troop force into Cambodia, announcing the operation publicly as one aimed at finding the supposed NLF command post.[5] Lon Nol, who by then was the Cambodian leader, and also a U.S. ally, complained that the invasion violated Cambodian sovereignty.[6] There was little evidence that the NLF used Cambodia to any significant extent;[7] even if a command post did exist, a short-term operation could destroy it but could not prevent it from being reestablished. The press, skeptical of Nixon's stated rationale, questioned whether he had some other, secret motive for the Cambodia invasion.[8]

In any event, Nixon kept the troops in Cambodia only a few weeks, declaring, as he pulled them out, that they had "completed successfully the destruction of enemy base areas" on the Cambodian side of the border with Vietnam.[9] Ellsworth Bunker, our ambassador in Vietnam, declared the invasion "perhaps the most successful of the war."[10] Vice President Spiro Agnew said that the operations resulted in "the cleaning out of the sanctuaries."[11]

Beyond these statements from official Washington, however, there was little to indicate that our troops had found any NLF bases. All that could be said for sure was that our troops had destroyed a number of Cambodian villages, apparently to keep any enemy forces from using them.[12]

After the ground invasion, the Nixon administration continued the aerial bombardment of Cambodia, no longer keeping it secret. Nixon did not immediately acknowledge, however, that we had bombed prior to the incursion.[13] In July 1973 the Defense Department admitted that it had bombed Cambodia before May 1970.[14] The bombing had been substantial. It was revealed at that time that from March 1969 to May 1970, American B-52s dropped 108,000 tons of bombs on Cambodia.[15]

When the Senate armed services committee finally learned that we had carried on secret bombing, it called in Defense Department officials to explain why. The air force had filed reports with the committee in 1969 on bombing activity in Indochina, but those reports reflected no raids over Cambodia. Senator Harold Hughes of Iowa, outraged at the omission, called it "official deception."[16]

What came out at the Senate hearings was that the air force kept the pre-1970 bombing a secret by failing to keep records of the raids.[17] When it bombed in Cambodia, the air force reported instead that it had bombed in South Vietnam, specifying some locations that had in fact not been touched.[18] Air force Major Hal Knight, who supervised the crews, told the committee that when he asked his superiors why he should falsify reports, they told him that it was for political reasons.[19]

Since Prince Sihanouk already knew that Cambodia was being bombed before 1970, Senator Hughes said that the only people the air force deceived "were the people of the United States of America."[20] Senator Stuart Symington of Missouri, referring to the power given to Congress to declare war, called the secret bombing unconstitutional. Symington bemoaned the fact that the air force "dropped a hundred thousand tons" on Cambodia when, as a Senator, "I had no idea you dropped one ton."[21] Symington thought that the bombing had "accomplished very little" from a military standpoint.[22]

As for the bombing in Cambodia after May 1970, President Nixon announced on June 30, 1970, that the sole purpose of further bombing raids would be to stop "enemy efforts to move supplies and personnel through Cambodia toward South Viet-Nam and to reestablish base areas relevant to the war in Viet-Nam."[23] But on June 13, 1970, a secret cable drafted by the Joint Chiefs of Staff authorized bombing in Cambodia "in any situation which involves a serious threat to major Cambodian positions."[24] By this the Joint Chiefs meant that bombing was to be done to support the government of Cambodia, which faced a rural guerrilla insurgency. Thus, contrary to what President Nixon had announced publicly, the bombing was meant to support the government of Lon Nol, which was sympathetic to the United States and a recipient of American military aid.[25] The opposition was a leftist insurgency led by the Khmer Rouge— Khmer being the predominant ethnic group of Cambodia, while Rouge ("red" in French) reflected their leftist orientation.

The Joint Chiefs' directive was not made public, however, and the administration continued to deny that it was intervening in Cambodia's civil war. It denied that there even was a civil war, claiming instead that the hostilities in Cambodia were between the Cambodian government on the one side, and the NLF and North Vietnamese forces on the other. Vice President Agnew declared in 1970, "this is not a civil war in Cambodia"; the fighting there was the result of "outrageous aggression by the North Vietnamese."[26] When in 1975 the Khmer Rouge marched into Phnom Penh and took over the country, it became obvious that the administration's story had been false.

As Congress debated Cambodian policy in 1970, the administration played down the extent of its bombing there.[27] In 1971, however, a Government Accounting Office (GAO) study of the Cambodia bombing found that two million Cambodians, of a total population of six million, had been forced to abandon their home areas. The air force's bombing, the GAO concluded, had wrought immense civilian casualties and was "a very significant cause of refugees."[28] As in Laos, the bombing was aimed at beating back a leftist insurgency by depriving it of a population within which to operate. If, as Mao Tse-tung said, guerrillas must swim like fish in the sea, the air force would dry up the sea.

In 1972, President Nixon stopped the bombing of Cambodia;[29] but when the January 1973 peace agreement for Vietnam ended our bombing campaign in that country, the Air Force redirected its B-52s back to Cambodia, bombing as much there in the first half of 1973 as it had done from 1969 to 1972.[30] As on the Laotian Plain of Jars, farming became impossible in much of Cambodia, with peasants streaming into cities to escape.[31] Under pressure from Congress, the air force finally put an end to the Cambodia bombing in August 1973.[32]

The bombing of Cambodia, first totally secret and then partially secret, led to enactment of the War Powers Resolution, requiring a president to notify Congress if he sends troops abroad for combat, and establishing a procedure for Congress to stop the operation if it disagrees.[33]

Our support for Lon Nol's government, as it turned out, was to no avail. As in Laos, the bombing did not stop the rural insurgency that was its target. If anything, the bombing helped the insurgents, because the Khmer Rouge called for a self-reliant, peasant-based society, which would build up Cambodia's economy without foreign investment or extensive export or import. The Khmer Rouge planned new and extensive peasant communities. The bombing only reinforced the Khmer Rouge's arguments of the futility of relying on the Western world.

Moreover, the bombing led to a mass influx of rural inhabitants into Phnom Penh, the country's capital city. Peasants lived in shanties on the outskirts of Phnom Penh, where the city could not provide them with services, and where disease was rampant. For the Khmer Rouge, these migrants formed the base for new peasant communities. Since many existing villages had already been emptied because of the bombing, the Khmer Rouge could shuffle the population at will.

Implementing its plan after taking Phnom Penh in April 1975, the Khmer Rouge drove out nearly the entire population—recent migrants and long-time residents alike—forcing the people to new locations to work in highly disciplined farming brigades. On any who protested, the Khmer Rouge inflicted harsh treatment, killing large numbers of people in an effort to stamp its mold on the population. The Khmer Rouge held power until 1979, when Vietnam sent troops to Cambodia and helped to power a dissident faction of the Khmer Rouge that opposed its harsh policies.

As for Phnom Penh, from 1975 to 1979 it was a ghost town. When I saw the city in 1979, I could tell that it had once been an attractive, sleepy colonial capital of broad, well laid-out avenues showing the influence of the French who built it. But in 1979 houses stood empty. Old Renaults, abandoned and inoperable, blocked driveways, where their owners had left them four years before.

I was in Phnom Penh as an expert witness at a trial organized by the new Cambodian government against the top two Khmer Rouge leaders, Pol Pot and Ieng Sary. Since they were both off in the Thailand-Cambodia border area leading the remnants of the Khmer Rouge against the new government, the trial was held without them. The charge against Pol Pot and Ieng Sary was genocide, a crime that had been defined by the 1948 Genocide Convention, drafted in the wake of the mass killings in Europe during World War II.

For four days, witnesses told of mass murder, and many instances of individual and small-group killings by Khmer Rouge cadres. Some of the killings were aimed at officials of the prior governments, others at persons who opposed the forced employment in highly disciplined agriculture. A parade of witnesses described how family members had been killed. Few could complete their testimony without losing their composure.

After the witnesses had completed their testimony, I gave the court an explanation of the law on genocide, describing how it was defined under the Genocide Convention, and giving my opinion that if the evidence presented at the trial was accurate, genocide had indeed been committed. I also mentioned the bombing of Cambodia by the U.S. Air Force, which, I said, "destroyed much of the Cambodian countryside through its bombing. The mass influx of people into Cambodia's cities as a result of that bombing led to shortage and disease in the cities." Those conditions, I concluded, set the stage for the genocide that followed.[34]

The air force's bombing of Cambodia facilitated a downward spiral for Cambodia. The American public could not question the bombing, because until 1970 it did not know it was occurring, and from 1970 to 1973, it did not have knowledge of the bombing's full scope.

The bombing, however, was not the last chapter in our military action in Cambodia. In a bizarre postscript, barely a month after the Khmer Rouge came to power in April 1975, a naval vessel of the new Khmer

Rouge government seized a U.S.-registered merchant vessel with an American crew. The SS *Mayaguez* was stopped and led to Koh Tang Island, off the Cambodian coast, where it was forced to anchor.[35] The reasons for the seizure were not made clear, as the *Mayaguez* was apparently on an ordinary commercial run, but the Khmer Rouge government, only just installed in power, may have suspected it of electronic surveillance of the Cambodian coast.

In any event, the Ford administration decided to retake the ship, and after demanding its return, sent U.S. Navy vessels to positions near Koh Tang Island. President Gerald Ford said that the deployment was to prevent the Cambodian navy from taking U.S. sailors to the mainland. On May 14, Cambodian authorities met Ford's demands, turning over to the navy first the *Mayaguez*, at 9:00 P.M., EDT, and then its crew, at 11:30 P.M., EDT.

The return of the *Mayaguez* and its crew did not end the episode, however. In the early hours of May 15, a force of U.S. Marines led an assault on Koh Tang Island. President Ford declared that its purpose was "to search out and rescue such other Americans as might still be held there." In addition, our jet fighters strafed a military airfield and other military targets on the Cambodian mainland, in order "to prevent reinforcement or support from the mainland of the Cambodian forces detaining the American vessel and crew."[36]

As this sequence shows, by the time we assaulted the island and bombed the mainland, we had already recovered both the *Mayaguez* and its crew.[37] Navy officials, when asked to explain, acknowledged that it was unnecessary to attack. They claimed they had not gotten word of the return of the vessel and crew soon enough to call off the raids, which, they said, had been planned prior to the return.

Several hours, in fact, had elapsed before the navy's subsequent raid. The assault on and bombing of the island, skeptics speculated, were a reprisal by an administration still smarting from the recent fall of its allied governments in both Cambodia and South Vietnam. Some thought the United States was trying to show that it was still tough even after its losses.[38]

Administration officials furthered these suspicions when they described the operation as a warning to North Korea and other communist countries that the United States, in the wake of the Vietnam war, "still stood ready to meet force with force to protect its interests."[39] Officials speaking on background said that the incident provided "a test of American determination in Southeast Asia." Demonstrating that determination was important after the collapse of the Cambodian and South Vietnam governments.[40] It was not, as the navy argued, that we could not stop a raid already set in motion. We strafed and assaulted Cambodian territory to make a point.

NOTES

1. William S. Turley, *The Second Indochina War: A Short Political and Military History, 1954–1975* (1986), p. 87.

2. *Bombing in Cambodia*, Hearings before the Committee on Armed Services, U.S. Senate, 93rd Cong., 1st sess. (1973), pp. 231–48, 493.

3. James William Gibson, *The Perfect War: Technowar in Vietnam* (1986), pp. 404–40

5; *Bombing in Cambodia*, pp. 80, 98, 104, 132, 279–80, 347, 482.

4. *Bombing in Cambodia*, pp. 158–59.

5. Robert B. Semple, Jr., "Nixon Sends Combat Forces to Cambodia to Drive Communists from Staging Zone," *New York Times*, May 1, 1970, p. Al, col. 8.

6. William Shawcross, *Sideshow: Kissinger, Nixon and the Destruction of Cambodia* (1979), p. 149.

7. Edward S. Herman and Noam Chomsky, *Manufacturing Consent: The Political Economy of the Mass Media* (1988), pp. 268–69.

8. Haynes Johnson, "The Irreconcilable Conflict between Press and Government: 'Whose Side Are You On?'" in Thomas M. Franck and Edward Weisband, eds., *Secrecy and Foreign Policy* (1974), pp. 165, 173.

9. Richard Nixon, "A Report on the Conclusion of the Cambodian Operation," DSB, vol. 63, p. 65 (1970).

10. Ellsworth Bunker, "A Review of Progress and Problems in Vietnam," DSB, vol. 64, p. 207 (1971).

11. "News Conference, September 1, San Clemente, California," DSB, vol. 63, p. 385 (1970).

12. Shawcross, *Sideshow*, pp. 150–52.

13. *Bombing in Cambodia*, p. 40.

14. Edgar O'Ballance, *The Wars in Vietnam, 1954–1980* (1981), p. 155; *Bombing in Cambodia*, p. 496.

15. *Bombing in Cambodia*, p. 487.

16. Ibid., p. 38.

17. Ibid., p. 11.

18. Ibid., pp. 98, 132, 352, 358, 483.

19. Ibid., p. 5.

20. Ibid., p. 160.

21. Ibid., p. 101.

22. Ibid., p. 180.

23. Richard Nixon, "A Report on the Conclusion of the Cambodian Operation," DSB, vol. 63, p.72 (1970).

24. Shawcross, *Sideshow*, p. 214.

25. "U.S. and Cambodia Sign Agreement Regulating Military Assistance," DSB, vol. 63, p. 387 (1970).

26. "News Conference, September 1, San Clemente, California," DSB, vol. 63, p. 386 (1970).

27. Shawcross, *Sideshow*, p. 214.

28. Terence Smith, "Refugee Problem in Cambodia Laid to Allied Bombs," *New York Times*, December 5, 1971, p. Al, col. 3.

29. Shawcross, *Sideshow*, p. 218.

30. "Pentagon's Statistics Underscore Intensity of Cambodia Bombing," *New York Times*, June 22, 1973, p. A2, col. 3.

31. Shawcross, *Sideshow*, p. 319.

32. *Bombing in Cambodia*, p. 482.

33. U.S. Code, vol. 50, §1541.

34. Statement of John Quigley, in Howard DeNike, John Quigley and Kenneth Robinson, eds., *Genocide in Cambodia: Documents from the Trial of Pol Pot and Ieng Sary* (2000), p. 518.

35. "Statement by White House Press Secretary," May 13, 1975, DSB, vol. 72, p. 719 (1975).

36. "Statement by President Ford," May 15, 1975, 12:27 A.M., E.D.T., DSB,

vol. 72, p. 721 (1975); Letters (identical) from Gerald Ford to the President Pro Tempore, U.S. Senate, and to the Speaker, U.S. House of Representatives, May 15, 1975, DSB, vol. 72, pp. 721–22 (1975).

37. "Secretary Kissinger's News Conference of May 16," DSB, vol. 72, p. 760 (1975); "A Chronology of the *Mayaguez* Episode," *New York Times*, May 16, 1975, p. A14, col. 2; Bob Woodward, *The Commanders* (1991), p. 175.

38. "Secretary Kissinger's News Conference of May 24," DSB, vol. 72, p. 802 (1975).

39. Bernard Gwertzman, "U.S. Sees Foray for Ship as Signal to Communists," *New York Times*, May 16, 1975, p. A14, col. 7.

40. "Thailand Reports Marines' Arrival in Ship's Seizure," *New York Times*, May 14, 1975, p. A1, col. 8.

17. ANGOLA: A GLOBAL MONROE DOCTRINE

In 1975, President Ford capitalized on the backing that earlier administrations had given to Colonel Mobutu in the Congo, which by then had been renamed Zaire. Mobutu, who remained our close ally, aspired to extend his influence elsewhere in Africa. Mobutu found support for these ambitions in Washington, where CIA Director William Colby viewed Zaire as "a future regional big power."[1] Both Colby and Secretary of State Henry Kissinger looked to Mobutu to oppose Soviet influence in Africa, and in particular to support us in Angola, where we were involved in a push-pull with the Soviet Union.[2]

Angola was of particular interest to Mobutu. An enclave called Cabinda, located on Zaire's Atlantic coast but belonging to Angola, had a huge pool of oil that Gulf Oil was busily tapping.[3] For Kissinger, Angola was of interest because in 1975 it was to gain independence from Portugal. In Angola three independence groups that had fought Portugal were vying for control: the Popular Movement for the Liberation of Angola (MPLA), the National Front for the Liberation of Angola (FNLA), and the National Union for the Total Independence of Angola (UNITA). Although the three did not differ markedly in outlook, the MPLA was more critical of the United States' support for Portugal during the years it refused to grant Angola independence.[4] All three had received Soviet-bloc aid, but the MPLA had tighter relations with the Soviet Union. The FNLA had close ties to President Mobutu, as it was based in Zaire, where it enjoyed Mobutu's encouragement.

Secretary Kissinger, smarting over losing Indochina to communism and determined not to let leftists win elsewhere, saw Angola as a cold war battlefield.[5] The Soviet Union had been giving arms to the MPLA when it was fighting Portugal, but ended that aid in 1973.[6] However, the Soviets resumed arms aid in the fall of 1974, leading Kissinger to fear that an MPLA-led Angola would become a Soviet beachhead in Africa.[7]

Kissinger's connection to U.S. policy on Angola went beyond his role as secretary of state. Kissinger also headed the so-called Forty Committee, an interagency body that oversaw U.S. covert operations around the world. In January 1975, the Forty Committee authorized aid to the FNLA to help it against the MPLA.[8] From bases in Zaire the FNLA attacked Angola in an effort to take territory around Luanda, the Angolan capital.[9] The Soviet Union responded in March 1975 by sending the MPLA a new quantity of arms.[10]

With Portugal scheduled to leave Angola in November 1975, Nathaniel Davis, assistant secretary of state for African affairs, proposed to Kissinger that the United States promote negotiations among the three rival parties. Unlike Kissinger, Davis thought that Angola was "basically an African problem," not a stage for East-West confrontation.[11] Along with Davis, other administration officials opposed Kissinger's approach of trying to "face off the Russians" in Angola.[12]

Kissinger, however, rejected these suggestions; in June and July 1975, he got the Forty Committee to approve another arms shipment to the FNLA and, for the first time, to supply arms as well to UNITA, which also opposed the MPLA and which leaned toward the West.[13] On the basis of the Forty Committee decision, President Ford signed a secret order authorizing aid to the FNLA and UNITA.[14]

In August, the aid began in earnest, when the CIA set up a task force in Washington to run the Angola operation. First the task force planned a propaganda-information campaign for the FNLA and UNITA. CIA propaganda experts in Zaire planted (true) stories in the wire services to expose Soviet arms shipments and (false) stories that Cuban soldiers operating with the MPLA had raped Angolan girls. CIA publicists also wrote position papers for the FNLA, which it used at the United Nations.[15]

The task force generated a flurry of activity. A CIA team flew to Zaire, where it briefed the FNLA and UNITA on tactics and set up radio systems for FNLA communications inside Angola. CIA cables flew between Zaire and Washington, as CIA officers brought in weapons and equipment and trained the FNLA and UNITA in their use.[16] In September, the administration allocated a new round of aid to the FNLA and UNITA; in November, it gave more aid.[17]

The Forty Committee set up a special supervisory group to oversee the CIA's handling of the Angola operation, with representatives from the State Department, Defense Department, and White House.[18] From Zaire, CIA personnel visited FNLA and UNITA positions in Angola to check on operations.[19] What they found convinced them that they needed to train and supervise the FNLA and UNITA more closely. So more CIA personnel went into combat areas in Angola.[20] There they advised and organized, drawing up battle plans and helping the FNLA and UNITA figure out how to put them into operation.[21]

When Assistant Secretary Davis testified on Angola policy before the Senate Subcommittee on Africa on July 14, he gave no hint of any American assistance to UNITA or FNLA.[22] Davis so opposed Kissinger's plans for the Angola operation that he resigned in protest shortly after testifying.[23] Kissinger replaced him with William Schaufele, who shared Kissinger's perspective on Angola.[24]

The CIA operation was not enough to put the FNLA and UNITA over the top, however, because the two groups needed more combatants. So the CIA recruited and hired mercenaries, mainly Portuguese and French, and sent them to FNLA and UNITA units in Angola.[25] The administration also convinced Mobutu to send in Zairian troops to help against the MPLA; Mobutu quickly obliged,[26] but his troops did so poorly that they were soon withdrawn.[27] For a time the operation made progress. CIA Director Colby took credit for "completely reversing" the momentum away from the MPLA. The MPLA had to ask for more help from the Soviet Union and approached Cuba, which sent several thousand troops to fight on its side.[28] For all the CIA activity in Angola, Congress and the public remained in the dark, as the Ford administration kept the Angola operation under close wraps. The media did not penetrate its veil of secrecy.

Over the summer a new factor emerged in the Angola picture: South Africa entered the war, sending a small troop force into southern Angola in mid-August.[29] The press reported South Africa's role in Angola, even while it remained unaware of our own. South Africa's entry, however, brought political risks for the administration, which did not want to appear to be collaborating with the apartheid government, for no one would believe that South Africa had Angola's interests at heart. When asked at a press conference in November about South Africa's role, Kissinger replied, "the South Africans are not engaged officially; that is, they are not engaged with their own military forces."[30] But even as Kissinger spoke, South African regular troops were fighting alongside UNITA forces.[31] In October, South Africa sent a large force into central Angola to support UNITA,[32] while two South African armored columns accompanied UNITA almost to the outskirts of Luanda.[33]

Kissinger's answer to the press obscured the fact that we were effectively allied with South Africa in supporting the FNLA and UNITA.[34] UNITA was obtaining arms and training from South Africa, and the FNLA was getting South African heavy artillery.[35] CIA Director Colby, concerned that if our collusion with South Africa became known, our reputation in independent Africa would plummet, claimed later that the CIA "stayed well away from" South Africa.[36] But CIA officials consulted regularly with South Africa's Bureau of State Security to coordinate Angola operations.[37] Under cross-examination in the U.S. Senate, Deputy Assistant Secretary of State for African Affairs Edward Mulcahy acknowledged that after South African forces entered Angola, we had "routine exchange of intelligence" with South Africa and that this included discussion of its troop movements in Angola.[38] South African officials even claimed that they entered Angola with our blessing.[39]

It was not only the South Africa connection that concerned the administration, however. After Vietnam, public sentiment would not have backed a war of any kind in Angola, and the administration knew it. So it went to great pains to keep the public from finding out about the CIA support to the FNLA and UNITA.[40] Kissinger publicly criticized the Soviet Union for helping the MPLA but gave no hint that the Soviet aid of March 1975 had come only in response to our own.[41] "Events in Angola have taken a distressing turn, with widespread violence," Kissinger said. "We are most alarmed at the interference of extracontinental powers who do not wish Africa well and whose involvement is inconsistent with the promise of true independence. We believe a fair and peaceful solution must be negotiated, giving all groups representing the Angolan people a fair role in its future."[42]

To the public, the administration denied providing any arms to the FNLA or UNITA, but to Congress, in secret briefings, CIA Director Colby admitted the deliveries, although he denied any involvement by CIA personnel.[43] The administration's secrecy ultimately doomed the operation, however, because there was no way to respond to the Soviet and Cuban counteraid without higher visibility. The operation came apart at the seams in late 1975, when the press finally exposed our activities, giving details on what the CIA was doing.[44] Pressure built in Congress to end the operation. Kissinger continued to view it in apocalyptic terms: if Congress forced termination, the Soviet Union and other countries might not take our warnings seriously in other parts of the world. Kissinger, invoking a doomsday scenario, claimed that Syria might invade Israel, with Soviet support.[45]

Hearings on Angola were called in the Senate, and Kissinger was summoned to testify. The senators wanted to know who had started the arms aid to Angola, the United States or the Soviet Union. Kissinger told the senators that our aid to the FNLA and UNITA began only in August 1975, making it seem like a response to the increase in Soviet aid to the MPLA in March.[46] But Schaufele, Kissinger's new assistant secretary, told the senators the truth—that we began funding the FNLA in January.[47]

Kissinger kept insisting that we were "responding" to "Soviet military moves" in Angola, to "outside interference initiated by the Soviet Union." Moreover, we were maintaining strict neutrality regarding the three Angola factions. "We are not opposing any particular faction," Kissinger argued. "In Angola we have consistently advocated a government representing all three factions. . . [and] never opposed participation by the Soviet-backed Popular Movement for the Liberation of Angola, the MPLA." Kissinger also denied that we collaborated with South Africa.[48]

Kissinger and other State Department officials, who testified in the Senate, and in the House as well, did not disclose the existence of the CIA Task Force, or the fact that CIA operatives operating out of Zaire worked with the FNLA and UNITA in the field in Angola. They denied that the CIA recruited mercenaries.[49] Senator John Tunney of California,who accepted Schaufele's version of events, decried the coverup, stating, "There is a pattern of American orchestration and involvement that goes far beyond what the administration has admitted."[50]

Senator Joseph Biden of Delaware objected that the administration twice changed the reason for its involvement in Angola. First, the CIA told him in a private briefing that the aim was to respond to a request from Zambia and Zaire, because they feared the MPLA. Then administration officials said that strategic issues were involved—the Atlantic sea lanes and the possibility of the spread of revolution to Brazil. But Kissinger gave the Senate a third reason as well—global considerations related to keeping the Soviet Union from dabbling in the Third World. Biden criticized Kissinger's approach of responding anywhere to the Soviet Union by calling it a "global Monroe Doctrine."[51]

A House committee also looking into the Angola operation decided that the CIA prompted Soviet and Cuban aid, not vice versa. The committee found that those two countries acted in "reaction to U.S. efforts," and that the aid we had given the FNLA in January 1975 "panicked the Soviets" into new aid to the MPLA in March.[52]

Disgusted over the administration's deception and opposed to the CIA operation, Congress ended the Angola operation in February 1976 by passing a statute that prohibited expenditure of funds in Angola for paramilitary operations.[53] By then the House Appropriations Committee was so suspicious of the administration that it did not trust the CIA to comply with this law, so it sent a special team of auditors to the CIA to make sure the agency would not cheat.[54]

With the CIA out of the picture, the FNLA soon collapsed, and UNITA withdrew to the southern reaches of Angola.[55] The Senate select committee on intelligence examining the operation complained that President Ford had not given Congress or the public a chance to assess the reasons for what it called "a large-scale covert paramilitary operation in Angola." The president had made a major foreign policy decision without telling anyone outside the administration, in an operation initiated, the committee said, "without any effort on the part of the executive branch to articulate, and win public support for, its overall policy in Africa."[56]

The Senate committee concluded that Secretary of State Kissinger had needlessly turned Angola into a cold war confrontation. The three Angolan factions, it said, were just three parts of an anticolonial movement trying to get Portugal to leave. The East-West confrontation scenario was the world as Kissinger had presented it in his lectures that I still remembered. In Kissinger's world, there were only two players. I understood why he viewed Angola as he did.

NOTES

1. Leslie Gelb, "Should We Play Direct Tricks in the World?" *New York Times Magazine*, December 21, 1975, p. 15.

2. Leslie Gelb, "U.S., Soviet, China Reported Aiding Portugal, Angola," *New York Times*, September 25, 1975, p. Al, col. 1; Bernard Gwertzman, "US Seeks Rapid Aid to Zaire but Congress Is Wary," *New York Times*, October 16, 1975, p. A2, col. 4; Michael I. Kaufman, "The U.S.–Zaire Connection: Substantial," *New York Times*, January 4, 1976, p. D2, col. 3.

3. *Angola*, Hearings before the Subcommittee on African Affairs of the Committee on Foreign Relations, U.S. Senate, 94th Cong., 2d sess., 1976, pp. 109–10 (statement of Stephen Weissman).

4. John Marcum, "Lessons of Angola," *Foreign Affairs* 54 (April 1976): 410–12; *United States Policy on Angola*, Hearing before the Committee on International Relations, U.S. House of Representatives, 94th Cong., 2d sess., 1976, p. 8 (statement of Asst. Secretary of State William Schaufele).

5. John Stockwell, *In Search of Enemies: A CIA Story* (1978), p. 43; Nathaniel Davis, "The Angola Decision of 1975: A Personal Memoir," *Foreign Affairs* 57, no. 1 (Fall 1978): 124.

6. Stockwell, *In Search of Enemies*, p. 68.

7. Marcum, "Lessons of Angola," p. 413.

8. *Final Report: Foreign and Military Intelligence*, U.S. Senate, Select Committee to Study Governmental Operations with Respect to Intelligence Activities, Book I, 94th Cong., 2d sess., April 26, 1976, p. 151; Seymour Hersh, "Early Angola Aid by U.S. Reported," *New York Times*, December 19, 1975, p. Al, col. 2; Stephen R. Weissman, "CIA Covert Action in Zaire and Angola Patterns and Consequences," *Political Science Quarterly* 94, no. 2 (Summer 1979): 282.

9. Stockwell, *In Search of Enemies*, p. 67; Marcum, "Lessons of Angola," p. 415.

10. Stockwell, *In Search of Enemies*, p. 68.

11. Davis, "The Angola Decision of 1975," p. 112.

12. Seymour Hersh, "Angola Aid Issue Opening Rifts in State Department," *New York Times*, December 14, 1975, p. Al, col. 4.

13. William Colby, *Honorable Men: My Life in the CIA* (1978), p. 422; Seymour Hersh, "Angola Aid Issue Opening Rifts in State Department," *New York Times*, December 14, 1975, p. Al, col. 4.

14. *Final Report: Foreign and Military Intelligence*, p. 152.

15. Stockwell, *In Search of Enemies*, pp. 72, 194–96.

16. Ibid., pp. 86–87.

17. *Final Report: Foreign and Military Intelligence*, p. 152.

18. Stockwell, *In Search of Enemies*, p. 94.

19. Ibid., pp. 121, 128, 138.

20. Ibid., p. 177.

21. Ibid.

22. "Department Discusses Situation in Angola," DSB, vol. 73, p. 212 (1975).

23. Seymour Hersh, "Angola Aid Issue Opening Rifts in State Department," *New York Times*, December 14, 1975, p. A1, col. 4; Davis, "The Angola Decision of 1975," p. 117.

24. *United States Policy on Angola*, p. 2.

25. Stockwell, *In Search of Enemies*, pp. 182–84, 220–25.

26. David B. Ottoway, "Zaire Conflict Poses Dilemma for U.S.," *Washington Post*, May 18, 1978, p. A18, col. 4; *Angola*, p. 165 (statement of Sen. John Tunney).

27. Madeleine Kalb, *The Congo Cables: The Cold War in Africa From Eisenhower to Kennedy* (1982), p. 382.

28. Colby, *Honorable Men*, p. 422; Marcum, "Lessons of Angola," p. 416.

29. *United States Policy on Angola*, pp. 22, 83.

30. "Secretary's News Conference of November 28," DSB, vol. 73, p. 897 (1975).

31. Stockwell, *In Search of Enemies*, p. 185; Fred Bridgland, "S. African Regulars Fight Inside Angola," *Washington Post*, November 23, 1975, p. A18, col. 1.

32. *Angola*, p. 165 (statement of Sen. John Tunney), 176 (statement of Asst. Secretary of State Schaufele).

33. David B. Ottoway, "Angola: Charges Prompt New Look at U.S. Role," *Washington Post*, May 10, 1978, p. A12, col. 1; Davis, "The Angola Decision of 1975," p. 122.

34. Gregory F. Treverton, *Covert Action: The Limits of Intervention in the Postwar World* (1987), p. 148.

35. Ottoway, "Angola"; *United States Policy on Angola*, p. 22 (statement of Deputy Secretary of State for African Affairs Edward Mulcahy).

36. Colby, *Honorable Men*, p. 422.

37. Stockwell, *In Search of Enemies*, pp. 187–88.

38. *Angola*, p. 187.

39. Marcum, "Lessons of Angola," p. 422.

40. Stockwell, *In Search of Enemies*, pp. 55, 170–71.

41. "Secretary's News Conference of November 28."

42. Henry Kissinger, "The United States and Africa: Strengthening the Relationship," DSB, vol. 73, p. 574 (1975).

43. Stockwell, *In Search of Enemies*, pp. 200, 227–30.

44. Ibid., p. 202; Hersh, "Angola Aid Issue Opening Rifts in State Department."

45. Bernard Gwertzman, "Kissinger Said to Warn Allon of Angola Danger," *New York Times*, January 9, 1976, p. A3, col. 3.

46. *Angola*, pp. 10, 17.

47. Ibid., p. 185.

48. Ibid., pp. 7–13, 20, 53.

49. Ibid., p. 27 (statement of Secretary of State Kissinger).

50. Ibid., p. 166.

51. Ibid., pp. 45–46.

52. *Report*, Select Committee on Intelligence, U.S. House of Representatives, 94th Cong., 2d sess., as published in *Village Voice*, February 16, 1976, p. 85.

53. U.S. Congress, *Statutes at Large*, vol. 90, p. 166 (1976).

54. Stockwell, *In Search of Enemies*, p. 242.

55. Ibid., p. 234.

56. Final Report: Foreign and Military Intelligence, p.445.

18. SHABA: A CONGOLESE REPRISE

In 1978, we again got involved in the Congo (Zaire), after a rebellion against U.S.-backed President Joseph Mobutu in Shaba, the new name for Katanga province. Following the turmoil the country experienced in the 1960s, which we reviewed in earlier chapters of this book, Zaire remained a fragile construct into the 1970s. The 1978 anti-Mobutu rebellion was led by former Shaba Province residents living in exile across the border in Angola; they were members of the Lunda tribe, whose territory extended across the Zaire-Angola border. This was one of many cases in which colonial borders had been drawn without regard for those who lived on the land. The rebels called themselves the Congo National Liberation Front, and their stated aim was to overthrow Mobutu.

Mobutu depicted the rebels as an outside group, which, from a nation-state standpoint, they were. When the rebellion broke out, Mobutu claimed that this outside contingent numbered between 3,000 and 4,000, but that estimate could not be verified.[1]

The situation was all the stickier because many of these Lunda rebels had fought for Katangan independence in 1960, when they still lived in the province. At that time, they fought alongside the Belgian mercenaries then employed by Moise Tshombe, who headed Katanga's government. After the Katanga secession failed, they, like the Belgian mercenaries,

183

took refuge in Angola, which was still a Portuguese colony. Angola was friendly territory for pro-Tshombe soldiers, since Tshombe was the champion of the Western mining companies.

After taking refuge in Angola, these Lunda fought on behalf of Portugal against the Zaire-based National Front for the Liberation of Angola (FNLA). When Portugal withdrew from Angola, the Lunda kept fighting the FNLA, but now on behalf of the Popular Movement for the Liberation of Angola (MPLA).[2] In 1977, there was a short-lived anti-Mobutu rebellion staged by Lunda in Shaba province; after it ended, many of those on the losing side joined their brethren in Angola, augmenting their numbers.[3]

The Lunda in Shaba province had ample reason to rebel against President Mobutu, because their province held the country's major mineral deposits, making it a particular focus of Mobutu's attention. The Lunda were upset because Mobutu took that wealth out of the province and put it into the national treasury. But worse, it was common knowledge that Mobutu used the proceeds less for the welfare of Zaire than to line his own pockets. From the copper, cobalt, and uranium of Shaba, Mobutu had amassed a fortune, much of which he kept in bank accounts abroad. At the expense of Shaba province, Mobutu became one of the world's wealthiest men.

After entering Shaba province, the Front quickly captured the key mining town of Kolwezi, where several thousand North Americans and Europeans, mainly Belgians, lived and worked. Mobutu, who could not handle the rebels with his own army, asked for outside intervention and found receptive ears. Belgian Prime Minister Leo Tindemans claimed that the Front was engaged in a "hunt against whites" in Shaba,[4] and one news report called it "the worst massacre of Europeans in modern African history."[5] The extent to which these American and European expatriates were victims of the violence remained unclear; but Belgium and France organized paratrooper forces, and the Carter administration agreed to fly in ammunition, trucks, and fuel for them.[6]

President Jimmy Carter expressed "abhorrence and distress over the violence and the killing that resulted from the Katangan invasion from

Angola into Zaire. As great as the human tragedy was, it could have been much worse for the European nationals and for the Zairians, and the consequences much more severe for that country, if we had not joined with our allies in a common effort."[7]

Ignoring the fact that the Front rebels were Lunda natives of Shaba province, the administration picked up Mobutu's claim that the Shaba rebellion was an outside job. Even with no evidence that Angola's government was actually inciting the Lunda, Secretary of State Cyrus Vance defended U.S. involvement because Shaba had been invaded from Angola.[8]

"The Government of Angola," Carter said, "must bear a heavy responsibility for the deadly attack which was launched from its territory, and it's a burden and a responsibility shared by Cuba. We believe that Cuba had known of the Katangan plans to invade and obviously did nothing to restrain them from crossing the border. We also know that the Cubans have played a key role in training and equipping the Katangans who attacked ."[9]

According to National Security Advisor Zbigniew Brzezinski, "the invasion of Katanga or Shaba from Angola could not have taken place without the full knowledge of the Angolan Government," or "without the invading parties having been armed and trained by the Cubans and, indeed, perhaps also the East Germans." "[W]e have sufficient evidence to be quite confident in our conclusion that Cuba shares the political and the moral responsibility for the invasion," Brzezinski said, "indeed, even for the outrages that were associated with it." When a reporter pointed out that no Cubans participated directly, Brzezinski replied, "there is a difference between direct involvement and responsibility. Direct involvement," he said, would mean "direct participation in the fighting, in command and control, presence on the ground." Brzezinski was charging Cuba with something different, responsibility for "a violation of territorial integrity, which in fact is a belligerent act," even though it was others who had physically entered Zaire: "[T]he Cuban Government and in some measure the Soviet Government bear the responsibility for this transgression."[10]

Thus, by the administration's account, European and American forces were on a rescue mission to save endangered Europeans and to drive out foreign invaders who were sponsored by Soviet-bloc countries. While there was some truth in this, it was not the whole truth. The administration had failed to mention that some of the participants in the rebellion were Lunda who still lived in Shaba province. Indeed, many local Lunda had joined their Angola-based brethren."[11]

Brzezinski and Carter argued that Angola and Cuba had known of the Lunda plans; indeed, in a message to Carter, Cuban president Fidel Castro admitted he did know in advance of the Lunda plan but that he had tried to stop them.[12] Angolan President Agostinho Neto said that his government had not trained or equipped the Lunda, and that neither the Soviet Union nor Cuba had done so in Angola.[13] Meanwhile the Front denied having received any Soviet or Cuban assistance.[14] There was little evidence of a Soviet or Soviet-bloc role in the Shaba rebellion. All that could be said for certain was that Angola was tolerating the Front's presence in its territory. In reply, Carter merely charged that Cuba could have done more to stop the invasion.[15]

The Belgian foreign minister, Henri Simonet, noted that Zaire was still aiding the FNLA, and that the FNLA was still active in northern Angola. If the Angolan government was aiding the Front, it would have been as a counterweight to the FNLA.[16]

Mobutu, for all his peccadilloes, was still "our man." We saw earlier how the Eisenhower, Kennedy, and Johnson administrations helped him to power, as someone who would side with the West. Thus, the Americans' role in suppressing the Shaba rebellion was a payback to Mobutu. We were also, of course, protecting our own position in Zaire, keeping it on our side in the cold war. While Brzezinski and Carter accused Angola and Cuba of responsibility, we bore responsibility ourselves. Had we not helped Mobutu gain power and helped keep him there over the years, despite his corruption, there might have been no cause for a rebellion in Shaba in 1978.

Secretary of State Vance gave justifications for our role that went beyond the protection of the Europeans. "We cooperated with other nations to rescue those trapped in the fighting," he said, but also, "to help preserve Zaire's territorial integrity, and to help prevent its economic collapse."[17] To talk of preventing Zaire's economic collapse when it was being pillaged by Mobutu personally must have made the words stick in Vance's throat. The United States had contributed to Zaire's sorry economic situation by promoting Mobutu, and protecting him against the Shaba rebellion only perpetuated Zaire's misery.

Mobutu was even more imaginative than the Carter administration in describing the Shaba events, claiming that Cuban troops had entered Zaire along with the Shaba natives.[18] Castro, however, denied the charge, and no evidence ever surfaced to back it.

As for Carter's professed concern over the safety of Europeans in Shaba, there was scant evidence of rebel atrocities. After the rebels took Kolwezi, the European community there was reported calm.[19] The Front denied targeting Europeans,[20] and even offered to cooperate with foreign governments to evacuate their nationals.[21]

One hundred thirty Europeans were killed during the Kolwezi fighting, which was heavy, resulting in 500 Zairian deaths.[22] But it was not clear that the Europeans would have been harmed if the paratroopers had stayed out. According to the rebel leader, most of the European deaths resulted from the occupation of European residential areas by French paratroopers. When that occurred, the rebels counterattacked, and residents were caught in the cross-fire.[23] Reports did emerge that a small number of French were killed intentionally by the rebels.[24] The best explanation that surfaced was that these killings were in reprisal for the landing of the French paratroopers.[25]

Within a short time the French and Belgian paratroopers drove the rebel forces out of Kolwezi.[26] As in Stanleyville in 1964, the paratroopers combined rescue with helping the central government regain control. The Carter administration acknowledged this second goal when it said that one aim of the landing had been to preserve Zaire's territorial integrity.

The French and Belgian paratroopers evacuated most of the Europeans from Kolwezi. Some doubtless left from fear, but others apparently departed simply because the fighting had so disrupted Kolwezi that making a living there became problematic. The United States citizens in Kolwezi were evacuated prior to the arrival of the paratroopers by the company for which they worked. As for France and Belgium, the French daily *Le Monde* suggested that a concern for French and Belgian investments prompted them to act.[27] Mobutu had been scrupulously respectful of their financial interests in Shaba.[28]

Speaking on background, administration officials acknowledged other motives for the Shaba action. Our decision to help Belgium and France had been motivated, they said, by concern over Soviet activity elsewhere in Africa, specifically Ethiopia. Showing a willingness to intervene in Shaba might curb the Soviet Union in other African countries. If this sounds like Kissinger's rationale for intervening in Angola in 1975, it was.

Carter was also concerned that he had acquired a reputation for being indecisive as the leader of the Western alliance.[29] He had not intervened abroad as aggressively as his predecessors, which put his cold war credentials in doubt. A modest intervention in Shaba provided a low-cost way for Carter to show the flag.

The Carter-Brzezinski rationale for the intervention gave the public the impression that Zaire was being invaded by an outside force with only a marginal connection to Zaire, and that Angola, and perhaps the Soviet Union and East Germany, were pulling the strings. Like previous administrations dealing with conflict situations, Carter exaggerated the role of the Soviet bloc. By depicting an event of local significance as a move on the cold war chessboard, he gave himself a pretext for an intervention whose real aim was to protect the loyal, if larcenous, Mobutu, and to enhance his own anti-Communist credentials.

NOTES

1. David B. Ottoway, "GIs on Alert as Fears Mount over Zaire War," *Washington Post*, May 17, 1978, p. Al, col. 1.

2. Jean Pierre Langellier, "Les anciens 'gendarmes katangais' ne jouent

plus qu'un rôle mineur parmi les rebelles du Shaba," *Le Monde*, May 21–22, 1978, p. 3, col. 1; David B. Ottoway, "Zaire Conflict Poses Dilemma for U.S.," *Washington Post*, May 18, 1978, p. A18, col. 4; *Angola*, Hearings before the Sub-committee on African Affairs of the Committee on Foreign Relations, U.S. Senate, 94th Cong., 2d sess., 1976, p. 183 (statement of Deputy Asst. Secretary of State for African Affairs Edward Mulcahy).

3. David B. Ottoway, "Zaire Says Rebels Backed by Angola Invade the South," *Washington Post*, May 15, 1978, p. Al, col. 5; "En 1977: Deux cent vingt mille Zaïrois se sont réfugiés en Angola," *Le Monde*, May 20, 1978, p. 3, col. 5.

4. William Claiborne and Don Oberdorfer, "Zaire Rescue Mission Launched," *Washington Post*, May 19, 1978, p. Al, col. 4.

5. David B. Ottoway, "Death & Destruction in a Terrorized City in Zaire," *Washington Post*, May 21, 1978, p. Al, col. 2.

6. Claiborne and Oberdorfer, "Zaire Rescue Mission Launched"; David B. Ottoway, "French Troops Parachute into Zaire," *Washington Post*, May 20, 1978, p. Al, col. 4.

7. "News Conference, May 25," DSB, vol. 78, pp. 17–18 (July 1978).

8. "The Secretary: U.S. Relations with Africa," DSB, vol. 78, p. 12 (August 1978).

9. "News Conference, May 25," pp. 17–18.

10. "National Security Adviser Brzezinski on 'Meet the Press,'" DSB, vol. 78, p. 26 (July 1978).

11. Pierre de Vos, "La France a une politique africaine qui n'est pas la nôtre," *Le Monde*, May 23, 1978, p. 3, col. 1.

12. David Binder, "Castro Says He Told U.S. He Tried to Halt Invasion into Zaire," *New York Times*, June 11, 1978, p. Al, col. 6; Jon Nordheimer, "Castro Says Carter Was 'Deceived' on Cuban Role," *New York Times*, June 13, 1978, p. A8, col. 1.

13. "Angola to Disarm Zaire Rebels," *New York Times*, June 11, 1978, p. A6, col. 5.

14. David B. Ottoway, "Zairians, Rebels Reportedly Battle in Mining Center," *Washington Post*, May 16, 1978, p. A1, col. 5.

15. "Transcript of the President's News Conference on Foreign and Domestic Matters," *New York Times*, June 15, 1978, p. A18, col. 1.

16. de Vos, "La France a une politique africaine qui n'est pas la nôtre."

17. "The Secretary: U.S. Relations with Africa," DSB, vol. 78, p. 12 (August 1978).

18. David B. Ottoway, "Zaire Says Rebels Backed by Angola Invade the South," *Washington Post*, May 15, 1978, p. Al, col. 5.

19. "Des parachutages ont été effectués par les gouvernementaux près de Kolwezi," *Le Monde*, May 17, 1978, p. 6, col. 1.

20. "Le sort de la communauté étrangère de Kolwezi reste très préoccupant," *Le Monde*, May 18, 1978, p. 4, col. 1.

21. René Lefort, "Dès que les parachutistes auront quitté Kolwezi nous serons capables de reprendre la ville rapidement, affirme un porte-parole du F.N.L.C.," *Le Monde*, May 23, 1978, p. 3, col. 1.

22. Paul Lewis, "French Troops Land in Zaire Battle Zone; U.S. Sees Cuban Role," *New York Times*, May 20, 1978, p. Al, col. 6.

23. "Le chef des rebelles affirme que des contacts avaient été établis pour assurer la sécurité des Européens," *Le Monde*, May 25, 1978, p. 3, col. 1.

24. David B. Ottoway, "French, Zairian Troops Patrol an Empty, Corpse-Strewn City," *Washington Post*, May 23, 1978, p. Al, col. l.

25. David B. Ottoway, "French, Belgian Get all Whites Out of Zaire City," *Washington Post*, May 22, 1978, p. Al, col. 5.

26. "Troops End Rebels' Hold on Zaire City," *Washington Post*, May 21, 1978, p. Al, col. 6; Jacques Isnard, "Une opération en trois temps," *Le Monde*, May 21–22,1978, p. 3, col. 4.

27. Philippe Decraene, "Qui sauver?" *Le Monde*, May 20, 1978, p. 3, col. 1.

28. Jean Pierre Langellier, "Les intérêts belges demeurent considérables dans l'ancien Congo," *Le Monde*, May 20, 1978, p. 3, col. 2.

29. Bernard Gwertzman, "Washington Acts to Show It Is Ready to Check Havana and Moscow in Africa," *New York Times*, May 20, 1978, p. Al, col. 5.

19. IRAN: HOSTAGES WILL DIE

In Iran a U.S. military operation of a most unusual kind was mounted in response to a most unusual situation. In November 1979, Iranians entered the American embassy in Tehran and took members of the staff hostage. Governments are normally protective of foreign embassies, but Iran's government refused to step in to help the embassy staff. Instead, it applauded the action. After fruitless demands on Iran, the Carter administration took legal action against Iran in the International Court of Justice, the UN's court. It ordered Iran to release the hostages, but Iran did not comply.

To free the hostages, President Carter decided on direct action, devising a plan that sounded as if it was taken from the plot of a spy novel. Carter would fly a handpicked team of ninety military personnel into Iran on eight helicopters from an aircraft carrier, while six C-130 transport planes flew into Iran from a base in Egypt. The helicopters and the C-130s would converge at a designated point in the Iranian desert, 200 miles from Tehran. From there the helicopters would fly to a site near Tehran, where they would be met by U.S. agents who had entered Iran clandestinely. These agents would assemble a fleet of small vehicles, in which the team would drive into Tehran, where they would get a night's sleep in prearranged hideouts.

The next day the team would drive to the U.S. embassy, and to several other locations to which some hostages had been removed. They would free the hostages from their guards, and the helicopters would fly in and pick up both team members and hostages.

The C-130s, meanwhile, would have flown to a location near Tehran; the helicopters would fly from the embassy to that location, where both team members and hostages would board the C-130s. The helicopters would be abandoned, and the entourage would fly out of Iran in the airplanes.[1]

On April 24, 1980, Carter put the plan into operation. The C-130s, as projected, arrived at the desert rendezvous point. But the helicopters were not so lucky: they encountered an intense desert dust storm. Of the eight helicopters, only six reached the rendezvous; once there, one of the six developed a mechanical problem. That left only five helicopters. The planners had decided that the mission could be completed with as few as five helicopters to accommodate the hostages and the team members. However, using just five helicopters left no margin for error.

Soon another problem emerged: the point chosen for the rendezvous was close to a highway, and while the team was on the ground a bus with fifty passengers happened by. Realizing that the passengers had gotten a good look at the transport planes and the helicopters, the team decided it could not risk the possibility that the passengers might inform authorities; therefore, it seized the bus and detained the passengers. Then a truck came along, followed by an automobile. Again, concerned about being detected, team members fired at the truck, trying to stop it. Its driver jumped out and climbed into the automobile, which sped off into the desert.[2]

All this time the team was in communication with Washington, with President Carter being advised of each mishap as it arose. The team had been detected, and with only five operating helicopters, any more mechanical problems would spell disaster. Moreover, they were guarding fifty bus passengers and had no idea what to do with them. Carter decided to cancel the mission.

The helicopters and C-130s prepared to leave Iran. As they were taking off, one of the helicopters flew into a C-130, bursting into flames, killing eight team members and severely injuring several others. Fearful of more problems with helicopters, the team abandoned them,leaving behind the bodies of the eight team members as well. They flew off in the C-130s.[3]

Carter's decision to abort the mission in the desert probably averted further disaster. Had the team reached Tehran, it might have been detected before it arrived at the embassy. With the embassy in a downtown location, slipping in unnoticed would not have been easy. Police or military forces might have confronted the team, and if that happened, the chances of getting the hostages out safely would have been truly remote.

While the mission was being developed, some of the planners thought the odds of success were poor. U.S. Marine Corps Commandant Robert Barrow, in particular, expressed serious doubts.[4] It was anticipated that the team would have to confront at least the armed Iranian civilians who guarded the hostages. Colonel Charles Beckwith, the operation commander, told Deputy Secretary of State Warren Christopher that the team planned to kill most or all of these guards. Beckwith also projected that some of the hostages and some team members would likely be killed when the shooting started.[5] Thus, even if the operation had been carried out as planned, it might not have saved all the hostages.

Had the hostages been under threat of death, the risks might have been worth running. But from what was known at the time, the Iranian captors had no intention of killing the hostages. Secretary of Defense Harold Brown thought there was a potential danger to the hostages from "the deteriorating security situation in Iran," because of disorder in the streets and tensions between Iran and Iraq.[6] But there was no reason to think the hostages were in immediate danger.

For President Carter, it was difficult to deal with the hostage situation without considering its political impact. Facing re-election in November 1980, Carter saw his popularity plummeting as the hostage crisis dragged on. He was under great pressure to secure the hostages' release. The Soviet government criticized the raid and accused Carter of being prepared to sacrifice the lives of American citizens for "his election interests."[7] Even after the raid failed, the administration did not explain to the public the risks that made success unlikely.

Carter had been reluctant to discuss prior U.S. policy in Iran, and that refusal may have reduced the chances of a peaceful resolution of the hostage crisis. Many Iranians harbored deep grievances against the United States for our attempts to control Iran's political life. In 1953, the CIA, in one of its most spectacular covert operations, collaborated with the shah of Iran, a figurehead monarch, to depose the prime minister and to assume power himself. The prime minister, Mohammed Mossadegh, an elderly landowner described by Secretary of State Dean Acheson as "rich, reactionary, [and] feudal-minded," had nationalized the Anglo-Iranian Oil Company.[8] Anglo-Iranian's parent company in the United States had once been represented by the law firm of Secretary of State Dulles, and President Eisenhower said that Mossadegh was not offering enough compensation.[9] Beyond the nationalization issue, Eisenhower worried that Iran might fall to the Soviet camp.

The shah had already tried once to dismiss Mossadegh, but street demonstrators supported Mossadegh and forced the shah to back down. The top CIA operative in Iran, Kermit Roosevelt, a grandson of President Theodore Roosevelt, urged the shah to try again, promising that the CIA would organize pro-shah street demonstrations.

Encouraged by Roosevelt, the shah declared Mossadegh fired. When, as expected, pro-Mossadegh crowds took to the streets, Roosevelt's recruits demonstrated for the shah. Roosevelt also encouraged the army to back the shah; when a pro-shah general named himself prime minister, Mossadegh resigned in fear.[10] The grateful shah gave our oil companies part of the British monopoly and oriented Iran's economy to the West; the political relationship became so cozy that the CIA built up an Iranian security police organization. The reputation these police developed for brutality became a major Iranian grievance against the United States.[11]

All this history figured heavily in the Iranian thinking about the hostage taking. Iran declared that the United States would have to "repent" for its misdeeds before the hostages were returned. President Carter refused to discuss the matter with Iran. He did not indicate to the American public that there was any truth to the points the Iranian government was raising.[12] Carter's silence is all the more enigmatic in light of the fact that in 1979, Kermit Roosevelt published his book explaining how he had engineered the overthrow of Mossadegh in 1953. Therefore, our prior interference in Iranian politics could not be disputed.[13]

In reaction to the past American interference, the Iranian government also asked the United States to "make a pledge and a promise that from now on she will in no way interfere, either directly or indirectly, politically or militarily, in the affairs of the Islamic Republic of Iran."[14] Carter did not respond to this demand, although a statement pledging noninterference would not have been difficult.

A few months before the hostage taking, in the midst of the anti-shah uprising that led to his overthrow, I happened to be flying home from the Far East via Tehran. I had a scheduled stopover before continuing to New York. While in the Far East, I followed news accounts of the anti-shah actions that would soon bring the Ayatollah Khomeini to power. Knowing the history of our support for the shah, I was not anxious to be an American in Tehran while the shah was being overthrown.

When the plane's doors opened on the ground in Tehran, my fears were confirmed, as Americans flocked into the plane to get out of the country, I pled with the steward to let me keep my seat to New York. The plane soon filled, but the steward somehow found me a seat. As we took off, I was happy to see the lights of Tehran fade in the distance.

NOTES

1. George C. Wilson and Michael Getler, "Raid Team Had Hoped to Surprise Hostage Captors in Ground Assault," *Washington Post*, April 26, 1980, p. Al, col. 5.

2. Richard Harwood, "Series of Mishaps Defeated Rescue in Iran," *Washington Post*, April 26, 1980, p. Al, col. 1.

3. "Secretary Brown's News Conference," April 25, 1980, DSB, vol. 80, p. 39 (June 1980).

4. David Martin and John Walcott, *Best Laid Plans: The Inside Story of America's War Against Terrorism* (1988), p. 32.

5. Ibid., p. 4.

6. "Secretary Brown's News Conference," April 25, 1980, p. 40.

7. Harwood, "Series of Mishaps Defeated Rescue in Iran."

8. Dean Acheson, *Present at the Creation* (1969), p. 504.

9. Text of the Letters by Mossadegh and Eisenhower," *New York Times*, July 10, 1953, p. A4, col. 3.

10. Kermit Roosevelt, *Countercoup: The Struggle for the Control of Iran* (1979), pp. 150–97; Jo

hn Prados, *Presidents' Secret Wars: CIA and Pentagon Covert Operations Since World War II* (1986), p. 97; Andrew Tul

ly, *CIA: The Inside Story* (1962), pp. 88–99.

11. Jonathan Kwitny, *Endless Enemies: The Making of an Unfriendly World* (1984), p. 12.

12. "Iran Chronology, September 1980," DSB, vol. 80, p. 55 (November 1980).

13. Roosevelt, *Countercoup*.

14. "Iran's Proposals for Release of American Hostages," DSB, vol. 80, p. 46 (December 1980).

20. NICARAGUA: WHO IS CONTRA?

Not long after the helicopter crash in the Iranian desert, another curious U.S. military action was taking shape in Central America. In the 1970s, a movement formed in Nicaragua to oppose long-time strongman Anastasio Somoza Debayle; it called itself Sandinista, after Augusto Sandino, a Nicaraguan general who had waged a guerrilla campaign against American Marines in Nicaragua in the 1920s. The Marines had occupied Nicaragua until 1933 and had oriented Nicaragua's economy to protect our companies operating there. To keep the peace after the Marines left in 1933, we organized a National Guard for Nicaragua, which was headed by Anastasio Somoza Garcia. As leader of the Guard, Somoza came to control the government, and his rule was heavy-handed. In the 1970s, his son, Anastasio Somoza Debayle was filling his shoes.

Relations between the Somozas and the United States were close. Recall that in 1961, President Kennedy launched the Bay of Pigs invasion from Nicaragua. In 1979, as the Sandinista party was poised to overthrow Somoza, President Carter tried to organize a military force from the Organization of American States to prop him up. But the Sandinistas took power in Nicaragua, and much of Somoza's National Guard fled Nicaragua and regrouped in neighboring Honduras. From there it started military raids back into Nicaragua, trying to regain power. A committee of Nicaraguans who had fled to Miami assumed nominal control of this effort and began to speak as a kind of government in exile. The media dubbed the force the Contras, Spanish for "against," because they opposed the new Nicaraguan government.

There was more to the Contras than met the eye, however. In 1981, President Ronald Reagan allocated funds for CIA covert operations in Central America, and one major project was to organize an army to fight the Sandinista government of Nicaragua.[1] In Honduras the CIA played a hand in forging the National Guard remnants into a fighting force. The committee in Miami had not formed spontaneously. The CIA had organized it as well.[2]

One of the Miami Nicaraguans picked by the CIA, Edgar Chamorro, explained later in a *New Republic* article that a CIA operative had told the Nicaraguans that the purpose of forming this leadership group was to deceive Congress. Congress was unlikely to fund the National Guard remnants, but the CIA thought it might support an anti-Sandinista movement headed by respectable businessmen who did not bear the taint of an affiliation with Somoza, even if the Guard remnants remained the fighting force. The CIA organized a press conference in Miami to announce the formation of the leadership group, after one of its agents briefed the Nicaraguans on what to say. The Nicaraguans followed their script well, denying any connection to the United States, denying even that their aim was to overthrow the Nicaraguan government. Although the Miami group announced itself as the political arm of the National Guard, it gained little control over the Guard. That remained the province of the CIA and its station in Honduras.[3]

For the Contras, the CIA set up training bases in Florida, Texas, and California, paid the soldiers' salaries, and planned their missions. Under the cover of military exercises, U.S. Army engineers built command posts for the Contras in Honduras. The CIA produced for the Contra soldiers a pamphlet explaining how to operate in Nicaragua, and included suggestions on how to assassinate local officials in order to show that the Sandinistas could not rule effectively.[4] Eventually a second Contra group sprang up in Costa Rica, also organized by the CIA.

All this, of course, was done on the quiet, which meant that, without any public debate, the administration had started a war.[5] Despite efforts by the CIA to keep its role undetected, in 1982 reporters figured out that the Contras were a CIA product. A congressional committee called in CIA Director William Casey to explain. Casey told the committee that, yes, the CIA was aiding the Contras, but the aim was only to stop arms shipments from Nicaragua to insurgents in El Salvador, where a civil war was in progress. Casey denied that we were trying to bring down the Nicaraguan government or put the Somoza forces back in power.[6]

Other administration officials contradicted Casey. They said that overthrowing Nicaragua's government was our aim.[7] Congress, upset over what the CIA was doing, tried to stop it. Congress wrote an amendment into a foreign appropriations bill that "none of the funds provided in this Act may be used by the Central Intelligence Agency or the Department of Defense to furnish military equipment, military training or advice, or other support for military activities, to any group or individual, not part of a country's armed forces, for the purpose of overthrowing the Government of Nicaragua."[8] Despite that law, the new administration of President Ronald Reagan found ways to keep the Contras in business.

The fall of 1983 and the winter of 1984 witnessed a series of spectacular military operations against Nicaragua. Aircraft bombed Nicaraguan economic installations; speedboats raided the Nicaraguan coast, blowing up oil depots; and undersea explosive mines appeared in the waters off Nicaragua's major port.[9] Ten ships were hit—ships registered in Nicaragua, the Netherlands, Liberia, Panama, and the Soviet Union. Nicaragua reported that the mines killed two crew members and injured fourteen, and it temporarily closed its ports. When asked by reporters whether our government had done the mining, government officials said no.[10]

In Moscow, Soviet Foreign Minister Andrei Gromyko called in our chargé d'affaires and called the mining "an act of banditry and piracy." Gromyko claimed we had done it using "mercenaries and terrorists." The State Department replied, "We note that anti-Sandinista forces have widely advertised that certain Nicaraguan ports have been mined. We have no further information on the incident." The Department expressed regret for "any injury to mariners or shipping," but blamed tensions leading to the mining on "Soviet encouragement of conflict in Central America and the Caribbean."[11] So we were not uninvolved, and the blame rested with the Soviet Union.

Meanwhile, Contra leader Chamorro announced by radio that they had planted the mines. But Chamorro later withdrew the claim. He admitted later that the CIA gave him a Spanish-language press release proclaiming Contra responsibility for the mining, which Chamorro read over a CIA-funded Contra radio station in Honduras.[12] Soon, evidence surfaced that the CIA had organized the operation.[13] The press even obtained a classified CIA report that gave dates and places of CIA speedboat attacks and the mining.[14] These activities were carried out by Latin American mercenaries recruited by the CIA. The CIA called them UCLAs: unilaterally controlled Latino assets. The UCLAs had attacked the port facilities. CIA trainers had launched the UCLAs into small boats from "mother ships" to take the mines in and plant them.[15]

Once Congress realized that the administration had kept it in the dark concerning the entire operation, Capitol Hill simmered with rage.[16] The Senate, 84 votes to 12, adopted a resolution "that no funds heretofore or hereafter appropriated in any act of Congress shall be obligated or expended for the purpose of planning, executing or supporting the mining of the ports or territorial waters of Nicaragua."[17]

During the summer following these raids, I inspected the oil depots that the UCLAs had at Corinto, Nicaragua's largest port. Children played in the charred remains of huge Esso tanks that had been the main repositories of fuel supplies for Nicaragua. The port director told me that the tanks had burned for three days after they were hit.

Nicaragua reacted to the attacks as Carter had to the hostage taking in Iran, by suing in the International Court of Justice. The court found that the United States had, as Nicaragua charged, organized the Contras, the raids, and the mining. It ruled in Nicaragua's favor, calling our attacks on Nicaragua acts of aggression.[18]

In 1984, a presidential election was held in Nicaragua. My wife and

I happened to be in Managua the day the Sandinista party opened its election campaign. We went to see an opening ceremony for the Sandinista campaign at a downtown shopping center. Daniel Ortega, leader of the Sandinistas, was the presidential candidate. Arriving a bit early, we spotted Ortega waiting for the ceremonies to begin. We were surprised that he had no security contingent around him, or even the entourage one expects of a politician making a public appearance.

My wife decided to approach him and strike up a conversation. She explained who we were. To our surprise, Ortega did not respond with small talk but raised a serious topic. He said that by its war the United States was making life unbearable for Nicaraguans. He could not understand how the public in the United States was letting the administration do this. "What will it take to make the public in North America pay attention?" he asked.

Thinking quickly through our military actions abroad, I told Ortega that the public usually gives the president free rein with military action abroad. Only when wars drag on too long, and our casualties are too high, as in Korea or Vietnam, does the public question a president.

My answer held little comfort for Ortega. He won the 1984 election, but he never found a way to get the American public aroused. That same year Congress did tighten the screws on President Reagan by passing a law that "no funds available to the Central Intelligence Agency, the Department of Defense, or any other agency or entity of the United States involved in intelligence activities" could be used to support "directly or indirectly, military or paramilitary operations in Nicaragua."[19] That sounded like the death knell for Contra funding; but Reagan evaded even this law by approving a National Security Council directive to create a surrogate network, nominally private, to finance and train the Contras.[20] The funding was creative, as administration officials convinced not only private citizens to contribute, but the governments of Saudi Arabia and Brunei. They asked Israel to contribute weapons, which it did.[21] The administration quietly sold arms to Iran and gave the Contras the proceeds.[22] It collected privately contributed equipment in the United States, while a CIA-owned airline, Southern Air Transport, ferried it to the Contras.[23]

On the return legs of some of these flights, Southern Air carried Contra cocaine and marijuana for the U.S. drug market, as still another way to add to the Contra coffers. When Drug Enforcement Administration agents confirmed the contents, the pilots told them that they had White House protection for the drug running.[24] A man named George Morales, who had recently been convicted of drug smuggling, had directed the pilots who flew arms to the Contras from southern Florida. Morales told the Senate Subcommittee on Terrorism, Narcotics, and International Operations that on return trips, he carried cocaine and marijuana under CIA protection.[25] Getting these drugs into our market gave the Contras the financial means for buying weapons and paying salaries.[26]

The CIA apparently had no more qualms about running cocaine and marijuana from Central America than it had about transporting opium in Laos for the Hmong. The CIA even helped the Medellin cartel of Colombia get drugs into Florida. When the cartel saw that the Contras had an easy route for getting drugs into the United States, it began renting space from the Contras on the CIA planes. The "rental" fees from the Medellin cartel generated even more revenue for the Contras.[27]

As part of its effort to bring down Nicaragua's government, the Reagan administration cut off trade with Nicaragua and imposed economic sanctions that made it difficult for Nicaraguans to get essential commodities. Then, in a major political coup, the White House turned Congress around in 1985 and got it to fund the Contras.[28] With thousands being killed in Nicaragua in Contra attacks, and with the economy generating few goods, markets stood half empty. Nicaraguans could not stand the war and the privation. In the 1990 presidential election, Nicaraguan voters turned Ortega and the Sandinista party out, preferring a coalition of parties that included some sympathetic to the Contras.[29] Nicaraguans wanted a normal life, which was impossible while the Yankees were trying to do them in. The only way to get rid of the Yankees was to vote out the Sandinistas.

NOTES

1. David Ignatius and David Rogers, "Why the Covert War in Nicaragua Evolved and Hasn't Succeeded," *Wall Street Journal*, March 5, 1985, p. 1, col. 1.

2. Leslie H. Gelb, "State Dept. Aides Said to Question Acts in Nicaragua," *New York Times*, April 7, 1983, p. Al, col. 1; Bob Woodward, *Veil: The Secret Wars of the CIA 1981-1987* (1987), pp. 229–30, 263.

3. Edgar Chamorro, "Confessions of a 'Contra,'" *New Republic*, August 5, 1985, pp. 18–19.

4. Peter Kornbluh, "The Covert War," in Thomas Walker, ed., *Reagan versus the Sandinistas: The Undeclared War on Nicaragua* (1987), pp. 23–27; Bob Woodward, "Middle-Level CIA Officials Cleared Manual," *Washington Post*, October 24, 1984, p. Al, col. 1.

5. "Should the U.S. Fight Secret Wars?" *Harper's Magazine*, September 1984, p. 45 (statement of Morton Halperin, former member of National Security Council).

6. Philip Taubman, "Moynihan Questions C.I.A.'s Latin Role," *New York Times*, April 1, 1983, p. A3, col. 4; Woodward, *Veil*, pp. 225–26.

7. Gelb, "State Dept. Aides Said to Question Acts in Nicaragua."

8. U.S. Congress, *Statutes at Large*, vol. 96, p. 1865 (1982).

9. David Rogers and David Ignatius, "How CIA Aided Raids in Nicaragua in '84 Led Congress to End Funds," *Wall Street Journal*, March 6, 1985, p. 1, col. 1.

10. "U.S. Denies Responsibility," *New York Times*, March 22, 1984, p. A4, col. 1.

11. Ibid.

12. Chamorro, "Confessions of a Contra," p. 22; Kornbluh, "The Covert War," p. 30.

13. Philip Taubman, "Americans on Ship Said to Supervise Nicaragua Mining," *New York Times*, April 8, 1984, p. Al, col. 6.

14. David Rogers and David lgnatius, "CIA Internal Report Details U.S. Role in Contra Raids in Nicaragua Last Year," *Wall Street Journal*, March 6, 1985, p. 20, col. 1.

15. Woodward, *Veil*, p. 281; Kornbluh, "The Covert War," p. 29.

16. Woodward, *Veil*, p. 320.

17. Martin Tolchin, "Senate, 84-12, Acts to Oppose Mining Nicaragua Ports; Rebuke to Reagan," *New York Times*, April 11, 1984, p. Al, col. 6.

18. Case concerning Military and Paramilitary Activities in and against Nicaragua (*Nicaragua v. USA*), International Court of Justice, Reports, pp. 46–51 (1986).

19. U.S. Congress, *Statutes at Large*, vol. 98, p. 1935 (1984).

20. Kornbluh, "The Covert War," p. 31.

21. Senate Select Committee on Intelligence, *Report on Preliminary Inquiry*, January 29, 1987, p. 49; President's Special Review Board, *Report of the Special Review Board*, February 26, 1987 (Tower Commission Report), p. B-123.

22. Kornbluh, "The Covert War," p. 32.

23. Ibid., pp. 32–33.

24. Joel Brinkley, "Contra Arms Crews Said to Smuggle Drugs," *New York Times*, January 20, 1987, p. Al, col. 4.

25. Keith Schneider, "Smuggler Ties Contras to U.S. Drug Network," *New York Times*, July 16, 1987, p. A13, col. 5.

26. Leslie Cockburn, *Out of Control* (1987), pp. 152–88.

27. Transcript, "Frontline" Special, "Guns, Drugs and the CIA," WGBH, Public Broadcasting System (1988), pp. 23–24.

28. U.S. Congress, *Statutes at Large*, vol. 100, p. 3341-299 (1986).

29. "Nicaraguan Opposition Routs Sandinistas; U.S. Pledges Aid, Tied to Orderly Turnover," *New York Times*, February 27, 1990, p. A1, col. 6.

21. EL SALVADOR: A TEXTBOOK CASE

For the Reagan administration, Nicaragua and El Salvador were of a piece. It claimed that its help to the Contras was aimed not at overthrowing the Nicaraguan government, but at stopping arms shipments from Nicaragua to insurgents in El Salvador. The administration justified aid that it gave to the government of El Salvador on the same basis, namely, that the El Salvador insurgents were getting arms from outside, especially through Nicaragua. For a time at least, the administration succeeded in convincing the public that our Contra funding was aimed at dealing with the civil war in El Salvador.

That war began in 1980, but it was a continuation of a conflict that had plagued the tiny Central American nation for generations. The name the Spanish colonists had given the country—"the Savior"—held more than a little irony. As of 1980, El Salvador was still waiting to be saved. Its economy was controlled by a small number of powerful families who had established plantations in the nineteenth century. The vast majority of the Salvadoran population who did not own land lived in poverty. Babies died of malnutrition at alarming rates, and unemployment was high.

The government and military in El Salvador were the domain of the small landowning group. When the peasants rebelled in 1932, the army killed them by the thousands. That kept the peasants quiet until the 1970s, when agitation resumed. Political parties supporting land reform contested national elections; but even when they did win at the polls, the army stepped in and kept them from taking office.

In 1980, when civil protest picked up, with political marches and general strikes, the government reacted harshly, killing or jailing protesters. Police and soldiers formed "death squads" that kidnapped and executed opponents. Finally, the opposition decided that it would not succeed through the political process, so it took to the hills and started an insurgency.[1] One of the insurgency leaders, Guillermo Ungo, had been a vice presidential candidate from whom the military stole an election in 1972.

To help it suppress the insurgency, the Carter administration began modest aid to the government of El Salvador. The landowning group that the Salvadoran government represented were the people in the country to whom we were linked, politically and financially. The night Ronald Reagan was elected to succeed Jimmy Carter, champagne flowed in the homes of El Salvador's elite, because they knew they would get even more help from him.

Reagan did not disappoint. He immediately gave more military equipment. He set up training for Salvadoran military personnel at bases in the United States and Panama. He sent military advisors, who planned counterinsurgency strategy with Salvadoran commanders.[2] The only thing the advisors would not do, the administration said, was to participate in actual combat operations. El Salvador's archbishop, a respected figure in the country, denounced the aid, arguing that it only encouraged the government to be repressive. Many Roman Catholic clergy espoused so-called "liberation theology," which viewed the poor as victimized by the rich.

The Reagan administration justified its aid and advisors to the Salvadoran government as a response to the aid the El Salvador insurgents were receiving from abroad. We were not interfering in a civil war, the administration argued, but protecting El Salvador from external interference. When this analysis was questioned by reporters, the State Department published a "white paper" to document its case.

The white paper made bold charges, stating that the El Salvador insurgents got arms and ammunition from Cuba, East Germany, Vietnam, Bulgaria, the Soviet Union, Hungary, Ethiopia, Czechoslovakia, and Nicaragua. Salvadoran communists were the conduit. A key item of evidence was a document supposedly captured from the insurgents listing armaments received from Ethiopia, Bulgaria, Czechoslovakia, and Hungary. The white paper concluded that "the insurgency in El Salvador has been progressively transformed into a textbook case of indirect armed aggression by Communist powers through Cuba."[3]

The white paper, which rang similar to the Vietnam white paper of 1965, brought firm denials from Nicaragua and the Soviet Union.[4] The insurgents themselves claimed that the white paper's documents were forged, and that their arms were captured from the government, or purchased abroad.[5] The white paper focused entirely on the Salvadoran Communist party, which was but one of five groups making up the insurgency.[6] Later the Bush administration would acknowledge that the Soviet Union had no connection with the other four.[7]

The information relating to the Communist party drew criticism as well, based as it was on documents supposedly captured from the party. The State Department was hard pressed to prove the authenticity of the documents. When challenged, it refused to make the documents public, although it did let several reporters review them and interview the paper's drafters.

Reporters concluded that several of the documents attributed by the white paper to insurgency leaders were obviously not written by them.[8] According to the *Washington Post*, many documents that the white paper identified by author and date contained no markings to indicate either date or author.[9] The white paper's principal author, Jon D. Glassman of the State Department, who had personally collected the documents in El Salvador, acknowledged to the *Wall Street Journal* that the intelligence analysts who examined them had to make guesses about their meaning. Glassman admitted that even the Salvadoran government expressed concern to the State Department about the white paper's accuracy; their message was, "You guys have made some mistakes."[10] Glassman admitted that the white paper contained errors on basic points, and that parts were "misleading" and "overembellished."

At the time the white paper was written, the U.S. ambassador in El Salvador was Robert White. White, who was removed from his post over policy differences with the Reagan administration, said the white paper did not give a credible presentation but "tries to prove more than the evidence warrants"; White called its conclusions "bizarre" and "tendentious." According to the *Wall Street Journal*, the white paper's authors "were making a determined effort to create a 'selling' document, no matter how slim the background material.'"[11]

The most important document in the white paper was one it identified as a report by Shafik Handal, head of the Salvadoran Communist party. The document, the white paper said, described a visit by Handal to Soviet-bloc countries. The white paper used the document as evidence that Handal had obtained commitments for arms shipments to the insurgents. The reporters, however, found that nowhere in the document did Handal's name appear, nor could they confirm that Handal was the person to whom the document related. In its English translation of this document, the State Department deleted a sentence that said that a particular shipment of arms "will leave in our ship the fifth of August." Since the Salvadoran Communist party had no ships, Handal would not likely have written such a statement. By deleting the sentence, the white paper's drafters apparently hoped to mask this inconsistency. Further research on the document showed it was written in Cuba, but at the time of its writing Handal was not in Cuba. When pressed by the *Wall Street Journal*, Glassman finally admitted that Handal could not have authored the report.

One of the white paper's most significant conclusions was that the Soviet Union was involved in the arms shipments to the insurgents. The paper claimed "definitive evidence of the clandestine military support given by the Soviet Union, Cuba and their Communist allies to Marxist-Leninist guerrillas now fighting to overthrow the established government of El Salvador." The white paper reported that Handal had received a commitment from Soviet officials to transport arms, which were to be made available by Vietnam. But the *Washington Post* found that while the documents did reflect discussions about arms, they said nothing about a Soviet commitment.

As for the quantity of arms supposedly received from abroad, the captured documents were reported to show the delivery to El Salvador of "nearly 200 tons of arms, mostly through Cuba and Nicaragua." But Glassman, when pressed by reporters, conceded that the documents did not bear out that figure, for which the Department apparently had no basis.[12]

Another of the white paper's claims of outside arms shipments was that the insurgents met in Managua with Yassir Arafat, head of the Palestine Liberation Organization, and that he "promised military equipment, including arms and aircraft." As Glassman acknowledged to the *Wall Street Journal*, however, the document said only that a meeting with Arafat occurred, with no mention of arms.

The *Washington Post* concluded from its review "that on several major points, the documents do not support conclusions drawn from them by the administration." When the criticisms were published, the State Department defended the paper's overall conclusion but did not reply point by point.[13]

The white paper also suffered from omission: in focusing on possible arms shipments, it ignored the causes of the Salvadoran civil war, failing to indicate the human rights violations and poverty that led to discontent, or that the opposition took to the hills only after electoral victory had been snatched from it by the military. The absence of such analysis made it appear that El Salvador was a happy country in which Cuba, Nicaragua, and the Soviet Union were stirring up trouble.[14]

The question of whether Nicaragua sent arms to the Salvadoran insurgency came up as well in the lawsuit Nicaragua filed against the United States in the International Court of Justice. The Reagan administration defended its military action against Nicaragua by arguing that Nicaragua was committing aggression against El Salvador, through aid to its insurgents, and that we were merely defending El Salvador. On this point the court decided that there had been "an intermittent flow of arms" from Nicaragua to the insurgents from late 1980 to early 1981, but no evidence to show that the government of Nicaragua promoted it. The court denied that the shipment of some arms from Nicaragua to the El Salvador insurgents meant that the Nicaraguan government was responsible.[15] The Court found no evidence of arms shipments after early 1981.

Neither in the white paper nor later did the administration make its case of massive outside arms shipments to the Salvadoran insurgents. It drew conclusions from questionable data in order to convince the public and Congress to fund the government of El Salvador. It did nothing to refute the insurgents' claim that they had obtained arms by purchase abroad and by capturing, stealing, or buying them from government troops.[16]

Even after the white paper's flaws were exposed, Reagan used the supposed arms shipments from Nicaragua to justify funding the Contras and aiding the Salvadoran government. He put out more public information, but none of it any more convincing than the white paper.[17] In 1983, David MacMichael, a CIA official responsible for analyzing data on El Salvador, resigned in protest, saying that the administration had "exaggerated the amount of arms" shipped from Nicaragua to the insurgents, "to justify our covert aid to the contras." MacMichael called the administration's hyperbole "plain prevarication."[18]

As the civil war in El Salvador dragged on, Congress from time to time challenged the administration over the Salvadoran government's sweeping measures to suppress opposition. Government-backed death squads roamed the country killing government opponents. Congress would allow the administration to send the aid only if the president periodically certified that El Salvador was improving its human rights record. Reagan duly gave the required certification, despite evidence of continuing brutality, and the aid continued to flow.

In addition to human rights, Congress was concerned over the Salvadoran government's military tactics, particularly in 1983, when the Salvadoran military began what appeared to be saturation bombing in rebel-held provinces, not unlike what the U.S. Air Force had done in Indochina.[19] Peasants reported apparently random aerial attacks on villages.[20]

Denying that the Salvadoran air force was bombing indiscriminately, or to drive the population from rebel-held areas, administration officials averred that the bombing was done with "surgical precision." Some members of Congress accused the administration of lying, but Congress continued the funding.[21]

Our support helped keep the Salvadoran government in power, and doubtless kept the war going. As the war intensified, the American embassy in San Salvador assumed the demeanor of a modern-day armed fast, with concrete barriers and heavy wire fencing protecting it from potential assaults.

The civil war in El Salvador took its toll, as thousands of combatants and noncombatants were killed and injured. Humanitarian organizations in the United States became concerned over the situation of wounded insurgent combatants who could not get medical attention. Insurgent field hospitals were rudimentary, but the wounded avoided government hospitals for fear of being killed. The archbishop intervened, and several times the government allowed small numbers of seriously wounded to leave the country for medical treatment, mostly amputees and others too seriously wounded to fight again. Finally an agreement was reached for the government to let the International Committee of the Red Cross evacuate all the seriously wounded, but the agreement broke down, and one hundred seriously wounded insurgents were left hiding in the bush. Some members of Congress expressed concern.

I was invited by humanitarian organizations to try to convince the Salvador government to let the evacuation proceed. With a group of other Americans, I went to El Salvador to hold talks. We visited military headquarters in San Salvador. The minister of defense was cordial and, to our delight, agreed to let the seriously wounded leave. Eventually, the president, Napoleon Duarte, also agreed, announcing that he was giving the order for the evacuation. But with Duarte dying of cancer, conservative members of parliament objected that letting the wounded leave would help the insurgents. So the order was canceled, Duarte died, the conservatives won the Salvadoran presidency, and the wounded remained in the field to fend for themselves.

In 1996, one detail regarding U.S. involvement in El Salvador was clarified. Reporters re-examined the exact role of our military advisors. Did they, as the Reagan administration claimed, avoid participation in combat? Film footage was found showing advisors in combat operations. The Pentagon had to acknowledge that it had lied. Our advisors had been in the field, directing Salvadoran government troops in operations against the insurgents.[22]

NOTES

1. James Petras, "Blots on the White Paper. The Reinvention of the 'Red Menace,'" in Marvin Gettleman et al., eds., *El Salvador: Central America in the New Cold War* (1986), p. 327.

2. Michael McClintock, *The American Connection* (1985), pp. 332–37; Reps. Jim Leach and George Miller, Sen. Mark Hatfield, "U.S. Aid to El Salvador: An Evaluation of the Past, a Proposal for the Future—A Report to the Arms Control and Foreign Policy Caucus," in Marvin Gettleman et al., eds., *El Salvador: Central America in the New Cold War* (1986), p. 231.

3. "Communist Interference in El Salvador," February 23, 1981, U.S. Dept. of State, Special Report no. 80.

4. Kevin Kose, "Soviets Deny Supply Weapons to Marxist Guerrillas in El Salvador," *Washington Post*, February 26, 1981, p. A30, col. 1.

5. Stephen Weeks, "International News," Reuters, February 26, 1981, AM cycle.

6. Robert G. Kaiser, "White Paper on El Salvador Is Faulty; Flaws in Salvador White Paper Raise Questions about Its Analysis," *Washington Post*, June 9, 1981, P. Al, col. 2.

7. Clifford Krauss, "U.S. and Soviets Jointly Urge Settlement in El Salvador," *New York Times*, October 19, 1990, p. A3, col. 3.

8. Jonathan Kwitny, "Apparent Errors Cloud U.S. 'White Paper' on Reds in El Salvador," *Wall Street Journal*, June 8, 1981, p. Al, col. 6.

9. Robert G. Kaiser, "White Paper on El Salvador Is Faulty."

10. Kwitny, "Apparent Errors Cloud U.S. 'White Paper' on Reds in El Salvador."

11. Ibid.

12. Ibid.

13. Kaiser, "White Paper on El Salvador Is Faulty."

14. Petras, "Blots on the White Paper," in Gettleman et al., *El Salvador*, pp. 327–28; Raymond Bonner, *Weakness and Deceit: U.S. Policy and El Salvador* (1984), pp. 259–60.

15. Case concerning Military and Paramilitary Activities in and against Nicaragua (*Nica. v. USA*), International Court of Justice, Reports, p. 86, § 160 (1986).

16. Bonner, *Weakness and Deceit*, pp. 267–68.

17. Ibid., p. 261.

18. "Should the U.S. Fight Secret Wars?" *Harpers Magazine*, September 1984, p. 44.

19. Mary Jo McConahay, "Living under El Salvador's Air War," in Gettleman et al., *El Salvador*, p.235.

20. James LeMoyne, "Salvador Air Role in War Increases," *New York Times*, July 18, 1985, p. Al, col. 3.

21. Reps. Leach and Miller, Sen. Hatfield, "U.S. Aid to El Salvador," in Gettleman et al., *El Salvador*, p. 367.

22. Juanita Darling and Ruth Morris, "Concerns grow about U.S. military aid to Colombia," *Los Angeles Times*, August 17, 1999, p. A1; William M. LeoGrande and Kenneth Sharpe, "Colombia: Is U.S. re-creating El Salvador?" *Los Angeles Times*, March 19, 2000, p. M1.

22. LEBANON: DEATH ON THE BEACH

I n August 1982, the American Marines returned to the beaches of Beirut. The Reagan administration sent a force to Lebanon into a civil war that pitted the pro-Western government representing Lebanese Christians against Muslim-based Arab nationalists. If this scenario sounds familiar, it was the same political lineup as during our 1958 intervention in Lebanon, and we were on the same side as in 1958.

This intervention was precipitated by Israel's invasion of Lebanon in June 1982. Israel's aim was twofold: to drive the Palestine Liberation Organization (PLO) out of Lebanon, and to install in Lebanon a government friendly to Israel.[1] Lebanon by this time had been rent by internal war for so long that it was in no position to repel Israel's attack. The Israeli army moved quickly northward to Beirut, the country's capital.

Once Israel's army was in occupation, the Lebanese parliament held a presidential election and chose Bashir Gemayel, of the rightist Phalange party. The Phalange, based in Lebanon's Christian population, was a rival for the Christian vote to the party of the more moderate Camille Chamoun, who had been president in 1958.[2] The Phalange party was founded in the 1930s by Bashir Gemayel's father, Pierre Gemayel, who named it after the fascist movements in Italy and Spain, which he admired.[3] More than Chamoun's party, the Phalange was prone to use force against its opponents, and it commanded a strong militia.

President Reagan called the election of Bashir Gemayel a positive development.[4] From Reagan's perspective, Gemayel presented advantages, because for some time he had been close to the United States, particularly to the CIA.[5] Indeed, the United States had given military aid to the Phalange militias and put Gemayel in contact with Israel.[6] Beginning in the mid-1970s, Israel and the Phalange had forged a virtual military alliance to oppose their common enemy, the PLO.[7] Israel also gave the Phalange military aid,[8] in return for which the Phalange provided Israel with intelligence information about Palestinians in Lebanon.[9] When Israel invaded Lebanon, Gemayel welcomed it, because he wanted the PLO out.[10]

Israel hit the PLO's stronghold, West Beirut, with massive bombardment, until the PLO agreed to withdraw from Lebanon. The Reagan administration, working with several other countries, sent troops to oversee the PLO evacuation, as well as to protect the many Palestinian refugees living in Beirut, who had relied on the PLO for protection against the Phalange.[11]

The PLO departed Beirut in early September,[12] and the Marines left one week later.[13] Calm, however, was not to return to Lebanon. Israel and the Phalange suspected that PLO combatants had stayed behind and hidden in Palestinian refugee camps in Beirut. They made plans for a Phalange search expedition into the camps.[14]

There was another reason for the joint Phalange-Israeli action: just a few days after the Marines left, Bashir Gemayel had been assassinated.[15] The Israeli army sealed off the Palestinian refugee camps in Beirut and let Phalange militiamen enter, ostensibly to search for PLO combatants. Once in the camps, however, the Phalange soldiers went on a rampage, killing Palestinian civilians indiscriminately.[16] Estimates of the dead ranged from 700 to 3,000.[17]

Gemayel's brother Amin was elected president by the parliament,[18] and President Reagan sent 1200 Marines back into Beirut.[19] Reagan declared that this second landing would "assist the Government of

Lebanon in reasserting authority over all its territory. Foreign forces and armed factions have too long obstructed the legitimate role of the Lebanese Government's security forces."[20] This was a longer-term and more complex objective than the August landing.

While Reagan tried to portray the U.S. function as neutral—helping restore Lebanon to the elected government—his backing of the "Lebanese Government's security forces" meant he would be opposing the Arab nationalists. Like Eisenhower in 1958, Reagan hoped to shore up the pro-Western government against nationalist militia forces that were arrayed against it.[21]

As president, Amin Gemayel cooperated with the United States and Israel.[22] In May 1983, he helped negotiate an agreement for an Israeli pullback from central Lebanon, which still left Israel in occupation of southern Lebanon.[23] This agreement anticipated a close military and intelligence partnership with Israel.[24] Reagan pressured Gemayel to hold conciliation talks with the other Lebanese militia in order to broaden the base of his government, but factionalism in Lebanon proved too strong. On October 19, 1983, Gemayel suspended the talks.[25]

On October 23, 1983, with the U.S. Marines in Beirut just over a year, a member of a Shia Muslim militia drove a truck laden with explosives to the door of an apartment building that served as a Marine barracks in Beirut, not far from the waterfront. The explosives detonated, the driver was blown up, and the building collapsed, killing 241 of the Marines inside.[26] Administration officials called the bombing an act of terrorism, while the press covered it as a senseless act against men who were trying to help Lebanon.

From the standpoint of the Shia militias, however, the Marines in Lebanon were the enemy, because we sided with the Phalange. We were backing the element in Lebanon that had traditionally been pro-Western and allied to the United States. To make matters worse, we were consolidating power for a Lebanese government that worked hand in glove with Israel, which was disliked by the nationalists for depriving the Palestinians of nationhood.

Even after the bombing of the Marines barracks, Reagan continued to back the Gemayel government. Since Syria had troops in the country arrayed against the Phalange, Reagan ordered the navy to shell Syrian positions in villages in central Lebanon from the USS *New Jersey*.[27] This angered the nationalists even more, as the shelling killed civilians. In February 1984, Reagan withdrew the Marines from Lebanon but kept the ships offshore.[28]

Throughout the Lebanon episode, the Reagan administration was successful in selling its version of the events, so Congress and the public did not realize that the Marines were acting in a partisan role. If our true objectives had been understood, the administration might have been forced to take an evenhanded approach, or it might have been forced to leave Lebanon. As it was, this second expedition of the Marines to the Lebanese beaches ended in disaster.

NOTES

1. David K. Shipler, "Israel and Lebanon Sign Agreement at 2 Ceremonies," *New York Times*, May 18, 1983, p. A16, col. 1.

2. John Kifner, "Lebanon Assembly Elects a Rightist to the Presidency," *New York Times*, August 24, 1983, p. Al, col. 6; Joe Stork, 'Report from Lebanon," *MERIP Reports* 13, no. 8 (October 1983): 4.

3. Edward A. Gargan, "Bashir Gemayel Lived by the Sword," *New York Times*, September 15, 1982, p. A8, col. 1.

4. Bernard Gwertzman, "Washington Hails Lebanon Outcome," *New York Times*, August 24, 1980, p. A6, col. 1.

5. Bob Woodward, *Veil: The Secret Wars of the CIA 1981–1987* (1987), p. 204.

6. Ibid., pp. 205, 217–18.

7. David K. Shipler, "Israeli Inquiry into Beirut Massacre to Focus on 2 Key Questions," *New York Times*, October 10, 1982, p. A14, col. 1.

8. Woodward, *Veil*, p. 203; "Maronist Leader Says He Started Israeli Link," *New York Times*, June 20, 1982, p. A12, col. 1.

9. Woodward, *Veil*, p. 249.

10. Gargan, "Bashir Gemayel Lived by the Sword."

11. Bernard Gwertzman, "Reagan Orders Marines to Beirut to Oversee Withdrawal by P.L.O.," *New York Times*, August 21, 1982, p. Al, col. 1; Helena Cobban, *The Making of Modern Lebanon* (1985), p. 185.

12. Colin Campbell, "Last Guerrillas Quit West Beirut," *New York Times*, September 2, 1982, p. Al, col. 5.

13. Colin Campbell, "U.S. Marines Leave Lebanese Capital," *New York Times*, September 11, 1982, p. A5, col. 1.

14. Shipler, "Israeli Inquiry into Beirut Massacre to Focus on 2 Key Questions."

15. Colin Campbell, "Gemayel of Lebanon Is Killed in Bomb Blast at Party Offices," *New York Times*, September 15, 1982, p. Al, col. 6; John Laffin, *The War of Desperation: Lebanon 1982–85* (1985), p. 169.

16. Thomas L Friedman, "Christian Militiamen Accused of a Massacre in Beirut Camps; U.S. Says the Toll Is at Least 300," *New York Times*, Septe

mber 19, 1982, p. Al, col. 6; Laffin, *War of Desperation*, pp. 170–71.

17. Linda A. Malone, "The Kahan Report, Ariel Sharon and the Sabra-Shatilla Massacres in Lebanon: Responsibility Under International Law for Massacres of Civilian Populations," *Utah Law Review* (1985): 396.

18. Colin Campbell, "Amin Gemayel Elected President in a Display of Unity by Lebanese," *New York Times*, September 22, 1982, p. A1, col. 4.

19. Steven R. Weisman, "Reagan Says U.S. Will Keep Its Marine Force in Lebanon Till Israelis and Syrians Go," *New York Times*, September 29, 1982, p. A1, col. 6; "Ambassador Dillon's Letter," September 25, 1982, DSB, vol. 82, p. 51 (November 1982); Cobban, *The Making of Modern Lebanon*, p. 190.

20. "President's Statement," September 20, 1982, DSB, vol. 82, p. 49 (November 1982).

21. Cobban, *The Making of Modern Lebanon*, pp. 199–202, Jonathan Randal, *The Tragedy of Lebanon: Christian Warlords, Israeli Adventurers and American Bunglers* (1983), p. 277; Francis A. Boyle, "International Law and Organizations as an Approach to Conflict Resolution in the Middle East," in Thomas Buergenthal, ed., *Contemporary Issues in International Law: Essays in Honor of Louis B. Sohn* (1984), p. 532; Stork, "Report from Lebanon," pp. 3–4, 12–13.

22. Stork, "Report from Lebanon," p. 4.

23. Ibid., p. 3; Shipler, "Israel and Lebanon Sign Agreement at 2 Ceremonies."

24. Shipler, "Israel and Lebanon Sign Agreement at 2 Ceremonies."

25. Cobban, *The Making of Modern Lebanon*, p. 202.

26. Ibid., pp. 202–203; Thomas L Friedman, "Beirut Death Toll at 161 Americans," *New York Times*, October 24, 1983, p. A1, col. 6.

27. Joseph B. Treaster, "Battleship's Guns Shell Syrian Sites in Lebanese War," *New York Times*, December 15, 1983, p. A1, col. 6.

28. Cobban, *The Making of Modern Lebanon*, p. 205; Steven R. Weisman, "President Asserts Marines in Beirut Still Have a Role," *New York Times*, February 23, 1984, p. Al, col. 6.

23. GRENADA: AN OCEAN VENTURE

On a Saturday evening in October 1983, I was at a dinner party with close friends, where the conversation turned to the Caribbean. In the tiny island nation of Grenada, with a population of 100,000, a leftist government was in crisis. One faction within the ruling party had just overthrown and killed the leader, a man named Maurice Bishop. In the ensuing fighting, seventeen others were killed. News broadcasts that Saturday aired rumors that the Reagan administration might move against Grenada, which, because of its close relations with Cuba, was something of a thorn in the administration's side. President Reagan had campaigned in 1980 on a platform of fighting communism, but after two years in office, he had scored no victory over communism.

The political weakness in Grenada that had been created by the internal dissension provided an opportunity. On that very evening, in fact, the Joint Chiefs of Staff were ordering Admiral Wesley McDonald, commander in chief of the U.S. Atlantic command, to land Marines and Army Ranger Paratroopers in Grenada.[1] Grenada had attracted Reagan's interest early in his administration. In 1981, he had the Atlantic command run a training exercise off the coast of Puerto Rico,[2] which the navy called Ocean Venture 1981. The exercise was based on a hypothetical invasion of an island country code-named "Amber and the Amberines." Grenada's full name is Grenada and the Grenadines. In Grenada, there was a location called Amber In the exercise, Amber was being supported by a country called Orange, which in turn was supported by Red. Orange apparently represented Cuba, and Red the Soviet Union. The commander of Ocean Venture 1981 explained at a press briefing that in the exercise scenario, Amber was "exporting terrorist activities to neighboring islands." His forces would rescue "twenty U.S. citizens held hostage there after negotiations with the Amber Government had broken down." The objective of Ocean Venture 1981 was to capture Amber and install a "government friendly to America."[3]

Grenada featured prominently in a speech President Reagan gave in March 1983 on U.S. military policy. Displayed behind the president as he spoke was an aerial photograph of a new airport under construction in Grenada. Reagan cited the new airport as an ominous sign that Grenada was preparing to let Cuba or the Soviet Union land military aircraft for military invasions in the Caribbean. "On the small island of Grenada," Reagan said, "the Cubans, with Soviet financing and backing, are in the process of building an airfield with a 10,000-foot runway. Grenada doesn't even have an air force. Who is it intended for?" The president elaborated:

> [T]he Caribbean is a very important passageway for our international commerce and military lines of communication. More than half of all American oil imports now pass through the Caribbean. The rapid build-up of Grenada's military potential is unrelated to any conceivable threat to this island country of under 110,000 people, and totally at odds with the pattern of other eastern Caribbean States, most of which are unarmed. The Soviet-Cuban militarization of Grenada, in short, can only be seen as power projection into the region.[4]

While the map made for good television, the cogency of Reagan's analysis was not self-evident. Reagan said that the airport was for Communist military aircraft. The Grenada government claimed it was for tourism. Other Caribbean island nations had airports that could accommodate large passenger jets on direct flights from New York and Miami.

Grenada's only airport had been a mountain airstrip that could not accommodate the big planes.

Since Cuba contributed construction workers to do the heavy work on the airport, Cuba was, in fact, building the airport. The general contractor on the job, however, wore no red star; it was Plessey, Ltd., a British contracting firm, whose executives explained to the press that they had designed the airport for civilian use. The buildings had not been reinforced to withstand shelling, nor had side runways or bunkers been built to protect military aircraft from attack.[5]

As for Reagan's point about Grenada's proximity to lines of communication, U.S. vessels did, as Reagan averred, use the Caribbean for transit, but Cuba was much larger and closer to our shores, and we never had trouble sailing around it.

On October 25, 1983, Ocean Venture 1981 was played out in the real world, in an invasion so remarkably similar to the exercise that the *Times* of London, in retrospect, called Ocean Venture a "rehearsal."[6] Admiral Wesley McDonald carried out President Reagan's orders, landing 6,000 troops in Grenada. Charging that Grenada was about to export revolution elsewhere in the Caribbean, Reagan purported to be rescuing American citizens who, he said, were in danger of being taken hostage by the Grenadan government. In fighting that lasted four days, McDonald defeated the Grenada army, captured Grenada's leaders, and asked a Grenadan official friendly to the United States—Sir Paul Scoon, who held the post of governor general*— to serve as caretaker until a new government could be formed. Thus, the script of Ocean Venture 1981 was carried out to the letter. The only major deviation was that Grenada did not accommodate the plot by taking any U.S. citizens hostage.

While the military action achieved its aim, the political fallout was troublesome. At the United Nations, the General Assembly called the assault on Grenada a "flagrant violation of international law," and a denigration of Grenada's "independence, sovereignty and territorial integrity."[7] The administration argued in justification that we had been invited into Grenada by the Organization of Eastern Caribbean States, a

---

*In Genada the governor general was a liaison officer with Great Britain, which ruled Granada until 1974.

regional association of island nations, and also by Governor General Scoon.[8] According to the State Department, Scoon made a request on October 23 for our intervention—not directly but via the Organization of Eastern Caribbean States (OECS).[9]

Scoon confirmed to the press that he had made such a request, but not on October 23. Rather, Scoon sent a request letter on October 24 to the OECS, addressed to Barbados Prime Minister Tom Adams.[10] While the time discrepancy could perhaps have been explained away, there was a more serious problem with Scoon's statement. Prime Minister Adams could not confirm having received any letter from Scoon prior to the invasion; Adams' press officer, when queried by the media, said that Adams received no such letter from Scoon, either before or after the invasion.

A request letter with Scoon's signature was later made public by the State Department, despite denials from Adams and his press officer. The press officer surmised that the letter had been composed by someone outside Grenada and hand-delivered to Scoon for his signature by U.S. paratroopers. As for who might have ghostwritten the request letter, no one ever found out for sure; but press speculation focused on the country most anxious to have the request, the United States.[11]

Available evidence gives little reason to believe that Scoon wrote and sent a request letter prior to the invasion. Although he had been in communication with regional officials in the days preceding, there is no indication that he had specifically requested it.[12] Britain's foreign secretary, Geoffrey Howe, affirmed that a British diplomat spoke with Scoon in person the day before the invasion. During that conversation, Scoon did not mention that he had made a request or was planning one. British Prime Minister Margaret Thatcher thought that Scoon had written no letter. Since these meetings were private, Scoon would have had no concern about his security in revealing that he had sent a request letter.[13] As for any contact with the United States before the invasion, Scoon denied there was any, direct or indirect. He said, in fact, that he had no idea the United States was involved until U.S. paratroopers knocked on his door.[14]

Whatever the true story about a possible eleventh hour request from

Scoon, the decision to land troops in Grenada had been made on October 22, three days before the landing.[15] So under any version of the alleged request by Scoon, Reagan ordered the intervention prior to a request.

The administration, however, did not rely only on a request from Scoon as justification for the Grenada landing; it also claimed that we had been invited to Grenada by the OECS under the authority of that organization.[16] Grenada was a member of the OECS, whose founding treaty had provisions about military intervention; therefore, on the face of it, the argument was plausible. And the OECS did ask us to intervene. At its meeting in Barbados on October 21, the OECS decided on the advisability of an intervention in Grenada and asked the United States to carry it out.

Reliance on the OECS request, like reliance on a Scoon request, had its problems. The OECS treaty allowed military intervention only in case of "external aggression" against one of the member countries, the idea being that the OECS countries would unite to help a member state if it was invaded from outside the area. Grenada, however, had not been invaded by a state outside the area. Indeed, it had been invaded by no state. The OECS treaty gave no right to invade over dislike of a member state's politics.

The administration's reliance on the OECS treaty faced one other obstacle. The treaty specified that before taking any military action to stop "external aggression," a unanimous vote of all the member countries was required. This was designed to prevent military action in a member country without its consent. Grenada was notably absent from the October 21 OECS meeting in Barbados, which meant that the other members could not vote for military action without violating the treaty. But this is precisely what they did.[17]

If the OECS did not have the right to intervene in Grenada, then it could hardly ask us to do so on its behalf. But why would the OECS violate its own treaty? From all evidence, Washington's gentle hand was at work. When the trouble started in Grenada, the State Department geared up, making plans for a Grenada intervention and approaching Caribbean leaders to sound them out.[18] Officials in Jamaica, one of the countries we approached, reported that the State Department pressured them to endorse a U.S. intervention to replace the government of Grenada.[19] The State Department acknowledged it held talks about Grenada with Caribbean leaders, but it denied encouraging them to make a request for intervention.

That denial was not universally believed. During the October 21 OECS meeting, Charles Gillespie, our deputy assistant secretary of state for Caribbean affairs, sat in an anteroom outside the meeting chamber.[20] As analyzed by reporters, Gillespie was too high an official to spend several hours sitting outside someone else's meeting, unless he had some role to play. In all probability, Gillespie was there either to make sure the delegates voted for intervention, or at least to let them know that if they requested our intervention, they would get it.[21] Since the OECS countries had no military forces of their own to speak of, they could not themselves have intervened in Grenada, which did have an army. The OECS decision to intervene, therefore, made sense only if it already knew that we would carry out the intervention.

When President Reagan announced the invasion, he gave the impression that the initiative had come from the OECS. We "acceded," Reagan said, "to the request to become part of a multinational effort with contingents from Antigua and Barbuda, Barbados, Dominica, Jamaica, St. Lucia, St. Vincent and the Grenadines and the United States. Early this morning, forces from six Caribbean democracies and the United States began a landing."[22]

Reagan stressed here the supposedly collective nature of the operation. Before the Organization of American States, too, our delegate took up this theme, saying that "a collective security force, made up of contingents from four member states of the OECS—Antigua and Barbuda, Dominica, St. Lucia, and St. Vincent and the Grenadines, supplemented by units from Barbados, Jamaica, and the United States—disembarked on Grenada yesterday [October 25] at dawn."[23]

These statements not only made the Grenada landing sound like an action to which we agreed only after being asked, but they depicted the invasion as having been carried out by a joint force. That depiction was pure fiction. The assault on Grenada was carried out by U.S. troops alone—Army paratroopers and Marines. After the American forces landed, they did bring in 300 Jamaicans and Barbadans, not for combat but to guard prisoners and to patrol streets.[24]

In convincing the OECS countries to ask for our help, we did not have to twist arms overly hard. Like the Reagan administration, the OECS governments, all right of center, worried about the leftists in Grenada. Already leftists in other OECS countries were looking to Grenada as a model; therefore, putting down Grenada would stop the virus before it spread. After the landing, OECS governments cracked down on leftists in what was described as a "climate of militant anti-radicalism."[25]

NOTES

1. Lt. Col. Michael J. Byron, U.S. Marine Corps, "Fury from the Sea: Marines in Grenada," 110/5/975 *U.S. Naval Institute Proceedings*, p. 124 (May 1984); "Ten Days of Urgent Fury," *All Hands* (U.S. Navy), p. 34 (May 1984).

2. Fred Hiatt, "U.S. Says Situation Still Unclear as Naval Force Nears Grenada," *Washington Post*, October 23, 1983, p. A24, col. 1.

3. Christopher Searle, *Grenada: The Struggle Against Destabilization* (1983), pp. 37–38.

4. "President's Speech on Military Spending and a New Defense," *New York Times*, March 24, 1983, p. A20, col. 1.

5. Rodney Cowton, "Plessey Say New Airport Not Military," *Times* (London), November 1, 1983, p. 6, col. 5; "L'aéroport de Point-Salines," *Le Monde*, November 1, 1983, p. 3, col. 1; "Firm Dismisses Claim Airport Was Military," *Toronto Globe and Mail*, November 2, 1983, p. 14, col. 1.

6. Nicholas Ashford, "U.S. Staged 'Invasion Rehearsal' in 1981," *Times* (London), November 7, 1983, p. 5, col. 1.

7. Res. 38/7, GAOR, 38th yr., *Resolutions and Decisions*, Supplement No. 47, p. 19 (1983).

8. Letter from Davis R. Robinson, Legal Adviser, U.S. Dept. of State, to

Prof. Edward Gordon, Chairman, Committee on Grenada, Section on International Law and Practice, American Bar Assn., February 10, 1984, in *International Lawyer* 18 (1984): 381.

9. Letter from Davis R. Robinson, p. 381.

10. Alex Brummer, "Scoon Tells of Rescue by Paras," *Guardian* (Manchester), November 1, 1983, p. 1, col. 6.

11. Alan George, "Did Washington Ghost-Write Scoon's Appeal?" *New Statesman*, November 11, 1983, p. 5.

12. Latin America Bureau, *Grenada: Whose Freedom?* (1984), p. 88.

13. Ian Aitken and Martin Wainwright, "Hurt Thatcher Widens Breach with Reagan," *Guardian* (Manchester), October 31, 1983, p. 1, col. 1.

14. Alex Brummer, "Scoon Tells of Rescue by Paras."

15. "D-Day in Grenada," *Time*, November 7, 1983, p. 27.

16. Letter from Davis R. Robinson, p. 381.

17. Treaty Establishing the Organization of Eastern Caribbean States, June 18, 1981, art. 8, *International Legal Materials* 20 (1981): 1166.

18. Patrick E. Tyler, "State Dept. Denies Reports that U.S. Sought Pretext for Invasion," *Washington Post*, October 28, 1983, p. A10, col. 1.

19. Juan Williams, "Jamaicans Indicate U.S. Signaled Will to Invade," *Washington Post*, October 27, 1983, p. A20, col. 1; Tyler, "State Dept. Denies Reports that U.S. Sought Pretext for Invasion."

20. Ralph Kinney Bennett, "Grenada: Anatomy of a 'Go' Decision," *Reader's Digest*, February 1984, p. 74.

21. Bob Woodward, *Veil: The Secret Wars of the CIA 1981–1987* (1987), p. 290.

22. "Grenada: Collective Action by the Caribbean Peace Force," DSB, vol. 83, p. 67 (December 1983).

23. "Grenada: Collective Action by the Caribbean Peace Force," p. 72.

24. Fred Halliday, "An Ambiguous Turning Point Grenada and Its Aftermath," in *North American Congress on Latin America Report on the Americas*, November–December 1984, p. 21.

25. Dennis Volman, "Antileftist Feeling Is Rising in Caribbean," *Christian Science Monitor*, November 28, 1983, p. 11, col. 1.

24. Grenada: Saving Our Students

The Reagan administration gave another reason for the Grenada landing: to protect American citizens residing there.[1] Saving citizens might not justify overthrowing Grenada's government, but it might justify getting a foot in the door. There were, in fact, U.S. citizens in Grenada, most of them students at a medical college run from New York. President Reagan said that it was "of overriding importance" to intervene to protect "innocent lives, including up to a thousand Americans, whose personal safety is, of course, my paramount concern."[2]

These students had not, however, come to any harm. They had not been seized. They had not been threatened, either by the Grenadan government or anyone else. What the administration claimed was that the Grenadans who overthrew Maurice Bishop might take these students hostage.[3] One official, who wished to remain anonymous, told reporters that the United States found documents in Grenada showing a government plan to seize some of the students. "It is clear from these documents and other information we now have," said the official, "that serious consideration was being given to seizing Americans as hostages and holding them for reasons that are not entirely clear, but seem to involve an effort to embarrass the United States and, more immediately, to forestall American military action in Grenada."[4] The administration never disclosed these supposed documents, even though the media pressed for them.[5] The official who claimed they existed never let his name be associated with the information.

Just prior to the invasion the administration did have information about the situation in Grenada. James Budeit was one of several State Department officials sent to Grenada two days before the invasion to talk to Grenadan officials and to the medical students. Budeit reported he found no reason to believe that the Grenada government would harm the students.[6] Violence had occurred in Grenada on October 19, but on October 20 the new government imposed a curfew, and from that date Grenada was quiet. The situation was calm enough that Leon Cornwall, a member of the new Grenadan government, invited Budeit to spend the evening at a disco. Although Cornwall "seemed a nice enough guy," Budeit related, he declined the invitation, explaining, "I can't go to discos with them. Our president called them a gang of leftist thugs."[7]

The administration could not present a logical explanation why the Grenadan government might take hostages. That government had every reason to treat the students with kid gloves. The medical school was a prime source of foreign exchange for the tiny nation, a key element in its economy. A government that lost the medical school would not likely survive politically. The school's vice chancellor, Geoffrey Bourne, in fact, received a visit soon after the anti-Bishop coup from the head of the new government, who asked if the students were doing well, and who gave Bourne his home telephone number to call in case of any difficulties.[8]

When President Reagan announced the invasion, he gave as one reason for thinking the students were in danger the fact that "we'd been informed of several hundred who wanted to leave."[9] The number given by State Department officials in Barbados on October 24 was 300.[10]

On October 22 and 23, however, according to Budeit and the vice chancellor, only 100 to 150 students wanted to leave, and their fear was prompted not by concern over the Grenadans, but by reports of an impending U.S. attack.[11] On the evening of October 23, radio stations from neighboring islands broadcast "rumors" that we would invade Grenada and, according to the vice chancellor, "this scared the students very much."[12] Understandably, they did not want to be caught in Grenada during an invasion. This concern was shared back in the United States by the students' parents, five hundred of whom sent President Reagan a telegram on October 24, asking him not to invade Grenada, because they did not want their children endangered.[13] Meanwhile, State Department officials in Barbados told the medical students that while the Grenadan government would likely not harm them, there could perhaps be a counter-coup against the new government, which might be a source of danger. Budeit, who apparently believed there might be a counter-coup, "scared the hell out of those people," leaving the wives of some of the students in tears.[14]

No evidence surfaced of any Grenadan group in formation to stage a countercoup, and even if there had been a counter-coup, there was no reason to believe the students would be harmed. In the fighting that accompanied the overthrow of Bishop, no medical students were injured; none were even reported to be in the fray, since most of them lived some distance from the downtown area where the violence occurred.

The State Department took one other tack to create the appearance of danger to the students. Peter Bourne, a professor at the medical school and son of the vice chancellor, happened to be in the United States at the time, when he got a phone call from a member of the school's board of trustees. The board member told Bourne that State Department officials were telephoning school officials in New York and pressing them to state publicly that the students were in danger.[15] The medical school declined to issue such a statement. School officials saw no danger to the students until they heard that the United States would invade.

There was one other flaw in President Reagan's position that an invasion was necessary to save the students. Even if there were a danger of a hostage-taking by the Grenadan government, or of a countercoup in which the students might be caught up, it remained unclear why a Marine landing was needed. In the days preceding the invasion, there were no hostilities in Grenada, and the Grenadan government was not preventing the students from leaving.

On October 22 and 23, in fact, State Department officials from Bar-

bados talked with the Grenadan government about possible ways to evacuate the students. But according to Secretary of Defense Caspar Weinberger, while "attempts were made to get Americans out," the Grenadan
government "failed to live up to its assurances that the airport would be
opened on October 24 and foreigners would be free to leave. Therefore,
the U.S. was unable to get any Americans out on charter flights prior to
the U.S. invasion."[16] Thus, in Weinberger's version of events, the
Grenadan government had rendered it impossible to get the students out
by normal means, making an invasion necessary. Deputy Secretary of
State Kenneth Dam made the same allegation: "Charter flights were not
allowed in."[17]

Weinberger was referring not to the new airport under construction,
but to the existing smaller airport, which was called Pearls. On October
24 it was open and functioning normally. By chance, a retired federal official, Robert J. Myers, who had been chief actuary in the Social Security
Administration, was in Grenada that day, and he reported taking a flight
out of Grenada from Pearls Airport on October 24.[18]

Four charter flights also flew in and out of Pearls Airport that day. A
fifth had been scheduled, but was canceled at the last minute by the char-
terer, Leeward Islands Air Transport, which was owned jointly by several
Caribbean island countries collaborating in the invasion.[19] Leeward
Islands canceled the flight because the Caribbean Community, a regional
economic group, decided on October 22 to ban all flights to Grenada as
an economic sanction.[20]

State Department officials apparently made no effort to get the medical students on these charter flights, or to organize others. The Grenadan
government, far from obstructing an evacuation, contacted the vice chancellor by phone on October 21, to ask whether any students wanted to
leave and to offer cooperation in transport arrangements if they did. Cornwall told State Department officials that charter flights could use Pearls to
evacuate students. The State Department declined, claiming that the
runway at Pearls was too short to accommodate large planes, and that the
road to Pearls was poor. The State Department proposed sending a battleship for the students, but Grenadan officials, fearing a ruse for an inva-

sion, insisted that any ships be civilian.[21] U.S. officials then told Cornwall that a Cunard cruise liner, the SS *Countess*, was scheduled to dock in Grenada October 25, and Cornwall agreed that any students wishing to leave could board. This plan was scotched in Washington, however, because the invasion was already set for October 25.[22]

The State Department thus was avoiding options for a peaceful evacuation. *Time* magazine reasoned that evacuation would have been better than invasion, "if their [the students'] safety was [our] primary concern."[23] "There was no evidence," wrote another observer, "that the Americans could not have been evacuated without military action."[24] The medical students, it would seem, were part of the administration's plan for invading Grenada. It needed the appearance of their being in danger as a reason to enter the country.

On October 25, as the invasion began, reporters were keen to know the fate of the students. When they asked President Reagan whether the students were safe, he replied, "As far as we know, the citizens are safe. We have been monitoring that very closely."[25] Two days later, on October 27, Reagan said in a televised speech, "Almost instantly our military seized the two airports, secured the campus where most of our students were and they're now in the mopping-up phase."[26]

These statements hardly reflected the reality. When Reagan spoke on October 27, our forces had not located many of the medical students. One reason, incredible as it may seem, was that no one had told the commanders where to find the students they were supposedly invading to save.

The first U.S. forces to arrive in Grenada were airborne U.S. Army Ranger units that parachuted into the new airport under construction at Point Salines. Next door was a campus where one hundred of the medical students lived. There was a second campus at a location called Grand Anse, where over two hundred students lived, and a residential area called Lance aux Épines, which housed two hundred more. Still other students lived in private apartments scattered around St. George's, the capital city. Secretary of Defense Weinberger, when asked in a House hearing whether "operation commanders were not aware that the Medical School in Grenada had two separate campuses," answered, "Initially it was not known that the medical school had two campuses."[27] One of the commanders, Major General Norman Schwarzkopf, who in 1990 would lead U.S. forces in the Persian Gulf, confirmed that the commanders had been told only about the campus at Point Salines. Schwarzkopf called the commanders' ignorance of the Grande Anse campus or the Lance aux Épines residential area a failure of intelligence.[28]

Admiral McDonald, the overall commander, recorded the snafu in his "after-action" report: "Evacuee locating information was not available except that they were generally located in the St. George area. During execution of the operation, interviews with the first evacuees provided location information for other potential evacuees."[29] The commanders themselves had information about the whereabouts of only one hundred out of nearly one thousand students. They had to ask the first students they encountered where their fellow students might be.

This so-called intelligence failure could have turned the Grenada "rescue" from low comedy to high tragedy: Grenada, after all, had an army, and fighting went on for four days. Just as their parents feared, the students wound up caught in a war zone. The Marines and Rangers engaged the Grenadan army, having no clue whether the medical students might be in the immediate vicinity.

Incredibly, the U.S. forces did not try, once they arrived, to contact even those students whose location they did know. Although the commanders knew about the Point Salines campus, the Rangers who landed at the Point Salines airport did not immediately approach it. They landed at 5:30 A.M. but did not enter the campus until 10:30 A.M.—five hours later—even though it was only a few yards away.[30] More incredibly still, after the Rangers reached that campus, they did not arrange an evacuation, even though fighting was continuing in the immediate area. Only on the following day did they begin to arrange transportation for the students.[31]

At the Point Salines campus, the firing was intense. The Grenadan army had gun emplacements around the airport construction site, and some of the Cuban airport workers living in dormitories nearby had rifles.

The Rangers attacked both groups by calling in helicopter gunships. Approaching from the sea, the gunships flew directly over the campus en route to Grenadan positions and the dormitories, where they inflicted heavy casualties.[32]

Seeing the helicopters firing overhead, the students were frightened out of their wits. Several students had ham radios. One of them broadcast that there was "quite a bit of fire" coming directly into the campus from the gunships.[33] Another student reported that shells fired by the gunships landed "less than 50 meters from our building on the campus."[34] Still another claimed that a bullet struck the pillow on his bed.[35] One frantic student sent out a message by radio to our forces, pleading that they divert the helicopters from the campus.[36]

If these students were being rescued, this was a strange way to go about it. When the medical school chancellor in New York received word that firing was occurring close to the campus, he said that if any students were hurt, President Reagan "should be held accountable."[37]

Meantime, our forces were still out of contact with the other nine hundred medical students. The next group to be reached was those at the Grand Anse campus, but that did not occur until the afternoon of October 26, thirty-five hours after the landing. Grand Anse was close to St. George's, in an area defended by the Grenadan army. To take those Grenadan positions, our bombers had to strafe heavily near the Grand Anse campus. They released what reporters called a "devastating barrage" that leveled two hotels near the campus.[38] To assault this area, Marines piloted the helicopters ferrying in Army Rangers. The return fire against the helicopters was so intense that some of the Marine pilots refused to land, hovering just above the ground, and forcing the Rangers to jump.[39]

While the fighting with the Grenada units near the Grand Anse campus continued, the Marines took helicopters in to evacuate the students. But these helicopters, too, met heavy fire, with students reporting that as they ran to the helicopters, "shots whizzed about them."[40] According to the Marine Corps "after-action" report, four helicopters were hit during the evacuation operation, although no one was injured. "Liftoff" with the Grand Anse campus students, the report said, "commenced at 1600" (4:00 P.M.) on October 26. "In less than an hour, 224 students were evacuated under fire without any friendly casualties. Three helicopters were damaged in the assault with one helicopter destroyed. There were no losses to passengers or crew."[41]

Our forces did not reach the students at the Lance aux Épines residential area until October 28, three days after landing in Grenada.[42] All this time these students remained behind Grenadan army lines. The same was true of those students who lived in private housing around St. George's, where our forces called in air strikes on Grenadan army positions.[43] One of the air strikes demolished, apparently by accident, a mental hospital, killing seventeen patients.[44] Fortunately, in the bombing of St. George's, no students were hit.

Robert Pastor, who had been a Latin American specialist in the National Security Council in the Carter administration, was doubtless correct when he told a House committee that "U.S. citizens were more likely to have been endangered by the invasion than by the Grenada Government."[45] While there was little reason to expect harm from the government, a fullscale military invasion with one thousand United States civilians in the line of fire was extremely hazardous. An army analyst wrote that had the Grenadan forces been so inclined, they could easily have retaliated against the students for the invasion.[46]

Many reporters understood that the administration had invented facts to justify the Grenada landing. The *New York Times* wrote that the administration put out "deliberate distortions and knowingly false statements of fact."[47]

Time magazine called the administration "disingenuous in its public explanations," and said that "American aims" went "well beyond those stated."[48]

Other media outlets accepted the administration statements at face value. The television networks broadcast and rebroadcast scenes of the medical students kissing the ground at U.S. airports after their return flights, giving the impression that our forces had saved them from danger. The networks did not explain who had put the students in danger.

NOTES

1. Letter from Davis R. Robinson, Legal Adviser, U.S. Dept. of State, to Prof. Edward Gordon, Chairman, Committee on Grenada, Section on International Law and Practice, American Bar Assn., February 10, 1984, in *International Lawyer* 18 (1984): 385.

2. "Grenada: Collective Action by the Caribbean Peace Force," DSB, vol. 83, p. 67 (December 1983).

3. Ibid., p. 80.

4. Philip Taubman, "U.S. Reports Evidence of Island Hostage Plan," *New York Times*, October 28, 1983, p. A14, col. 5.

5. John Quigley, "The United States Invasion of Grenada: Stranger than Fiction," *University of Miami Inter-American Law Review* 18 (1986–87): 281.

6. Jonathan Kwitny, *Endless Enemies: The Making of an Unfriendly World* (1984), p. 417.

7. Ibid., p. 416.

8. *U.S. Military Actions in Grenada: Implications for U.S. Policy in the Eastern Caribbean*, Hearing before the Subcommittees on International Security and Scientific Affairs and on Western Hemisphere Affairs of the House Committee on Foreign Affairs, 98th Cong., 1st sess. (1983), pp. 187–91.

9. "'U.S. Had to Act Strongly, Decisively,'" *Washington Post*, October 26, 1983, p. A7, col. 1.

10. Michael T. Kaufman, "50 Marines Land at Barbados Field," *New York Times*, October 25, 1983, p. Al, col. 1.

11. Kwitny, *Endless Enemies*, p. 413.

12. *U.S. Military Actions in Grenada*, p. 193.

13. Michael T. Kaufman, "50 Marines Land at Barbados Field," *New York Times*, October 25, 1983, p. Al, col. 1.

14. Kwitny, *Endless Enemies*, p. 414.

15. P. Bourne, "Was the U.S. Invasion Necessary?" *Los Angeles Times*, November 6, 1983, p. IV3, col. 4.

16. *Situation in Lebanon and Grenada*, Hearing before a Subcommittee of the House Committee on Appropriations, 98th Cong., 1st sess. (1983), p. 58.

17. *The Situation in Grenada*, Hearing before the Senate Committee on Foreign Relations, 98th Cong., 1st sess. (1983), p. 6.

18. Hedrick Smith, "Ex-U.S. Official Cites Ease in Leaving Grenada Day Before Invasion," *New York Times*, October 29, 1983, p. A7, col. 3.

19. "Ottawa Probing if Grenada Flights Purposely Scuttled," *Toronto Globe and Mail*, November 12, 1983, p. 1, col. 2.

20. Christopher Thomas, "Marines Sent to Three Islands near Grenada," *Times* (London), October 25, 1983, p. 1, col. 2.

21. *U.S. Military Actions in Grenada*, p. 193.

22. Hedrick Smith, "Reagan Aide Says U.S. Invasion Forestalled Cuban Arms Buildup," *New York Times*, October 27, 1983, p. A1, col. 3; Kwitny, *Endless Enemies*, p. 413.

23. "Now to Make It Work," *Time*, November 14, 1983, p. 19.

24. Edwin C. Hoyt, *Law and Force in American Foreign Policy* (1985), p. 144.

25. "'U.S. Had to Act Strongly, Decisively.'"

26. "Transcript of Address by President on Lebanon and Grenada," *New York Times*, October 28, 1983, p. A10, col. 1.

27. *Situation in Lebanon and Grenada*, p. 56.

28. Edward Cody, "Estimates of Casualties in Grenada Are Raised," *Washington Post*, November 9, 1983, p. A1, col. 6.

29. Commander in Chief, U.S. Atlantic Command, *Operation Urgent Fury Report* (1984), p. II-9.

30. U.S. Marine Corps Development and Education Command Newsletter: *Operational Overview*, January–March 1984, p. 12.

31. Quigley, "The United States Invasion of Grenada," p. 296.

32. Drew Middleton, "Operation on Grenada: How Forces Performed," *New York Times*, October 28, 1983, p. A12, col. 1.

33. Judith Valente, "Beltsville Ham Operator Monitors Eyewitness Reports on Invasion," *Washington Post*, October 26, 1983, p. A10, col. 1.

34. Ward Sinclair, "Medical Students Recount Tale of Tense Escape from Grenada," *Washington Post*, October 28, 1983, p. A17, col. 1.

35. "D-Day in Grenada," *Time*, November 7, 1983, p. 23.

36. "Under Fire, Ham Radio Operators Describe Invasion," *New York Times*, October 26, 1983, p. A20, col. 2.

37. John T. McQuiston, "School's Chancellor Says Invasion Was Not Necessary to Save Lives," *New York Times*, October 26, 1983, p. A20, col. 5.

38. "Battle for Grenada," *Newsweek*, November 7, 1983, p. 72.

39. *U.S. Military Actions in Grenada*, p. 83.

40. "D-Day in Grenada," *Time*, November 7, 1983, p. 25.

41. *Operational Overview*, p. 18.

42. Cody, "Estimates of Casualties in Grenada Are Raised."

43. Ward Sinclair, "Medical Students Recount Tale of Tense Escape from Grenada," *Washington Post*, October 28, 1983, p. A17.

44. B. Drummond Ayres, Jr., "U.S. Concedes Bombing Hospital in Grenada, Killing at Least 12," *New York Times*, November 1, 1983, p. Al, col. 1; "Pentagon Account of Attack," *New York Times*, November 1, 1983, p. A16, col. 3.

45. *U.S. Military Actions in Grenada*, p. 73.

46. Charles Doe, "Grenada: Will Its Lessons Be Taught?" *Army Times*, November 5, 1984, p. 32.

47. Stuart Taylor, Jr., "In Wake of Invasion, Much Official Misinformation by U.S. Comes to Light," *New York Times*, November 6, 1983, p. A20, col. l.

48. "Weighing the Proper Role," *Time*, November 7, 1983, p. 48.

25. GRENADA: THE CUBANS WERE FEROCIOUS

One other aspect of the Grenada operation found the administration anxious to press its version of events. As we saw, Cuban workers were housed in dormitories near the Point Salines airport site. The administration claimed that they were a military unit masquerading as construction workers, and that they fought in alliance with the Grenadan army to repel our attack.[1]

The Cuban workers, at least some of them, did fight against the Army Rangers who parachuted into Point Salines, but it is not clear how that fighting started. The Defense Department claimed that it did not intend to engage the Cubans, and that the Cubans fired first.[2] According to Secretary of Defense Caspar Weinberger, "we broadcast to the Cubans as quickly as possible that we were not attacking Cubans, and that they should not shoot at us, because our aim was to liberate the American students—American civilians there, and that we were dealing only with the Grenadian Armed Forces. They didn't heed that, and as a result, we had to use force." The Cubans, to whom Weinberger referred as "the Cuban forces," had been readied to "resist a landing" by our forces.[3]

Other U.S. officials painted a similar picture. Admiral Wesley McDonald called the Cubans "well-trained professional soldiers" who were impersonating construction workers.[4] Deputy Secretary of State Kenneth Dam said they were "organized Cuban units. These were not just construction workers helping out the poor Grenadian people to build a little airfield."[5] At first the Defense Department estimated that there were 1,100 Cubans in Grenada but later reduced the estimate to 750, which was close to the number of 784 given by the Cuban government.[6]

The version of events provided by Cuban sources differed from the Defense Department's. Within a few hours after the landing, Cuba sent a diplomatic note to the United States, charging that the Rangers had assaulted the workers without provocation.[7] At the United Nations, Cuba called it a "cowardly surprise attack."[8] Cuba said that the workers had fired back at the Rangers in self-defense.

In the spring of 1984, I was able to visit Cuba. The conflicting stories about the Ranger-Cuban fighting had piqued my interest. I had learned that the Cubans from Grenada were back in Cuba at a construction project. Our media had not interviewed them to get their version of events, so I arranged to meet them to see what I could learn.

I found that they were still employed, as they had been in Grenada, by the National Union of Enterprises (Caribbean), a parastatal construction firm. I found them in a little town called Puerto Escondido, just east of Havana, where they were at their first post-Grenada job, building a swimming pool. The only visible sign of their Grenada experience was a display they had set up of portrait photographs of their twenty-four colleagues who had been killed in the Grenada fighting.

From the Defense Department accounts, I expected the workers to be brawny young specimens. The men and women I met at Puerto Escondido did not look like a match for Army Rangers. Some were female clerical workers. Some were female schoolteachers, whose assignment in Grenada had been to teach high school equivalency classes for crew members. Of both the women and the men, quite a few were middle-aged. Of the men in particular, quite a few were overweight.

These Cubans did not look to be the "well-trained professional soldiers" described by Admiral McDonald. Some had carried rifles during the hostilities, they told me, although most, they said, did not. They had made preparations to defend their dormitories if attacked, but not to repel the invasion of Grenada.

After returning to the United States, I checked accounts of the Grenada operation by our military officers—what the Defense Department calls "after-action" reports—to see if they might shed light on the Cubans they confronted. "After-action" reports are written for use within the military to assess their strategy, and they are more frank than the public statements of the Pentagon. What I found in these reports accorded more with what I observed at Puerto Escondido than with the characterizations by Secretary Weinberger and Admiral McDonald.

One Marine Corps report referred to "the low state of training on the part of the Cuban troops (actually only construction workers)."[9] The phrase in parentheses was telling. The report referred to the Cubans first as "troops," as the Pentagon did in public statements, but the author then gave a more accurate characterization.

One of the operation's intelligence officers, Captain Thomas A. Brooks, wrote that the Cubans were but lightly armed with personal weapons, and that there were only "three to four dozen Cuban Army regulars" in Grenada. These "were not organized into a regular military unit, but were primarily advisers and instructors to the Grenadian military."[10]

The Cubans were not a combat unit, or even a military construction unit. I learned that the medical students had gotten on well with the Cubans, who were their neighbors at Point Salines. Professor Peter Bourne of the medical school reported that the students and the workers sometimes played softball together.[11]

I asked the workers at Puerto Escondido how the fighting with the Rangers started. Roberto Abreu Cruz, a 38-year-old bricklayer, told me that the Rangers "landed on the airstrip we had built. We thought they would go to the end of it where the U.S. university was. Instead they surrounded our camp." In a Cuban newspaper, I found a similar account by another bricklayer. Alberto Díaz said that the Rangers "occupied a hill and took up attack positions. I was watching them and I thought they were doing this to take the U.S. students away, but they advanced to where we were."[12] What did the Rangers do next? They started shooting, several of the workers told me, and they "took over the whole area. They took our bulldozers and construction tools."

I found more information on the fighting between the Rangers and the workers in a diplomatic note the United States sent to Cuba during the fighting. Curiously, the notes that the two countries exchanged—and there were several—were not published in the United States. In Cuba, they were reproduced in a book on Grenada.

Even before receiving the Cuban protest note on October 25, the United States sent a note to Cuba, through John Ferch, who headed the U.S. diplomatic office in Havana. The note, delivered at 5:00 P.M., October 25, urged Cuba to have the workers stop fighting. It said that the United States "regrets the armed clashes between men from the two countries and considers that they have occurred due to confusion and accidents brought about by your men's proximity to the area of operations of the multinational troops."[13]

That was tantamount to an apology, almost an acknowledgement that the Rangers had started the fighting, although it seemed to excuse the Rangers for shooting at the workers while the Rangers were engaging the Grenada forces. The administration never published this or any of the other communications between the United States and Cuba during the Grenada hostilities. It did not even inform the press that Cuba had contacted us during the crisis. So was this text authentic as published in Cuba, or could it have been a forgery to make the United States look bad?

When I visited Havana, I wondered if Ferch could authenticate the message texts, which, according to the Cuban account, all went through his hands. So I contacted Ferch's office and asked if I could meet with him. Ferch's office was in a large building that had been under construction as a new embassy when President Eisenhower broke diplomatic relations with Cuba. To carry on contacts, at least at a minimal level, the State Department arranged with the Swiss government to have this office be considered a part of its embassy in Havana. We dubbed it the U.S. interests section of the Swiss embassy. In Washington, Cuba did the same, using the Czech embassy. The building in Havana was now completed, and the interests section moved in on two upper floors. Otherwise the building stood empty, which lent it an eerie quality. Ferch's office had a window with a northern exposure, at which he kept a telescope trained on Miami.

When I asked Ferch about the diplomatic notes as published in Cuba, he readily affirmed their accuracy. While he could not be sure of every word, he said, the Spanish translation appearing in the book published in Cuba had not changed the meaning. This meant that the scenario as portrayed publicly by the Defense Department about the encounter with the Cubans was quite different from the scenario as it appeared in the communications between the State Department and Cuba.

Although the media had not focused on the details of the encounter with the Cubans, one Ranger commander had been interviewed. His version of events had us initiating the action. Major Jim Holt, who arrived at Point Salines on the morning of October 25 as a battalion executive officer, told a reporter that it was part of the Rangers' battle plan to seize the Cuban dormitory area. The first objective Holt's unit was assigned after landing, he recounted, was to seize the Cuban workers' living area.[14]

More light was shed on the question when Congress became interested in the Grenada operation. William S. Lind, an aide to Senator Gary Hart of Colorado, wrote a report critical of our tactics in Grenada. The Joint Chiefs of Staff, over the signature of Chairman John W. Vessey, Jr., sent a point-by-point rebuttal to the House Armed Services Committee.

One of Lind's charges was that the Rangers attacked the Cubans frontally, whereas, he said, they should have attacked from the flanks. The Joint Chiefs responded:

> B Co., 1st Ranger Battalion, 75th Infantry, on the western flank of the runway, started rolling up the flank of the Cuban defensive position from west to east by 0700. The company first sergeant led a three-man team to assault a Cuban position, killing two Cubans and capturing 28 more. B Co. rolled up the Cuban defenses until they reached the main Cuban camp. Ranger snipers took Cuban mortar positions under fire and killed or wounded 18 Cubans at ranges of 600–1,000 meters.[15]

So the Joint Chiefs were saying that the Rangers did not attack the Cubans frontally but from the western flank. This was an acknowledgement that it was the Rangers who had initiated the attack. The Joint Chiefs admitted, in fact, that although "the principal military mission" was "to rescue U.S. citizens and other foreign nationals," "in order to achieve this objective, Cuban and Grenadian forces would have to be neutralized and a stable situation on the island achieved." As for the Cuban workers housed at Point Salines, "the plan called for the capture of the two air-fields on Grenada to include the immediate neutralization of Cuban forces at Point Salines Airfield." This confirmed Major Holt's statement that his unit had been ordered to take the Cuban dormitory area. Moreover, the Joint Chiefs acknowledged that the Rangers had succeeded: "The surprise airborne assault on Point Salines Airfield by the Rangers effectively neu-tralized Cuban forces at the outset and led to the capture of several hun-dred Cubans despite stiff resistance."[16]

I asked the workers at Puerto Escondido how their twenty-four fellow workers had come to be killed at Point Salines. They were shot, I was told, "at different times during the day, mostly in the afternoon. Most were shot from helicopters." News accounts confirmed that the Cubans had been killed by "naval guns, land-based artillery, Cobra helicopter gunships, AC130 gunships and jets from the carrier."[17] The Rangers, anx-ious to avoid close combat, called in jets and helicopter gunships to strafe the workers. The gunships "operated with impunity, destroying, with heavy casualties, the main Cuban position at the Point Salines airfield."[18]

Early reports on the Ranger-Cuban fighting were that it was heavy, reinforcing the impression the Defense Department was suggesting, that the Cubans were part of the defense of Grenada. But the *Washington Post* wrote later that "early impressions and reports on the scale and intensity of the action" were "exaggerated by the military, by the news media whose information initially was limited to what the Pentagon provided, and by pre-invasion reports by the Grenadian junta of a coming blood-bath, coupled with post-invasion Cuban propaganda about the fighting."[19]

Why would the Defense Department exaggerate the numbers and ferocity of the fighting by the Cuban workers? Military action that could be attributed to Cuba supported the administration's claim that Cuba was building up Grenada as a bastion to export revolution. The Cuban government did, to be sure, order the workers to fire back if fired upon, and a Cuban colonel even went to Grenada shortly before the invasion to help the workers plan a defense. Cuban leader Fidel Castro, when he learned that a U.S. armada was approaching Grenada, sent the workers a message dated October 22, which he made public at a press conference:

> If the United States intervenes, we must vigorously defend ourselves as if we were in Cuba... in our camp sites and our work places close by, but only if we are directly attacked. I repeat: only if we are directly attacked. We would thus be defending ourselves, not the Government or its deeds. If the Yankees land on the runway section near the university or on its surroundings to evacuate their citizens, fully refrain from interfering.[20]

This message had apparently been conveyed to the workers as well. The NBC television program "First Camera," which aired on October 30, interviewed Dr. Raul Jimenez, an instructor at the medical school, who said he encountered a Cuban worker near the Cuban dormitories early in the morning of October 25, just before the Rangers landed. Dr. Jimenez saw that the Cubans had taken up positions with weapons; when he asked one of them what they were doing, the worker replied that the United States was going to land, but that the Cubans "would not fire unless they were fired upon."

Castro's statement that the Cubans should defend themselves but "not the Government or its deeds" seems curious at first blush, but is understandable in the context of the complex politics of the situation. Castro had been close to Maurice Bishop, the assassinated Grenadan leader, and he was appalled at Bishop's overthrow and death. The new Grenadan leaders, who, like Castro, knew we were about to attack, asked Castro to help defend them, at least by having the construction workers participate in the defense of Grenada alongside the Grenadan army. Castro refused, telling them, "the political situation created inside the country due to the people's estrangement on account of the death of Bishop and other leaders, isolation from the outside world, etc., considerably weakens the country's defense capabilities."[21]

The administration had tried to make it appear that Cuba was the major support behind the new Grenadan government, suggesting that those who overthrew Bishop were even more in the Cuban camp than Bishop himself had been.[22] But Cuba was not willing to defend the new Grenadan government from an invasion. Castro reasoned that because the Grenadan people were not supportive of this new leadership group, "the present military and political conditions are the worst for organizing a firm and efficient resistance against the invaders, an action which is practically impossible without the people's participation."[23] Recalling the Bay of Pigs, and how Cubans rushed to the beach to defend Cuba, Castro did not expect Grenadans to do the same. Disgusted with the new Grenadan leaders, Castro began to withdraw technical aid personnel.[24]

Although Castro was unwilling to defend Grenada, he did not want U.S. forces to capture the Cuban workers. In a message to Ferch on October 22, the first in the series of communications the two sides would exchange, Castro expressed concern about the construction workers. Like the other notes, it was not published, or publicly acknowledged, by the administration. In the note, Castro said he wanted to avoid any confrontation between the Cuban workers and our forces if they invaded Grenada. Castro was aware of the administration's "concern about the numerous U.S. residents there," adding, "we are also concerned about the hundreds of Cuban cooperation personnel working there in different fields and about the news that U.S. naval forces are approaching Grenada." Castro suggested that Cuba and the United States should "keep in touch on this matter, so as to contribute to solve favorably any difficulty that may arise or action that may be taken relating to the security of these individuals, without violence or intervention in the country."[25]

Thus, Castro offered to remain in communication to avert conflict with the workers. The administration did not reply to that message. I asked Ferch why. Ferch told me that he thought Castro's message was "bizarre," and that it did not require a response.

While it told the workers not to defend Grenada, the Cuban government did advise them to fire back if fired upon. That seemed to me a foolhardy decision, given the overwhelming firepower of the U.S. forces.

I asked Cuban Deputy Foreign Minister Ricardo Alarcón about this when I was in Havana, and he told me what he had said in a published interview: the defense was "intended to have a demonstration effect. The Americans now have to think of how many thousands of battalions they would need to subjugate Cuba or Nicaragua if all their technical and logistical strength hasn't enabled them to take Grenada."[26] So Cuba had not forgotten the Bay of Pigs.

Early in the invasion, the Defense Department claimed that up to five hundred Cuban workers fled from their dormitories into mountainous areas to take up a Che Guevara-style guerrilla campaign against the U.S. forces. For several days after the invasion the press carried these reports. Later the Defense Department acknowledged that it never had information about such a guerrilla campaign. It did not explain why the story had been released in the first place. During the fighting, however, these stories served a useful purpose for the Reagan administration by reinforcing the impression that Grenada was a Cuban bastion.[27]

While the fighting continued, the Defense Department excluded the press from Grenada, giving the administration "full opportunity to manage the news to its best advantage," as one reporter complained. The administration distorted events to create "the impression conveyed to the world that the bulk of the fighting was done by Cuban troops and that Grenadian resistance had been minimal."[28]

Another black mark against Cuba was accounts of large caches of arms in Grenada. According to President Reagan, we encountered "weapons and ammunition...enough to supply thousands of terrorists."[29] Since Grenada did not need such weaponry for defense, Reagan inferred that it must have been planning to invade other Caribbean islands. According to an assessment later by the CIA, however, the arms were too few and too outdated for much offense.[30] When reporters were allowed to see them in a warehouse in Grenada, they concurred with the assessment. Later the Defense Department displayed captured weapons at Andrews Air Force Base near Washington, but soon closed the exhibit because no one was impressed.

After the Grenada invasion, the new government completed the Point Salines airport, which began handling tourist flights. Thus, as the prior government had said, the long new runway was to bring in those who would drink rum and coke. The CIA provided money to organize elections in Grenada, but in a way that would bring in a friendly government.[31] That was hardly necessary, because most Grenadans welcomed the invasion. Had we invaded while Bishop was alive, Grenadans might have objected; but when we did strike, they were, as Reagan well knew, angry over the assassination of Bishop and the violence that accompanied his overthrow. Once we were in occupation, Grenadans hoped we would take the tiny country under our wing and pour in investment and aid. Perhaps they had struck it rich. A year passed, however, and then two and three, without much investment or aid. The glow began to fade.

NOTES

1. John Quigley, "Parachutes at Dawn: Issues of Use of Force and Status of Internees in the United States-Cuban Hostilities on Grenada, 1983," *University of Miami Inter-American Law Review* 17 (1986): 199.

2. Stuart Taylor, Jr., "Treatment of Prisoners Is Defended," *New York Times*, October 29, 1983, p. A7, col. 1.

3. *Situation in Lebanon and Grenada*, Hearings before a Subcommittee of the House Committee on Appropriations, 98th Cong., 1st sess. (1983), pp. 39–40.

4. Taylor, "Treatment of Prisoners Is Defended."

5. *Situation in Grenada*, Hearings before the Senate Committee on Foreign Relations, 98th Cong., 1st sess. (1983), p. 16.

6. Fred Hiatt and David Hoffman, "U.S. Drops Estimate of Cubans on Island," *Washington Post*, October 30, 1983, p. Al, col. 5.

7. Editorial de Ciencias Sociales (Havana), *Grenada: The World Against the Crime* (1983), p. 41.

8. "Situation in Grenada," *UN Chronicle* 20 (December 1983): 18.

9. U.S. Marine Corps Development and Education Command Newsletter: *Operational Overview*, January–March 1984, p. 31.

10. William Berry, "Ten Days of Urgent Fury," *All Hands*, May 1984, p. 23.

11. P. Bourne, "Was the U.S. Invasion Necessary?" *Los Angeles Times*, November 6, 1983, p. IV3, col. 4.

12. "National and Foreign Press Interview Cuban Wounded in Grenada," *Granma Weekly Review*, November 13, 1983, p. 7, col. 1.

13. *Grenada: The World Against the Crime*, p.41.

14. "Grenada: Now the American Model," *Los Angeles Times*, November 6, 1983, p. Al, col. 5.

15. "JCS Replies to Criticism of Grenada Operation," *Army*, August 1984, p. 32.

16. Ibid., pp. 29–30.

17. Richard Harwood, "Tidy U.S. War Ends: 'We Blew Them Away,'" *Washington Post*, November 6, 1983, p. Al, col. 4.

18. Drew Middleton, "Operation on Grenada: How Forces Performed," *New York Times*, October 28, 1983, p. A12, col. 1.

19. Harwood, "Tidy U.S. War Ends: 'We Blew Them Away.'"

20. *Grenada: The World Against the Crime*, p. 34; "Cuba Says Troops End Resistance," *Washington Post*, October 27, 1983, p. Al, col. 6.

21. *Grenada: The World Against the Crime*, pp. 34–35.

22. Jonathan Kwitny, *Endless Enemies: The Making of an Unfriendly World* (1984), p. 409.

23. *Grenada: The World Against the Crime*, pp. 34–35.

24. Kwitny, *Endless Enemies*, p. 417.

25. *Grenada: The World Against the Crime*, pp. 35–36.

26. Alma Guillermoprieto, "Havana Seeks to Turn Loss in Grenada into a Moral Victory," *Washington Post*, October 30, 1983, p. A10, col. 1.

27. Hugh O'Shaughnessy, *Grenada: Revolution, Invasion and Aftermath* (1984), p. 210.

28. Ibid., p. 204.

29. Ronald Reagan, "America's Commitment to Peace," October 27, 1983, DSB, vol. 83, p. 4 (December 1983).

30. Bob Woodward, *Veil: The Secret Wars of the CIA 1981-1987* (1987), p. 299.

31. Ibid., p.300.

26. LIBYA: QADDAFI'S AIR CONDITIONER

On the night of April 14, 1986, thirty-three American bombers lit up the skies over Libya. While navy jets flying from an aircraft carrier in the Mediterranean bombed two military bases near the city of Benghazi, air force F-111 bombers flying from Great Britain hit three targets in

Tripoli, the capital city. President Reagan described the targets as "terrorist facilities," by which he meant that they were connected with terrorist attacks abroad by Libya. The Tripoli targets, said the White House, were command and control systems: intelligence-gathering, communication, and logistics and training facilities.[1]

The Libyan government said the bombing killed 37 people and wounded 93.[2] Hit, apparently by accident, was a residential district of Tripoli near the French embassy, which accounted for many of the casualties.[3]

As justification for the raid, the administration accused Libya of arranging an explosion, on April 5, 1986, in a West Berlin nightclub, in which an American serviceman and a Turkish woman were killed, and two hundred other patrons were injured.[4] The White House claimed to have intercepted a message between Libya and the Libyan mission in East Berlin acknowledging the Libyan government's role.[5] The intercepts reportedly had unnamed persons in Berlin transmitting to Libya on April 4 that "we have something planned that will make you happy," and several hours later, "an event occurred. You will be pleased with the result."

Secretary of Defense Caspar Weinberger and Secretary of State George Shultz claimed that only minutes prior to the explosion at the nightclub, police, acting on the basis of the intercepts, were on the streets in Berlin and nearly prevented the explosion.[6] But the deputy chief of West Berlin's military police said that the information in the intercepts was too general for any such operation. Despite Weinberger and Shultz's claim, there had been no police on the streets as a result of intercepts.[7]

Libya denied involvement. The West German government, although it knew what information we had, could not immediately trace a Libyan hand.[8] The chief of Germany's anti-terrorist police doubted that Libya was responsible.[9]

In the United Nations Security Council, a number of delegates criticized the U.S. raid and expressed doubts about its evidence. A Security Council resolution to condemn the United States for aggression received nine votes out of fifteen; but it was vetoed by France, Great Britain, and the United States.[10] In November, the UN General Assembly passed a resolution condemning the raid.[11]

Some Reagan administration officials doubted the information about Libya and the disco bombing. Journalist Seymour Hersh reported that a number of them, although refusing to speak for attribution, expressed skepticism. The intercepted messages were vague, they said, and they doubted that Libya would target the particular nightclub, because it was frequented by many black GIs. In addition, the intercepts had been speeded from the National Security Agency, which first obtained them, to the White House, without being evaluated by experts. Normal procedure is to analyze such information carefully before going public with it.[12] Thus, at the time of the raid the information on which the administration acted was not overwhelming.[13]

German police continued to investigate, and in 2001, a German court convicted four persons in the disco bombing. Two of them had connections to the Libyan bureau in East Berlin.[14] Judge Peter Marhofer, announcing the conviction, cited the intercepts from the Libyan bureau in East Berlin, including one that referred to an attack "with as many victims as possible." Whether the court was able to assess these intercepts appropriately was not clear, because German and US authorities had declined to provide more detailed information that Judge Marhofer thought should have been given to the court. Marhofer referred to the lack of cooperation as a "disappointment." Nonetheless, Marhofer said there was enough evidence to convict. The court also cited an incriminating statement from one of the suspects.[15]

The intercepted message of April 4 from the Libyan East Berlin bureau to Libya was assessed and translated by German police in 1986. The *London Observer* reported at the time that the German police version of the intercept was less specific than President Reagan's. According to the *Observer*, the message simply read, "Something will happen tomorrow when Allah wills." The *Observer* obtained the actual intercepts in Washington and concluded that President Reagan made the messages seem more directly related to the disco bombing than they actually were. Wrote the *Observer*, "on the basis of extracts of the messages leaked in Washington and Bonn last week, it appears that the American government massaged the evidence."[16]

In 2004, at a time when Libya was mending fences with the West, Libya agreed with the German government to pay compensation for German and other, though not American, victims of the disco bombing. It still disclaimed responsibility for the bombing, however.[17]

As additional justification for the Libya raid, the administration claimed that Libya planned to attack thirty U.S. targets in various countries. Libyans, it said, had surveilled embassies and commercial installations in Africa, Europe, the Middle East, and Latin America. The White House said it could not, on security considerations, give details about these plans.[18] The media did not press the matter, and no evidence to prove or disprove this charge ever surfaced.

Skepticism about the administration's information abounded, however, because of our long-standing efforts to get rid of the Libyan leader,

Colonel Moammar Qaddafi. For several years, the CIA had encouraged Libyan exile groups to overthrow Qaddafi, and to kill him if necessary.[19] In 1985, the Reagan administration asked Egypt to invade Libya to overthrow Qaddafi, but Egyptian President Hosni Mubarak declined.[20]

Some evidence that the disco bombing may have been a makeweight comes from the fact that in January 1986, Donald Fortier, an aide to National Security Advisor John Poindexter, told *Newsweek* magazine that the administration was preparing military action against Libya and was merely waiting for a pretext to strike. At that time, Libyan assets in the United States were frozen and U.S. citizens ordered out of Libya, so that they would not be hurt during an attack.[21] Also in January 1986, the administration said that Libya was responsible for shootings the previous December at the ticket counters of the Israeli El Al airline at the Vienna and Rome airports. The shootings left twenty dead, including five American citizens. It was apparently immediately after the Rome and Vienna incidents that the White House geared up for the attack it launched on April 14.[22]

In early 1986, apparently to lay a foundation for the planned raid, Secretary of State Shultz argued that the United States had a right to use military force against states that support terrorism, and in particular to deter anticipated terrorist attacks. State Department lawyers elaborated on Shultz's argument, setting the legal groundwork for a military attack on Libya. At the same time, to better monitor Libyan communications, the administration sent a new spy satellite into orbit over Libya.[23]

In February and March 1986, the administration positioned planes and ships near Libya in a campaign of pressure. On March 24, it sent a guided missile cruiser into waters claimed by Libya, accompanied overhead by jet fighters.[24] The alleged message about the disco bombing was intercepted March 25.[25] If Libya was indeed responsible for the bombing, it might have acted in response to what it considered provocative military action by the United States.

Suspicions about U.S. intentions heightened four months after the raid, when the administration released reports that Libya was increasing terrorist activity, and that we might attack again, or else that Colonel

Qaddafi might be overthrown. The stories apparently were "plants," in the jargon of the propaganda business, as the administration knew that Libya was not increasing terrorist activity, nor did it have information that Qaddafi was about to be toppled. According to a memorandum that John Poindexter sent to President Reagan, the idea was to mount a "disinformation program" (Poindexter's term) to make Colonel Qaddafi think that internal opposition to him was growing, that key aides were disloyal, and that we would move against him militarily. This would make Colonel Qaddafi "paranoid and ineffective" and "embolden" forces in Libya that might overthrow him.[26] The administration said that its purpose was to deceive Qaddafi, not to deceive the public. However, the fact that it had planted false stories regarding Libyan terrorism raised the question whether earlier accusations against Libya were also part of a disinformation campaign.

For several years previously, in fact, the Reagan White House had been making questionable allegations against Qaddafi. In 1981, CIA Director William Casey was the intelligence officer for a secret task force the administration had set up on Libya. Casey told the task force he had information that Libya was organizing "hit teams" to assassinate administration officials. News stories began to appear, apparently based on leaks from the administration, that such teams had arrived in the United States. Some members of the task force suspected that Casey had fabricated the information, and no evidence came to light to confirm it.[27]

In January 1986, when the administration imposed economic sanctions on Libya, it allegedly had "irrefutable evidence" that Libya was behind the recent shootings at the Vienna and Rome airports. When asked to describe his evidence, President Reagan replied, "There are things that should not be revealed." While the perpetrators had not been Libyan, Reagan said, "these murderers could not carry out their crimes without the sanctuary and support provided by regimes such as Col. Qaddafi's in Libya."[28]

It appeared from other sources that the "evidence" the administration had on the Rome and Vienna operations was three passports found on the Vienna attackers. One passport had been lost in Libya eight years before by a Tunisian laborer, and the other two had been seized by Libyan authorities from Tunisians earlier in 1985. The interior ministers of Italy and Austria said at a joint news conference that they did not think that this or other evidence established Libyan involvement in the Rome or Vienna incidents.[29] The White House urged the foreign ministers of Greece and Germany to make formal accusations against Libya, but they declined.[30] The fact that other governments with an interest in finding the perpetrators did not take the administration's information suggested that the administration was overplaying its evidence.

Responsibility for the Rome and Vienna attacks was never determined. Some information that emerged suggested they were carried out by Palestinians recruited by the organization of Abu Nidal, who were from the refugee camps in Beirut where the Lebanese Phalange militia killed Palestinian civilians during Israel's 1982 invasion.[31] As we saw earlier, Palestinians held the United States to blame for those killings, because it did not protect the refugees after the PLO withdrew from Beirut. The Palestinians reportedly trained in the Bekaa Valley of Lebanon, a territory under the occupation of Syria, the country in which the Abu Nidal group is based.[32]

The Reagan administration was less than candid about what our bombers hit in Libya. It said that we were going after "terrorist infrastructure," and announced three targets in Tripoli and two in Benghazi.

Of these five targets, the one to which the administration directed the greatest firepower was the El-Azziziya barracks in Tripoli. Although the White House did not admit this publicly, this barracks contained the family compound of Colonel Qaddafi. The administration denied that it was trying to kill Qaddafi,[33] but circumstances suggested the contrary. According to one official, "we hoped we would get him, but nobody was sure where he would be that night."[34] Seymour Hersh, who interviewed seventy administration officials about the raid, concluded that Qaddafi was the primary target.[35]

The administration sent nine F-111s to bomb the El-Azziziya barracks, the highest number of planes for any of the five targets. In the planning for the raid, President Reagan picked El-Azziziya at the last minute from a list of potential targets. El-Azziziya was not favored as a target by the Defense Department because it had minimal military significance and was in a crowded downtown area of Tripoli.[36] Of the nine planes slated to hit El-Azziziya, two were to target Colonel Qaddafi's house, aiming for an air conditioning unit on the roof that was visible from the air.[37] Although the F-111s did not manage a direct hit on Qaddafi's residence, they landed several bombs within a few yards of it, injuring several family members and killing an adopted daughter of Qaddafi.[38]

Whatever the targets, the Libya raid was structured in a way that made it almost certain there would be civilian casualties. One target was a command post in a densely populated section of downtown Benghazi, while the El-Azziziya barracks was located in a densely populated section of Tripoli.[39]

It was one of the F-111s aiming for El-Azziziya, in fact, that hit the neighborhood near the French embassy. The administration called this a mistake, and Secretary Shultz "regretted" the casualties.[40] Secretary of Defense Caspar Weinberger, however, denied that it was the F-111s that had killed civilians near the French embassy, claiming instead that the deaths could have been caused by Libyan anti-aircraft missiles falling to earth.[41]

The administration planned the raid for nighttime hours, because it expected Libyan anti-aircraft defenses to be down. Operating at night, however, made visibility more difficult and made it more likely that bombs would miss their targets. The F-111s were to bomb while flying at 600 m.p.h., so that any timing error would put a bomb off target. The fact that El-Azziziya was chosen as a target only a few days before the raid meant that there was no time for precision planning.[42]

During the early months of 1986, the air force trained highly experienced pilots for the Libya raid, giving them practice on long-range flights from England to Turkey. Late in the preparations, however, when the White House learned it would not be able to use French airspace to fly from England to Libya, it decided to increase the number of F-111s from six to eighteen. This meant that the air force had to use less experienced pilots who had not been trained for the mission. This change increased the chance of bombing errors.[43] Bombing at night, at high speed, in congested areas, by pilots with inadequate training, meant that mistakes and civilian casualties were to be anticipated.

NOTES

1. "Announcement by Speakes," *New York Times*, April 15, 1986, p. A13, col. 5.

2. "Pentagon Details 2-Pronged Attack," *New York Times*, April 15, 1986, p. Al, col. 5.

3. Seymour Hersh, "Target Qaddafi," *New York Times*, February 22, 1987, p. F17, col. 1.

4. "Announcement by Speakes."

5. Bob Woodward, *Veil: The Secret Wars of the CIA 1981–1987* (1987), pp. 444–45.

6. "Joint News Conference by Secretary Shultz and Secretary Weinberger, April 14,1986," DSB, vol. 86, p. 5 (June 1986).

7. Bill Schaap, "Disinforming the World on Libya," *Covert Action Information Bulletin*, No. 30 (Summer 1988): 71.

8. Bernard Gwertzman, "Plots on Global Scale Charged," *New York Times*, April 15, 1986, p. Al, col. 3.

9. Hersh, "Target Qaddafi."

10. SCOR, 41st yr., 2682nd mtg., p. 43, UN Doc. S/PV.2682 (1986).

11. Res. 41/38, GAOR, 41st yr., Supplement No. 53, p. 34, UN Doc. A/41/53 (1987).

12. Hersh, "Target Qaddafi."

13. Schaap, "Disinforming the World on Libya," p. 76.

14. Steven Erlanger, "4 Guilty in Fatal 1986 Berlin Disco Bombing Linked to Libya, *New York Times*, November 14, 2001, p. 7.

15. Derek Scally, "West Berlin Disco Bombers Sentenced," *Irish Times*, November 14, 2001, p. 11.

16. Catherine Field, Tony Catterall, and Ian Mather, "Disco Bomb Evidence 'Massaged,'" *Observer* (London), April 27, 1986, p. 14.

17. Tony Czuczka, "Libya Pays Pounds 19m to Disco Bomb Victims" *Independent* (London), August 11, 2004, p. 21.

18. Gwertzman, "Plots on Global Scale Charged."

19. Hersh, "Target Qaddafi."

20. David Martin and John Walcott, *Best Laid Plans: The Inside Story of America's War against Terrorism* (1988), pp. 265–66; Bob Woodward and Don Oberdorfer, "State Dept. Acted to Block U.S.-Egypt Attack on Libya; White House Envisioned Aiding a 1985 Invasion," *Washington Post*, February 20, 1987, p. Al, col. 1.

21. Harry Anderson, "Get Tough: The Reagan Plan: Clearing the Way for Military Action—If Necessary," *Newsweek*, January 20, 1986, p. 16.

22. Martin and Walcott, *Best Laid Plans*, p. 268; Bill Keller, "State Dept. Study on Terror Group Cites Libyan Link," *New York Times*, January 1, 1986, p. Al, col. 3.

23. Hersh, "Target Qaddafi."

24. Martin and Walcott, *Best Laid Plans*, pp. 279–81.

25. Ibid., p. 289.

26. Bob Woodward, "Gadhafi Target of Secret U.S. Deception Plan; Elaborate Campaign Included Disinformation that Appeared as Fact in American Media," *Washington Post*, October 2, 1986, P. Al, col. 2.

27. Hersh, "Target Qaddafi."

28. "President's News Conference on Foreign and Domestic Issues," *New York Times*, January 8, 1986, p. A6, col. 1.

29. Loren Jenkins, "Airport Terrorists Reportedly Trained in Syrian-Controlled Area," *Washington Post*, January 11, 1986, p. Al, col. 2.

30. John Tagliabue, "West Germans Decline U.S. Bid to Join in Moves against Libya," *New York Times*, January 22, 1986, p. A4, col. 1 (Germany); Paul Lewis, "The French Offer a Pledge on Libya," *New York Times*, January 23, 1986, p. A6, col. 1 (Greece).

31. Lou Cannon and Don Oberdorfer, "U.S. Seeks to Temper Response by Israel," *Washington Post*, December 29, 1985, p. Al, col. 6; Martin and Walcott, *Best Laid Plans*, p. 267.

32. Martin and Walcott, *Best Laid Plans*, pp. 268, 289.

33. "Joint News Conference by Secretary Shultz and Secretary Weinberger, April 14, 1986," DSB, vol. 86, p. 4 (June 1986).

34. George C. Wilson, "Qaddafi Was a Target of U.S. Raid," *Washington Post*, April 18, 1986, p. Al, col. 6.

35. Hersh, "Target Qaddafi."

36. Martin and Walcott, *Best Laid Plans*, pp. 287–88.

37. Ibid., pp. 293–95.

38. Bernard Weinraub, "U.S. Jets Hit 'Terrorist Centers' in Libya," *New York Times*, April 15, 1986, p. Al, col. 6; Martin and Walcott, *Best Laid Plans*, p. 310.

39. Martin and Walcott, *Best Laid Plans*, p. 287.

40. "'Worldnet' Interview with Secretary Shultz, April 16, 1986," DSB, vol. 86, p. 9 (June 1986).

41. Martin and Walcott, *Best Laid Plans*, p. 309.

42. Ibid., pp. 286–87.

43. Ibid., p. 293.

27. The Philippines: Shoring Cory

While many U.S. administrations have elected to use force to try to remove an unwanted government, rarely has force been used to keep a favored government in power. That, however, is what the President George H.W. Bush did in December 1989 in the Philippines when elements of the Filipino army mounted a coup attempt against the new and fragile government of President Corazon Aquino. The Reagan administration had helped facilitate Aquino's accession to power to replace former strongman Ferdinand Marcos, and Bush was anxious to keep her from being removed. Shortly after the coup plotters made their move, Bush ordered jet fighters at our Clark Air Force Base in the Philippines into the air to shoot down any rebel planes that might get off the ground.

At that point, the rebels had not used any aircraft, but Bush wanted to make sure they did not strafe ground troops loyal to Aquino. The tactic worked: the rebels did not get any planes into the air, and quickly the coup attempt ended.[1] While our scrambling of jets predictably drew a favorable reaction from the Aquino government, several Manila newspapers criticized us for interfering in Philippines politics.[2] A former spokesperson for the late President Ferdinand Marcos said President Aquino's "most urgent and nearly exclusive concern is her physical and political survival, and only Washington's continued support can ensure it," by which he meant that Aquino's request for U.S. protection revealed a shaky political posture.[3]

The White House did not disguise our role. It explained why we decided to get involved. At President Aquino's request, President Bush had "authorized U.S. military assistance to the government of the Philippines in defending itself against a coup attempt," adding, "This assistance is intended to allow the democratically elected government of the Philippines to restore order. The President also is determined to protect the lives of Americans in the Philippines."[4] Thus, the stated aims were twofold: to protect an elected government and to protect U.S. citizens.

President Bush was, indeed, trying to keep President Aquino in power; like Reagan before him, Bush viewed the Aquino government as one that would protect U.S. interests without being as authoritarian as the Marcos government had been. In particular, the administration thought that Aquino could effectively combat a long-standing leftist insurgency in the Philippines that was a potential threat to American investments and commercial interests. In addition, Bush viewed Aquino as being favorable to our continued use of two large military bases in the Philippines.

As for the second reason for intervening, the White House statement did not explain how our intervention would protect "the lives of Americans." No Americans in the Philippines had been harmed or threatened. The administration did not indicate what danger our citizens might be in, or how the jet overflights or the defeat of the rebels might avert it. Bush did not organize an evacuation of American citizens or take any measures to protect them in the places where they lived and worked.

Street fighting had occurred, to be sure, in a commercial district of Manila, and that district included hotels and apartments occupied by Americans. The administration might have been concerned that the rebels would harm our citizens, but the rebels were politically to the right of President Aquino. Their political position was not hostile to the United States; to allay fears—and probably in the hope of stopping U.S. intervention—they issued a statement that "the United States of America is not our enemy."[5] If the rebels did harbor any grievance against the United States, it was that we were intervening to keep them down.

Because of the street fighting, there was a potential danger that U.S. citizens might be caught up in it; indeed, at one point in the fighting, the rebels took over Manila's commercial district. Had the Aquino government tried to retake it by force, civilians might have been caught up. However, that danger never came to pass, because on December 5, a truce was negotiated to allow foreign nationals to leave, including those from the United States.[6]

Even if there had been a real danger, flying jets overhead was not likely to help, since overflights would not get American citizens out of the commercial district. Bush might have thought that by helping to put down the rebellion, Manila would more quickly become safer for our citizens; but at the same time, intervening ran the risk of turning the rebels against us. From what information is available, it seems unlikely that protecting Americans residing in the Philippines was a genuine aim of the intervention. As we have seen, prior administrations sending troops abroad invoked the need to protect U.S. citizens, a rationale that strikes a sympathetic chord with the American public.

Beyond shoring up the Aquino administration, there was another likely motivation for the intervention that Bush did not mention. In 1989, the United States and the Philippines were about to begin negotiations to extend the lease in the Philippines on the Clark Air Force Base and the Subic Naval Base.

These two bases were the largest U.S. military facilities outside the United States, and in the Philippines they were a political hot potato. Many Filipinos objected to the bases and wanted the leases terminated, seeing in them an unnecessary militarization of their country. Some Filipinos feared that, just as with the 1989 coup attempt, the United States would interfere in Philippines politics by using the forces stationed at these bases. Even if the United States did not actually use the troops, their presence and potential use was an ever-present threat looming over the Philippines' political scene.

The bases themselves were the product of prior military intervention in the Philippines. During the Spanish-American war, we drove Spain out as ruler of the Philippines. The Filipinos, happy to be free from

Spanish control, expected us to leave as well. When we did not, Filipino guerrillas waged a bloody campaign against us. We put it down, inflicting several hundred thousand casualties on the Filipinos, and then we turned the Philippines into a colony. In 1946, we withdrew; but as a condition of our leaving, we made the Philippines give us leases for military bases.

Filipino critics of the bases charged that by asking for our help to put down the 1989 coup attempt, President Aquino jeopardized her bargaining position regarding the bases.[7] The *New York Times* saw the situation that way too: the intervention, it said approvingly, "created a new atmosphere for negotiations on the future of United States military bases in the Philippines."[8] Rep. Stephen Solarz, chair of the House foreign affairs subcommittee on Asia and the Pacific, said that our intervention would put the base negotiations "in an entirely different context," because it showed the Filipinos that we could intervene quickly to protect democracy.[9] By saving President Aquino from the coup, the Bush administration increased her dependence on the United States and thus strengthened our hand in the base negotiations.

Any advantage the United States gained from putting down the coup turned out to be ephemeral, however. The differences between the United States and the Philippines on the bases issue were sharp, even with Aquino at the helm. While Philippines Foreign Secretary Raul Manglapus called for our departure from Clark Air Force Base by late 1991, and from Subic Naval Base by 1996 to 1998, U.S. negotiator Richard Armitage insisted that we keep both bases until 2001 or 2003, with a continued lower-level presence indefinitely into the future.[10]

In June 1991, Mount Pinatubo, a long-dormant volcano, erupted, virtually destroying Clark Air Force Base and seriously damaging Subic. The eruption, plus the Aquino government's opposition to the bases, led the Bush administration to abandon them.

NOTES

1. Criselda Yabes, "Manila Turns Back Coup Bid with Help of U.S. Air Power," *Washington Post*, December 2, 1989, p. Al, col. 6; Bob Woodward, *The Commanders* (1991), pp. 146–52.

2. Sheila Coronel, "Coup Fails, Manila Says amid Fighting," *New York Times*, December 4, 1989, p. Al6, col. 1.

3. Jeremy Clift, "U.S. and Philippines Far Apart on Future of Bases," *Reuters*, September 21, 1990, BC cycle.

4. "Bush OKs Military Aid for Aquino; U.S. Jets Fly over Filipino Bases," *Chicago Tribune*, December 1, 1989, p. Al, col. 2.

5. David E. Sanger, "Cease-Fire in Manila Allows for Evacuation of Foreigners," *New York Times*, December 6, 1989, p. Al, col. 1.

6. Bob Drogin and Mark Fineman, "Foreigners Evacuated under Truce in Manila," *Los Angeles Times*, December 6, 1989, p. Al, col. 3.

7. "Philippine Bases Negotiator Defends U.S. Military Help," *Reuter Library Report*, BC cycle, December 17, 1989.

8. Robert Pear, "The U.S. Stake in the Philippines," *New York Times*, December 17, 1989, p. D3, col. 3.

9. David B. Ottoway, "U.S. Bases Rarely Used to Save Host Government; Effect on Philippine Negotiations Unclear," *Washington Post*, December 3, 1989, p. A30, col. 5.

10. Fernando Del Mundo, "Philippines Favors Extension of Subic Lease," *UPI*, November 15, 1990, BC cycle.

28. Panama: Slaying a Monster

The Panama Canal lifts huge tankers up over the hills that separate the Atlantic Ocean in the west from the Pacific Ocean in the east. Yes, in Panama, the Atlantic is west of the Pacific—check your atlas. The Panama Canal is by any lights an engineering marvel. The canal is the more remarkable for having been built between 1904 and 1914, before modern earth-moving equipment. A French crew had tried to build a canal across Panama in the 1880s, but it was decimated by malaria and gave up. Our own crew overcame malaria before it could overcome the earth and rock.

On the political side, we did not match our human and engineering accomplishment. To obtain the right to build the canal, we wrested the territory away from Colombia, of which Panama was a part. First we negotiated with Colombia and got its government to sign a treaty to let us build a canal across Panama.[1] But Colombia's Senate called the treaty a giveaway because it granted us virtual sovereignty for the area of the canal; therefore, the treaty was turned down.[2]

At that point the administration of Theodore Roosevelt approached some of Panama's prominent citizens, professional people of Spanish ancestry, who had aspirations to independence from Colombia. The administration told them that if they rebelled, our destroyers would stand

269

by offshore to neutralize the Colombian navy.[3] A rebellion was soon staged, and Colombia, as expected, sent ships to put it down. As the Colombian fleet approached Panama, they were met by American destroyers. The Roosevelt administration was true to its word.

The saga of how the U.S. Navy came out to meet the Colombian navy is omitted from many history books, but to me it was a childhood story. My grandfather, as a seventeen-year-old orphan, ran away to join the navy in 1903, lying about his age. His first ship was the USS *Wyoming*. Thin and agile, he could scamper up the ship's tall masts, a feat he was happy to recount to me. I had no reason to doubt him, because even in his eighties he could climb the apple trees in his yard. My grandfather was also fond of describing the ship's mortars, which he had studied and practiced hard to master.

In November 1903, before my grandfather had time to adjust fully to life on board ship, the *Wyoming* was dispatched to Panama as part of the armada sent by President Roosevelt. When the *Wyoming* came within sight of the Colombian ships, my grandfather was at the ready by his mortar. He was ordered to fire and did. The sounds and smells were as real to him when he related the story to me, as they had been when he stood on the ship's deck. He described the measurements of the mortar, how he aimed, and how the Colombian ships backed off.

The political issues did not attract my grandfather's attention at the time; but when the *Wyoming* and the rest of our fleet had accomplished their mission, Colombia had conceded Panama, and a new country was born.[4] Not unexpectedly, President Roosevelt found Panama more willing than Colombia to meet our terms. We drafted a treaty called the Isthmian Canal Convention. While the treaty did not quite give us the territory to build a canal, it came close: Panama granted the United States the rights it would have "if it were sovereign" in a ten-mile strip across Panama, "to the entire exclusion of the exercise by the Republic of Panama of any such sovereign rights, power or authority."[5]

We built the canal within our "sovereign" zone, and some years later we found room there for military bases as well. In the 1960s, these bases became the headquarters of the U.S. Southern Command, which used them as a center of operation for military action elsewhere in Latin America. We also used the bases to train Latin American troops in counterinsurgency tactics.

If the treaty deal seemed too good to be true, in the long run it turned out to be just that. The treaty left an undercurrent of resentment in Panama. In the 1960s, with anti-colonialist sentiment sweeping Africa, Asia, and Latin America, some Panamanians, largely from the lower (mixed-race) classes—not the professional classes on whom we had relied—took to the streets to protest our control of the canal and the zone.[6] The United Nations, now including African, Asian, and Latin countries as members, pressured us to give the zone back to Panama.

In 1977, President Carter, seeing the handwriting on the wall, signed two new treaties to redesign our relation with Panama. One was the Panama Canal Treaty, by which we gave the zone back to Panama immediately and agreed to phase out our control, turning it over completely to Panama on December 31, 1999.[7] The other agreement was the Treaty Concerning the Permanent Neutrality and Operation of the Panama Canal, which stipulated that Panama and the United States would jointly keep the canal open to world shipping, even after 1999, and that after 1999 we would close our military bases.[8]

For a time, all went well under the new treaties. In the 1980s, Panama's leader was General Manuel Noriega, a man with whom we could deal. Early in his military career, Noriega had moonlighted by informing U.S. intelligence agencies about leftist activities in Panama.[9] Once in power, General Noriega helped us fight the insurgency in El Salvador, and gave the CIA information about Nicaragua to help in our attacks there.[10]

Most important, General Noriega lent a hand with our Contra army, helping the CIA setup the second Contra army in Costa Rica and allowing Contras to train in Panama.[11] He also cooperated with the Drug Enforcement Administration (DEA), which was trying to stop cocaine from being smuggled through Panama from South America. The DEA learned, however, that even while General Noriega was helping us in anti-drug efforts, he was making a tidy profit for himself in the cocaine traffic.[12] Cuban accountant Ramón Milian Rodriguez, who was convicted of cocaine possession and drug-money laundering, testified before the Senate Foreign Relations Committee's Subcommittee on Terrorism, Narcotics, and International Operations that he delivered to General Noriega money from both the CIA and the Colombian drug cartel.[13]

Since, however, General Noriega was helping with the Contras, he was "our man" in Panama, because the Contras were our top priority.[14] When anyone in Washington raised concerns about General Noriega, CIA Director William Casey intervened to mention the Contras, which effectively ended the discussion.[15] And as we saw in our chapter on Nicaragua, the CIA itself was involved in the cocaine traffic as part of the aid package to the Contras.

Eventually, however, General Noriega apparently balked at some of the things we asked him to do. After the Contra southern front against Nicaragua in Costa Rica collapsed, the CIA wanted to reopen it; when the agency asked Noriega to help, he declined.[16] By 1986, the relationship with General Noriega had begun to sour.[17] When Noriega reportedly threatened to blow the lid off the CIA drug trafficking, a federal prosecutor in Florida indicted him *in absentia* in 1988 for cocaine smuggling.[18]

Concerned over a leader in a key country who now seemed recalcitrant, we huddled with Panamanian military officers who wanted to overthrow General Noriega.[19] To put pressure on Noriega, and hopefully to secure either his resignation or removal, the Reagan administration froze Panamanian government assets in American banks[20] and instructed U.S. citizens and companies in Panama not to pay their taxes there.[21] Although these sanctions put a crimp in Panama's economy, General Noriega remained in power.

Unlike Carter, Reagan had reservations about giving up the canal and our military bases in Panama in 1999. In 1987, J. Edward Fox, assistant secretary of state for legislative and intergovernmental affairs, thought that the State Department might try to renegotiate the 1977 treaties, in particular to continue our base rights after 1999. Fox stated that the domestic political situation in Panama might threaten stability in Central America, and that "steps should be taken to bring about the resignation of

General Noriega," replacing him with other military officers committed to "the safeguarding of U.S. strategic interests."[22] To the Reagan State Department, General Noriega had become an obstacle to renegotiating the canal treaties.

In May 1989, a presidential election was held in Panama, and a candidate loyal to General Noriega was challenged by Guillermo Endara, around whom most opposition groups stood united. By then our economic sanctions were causing havoc in Panama, and voters knew that if Endara was elected, we would lift them. Toward the end of the presidential campaign, the press reported that President Bush issued a secret finding to the CIA to funnel $10 million to Endara.[23] Although Bush refused to comment on the report, administration officials, speaking not for attribution, said that Bush approved the plan in February 1989 as part of his effort to bring Noriega down. Endara denied that he had received the funds.[24]

As Panamanians voted to choose a president in May 1989, international observers flooded the isthmus to watch the vote tally. Almost to a person, the observers said that Endara won. General Noriega, however, declared the elections null, citing the reports of CIA funding to Endara.[25] The Bush administration then asked the Organization of American States (OAS) to approach General Noriega on the matter,[26] and over a period of months the OAS repeatedly urged Noriega to yield authority to Endara.[27]

Relations with Panama went from bad to worse, as our military personnel stationed there experienced run-ins with Panamanian soldiers. Some of our civilian personnel working at the canal experienced harassment as well, and we complained to the UN Security Council.[28] We kept up political pressure on General Noriega, taking our case to the OAS that he had turned Panama into a "haven for drug traffickers."[29]

As an object lesson to General Noriega, and perhaps to provoke him, the U.S. Southern Command conducted highly visible military maneuvers in Panama, sending armored personnel carriers rumbling through city streets.[30] The Panamanian administration called this tactic intimidation, and complained to the Security Council that the maneuvers created "a state of imminent war" between Panama and the United States.[31]

Despite its efforts to convince General Noriega to resign, the OAS criticized our maneuvers as "inopportune."[32]

Conflict also developed over the administration of the canal. Under the Panama Canal Treaty, a Panamanian was to replace a U.S. citizen as canal administrator on January 1, 1990.[33] But the State Department refused to accept a canal administrator appointed by General Noriega, nor would we recognize the administration that took office in September 1989, since General Noriega had annulled the May presidential election. President Bush would accept no diplomatic correspondence from the Panamanian administration, including correspondence about the appointment of a canal administrator.[34] By refusing to accept a Noriega-appointed administrator, Bush hoped to bring down the Panamanian administration.[35]

As a further means of undermining Noriega, President Bush issued an order to halt the import of Panamanian sugar.[36] When an insurgent group formed among Panamanian military officers in neighboring Costa Rica to overthrow General Noriega, the CIA lent a hand.[37] In October, some Panamanian officers tried to raise a coup against General Noriega. We helped by blocking some roads; but the coup failed.[38]

By then, however, the Pentagon had begun final planning for an invasion to overthrow Noriega, and during November 1989, the assigned units rehearsed.[39] On December 1, Bush stepped up the economic pressure by announcing that we would not let Panama-registered ships dock at U.S. ports.[40] This was a major blow, because Panama turned a tidy profit by letting out its flag to foreign shippers as a "flag of convenience."[41] Viewing this as one more hostile act, Panama's National Assembly of District Representatives passed a resolution on December 15 "that the Republic of Panama is in a state of war while there is aggression against the people of Panama from the United States of America."[42] By "aggression," the Assembly meant our military maneuvers and economic sanctions.[43]

On December 16, a shooting incident occurred in Panama City. According to the Defense Department's account, four unarmed off-duty U.S. military officers driving in an automobile were out for dinner and got lost on their way home. Not knowing where they were, the officers drove up to a military checkpoint at the headquarters of the Panama Defense Force (PDF). PDF soldiers pointed weapons at them and reached into the automobile in a menacing fashion. In fear, the driver started up the car and drove through the checkpoint. The PDF soldiers fired after the car, killing one of the officers and wounding another.[44]

The PDF gave a different version of the shooting incident. According to its communique, the four U.S. officers were armed, and it was they who fired first, wounding two Panamanian civilians and one soldier.[45] Neither version of the story could be confirmed. The PDF said that there were witnesses who could back up its version, but it did not produce any. The Defense Department's claim that the officers did not realize they were at an important checkpoint raised eyebrows, because before arriving at the checkpoint, the officers had to drive past two other barricades that should have alerted them that they were in a restricted area.

As it happened, a U.S. Navy officer and his wife were near the checkpoint and saw the incident. Other PDF soldiers were nearby, reportedly intoxicated.[46] They stopped the officer and his wife and took them to a nearby building where they questioned them for four hours. In the process, according to the Defense Department account, the PDF soldiers beat the officer and threatened his wife with sexual attack.[47]

President Bush called the checkpoint shooting and the treatment of the navy officer and his wife an "outrage"; the president's spokesperson said that this, together with the December 15 Panamanian resolution about a state of war with the United States, created a "climate of aggression."[48] Although the PDF did not consider its soldiers at fault for the incident, it reportedly told U.S. representatives that whatever the PDF soldiers might have done, it was not intended as an affront to the United States.[49] While not quite an apology, this stance bespoke an expression of regret.

In any event, shortly after the checkpoint incident President Bush decided to put the invasion plan into action. With 12,000 troops already stationed in Panama, on December 20, Bush sent an equal number to make an invasion force of 24,500. This force took over Panama in several days of fighting.[50] We contacted Endara and asked him to assume the presidency.[51]

U.S. forces suffered 26 dead and 300 wounded in the invasion. For Panama the toll was more severe. A prime target of our forces was the PDF headquarters in Panama City, located in a densely populated lower-class district. In bombing the headquarters, our planes leveled several city blocks of nearby housing, killing many residents.[52] Overall, several thousand Panamanians were hospitalized for injuries suffered during the invasion.[53] The Red Cross reported that hospitals in Panama City were "inundated with civilian and military casualties," that "over 800 people were treated during the first few days," and that "medicines and medical material were in short supply." The Red Cross brought in two planeloads of medical supplies to make up the shortfall.[54]

As for deaths, Deputy Secretary of State Lawrence Eagleburger estimated 400 Panamanians killed, a figure that most observers considered low.[55] The overthrown government estimated 7,000 killed, but that figure could not be substantiated.[56] According to a Red Cross official, there were "at least two thousand killed; the morgues of the hospitals are overflowing and there is no more room." He accused the United States of covering up a massacre.[57]

I had an opportunity to visit Panama after the invasion. In Panama City, I spoke with survivors of the bombing in the neighborhood around the PDF headquarters. For them it was a night of horror, with houses in flames all around, uncertainty over whether they would be hit, and worry over relatives living nearby. Survivors of the bombing told of psychological trauma and of children who afterward became frantic at the sound of a helicopter.

I was in Panama to sit as a hearing officer in an inquiry organized by Panamanian human rights organizations to assess responsibility for the damage suffered by Panama's civilian population during the invasion. The case files prepared by investigators recounted bombing deaths and fatal shootings of civilians by U.S. soldiers.

One reason the number of fatalities was not immediately apparent was that our forces sealed off the heavily damaged area around the PDF headquarters for the first four days, keeping out the media and the Red Cross. They forced the residents out of the houses, which they then demolished. When I visited the area, there were no standing structures in the area. Mass graves discovered months after the invasion led to the revelation that U.S. forces had collected bodies in the streets and carted them off without identifying them. Some Panamanians reported seeing our soldiers incinerating bodies in the streets with flame throwers.[58] The apparent aim of all this activity was to hide the human and material damage caused by the bombing. Under pressure from Panamanian human rights groups, the Endara government exhumed from the mass graves many bodies, some of which could be identified.

Once in occupation, our soldiers set up roadblocks to try to identify members of the PDF; they had trouble distinguishing friend from foe. At roadblocks, the soldiers might hear a shot and fire in return, not knowing where the shot originated. A number of passersby were killed in this way.

In one well-documented case, our forces pulled five young Panamanian men out of a van and shot them execution-style as they lay face down on the ground; it was unclear whether the soldiers suspected the men of hostile activity. In many cases of civilians killed by shooting, the Panamanian courts conducted a coroner's inquest and determined that the person had been shot by an American soldier, but one who could not be identified. Despite requests, U.S. officials in Panama refused to determine the circumstances or the identity of the soldier, and the Panamanian courts had no access to U.S. military personnel

In its early statements after the invasion, the Bush administration painted a picture of normalcy in Panama, but several newspapers told a different story: "North American Invasion Leads to Total Chaos in Panama," screamed a headline in the Madrid daily *El País*.[59] "Looting and Bombs Turn Panama into a No Man's Land," said Argentina's *La Prensa*.[60] "Chaos Grips Streets," said the *Los Angeles Times*.[61] Looters emptied shops, as Panama City experienced a wave of robbery and violence by criminal elements.[62] One reason for the chaos was that American forces disbanded the existing police force without substituting other security measures.[63] Damage from the bombing and looting combined was estimated at $1 billion.[64] After several weeks of direct military rule, our forces turned control over to Endara, although we maintained advisors in government departments as a kind of shadow administration.[65]

NOTES

1. Construction of a Ship Canal (Herran-Hay Treaty), January 22, 1903, *Unperfected Treaties of the United States of America: 1776–1976* (1977), 3: 447.

2. Antonio Jose Uribe, *Colombia, Estados Unidos y Panamá* (1976), pp. 90–98; Manuel Arteaga Hernandez and Jaime Arteaga Carvajal, *Historia política de Colombia* (1986), p.501. German Cavelier, *La política internacional de Colombia* (1960), 2: 305–307.

3. Uribe, *Colombia, Estados Unidos y Panamá*, pp. 103–105; Cavelier, *La politica internacional de Colombia*, 2: 308–309.

4. John Bassett Moore, *Digest of International Law* (1906), 3: 46; Uribe, *Colombia, Estados Unidos y Panamá*, p. 105; Arteaga and Arteaga, *Historia política de Colombia*, p.502; David Howarth, *Panama* (1966), p. 23

5. Albert Edwards, *Panama: The Canal, the Country, and the People* (1912), p. 471.

5. Isthmian Canal Convention, art. 3, November 18, 1903, Treaty Series 431, U.S. Congress, *Statutes at Large*, vol. 33, p. 2234 (1904).

6. "Panama Suspends U.S. Tie and Charges Aggression After Riot in Canal Zone," *New York Times*, January 10, 1964, p. A1, col. 8.

7. Panama Canal Treaty, arts. 2–3, September 7, 1977, TIAS No. 10030, in *International Legal Materials*, vol. 16, p. 1022 (1977).

8. Treaty Concerning the Permanent Neutrality and Operation of the Panama Canal, arts. 1, 5, September 7, 1977, TIAS No. 10029, in *International Legal Materials*, vol. 16, p. 1040 (1977).

9. Frederick Kempe, "Ties That Blind: U.S. Taught Noriega to Spy, but the Pupil Had His Own Agenda," *Wall Street Journal* October 18, 1989, p. Al, col. 1.

10. Seymour Hersh, "Panama Strongman Said to Trade in Drugs, Arms and Illicit Money," *New York Times*, June 12, 1986, p. A1, col. 1.

11. "A Man, a Plan, a Canal, Panama," *Economist*, January 6, 1990, p. 17;

Stephen Engelberg, "U.S. Said to Ignore Noriega Drug Role," *New York Times*, April 5, 1988, p. A1, col. 1; Stephen Engelberg, "Officials Say Bush Heard '85 Charge Against Noriega," *New York Times*, May 8, 1988, p. A1, col. 4; David Johnston, "Papers Seized from Noriega Could Help Iran-Contra Case," *New York Times*, January 12, 1990, p. A8, col. 1.

12. Hersh, "Panama Strongman Said to Trade in Drugs, Arms and Illicit Money", Transcript, "Frontline" Special, "Guns, Drugs and the CIA," WGBH, Public Broadcasting System (1988), p. 22.

13. Dennis Volman, "Money Courier Tells of Services for CIA," *Christian Science Monitor*, July 16, 1987, p. 3, col. 2.

14. Connie Bruck, "How Noriega Got Caught and Got Away," *American Lawyer*, July–August 1988, p. 35.

15. Transcript, "Frontline" Special, "Guns, Drugs and the CIA," p. 23.

16. Milton Martinez, *Panama 1978–1990: Una Crisis sin Fin* (1990), p. 97; Independent Commission of Inquiry on the U.S. Invasion of Panama, *The U.S. Invasion of Panama: The Truth Behind Operation 'Just Cause'* (1990), p. 22.

17. "The OAS and the Panama Crisis," DSB, vol. 89, p. 72 (November 1989).

18. Philip Shenon, "Noriega Indicted by U.S. for Links to Illegal Drugs," *New York Times*, February 6, 1988, p. A1, col. 2.

19. Neil A. Lewis, "U.S. Withholds a Canal Payment in New Steps to Oust Panamanian," *New York Times*, March 12, 1988, p. A1, col. 4.

20. "Prohibiting Certain Transactions with Respect to Panama," Exec. Order. 12635, April 8, 1988, *Federal Register*, vol. 53, p. 12134 (April 12,1988); Lewis, "U.S. Withholds a Canal Payment in New Steps to Oust Panamanian"; Julie Johnson, "Reagan Halts All Payments to Panamanian Government," *New York Times*, April 9, 1988, p. A1, col. 5; "Contemporary Practice of the United States Relating to International Law: Economic Sanctions," *American Journal of International Law* 82 (1988): 573.

21. "Prohibiting Certain Transactions with Respect to Panama"; Johnson, "Reagan Halts All Payments to Panamanian Government."

22. Letter of J. Edward Fox to Sen. Jesse Helms, March 26, 1987, reprinted in Independent Commission of Inquiry on the U.S. Invasion of Panama, p. 20.

23. "Taking Aim at Noriega: Will CIA Campaign Funds Topple a Dictator in Panama's Election?" *U.S. News & World Report*, May 1, 1989, p. 40.

24. Stephen Engelberg, "C.I.A. Funnels Aid to Noriega's Election Foes," *New York Times*, April 23, 1989, p. A14, col. 4.

25. Lindsey Gruson, "Noriega Stealing Election, Carter Says," *New York Times*, May 9, 1989, p. A1, col. 6; Bernard Weinraub, "Bush Urges Effort to Press Noriega to Quit as Leader," *New York Times*, May 10, 1989, p. A1, col. 6; "Transcript of Bush's News Conference on the Panama Vote," *New York Times*, May 10, 1989, p. A10, col. 1.

26. Robert Pear, "Hemispheric Group Asks Noriega to Yield Power," *New York Times*, May 18, 1989, p. A8, col. 3.

27. Larry Rohter, "O.A.S. Draws Latin Fire for Stand on Panama," *New York Times*, June 4, 1989, p. A10, col. 1; Robert Pear, "Latin Envoys Report No Progress in Their Effort to Dislodge Noriega," *New York Times*, June 20, 1989, p. A8, col. 1; Robert Pear, "Diplomats Urge Noriega to Resign by September 1," New York Times, July 20, 1989, p. A6, col. 4; Robert Pear, "Washington Talk; Diplomacy," *New York Times*, August 22, 1989, p. A20, col. 5. Robert Pear, "U.S. Is Faulted on Military Maneuvers in Panama," *New York Times*, August 24, 1989, p. A3, col. 1.

28. "Panama, United States Again Before Council," *UN Chronicle* 26 (December 1989): 20.

29. Robert Pear, "U.S. Renews Attack on Noriega, Offering Evidence of Ties to Drugs," *New York Times*, September 1, 1989, p. A1, col. 1.

30. Bob Woodward, *The Commanders* (1991), pp. 92, 99–100.

31. "Panama, United States Again Before Council"; Paul Lewis, "Panama Urges U.N. to Send Observers," *New York Times*, August 12, 1989, p. A3, col. 4; Pear, "U.S. Is Faulted on Military Maneuvers in Panama."

32. Pear, "U.S. Is Faulted on Military Maneuvers in Panama."

33. Panama Canal Treaty, art. 3(3)(c).

34. Robert Pear, "Aide to Noriega Is Sworn In: U.S. Won't Recognize Him," *New York Times*, September 2, 1989, p. A3, col. 5.

35. John Pearson, "Panama," *Business Week*, December 25, 1989, p. 70.

36. "U.S. Severs Diplomatic Contact with Noriega Regime," DSB, vol. 89, p. 69 (November 1989); "Economic Measures Against Panama," Department Statement, September 12, 1989, DSB, vol. 89, p. 69 (November 1989); "U.S. Expands Its Sanctions Against Panama," *New York Times*, September 13, 1989, p. A5, col. 1.

37. Tony Avirgan, "Panama Contras?" *Nation*, September 18, 1989, p. 263; Mark A. Uhlig, "An Untold Guerrilla War: Noriega Foes Rule Border," *New York Times*, January 10, 1990, p. A8, col. 5.

38. Stephen Engelberg, "Bush Aides Admit a U.S. Role in Coup, and Bad Handling," *New York Times*, October 6, 1989, p. A1, Col. 6; Woodward, *The Commanders*, pp. 119–24.

39. Woodward, *The Commanders*, pp. 132–45.

40. "U.S. Imposes Ban on Ships under Panamanian Flag," *Wall Street Journal*, December 1, 1989, p. B2, col. 5

41. Don A. Shanche, "Rivals Try to Flag Down Panama Ship Business," *Los Angeles Times*, December 19, 1989, p. A8, col. 1.

42. Andrew Rosenthal, "U.S. Forces Gain Wide Control in Panama, New Leaders Put In But Noriega Gets Away," *New York Times*, December 21, 1989, p. Al, col. 6.

43. William Branigin, "Noriega Appointed 'Maximum Leader,'" *Washington Post*, December 16, 1989, p. A21, col. 1; William Branigin, "Noriega's 'State of War' Seen as Quest for Backing," *Washington Post*, December 20, 1989, p. A32, col. 1.

44. "Excerpts from U.S. Account of Officer's Death in Panama," *New York Times*, December 18, 1989, p. A8, col. 3.

45. William Branigin, "U.S. Assails Panama in Killing of GI," *Washington Post*, December 18, 1989, p. A1, col. 6.

46. Walter Pincus, "Pair of Incidents Pushed Bush Toward Invasion," *Washington Post*, December 24, 1989, p. A16, col. 2.

47. "Excerpts from U.S. Account of Officer's Death in Panama."

48. Andrew Rosenthal, "President Calls Panama Slaying a Great Outrage," *New York Times*, December 19, 1989, p. A1, col. 1.

49. Ibid.

50. Molly Moore and Ann Devroy, "Officials Say Panama Taking More Time and Troops Than Expected," *Washington Post*, December 23, 1989, p. A6, col. 6.

51. Rosenthal, "U.S. Forces Gain Wide Control in Panama, New Leaders Put In But Noriega Gets Away."

52. Brook Larmer, "With the Dictator Disabled, Panama Looks to Rebuild," *Christian Science Monitor*, December 27, 1989, p. 1, col. 4.

53. Brook Lamer, "In Invasion's Wake, Disorder Reigns in Panamanian Capital," *Christian Science Monitor*, December 22, 1989, p. 1, col. 1.

54. "U.S. Military Intervention in Panama," International Committee of the Red Cross Bulletin, No. 169 (February 1990): 2.

55. J. D. Gannon, "Invasion Took Its Toll in Deaths, Human Suffering," *Christian Science Monitor*, December 29, 1989, p.3, col. 1; Andrew Rosenthal, "No More Panamas, Bush Aides Predict," *New York Times*, January 8, 1990, p. A9, col. 1; David E. Pitt, "The Invasion's Civilian Toll: Still No Official Count," *New York Times*, January 10, 1990, p. A9, col. 3.

56. "Panamá sumida en el caos y Noriega continua prófugo," *La Prensa* (Buenos Aires), December 23, 1989, p. 1, col. 3.

57. "Acusan a EE.UU. de esconder una matanza," *La Prensa* (Buenos Aires), December 26, 1989, p. 2, col. 3.

58. Independent Commission of Inquiry on the U.S. Invasion of Panama, pp. 41–43.

59. "La invasión norteamericana provoca el caos total en Panamá," *El País* (Madrid), December 25, 1989, p. 1, col. 2.

60. "Panamá sumida en el caos y Noriega continua prófugo"; "Saqueos y bombas han convertido a Panamá en 'tierra de nadie,'" *La Prensa* (Buenos Aires), December 23, 1989, p. 3, col. 1.

61. "Noriega Loyalists Hit Back at U.S. Military as Chaos Grips Streets," *Los Angeles Times*, December 24, 1989, p. A1, col. 5.

62. William Branigin, "Looters Lay Waste to Panama City Shops," *Washington Post*, December 23, 1989, p. A1, col. 1; Michael R. Gordon and David E. Pitt, "Panama Crime Wave Shakes Faith in Police," *New York Times*, February 2, 1990, p. A10, col. 1.

63. Larmer, "With the Dictator Disabled, Panama Looks to Rebuild"; Brook Larmer, "Panama Forges Police Force From Members of Noriega's Military," *Christian Science Monitor*, December 28, 1989, p. 1, col. 1.

64. Larmer, "With the Dictator Disabled, Panama Looks to Rebuild"; Douglas Wailer and John Barry, "Inside the Invasion," *Newsweek*, June 25, 1990, pp. 29–31.

65. Independent Commission of Inquiry on the U.S. Invasion of Panama, p. 49.

29. PANAMA: EXPLAINING WHY

In the words of the White House announcement of the Panama invasion, "Last Friday [December 15, 1989], [General Manuel] Noriega declared a state of war with the United States. The next day, the P.D.F. [Panama Defense Force] shot to death an unarmed American serviceman, wounded another, seized and beat another serviceman and sexually threatened his wife. Under these circumstances, the President decided he must act to prevent further violence."[1] President Bush said that these incidents showed that "the lives of American citizens were in grave danger," and that the December 15 resolution had been a declaration of war.[2] Secretary of State James Baker said that we had information that General Noriega was preparing "an urban commando attack on American citizens in a residential neighborhood" in Panama City. Baker acknowledged he could not prove this information. He also acknowledged that he had received it only after President Bush ordered the invasion.[3]

How solid was the administration's information about Panama? Did it provide, as the administration argued, a "just cause" for invasion? As for the December 15 National Assembly resolution, it was not Panama's first reference to a "state of war" with the United States. In August 1989, as we saw, Panama's government declared that our military maneuvers created "a state of imminent war," although Bush did not make much of this statement.[4] The December 15 resolution was open to varying inter-pretations. The *Christian Science Monitor* took it as a statement that the United States had initiated an economic war against Panama, but not a declaration of a Panamanian intent to initiate a shooting war.[5] One reason for skepticism about President Bush's reading of the resolution was that we had 12,000 troops already stationed in Panama. It would have been foolhardy for Panama to start anything. Noriega had been accused of many things. Stupidity was not one of them.

Why, in fact, did the National Assembly pass the resolution, and why did it refer to a "state of war"? In all likelihood, the motive was to rally the population behind General Noriega by showing that the United States was trying to bring him down. The resolution appealed to Panamanian patriotism; to say that the United States had created a "state of war" was an eloquent way of denouncing our actions.

The notion of war by economic means is common in hemispheric relations: one of the perennial fears of the Latin states is that the United States may use its economic clout against them. To stop this, in fact, they wrote a provision into the Charter of the Organization of American States (OAS) that equates economic sanctions with war. The provision reads, "No State may use . . . coercive measures of an economic . . . character in order to force the sovereign will of another State."[6]

The conclusion that the December 15 resolution was a document for internal consumption is reinforced by the fact that the resolution went on to name General Noriega "chief of government" and "maximum leader of national liberation" to oppose the United States. The pronouncement about a state of war was a rationale for giving General Noriega these new titles and new roles.[7]

The Bush administration kept close enough watch on Panamanian politics that it must have understood that this was the import of the December 15 resolution. While the administration knew that the resolution was not a formal declaration of war, it seized on the opportunity to take the phrase "state of war" out of context, to find a reason to invade.

Beyond the matter of the December 15 resolution, the White House relied as well on the checkpoint incident of December 16 to prove that the

Panamanian administration was carrying out its "declaration of war" by attacking U.S. citizens. But there was little reason to take the December 16 incident as part of a plan to attack Americans in Panama, even if the U.S. version of the incident was accurate. Since the four American officers drove up to the checkpoint unannounced, the attack could not have been planned in advance. As for the treatment of the navy officer and his wife, the Defense Department conceded that the PDF soldiers responsible were intoxicated at the time, a fact that suggested that the incident was generated by the PDF soldiers involved and was not part of a governmental plan.

Although President Bush insisted that the invasion was prompted by the "declaration of war" and the checkpoint incident, he had been planning it for months. Military officers posing as tourists had spread through Panama to reconnoiter locations they planned to attack. Fred Hoffman, a former Pentagon official, referring to classified planning documents for the invasion, said the administration "had a plan" and was "just waiting for an excuse to use it."[8]

The Bush administration gave three other justifications for the invasion. One objective, according to Secretary of State Baker, was "to seize and arrest an indicted drug trafficker"—a reference to General Noriega and his indictments in Florida.[9] The army did capture General Noriega and take him to Florida for trial. But the United States had known of Noriega's drug involvement even during the years we befriended him. The impression that the administration was trying to give of coming down hard on a cocaine trafficker was disingenuous. Beyond that, arresting a drug trafficker is hardly a reason to invade a country, even if the trafficker heads the government.

A second justification was given by President Bush, who said that we invaded "to defend democracy in Panama."[10] Secretary Baker averred that "in taking the actions that we've taken, we consulted the legitimate, democratically elected government of Panama, which welcomed our actions."[11] This suggested that Guillermo Endara, who had been denied his seat as president, requested the intervention, or at least that his opinion was sought. However, Endara said that the administration never asked him if he *wanted* an invasion; the White House only informed him when the invasion was imminent and told Endara that he should get ready to take over as president. Endara's UN representative also denied that Endara had requested or authorized the invasion, calling it a unilateral decision by the U.S., in which the Endara government had no part.[12]

Was Bush truly moved by a desire for democracy in Panama in his decision to invade? In Latin America, the rationale was met with skepticism, because the United States has often supported undemocratic governments in Latin America if they were safely in our camp. In the Dominican Republic, as we have seen, the Johnson administration intervened against an elected president to keep him from reclaiming his office. In Chile in 1973, we helped overthrow a democratically elected government. Our history has been to favor governments on the basis of national interest, not on the basis of democracy. This could have been an instance of the leopard changing its spots, but there was little reason to believe it.

A third justification given by the administration is that we invaded Panama to protect our interests in the Panama Canal; as Secretary of State Baker put it, "to defend the integrity of United States' rights under the canal treaties."[13] The smooth functioning of the canal, Baker argued, was at stake, because Panama was harassing canal workers and attacking our military personnel who were there to defend the canal. Baker declared that "the United States has both the right and . . . the duty to protect and defend the Canal under Article 4 of the Panama Canal Treaty."[14] Article 4 states that Panama and the United States should defend the canal, in particular "to meet the danger resulting from an armed attack or other actions which threaten the security of the Panama Canal or of ships transiting it."[15]

Baker, referring to "the continuing pattern of harassment that we've seen going on down there against Americans in the exercise of our treaty rights," said that we "anticipated that there might be problems with respect to the canal if Noriega continued to retain power illegitimately."[16] Baker's statement focused less, however, on the impact of those incidents on canal operations than on a concern that the incidents might increase in the future, in which case they might affect operations. In congressional testimony a month earlier, Michael G. Kozak, deputy assistant secretary of state for inter-American affairs, cited instances of harassment but said that they had not adversely affected the canal. Kozak said, "Despite regime efforts to change U.S. nonrecognition policy by harassing U.S. and Panamanian employees of the U.S. forces and the Panama Canal Commission, Noriega has seemingly sought to avoid a direct threat to the canal or a direct challenge to the proper exercise of U.S. rights." Like Baker, Kozak saw a possible future threat: "Nevertheless, it becomes clearer each day that Noriega's continuation in power is a threat not only to the interests and freedom of his own people, but also to the canal."[17]

Despite the problems between General Noriega and the Bush administration, wrote the *New York Times*, "ship traffic on the canal was hardly disrupted."[18] "The security of the canal," according to the *Economist*, "was not at stake" in the administration's confrontation with Noriega.[19] Ships were going through, and prospects were that they would continue to go through. "There is no evidence," wrote the Madrid daily *El País*, "that might prove that Noriega or his forces had any intention of attacking the installations of the waterway."[20] Even after the invasion began, our forces showed no concern that the canal might be sabotaged. They took no precautions to protect the canal, and the PDF made no moves against it.[21]

Of the long list of reasons Bush gave for invading Panama, none withstood scrutiny, and although the American public did not raise much objection, the administration's rationale for intervening in Panama did not play well abroad.[22] The OAS, which had repeatedly urged General Noriega to cede power, issued a resolution in which it "deeply deplored" the invasion and called the American action a violation of "the right of the Panamanian people to self-determination without outside interference."[23] The OAS resolution was adopted by a vote of 20 to one, the only negative vote being our own.[24]

In the UN Security Council, a majority voted a condemnation, but we vetoed it, along with our allies Britain and France.[25] The UN General Assembly "strongly deplored" the intervention and demanded the immediate withdrawal of U.S. forces from Panama. This resolution passed

75–20. Most of the states that voted against it agreed that the invasion was unjustified. They voted against because they wanted the resolution to mention misdeeds by General Noriega.[26] The Bush administration reportedly anticipated the negative reaction abroad but decided it could live with it.[27]

International condemnation was so strong because the Bush administration's various rationales for the Panama invasion did not ring true. But if these were not the real reasons, why then did we invade Panama? The drug-trafficking angle may have been a factor, but not quite for the reason the administration gave. As vice president, Bush had been responsible for drug policy, and as president he declared a "war on drugs"; but he had registered no major successes against drug trafficking.[28] Cocaine came from Colombia to the United States, and Panama was a transit point.[29] A high-visibility move like arresting General Noriega might appear to be a victory in the "war on drugs."

Another possible factor in the administration's decision to invade was its war in Nicaragua. At the time we were still financing the Contras. With elections scheduled in Nicaragua for February 1990, President Bush may have hoped, by an invasion of Panama, to reemphasize to Nicaragua's voters that you can't cross Uncle Sam. The anti-Sandinista candidate, Violeta Chamorro, whom we supported, promised close relations with the United States. Chamorro did win the election. So perhaps this strategy worked.[30]

In London, the *Economist* theorized along a different line: "Robbed of a plausible threat in the shape of the Evil Empire [a term President Reagan had used for the Soviet Union], the United States Defence Department needs new enemies to take on. Who better than beastly drug runners like General Noriega?"[31] With the cold war ending, the administration was under pressure to justify its arms budget, which had nearly doubled during the 1980s. One weapon the Defense Department used in Panama was the "stealth" bomber, which, said the *Economist*, "reinforced the impression that the Pentagon is treating Panama as a playground in which to practise its new arts."[32] Defense Department critics charged that the only reason we used the stealth bomber in Panama was to buttress the case for buying more of them, in the face of serious congressional opposition to the aircraft.[33] This suspicion heightened when it was revealed that the Defense Department lied about the number of stealth bombers it used in Panama. At first the Department acknowledged only two, but later Army Lieutenant General Carl Stiner, who commanded the invasion, revealed that six were used.[34]

The canal may have been a factor in the United States' decision to invade, although not quite for the reason the administration gave. As we saw, Panama was to have the right, beginning January 1, 1990, to appoint the canal administrator. Bush did not want a Noriega appointee. Invading ten days before that deadline ensured that the administrator would be appointed by a friendly government.

Also, the Panama Canal Treaty called for the complete transfer of the canal and the withdrawal of U.S. troops by December 31, 1999. The treaty, negotiated by a Democrat, President Jimmy Carter, was controversial. In 1989 some in Congress thought we should keep the canal.[35] Republicans were prominent in taking this view. They wanted to ask Panama to renegotiate, but with General Noriega in power, that was not likely. A Panamanian government that owed us its position might be more amenable. Although President Bush reaffirmed our commitment to turn the canal over on schedule,[36] he did not rule out the possibility of renegotiation. The press reported from inside sources that renegotiation figured in the administration's thinking about the invasion.[37]

Endara was also more likely to cooperate because he represented the white upper stratum of Panamanian society, the group we had approached in 1903 to separate Panama from Colombia. That group ruled until 1968, when a military coup brought in an administration oriented to lower-class black and brown Panamanians, who were more nationalistic, more concerned about Yankee domination. It was they who rioted in 1964 to demand that we turn over the canal. General Noriega, although he collaborated with us early in his career, drew his support from the lower class. When Endara took office, he showed his colors by appointing a cabinet almost entirely from the upper class.

Possible renegotiation of the 1977 treaties remained a hot political topic in the United States through the 1990s. In 1993, the Academy Award for best documentary went to a film titled *The Panama Deception*, which focused on the 1989 invasion and the reasons behind it. The film presented information to show that the aim was to get a better deal on the canal. Most attention focused on the issue of U.S. troops. While there was little dispute that we should turn over canal operations in 1999, many thought we should re-negotiate the second canal treaty to allow for U.S. troops to remain in Panama.

Endara, after taking office, showed no inclination to renegotiate. Nor did his successor, who took office in 1995. By then a Democrat was president of the United States. President Clinton did not rule out the possibility of renegotiation to let U.S. troops remain, but in the end no renegotiation took place. We turned over the canal, and our troops left Panama.

We may have to wait for memoirs by Bush administration insiders to learn the real reasons for the Panama invasion. All I know for sure is that I still have my grandfather's sailor hat from the USS *Wyoming*. "Wyoming" is emblazoned, still brightly, on the bill.

NOTES

1. "Text of Statement by Fitzwater," *New York Times*, December 21, 1989, p. A19, col. 2.

2. "A Transcript of Bush's Address on the Decision to Use Force in Panama," *New York Times*, December 21, 1989, p. A19, col. 1.

3. Andrew Rosenthal, "U.S. Forces Gain Wide Control in Panama, New Leaders Put In But Noriega Gets Away," *New York Times*, December 21, 1989, p. Al, col. 6; "Excerpts from Statement by Baker on U.S. Policy," *New York Times*, December 21, 1989, p. A19, col. 3.

4. Paul Lewis, "Panama Urges U.N. to Send Observers," *New York Times*, August 12, 1989, p. A3, col. 4; "Panama, United States Again Before Council," *UN Chronicle* 26 (December 1989): 20.

5. Lucia Mouat, "U.S. Policy of Grinding Down Noriega Stalls," *Christian Science Monitor*, December 20, 1989, p. 1, col. 4.

6. Charter of the Organization of American States, 1948, art. 16, *United States Treaties and Other International Agreements*, 2: 2394; *United Nations*

Treaty Series, 119: 3.

7. William Branigin, "Noriega Appointed 'Maximum Leader,'" *Washington Post*, December 16, 1989, p. A2l, col. 1; William Branigin, "Noriega's 'State of War' Seen as Quest for Backing," *Washington Post*, December 20, 1989, p. A32, col. 1.

8. Douglas Wailer and John Barry, "Inside the Invasion," *Newsweek*, June 25, 1990, pp. 29–31.

9. "Excerpts from Statement by Baker on U.S. Policy."

10. "A Transcript of Bush's Address on the Decision to Use Force in Panama."

11. "Excerpts from Statement by Baker on U.S. Policy."

12. Ethan Schwartz, "World Criticism of U.S. Intervention Mounts," *Washington Post*, December 22, 1989, p. A29, col. 2.

13. "Excerpts from Statement by Baker on U.S. Policy."

14. Ibid.

15. Panama Canal Treaty, art. 4, September 7, 1977, entered into force October 1, 1979, TIAS No. 10030, in *International Legal Materials* 16 (1977): 1022.

16. "Excerpts from Statement by Baker on U.S. Policy."

17. "Panama Canal: The Strategic Dimension," U.S. Dept. of State, Current Policy No. 1226, p. 3 (November 1989) (statement before Subcommittee on Panama Canal and Outer Continental Shelf, Committee on Merchant Marine and Fisheries, U.S. House of Representatives, November 2, 1989).

18. David E. Pitt, "Challenge for Panamanians: A Canal in Transition," *New York Times*, January 29, 1990, p. A11, col. 1.

19. "A Man, a Plan, a Canal, Panama," *Economist*, January 6, 1990, p. 17.

20. "George Bush, contra reloj," *El País* (Madrid), December 25, 1989, p. 2, col. 1.

21. Peter Grier, "U.S. Forces Strike Panama in Bid to Oust Strongman," *Christian Science Monitor*, December 21, 1989, p. 1, col. 4.

22. Schwartz, "World Criticism of U.S. Intervention Mounts"; Bill McAllister, "U.S. Cites Self-Defense; Legal Scholars Skeptical," *Washington Post*, December 21, 1989, p. A36, col. 3; "Generalizada condena a la intervención estadounidense," *La Prensa* (Buenos Aires), December 22, 1989, p. 3, col. 1.

23. "La OEA deplora la invasión y exige un cese del fuego," *La Prensa* (Buenos Aires), December 23, 1989, p. 4, col. 1.

24. "Criticism of U.S. Action Is Supported in 20–1 Vote," *New York Times*,

December 23, 1989, p. A15, col. 5; John M. Goshko and Michael Isikoff, "O.A.S. Votes to Censure U.S. for Intervention," *Washington Post*, December 23, 1989, p. A7, col. 5.

25. Paul Lewis, "Two Delegates Vying to Be the Voice of the New Government," *New York Times*, December 29, 1989, p. A12, col. 1.

26. Ethan Schwartz, "U.N. Assembly Blasts Invasion of Panama," *Washington Post*, December 30, 1989, p. A 17, col. 1.

27. Bob Woodward, *The Commanders* (1991), p. 170.

28. Richard L. Berke, "Bush Endorses Outline of Plan for Drug Battle," *New York Times*, August 16, 1989, p. A1, col. 5.

29. Ann B. Wrobleski, "Presidential Certification of Narcotics Source Countries," DSB, vol. 88, pp. 47–50 (June 1988).

30. "Nicaraguan Opposition Routs Sandinistas; U.S. Pledges Aid, Tied to Orderly Turnover," *New York Times*, February 27, 1990, p. A1, col. 6.

31. "A Man, a Plan, a Canal, Panama," p. 17.

32. Ibid., p. 18.

33. "Stealth Fighter's Mission Reported Marred by Error," *New York Times*, April 4, 1990, p. A1, col. 2.

34. "Panama Alerted to Attack, General Says," *New York Times*, February 27, 1990, p. A7, col. 1.

35. "Combat in Panama," *Los Angeles Times*, December 21, 1989, p. A9, col. 1.

36. Ibid.

37. "Quayle Trip: Resentment Dramatized," *New York Times*, January 31, 1990, p. A16, col. 4.

30. Liberia: Just in Case

J ust as the U.S. invasion of Panama got underway, a civil war broke out in the west African nation of Liberia. The Bush administration's antennae went up. After five months of watching from a distance, on May 31, 1990, we sent to Liberia's coast a flotilla of six battleships with 2,100 U.S. Marines, carrying tanks, helicopter gunships, and vertical takeoff jet fighters. According to a Defense Department spokesperson, Commander David Thomas, as the ships cast anchor offshore, they were under orders to "be prepared to evacuate American citizens" from Liberia. When the civil war began, 5,000 Americans were in Liberia. By the time the flotilla arrived, all but about 1,200, including one hundred embassy personnel and dependents, had left.[1]

The Defense Department was concerned, it said, over the possible danger to U.S. citizens in Liberia. Two separate rebel forces were challenging the government of President Samuel Doe. Pete Williams, another Defense Department spokesperson, explained the Marine presence "as a precaution to take up a position in international waters in the event they are needed to help American citizens and other noncombatants who need to leave and cannot do so by commercial means."[2]

Liberia was a nation in which the United States had long had a substantial interest. Unique among African countries, Liberia was founded in the nineteenth century by emancipated slaves from the American south. It had long been our close ally. American companies were heavily invested there, and we gave Liberia substantial aid.[3] During the early 1980s, Liberia was the largest per capita recipient of U.S. foreign aid in sub-Saharan Africa.[4]

One reason for our generosity was that Liberia let us maintain vital facilities there. On Liberian territory we had set up a navigation station to guide nuclear powered missile-launching submarines in much of the Atlantic Ocean. We had sophisticated communications equipment in Liberia that relayed all CIA and State Department radio messages to and from sub-Saharan Africa. The Voice of America radio station had its transmitter for sub-Saharan Africa there as well;[5] officials put the value of the facilities at $200 million.[6] None of these facilities had been damaged or immediately threatened by the fighting, but they were not under military guard and could have been entered by troops, many of whom were not under tight discipline.

In its explanation of why it sent the flotilla, the Bush administration did not mention these facilities, or say why it needed so many heavily equipped ships to rescue a small number of civilians. One skeptical reporter asked whether the communications facilities might be the reason for the deployment, and whether we might land troops or launch aircraft from the flotilla to protect the facilities. Intriguingly, Herman Cohen, assistant secretary of state for African affairs, did not deny the possibility. Cohen answered, "I wouldn't want to reject any options." Cohen acknowledged that "they are important installations," and that "it would be difficult and very expensive to move them to another country."[7]

As the flotilla rested offshore, the civil war reached Monrovia, Liberia's capital; small numbers of American citizens were evacuated to the ships from time to time, but others continued to leave Liberia on their own. By early August, only 300 Americans remained in the country. As the fighting intensified, the Liberian death toll mounted, and Monrovia was left with little water, electricity, or food. Prince Johnson, commander of the smaller of the two rebel groups, threatened to arrest foreign nationals, apparently as a way of bringing about international intervention in the civil war.[8]

On August 5, Johnson seized a dozen foreigners, including one American, from a Monrovia hotel.[9] At that point, President Bush, citing "an increased threat to our embassy and its facilities" from the fighting, ordered 225 of the Marines from the flotilla to fly into Monrovia via helicopter. The helicopters carried back to the flotilla personnel from the embassy, from the Voice of America station, and from a communications facility—eighty persons in all.[10]

Charles Taylor, the leader of the larger rebel group, protested the landing. A Taylor aide charged that the landing created "a situation where an accident will be caused and someone will blame us."[11] Cuba also protested the landing, fearing we might help the government forces of President Doe.[12]

Several members of Congress suspected that the administration had organized the Liberia landing for reasons other than rescue. Iraq had invaded Kuwait just three days before, leaving many U.S. citizens under Iraqi occupation there, with Iraq's intentions uncertain. Representative Les Aspin of Wisconsin called the Liberia landing "a marvelous opportunity for George Bush to send a message to [Iraqi president] Saddam Hussein."[13] The *New York Times* took up the same theme. The *Times* editorialized that the landing "sends a useful signal about America's willingness to use appropriate military force in defense of clear national interests."[14] The Liberia landing might well have been intended as an object lesson to Iraq.

After the Marines landed, they took up positions around the American embassy but stayed clear of the civil hostilities. Giving little justification to Cuba's fear, they did not assist President Doe.[15] They remained for several months, however, evacuating small numbers of Americans from time to time. In January 1991, the Defense Department removed the flotilla, leaving only a handful of Marines at the embassy. By that time, the Marines had evacuated 224 U.S. citizens, a figure that included eighty official personnel.[16]

Therefore, most of the 1,200 Americans still in Liberia at the flotilla's arrival left the country while it sat offshore, with only 224 using its services, nearly a third of whom were official personnel. During the Liberian hostilities, only one U.S. citizen was killed, and that occurred outside Monrovia in April 1990, before deployment of the flotilla.[17]

Although few private citizens used the flotilla, it remained off Liberia's coast for over seven months. When the Defense Department finally removed the flotilla, spokesperson Pete Williams gave the operation a curious epitaph, calling it the "longest evacuation of its kind in U.S. naval history."[18] The fact that the flotilla stayed so long with no harm or threatened harm to U.S. citizens led observers to wonder about the administration's characterization of the action as a rescue. If our citizens had been desperate to leave, they would have gotten to the flotilla as soon as it arrived. They did not. The flotilla sat offshore much longer than would have been required for an evacuation of Americans.

Moreover, rescue, even in the midst of serious civil turmoil, can usually be accomplished without sending military forces into a country. We saw that done in the Dominican Republic, prior to the Marine landing. Similarly, during a civil war in Somalia in 1991, we flew in helicopters from offshore ships to evacuate eighty American citizens, and Marines who flew in on the helicopters to protect the evacuation flew out with the evacuees.[19] Later, in 2006, Marines evacuated Americans from Lebanon simply by sailing into port.

But for Liberia we sent six large ships with sophisticated assault equipment and left them there for seven months. Into Liberian territory we sent 225 Marines who stayed for five months. Our aim was less to rescue our citizens than to be on hand in case the civil war threatened our facilities. By January 1991, no harm had come to the installations. With the outbreak of the Persian Gulf war we needed the ships elsewhere, so we left.

NOTES

1. "Liberian Rebels Gain; U.S. Forces Poised," *Los Angeles Times*, June 2, 1990, p. A6, col. 1.

2. Patrick E. Tyler, "U.S. Sends Ships to Liberia, Orders Most Personnel Out," *Washington Post*, June 1, 1990, p. A1, col. 5.

3. J. Gus Liebenow, *Liberia: The Quest for Democracy* (1987), pp. 135–37.

4. Gordon C. Thomasson, "Liberian Disaster Made in the U.S.A.," *New York Times*, July 14, 1990, p. A21, col. 2.

5. Liebenow, *Liberia: The Quest for Democracy*, p. 137; Thomasson, "Liberian Disaster Made in the U.S.A."

6. Clifford Krauss, "U.S. Worried Over Safety of Americans in Liberia as Crisis Grows," *New York Times*, June 2, 1990, p. A3, col. 1.

7. Clifford Krauss, "Strategic Interests Tie U.S. to Liberia," *New York Times*, June 13, 1990, p. A3, col. 1.

8. John W. Mashek, "Marines Evacuate Americans from Liberia amid Rebel Threats," *Boston Globe*, August 6, 1990, p. A1, col. 1.

9. Eric Schmitt, "Liberian Rebel Seizes Foreigners, Including American," *New York Times*, August 7, 1990, p. A3, col. 3.

10. "Department of State Statement," August 5, 1990, *Foreign Policy Bulletin* 1, no. 2 (1990): 30; Michael A. Hiltzik, "Marines Fly Americans from War-Torn Liberia," *Los Angeles Times*, August 6, 1990, p. Al, col. 2.

11. Mashek, "Marines Evacuate Americans from Liberia amid Rebel Threats."

12. "Cuba's Castro Condemns U.S. Marine Landing in Liberia," *Reuter Library Report*, August 6, 1990.

13. Hiltzik, "Marines Fly Americans from War-Torn Liberia."

14. "The Uses of Force," *New York Times*, August 6, 1990, p. A12, col. 1.

15. "Department of State Statement," p. 30.

16. "Defense Department Briefing," Federal Information Systems Corp., January 10, 1991.

17. Krauss, "U.S. Worried Over Safety of Americans in Liberia as Crisis Grows."

18. "Defense Department Briefing."

19. "Americans Are Evacuated from Somalia," *Los Angeles Times*, January 6, 1991, p. A16, col. 1.

31. IRAQ: BLOOD FOR OIL?

When Iraq invaded Kuwait in 1990, President George Bush explained to the public that Iraq was about to do the same to Saudi Arabia. Bush sent 200,000 troops to the deserts of Saudi Arabia. Although Bush did not have hard evidence that Iraq would invade Saudi Arabia, he said it was a fair supposition that it would, since it had just invaded Kuwait, and since it had put into Kuwait large numbers of troops that could be used against Saudi Arabia. To show Iraq's bad intent, Bush reminded the public that in 1980 Iraq had invaded Iran. Iraq, he said, was on a path of conquest.

President Bush's assertion that Iraq was about to invade Saudi Arabia was hardly airtight. Iraq's invasion of Kuwait had grown out of a specific dispute between Iraq and Kuwait. Iraq harbored grievances against Kuwait, one being that Kuwait had been taking oil from a pool lying under a piece of land on the two countries' common border. Iraq claimed that Kuwait was siphoning its oil.

Iraq owed Kuwait for loans Kuwait had made to Iraq during the decade-long Iran-Iraq war that had just ended. Iraq thought Kuwait should forgive the loans because Kuwait had reaped profit from Iraq's inability to export oil during the war. Iraq accused Kuwait of "economic warfare."[1]

Beyond that, Iraq objected that Kuwait was keeping world oil prices low, and that this made it difficult for Iraq to survive. Finally, Kuwait held two islands in the Persian Gulf that Iraq claimed, and which it wanted in order to have better access to the waters of the Persian Gulf. Iraq and Kuwait were in closed talks on all these issues during July 1990, but no resolution emerged.

In addition to these specific grievances, Iraq had a longstanding territorial claim to all of Kuwait. Early in the twentieth century Great Britain controlled the area, and the Iraqi view was that Britain unfairly carved Kuwait out of Iraqi territory as the old Ottoman Empire fell apart. When Britain gave Kuwait its independence in 1962, Iraq made a claim to Kuwait, and both Britain and the Arab League put troops in Kuwait to prevent an Iraqi takeover.

While Iraq had all these issues with Kuwait, it had no similar grievances against Saudi Arabia, except perhaps on oil prices. Iraq had indeed drawn troops up close to the border with Saudi Arabia when it sent troops into Kuwait. U.S. intelligence reported a small contingent of Iraqi troops entering the Saudi portion of a neutral zone between Kuwait and Saudi Arabia. According to the story, Iraqi troops had entered the neutral zone in force.[2] If true, this might have indicated preparation for an Iraqi invasion of Saudi Arabia. But this report, whose origin was unclear, turned out to be false.[3]

A small Iraqi force apparently had entered the zone on the night of August 3, but left when confronted by Saudi border forces.[4]

Newsday quoted a "senior State Department official" saying that while Iraqi troops had entered the neutral zone, they "have made no threatening movements toward the south," no "massing of troops...as they did before the invasion of Kuwait."[5] Although the reports of an Iraqi buildup in the neutral zone were false, they added to the impression that Iraq might be planning to move against Saudi Arabia.

Bush was claiming that Iraqi troops in Kuwait were threatening Saudi Arabia, but satellite photographs obtained by the *St. Petersburg Times* of the Kuwait-Saudi border, taken August 8, 1990, showed no buildup of Iraqi forces.[6] "Two commercial satellite photographs of Kuwait and Saudi

Arabia purchased by this newspaper pose a mystery the Pentagon has a duty to clear up," editorialized the newspaper, "otherwise, the credibility of the U.S. mission in the Persian Gulf region will be undermined."[7]

Iraq denied any intent to invade Saudi Arabia. Saudi officials, while concerned that Iraq might attack some time in the future, did not expect an imminent invasion.[8] They said that the Iraqi deployment near the Kuwait-Saudi border did not presage an Iraqi invasion of Saudi Arabia. They thought that the deployment was aimed at consolidating Iraq's hold on Kuwait against a possible counter-offensive staged from Saudi Arabia. Or, they thought, it might be aimed at creating fear of an invasion of Saudi Arabia, so that the West and the Arab states would accept Iraq's occupation of Kuwait. They did not think Iraq so foolhardy as to go after Saudi Arabia, a much more difficult military target than tiny Kuwait.[9] Administration officials speaking "on background" concurred with the Saudi assessment.

Anxious to insert troops into Saudi Arabia, President Bush dispatched Secretary of Defense Richard Cheney to Riyadh, where he spent several days trying to convince Saudi leaders they were about to be attacked by Iraq, and that they should invite the United States to send in troops.[10]

Whether an imminent Iraqi invasion of Saudi Arabia was in the works turned into a sticky issue for President Bush. To convince Saudi Arabia, and the American public, of the need to send US troops to Saudi Arabia, there had to be an Iraqi threat. But if he sent troops, and there was such a threat, Congress had a right to second-guess him. By law, the president must notify Congress if he sends troops into "imminent involvement in hostilities," and Congress may then force the president to withdraw the forces within sixty days.[11]

When President Bush announced August 7 that he was sending troops to Saudi Arabia, State Department spokesperson Marlin Fitzwater, citing unspecified intelligence information, probably the erroneous report about the neutral zone, said there was "an imminent threat to Saudi Arabia" from the way that the Iraqi forces were "positioned and located in Kuwait."[12] That raised the fear, Bush said, that Iraq would control a hefty percentage of Persian Gulf oil.

President Bush, however, in a less publicized communication, said just the opposite. On August 9 Bush sent a letter to Congress, informing it, as the law required, that he had sent troops to foreign territory. As for what they might face there, Bush wrote, "I do not believe involvement in hostilities is imminent; to the contrary, it is my belief that this deployment will facilitate a peaceful resolution of the crisis."[13] Elaborating for the press, Bush said, "There is no evidence right now that Saddam Hussein would be foolish enough to cross that border (into Saudi Arabia)."[14]

Thus, the administration's assessment on August 7 was that there was an imminent threat of an Iraqi attack on Saudi Arabia, but by August 9 there was no such threat. The media did not press the administration on the discrepancy. For selling the deployment to the public, an imminent Iraqi threat was an advantage, but with Congress it was a liability.

Bush's call to arms to fight to preserve access to oil met a mixed response. At public speeches Bush was dogged by placard slogans like "No blood for oil." Bush changed his emphasis in public statements from oil to the defense of Kuwait. We must stand up against aggression, he said, because if it can happen in one place it can happen anywhere.

The aggression rationale was potentially a better selling point for Bush, but it involved the United States in something of a change of view. In late July our ambassador in Baghdad, April Glaspie, discussed with Iraqi President Saddam Hussein the issues between Iraq and Kuwait. She asked what he would do if his negotiations with Kuwait failed. When Hussein hinted that Iraq might invade Kuwait, Glaspie replied that the United States had no opinion on Iraq's territorial dispute with Kuwait and did not want to be involved. Analysts thought that Hussein might have taken Glaspie's reply to mean that Bush would view an Iraqi invasion of Kuwait as a matter of no great consequence.[15] Iraq and the United States had, after all, practically been allies against their common enemy, Iran. Iraq had attacked Iran, with U.S. blessing, in 1980. Why would Kuwait be any different?

When Iraq invaded Iran in 1980, we supplied it with weapons. With that war, disdain for Iran took precedence over concern about aggression.

Kuwait, to the contrary, had been our ally in the ongoing war over oil prices, raising production from time to time to undermine OPEC. Bush feigned surprise when Iraq invaded, but he was well aware of Iraq's grievances against Kuwait. Glaspie's assurance to Saddam Hussein made it appear that we were inviting an invasion.

Even after Iraq invaded Kuwait, peace feelers were made by Egypt, and Saddam Hussein agreed to discuss withdrawing from Kuwait. But the Bush administration pressed Egypt to issue a public condemnation of Iraq. It did, and that killed the peace effort.[16] That action by the administration suggested that it did not want Iraq to leave Kuwait on its own.

Skeptics suspected that Bush's actual motive in sending troops to Saudi Arabia was to show a need for a large military establishment. The Soviet Union had just bowed out of the arms race, leaving the West with little reason for major weapon systems. We saw the same suspicion about Bush in his invasion of Panama. New enemies would justify the need for weaponry.

Whatever the administration's aims, the Persian Gulf plot thickened in November 1990 when Bush doubled our force in Saudi Arabia to give it, as he said, an offensive capability to drive Iraq out of Kuwait. To justify this new and larger deployment, President Bush floated a new rationale for our involvement. Iraq, he said, was developing nuclear weapons, and in the hands of a country bent on aggression, this would pose a danger to world peace. While this new rationale held some appeal, it too had its flaws. Iraq had undertaken some development aimed at nuclear weaponry but, from what was known, Iraq was some years away from being ready to deliver a nuclear weapon against an enemy.

Bush's nuclear rationale gained some public following, but each change of focus cast doubt on his motivation. Later in November, Bush followed up on the Saudi troop deployment by getting United Nations backing for an invasion of Iraq. At Bush's initiative, the UN Security Council adopted Resolution 678 authorizing any UN member country to use "all necessary means" to get Iraq out of Kuwait if it didn't leave by January 15, 1991. Council members, although they agreed to this language, said that military force was to be only a last resort. Council members said that intensive diplomacy should precede any hostilities.[17]

President Bush, his offensive formation in place, did not negotiate with Iraq. After the Security Council vote, his administration held only one meeting with Iraq, a session in Geneva during which Secretary of State James Baker simply told Iraq to leave Kuwait. Baker, by his own account, did not explore ways of resolving Iraq's differences with Kuwait.[18] Iraq floated peace feelers, but the administration ignored them.

Bush drummed up support for an invasion of Iraq. His standard remarks on Iraq during October and November 1990 included a story he said he had heard from the Emir of Kuwait, who visited the White House. Iraqi soldiers, after occupying Kuwait, tore babies off incubators in a Kuwait hospital and left them to die, taking the incubators back to Iraq.[19] Also in October, a Kuwaiti girl, 15 years old, told the same story to a caucus hearing in the U.S. Congress. What she did not tell Congress when she testified was that she was the daughter of the Kuwaiti ambassador in Washington, and that her story had been put together with the help of a professional consulting firm.[20] After Iraq withdrew from Kuwait, staff members at the Kuwaiti hospital were asked by reporters about the story. They said that the incubators that had been in the hospital before Iraq's invasion were still there, and that no babies had been removed from them by Iraqi soldiers.[21]

On January 16, 1991, the United States launched a blistering aerial attack on Iraq. President Bush explained that he acted "in accord with United Nations resolutions," and that the attack followed "months of constant and virtually endless diplomatic activity."[22] But if there had been "endless diplomatic activity," Bush had not involved Iraq in it.

The manner in which the air campaign against Iraq was conducted raised further questions about American aims. The Security Council had anticipated that the United States would attack Iraqi forces in and near Kuwait. It did not expect bombing of the Iraqi heartland. Malaysia's Security Council delegate, for example, in explaining his vote in favor of the resolution authorizing force against Iraq, said that the resolution "does not provide a blank cheque for excessive and indiscriminate use of force," and cautioned "against any action purportedly taken under this resolution that would lead to the virtual destruction of Iraq."[23]

The United States, however, when it attacked Iraq, nearly accomplished what Malaysia had feared. Arguing that it needed to destroy support facilities that allowed the Iraqi forces to occupy Kuwait, the United States conducted massive aerial bombardment of Iraq, running 92,000 air sorties and dropping 88,500 tons of bombs.[24]

The bombs were dropped primarily on urban areas, and many misdirected bombs hit civilians. According to General Merrill McPeak, Air Force Chief of Staff, 70 percent of the bombs missed their targets.[25] On February 9, UN Secretary-General Javier Pérez de Cuellar called it "disturbing" that "civilian casualties are mounting and that damage to residential areas throughout Iraq has been widespread."[26] Mahathir Mohammed, prime minister of Malaysia, said that the rapid escalation was taking the action beyond what was authorized in Resolution 678.[27]

One analyst wrote, "The wanton destruction of mosques, schools, invalid homes, institutes for the disabled, civilian shelters and agricultural plant had nothing to do with the eviction of the Iraqi forces from Kuwait."[28] After the fighting ended, a UN team visited Iraq to investigate its condition. The team found Iraq unable to produce industrial goods to any significant degree as result of the bombing. Calling the bombing "near apocalyptic," the team said that life in Iraq had been reduced to a "pre-industrial stage."[29] The bombing damaged electrical generating plants and water and sewage treatment facilities, leading to a shortage of clean drinking water and a rise in waterborne diseases. Tens of thousands of children reportedly died as a result.[30] According to military personnel who chose bombing targets, the U.S. military planners understood that they were destroying civilized life in Iraq.[31]

After a month of air strikes, Iraq was still in Kuwait. On February 23, 1991, President Bush launched a ground assault on Iraqi forces, explaining that his aim was "to eject the Iraqi Army from Kuwait."[32] The previous day, however, the administration had demanded that Iraq leave Kuwait over a one-week period, and the Soviet Union, which was in intense talks with Iraq, got it to agree to leave Kuwait over a three-week period. Bush said he could not wait three weeks, because Iraq was following a "scorched-earth" policy in Kuwait.

Bush's rejection of a three-week withdrawal created doubt that he was being truthful when he said that an Iraqi withdrawal from Kuwait was his only objective. Even if Iraq was causing damage in Kuwait, a ground offensive would likely cause more. When National Security Adviser Brent Scowcroft was asked about our aims, he acknowledged a purpose that Bush had not mentioned, saying the administration hoped to leave Iraq with "no offensive capability."[33] This aim was confirmed by General Thomas Kelly, director of operations for the Joint Chiefs of Staff. Kelly said that Bush had asked the JCS both to get the Iraqis out of Kuwait and to "destroy their ability to conduct offensive operations" outside Iraq in the future.[34] If Scowcroft and Kelly were accurate, the rationale Bush gave the public for the ground offensive was only part of the truth.

Secretary of State Baker hinted at yet one other reason for the ground offensive when he suggested that removing Iraqi President Saddam Hussein from power might be authorized by the Security Council resolutions.[35] In any event, the administration's aims went well beyond what it explained to the public.

Shortly after the ground offensive began, Iraq decided it had had enough and ordered its forces to withdraw from Kuwait immediately. The troops began a pullout. The administration, however, refused to stop its offensive, saying that Iraq must comply not only with the Security Council resolution calling on it to leave Kuwait, but with other resolutions the Council had passed about the situation.[36] The other resolutions, however, related to Iraq's occupation of Kuwait, and to sanctions aimed at getting it to leave. One resolution demanded that Iraq allow foreign nationals to leave Iraq, but Iraq had already done that. One other held Iraq responsible for financial loss resulting from the invasion, but that was hardly an issue that could be resolved overnight. The administration's reference to the other resolutions was an apparent smoke screen to allow it more time to destroy Iraq's military infrastructure.

The United States, wrote one military analyst, fought on longer than necessary to drive Iraq from Kuwait, keeping the conflict going "despite a series of frantic peace bids until they were confident that they had shattered Mr. Hussein's best divisions."[37] This approach was most apparent as Iraq began to withdraw from Kuwait. Of the withdrawal, President Bush said, "This changes nothing. The allied assault will continue with undiminished intensity."[38]

As Iraqi troops fled from Kuwait, the United States fired on them in what was described by eyewitnesses as a "turkey shoot." Iraqi forces were fleeing for their lives and were unable to return fire.[39] The U.S. firing destroyed a large convoy of Iraqi vehicles and resulted in the deaths of thousands of fleeing Iraqis.[40] One senior Air Force analyst called the bombing "an outrage," because the fleeing Iraqis "were whipped."[41]

U.S. commanders justified the slaughter on the ground that the Iraqi forces were taking their equipment and arms with them. General Merrill McPeak, Air Force Chief of Staff, explained, "When enemy armies are defeated, they retreat, often in disorder, and we have what is known in the business as the exploitation phase." General McPeak said, "It's during this phase that the true fruits of victory are achieved from combat."[42]

A year after the end of the Gulf war, the Pentagon produced a policy paper outlining U.S. aims in various parts of the world. "In the Middle East and Southwest Asia," the document recited, "our overall objective is to remain the predominant outside power in the region and preserve U.S. and Western access to the region's oil."[43]

While the paper did not say that this objective had been the reason for the Gulf war, it took little reading between the lines. Iraqis who remembered the 1960s would have needed little convincing. A nationalist government that took power in Iraq in 1958 was involved in founding OPEC and in seeking a better deal for Iraq on its oil. In 1963, the CIA helped overthrow that government.[44]

NOTES

1. Martin Yant, *Desert Mirage: The True Story of the Gulf War* (1991), pp. 18–19.

2. John Kifner, "Arabs' Summit Meeting Off; Iraqi Units in Kuwait Dig in; Europe Bars Baghdad's Oil," *New York Times*, August 5, 1990, p. A1.

3. "Chronology of the Crisis," *Middle East International*, August 31, 1990, p. 24.

4. "British Troops Feared Held by Saddam's Men," *Daily Telegraph*, August 5, 1990, p. 1.

5. Fred Bruning, "Enter `Neutral Zone'; Won't Attack Saudi Land, Top Arabs Say," *Newsday*, August 5, 1990, p. 3.

6. Jean Heller, "Photos Don't Show Buildup," *St. Petersburg Times*, January 6, 1991, p. 1A.

7. Editorial, "Explain the Mystery," *St. Petersburg Times*, January 8, 1991, p. 8A.

8. Youssef M. Ibrahim, "Bush Sends U.S. Force to Saudi Arabia as Kingdom Agrees to Confront Iraq," *New York Times*, August 8, 1990, p. A1.

9. Thomas Friedman, "Bush, Hinting Force, Declares Iraqi Assault `Will Not Stand'; Proxy in Kuwait Issues Threat," *New York Times*, August 7, 1990, p. A1.

10. Andrew Rosenthal, "Bush Sends U.S. Force to Saudi Arabia as Kingdom Agrees to Confront Iraq," *New York Times*, August 8, 1990, p. A1; Bob Woodward, *The Commanders* (1991), pp. 263–77.

11. US Code, vol. 50, §§1543–44.

12. Rosenthal, "Bush Sends U.S. Force to Saudi Arabia as Kingdom Agrees to Confront Iraq."

13. Letter to the Speaker of the House and the President Pro Tempore of the Senate on the Deployment of United States Armed Forces to Saudi Arabia and the Middle East, Aug. 9, 1990, *Weekly Compilation of Presidential Documents*, August 13, 1990, p. 1225; R. W. Apple, Jr., "U.S. Says Its Troops in the Gulf Could Reach 100,000 in Months," *New York Times*, August 11, 1990, p. A1, col. 4.

14. Dan Balz, "Bush Warns Iraq Against Sending Out Oil Tankers," *Washington Post*, August 11, 1990, p. A23.

15. Elaine Sciolino, "U.S. Gave Iraq Little Reason Not to Mount Kuwait Assault," *New York Times*, September 23, 1990, p. A1.

16. Pierre Salinger and Eric Laurent, *Secret Dossier: The Hidden Agenda Behind the Gulf War* (1991), pp. 112–13.

17. SCOR, 45th yr., 2963d meeting, UN Doc. S/PV.2963 (1990).

18. "Excerpts from Bush's Remarks on Baker's Mission and Diplomacy's Fate," *New York Times*, January 10, 1991, p. A16.

19. Linda Diebel, "Bush Warns Saddam of War-crimes Trial," *Toronto Star*, October 16, 1990, p. A15.

20. John R. MacArthur, *Second Front: Censorship and Propaganda in the Gulf War* (1992), pp. 58–61.

21. Robert L. Koenig, "Testimony of Kuwaiti Envoy's Child Assailed," *St. Louis Post-Dispatch*, January 9, 1992, p. 1C.

22. "Transcript of the Comments by Bush on the Air Strikes Against the Iraqis," *New York Times*, January 17, 1991, p. A6.

23. SCOR, 45th yr., 2963d mtg., pp. 76–77, UN Doc. S/PV.2963 (1990) (Mr. Abu Hassan, Malaysia).

24. Fred Kaplan, "General Credits Air Force with Iraqi Army's Defeat," *Boston Globe*, March 16, 1991, p. A1; Geoff Simons, *The Scourging of Iraq: Sanctions, Law and Natural Justice* (1998), p. 4.

25. Barton Gellman, "U.S. Bombs Missed 70% of Time," *Washington Post*, March 16, 1991, p. A1.

26. Nikolai Maslov, "UN Chief Informs Security Council on Gulf Situation," Tass News Agency, February 9, 1991.

27. Thalif Deen, "Third World Charges Security Council Meeting Blocked," Inter Press Service, February 4, 1991.

28. Simons, *The Scourging of Iraq*, p. 13.

29. "Excerpts from U.N. Report on Need for Humanitarian Assistance in Iraq," *New York Times*, March 23, 1991, p. A5; Paul Lewis, "UN Survey Calls Iraq's War Damage Near-Apocalyptic," *New York Times*, March 22, 1991, p. A1.

30. Roger Normand and Chris af Jochnick, "The Legitimation of Violence: A Critical Analysis of the Gulf War," *Harvard International Law Journal* 35 (1994): 399.

31. Barton Gellman, "Allied Air War Struck Broadly in Iraq: Officials Acknowledge Strategy Went beyond Purely Military Targets," *Washington Post*, June 23, 1991, p. A1.

32. "Announcement by Bush on Start of Ground War," *New York Times*, February 25, 1991, p. A13.

33. Interview, Meet the Press, NBC-TV, February 24, 1991.

34. Interview, Sunday Today, NBC-TV, March 31, 1991.

35. Interview, This Week, ABC-TV, February 24, 1991.

36. Patrick E. Tyler, "Baghdad Cites Soviets' Plan; Administration Wants More," *New York Times*, February 26, 1991, p. A1.

37. R.W. Apple Jr., "Another Gulf War?" *New York Times*, March 10, 1991, p. A16.

38. "Countdown to Iraq's Defeat," *Middle East International*, March 8, 1991, p. 7.

39. Christopher Hitchens, "Minority Report," *Nation*, March 25, 1991, p. 366.

40. Simons, *The Scourging of Iraq*, pp. 8–9.

41. Knut Royce and Timothy M. Phelps, "Rout of Iraqis Became Savage `Turkey Shoot,'" *Newsday*, March 31, 1991, p. 7.

42. Fred Kaplan, "General Credits Air Force with Iraqi Army's Defeat," *Boston Globe*, March 16, 1991, p. A1.

43. "Excerpts from Pentagon's Plan: Prevent the Emergence of a New Rival," *New York Times*, March 8, 1992, p. A14.

44. Ramsey Clark, *The Fire This Time: U.S. War Crimes in the Gulf* (1992), p. 4.

32. SOMALIA: BLACKHAWK DOWN

In 1992, the United States intervened in Somalia in a situation of breakdown of domestic order. The country's central government had collapsed after Somalia's authoritarian ruler Siad Barre was challenged by local clans and fled the country in 1991. After Barre's departure, clan-based militias assumed control in various parts of the country. As order broke down, the population was unable to feed itself or take care of other basic needs. Humanitarian relief organizations tried to assist, but they found themselves under attack by the clan-based militias.

In this context, the UN Security Council adopted a resolution authorizing member states to intervene militarily. Resolution 794 determined that a threat to the peace existed in the Somalia situation and "authorize[d] the Secretary General and Member States cooperating to implement the offer referred to in paragraph 8 above to use all necessary means to establish as soon as possible a secure environment for humanitarian relief operations in Somalia."[1] Paragraph eight referred to an offer made by the United States to establish a military force to enter Somalia. The Bush administration had decided it wanted to intervene, and it got the Security Council to adopt a resolution to allow it. Resolution 794 was adopted unanimously; Council members expressed concern about the breakdown of order in Somalia and the risk to the population since basic needs were not being met.[2]

In the debate that preceded the vote on Resolution 794, a number of Security Council members expressed concern that the operation was being handled in the same way as the Iraq operation had been handled in 1990, namely, by giving over control to unnamed member states. They knew that the United States would be the prime actor, since, as in the Iraq situation, it was the United States that had lobbied the Council for authorization and had offered to intervene if the Council authorized.[3]

Under the UN Charter, the Security Council is to organize and control military action it takes in the name of international peace. Here it would have no control. Belgium in particular said it "would have preferred this to be a purely United Nations operation."[4] China said, "in spite of the fact that the Secretary-General has been given some authorization [to control the operation], the draft resolution has taken the form of authorizing certain countries to take military actions, which may adversely affect the collective role of the United Nations. We hereby express our reservations on this."[5]

India, too, complained that the Council was giving the United States too free a hand: "The present actions should not," it said, "set a precedent for the future. We would expect that, should situations arise in the future requiring action under Chapter VII, it would be carried out in full conformity with the Charter provisions."[6]

President Bush stressed the depths of the humanitarian disaster in Somalia. "One and a half million people could starve to death," he said, explaining his decision to intervene. Delivery of relief supplies had broken down: "Truck convoys from Somalia's ports were blocked. Sufficient food failed to reach the starving in the interior of Somalia." "There is no government in Somalia. Law and order have broken down. Anarchy prevails."

Bush disavowed any ulterior motives in Somalia: "We have no intent to remain in Somalia with fighting forces, but we are determined to do it right, to secure an environment that will allow food to get to the starving people of Somalia." He said, "We do not plan to dictate political outcomes. We respect your sovereignty and independence."[7]

Neither our own troops nor those of other nations that joined found any great success in meeting Bush's objectives. The situation in Somalia was so chaotic that the U.S. forces were unable to protect even themselves. President Clinton, who took office six weeks after the intervention began, decided at one point to target the forces of one of the principal warlords, Mohammed Aidid. U.S. forces successfully detained some of Aidid's militia personnel in October 1993 in downtown Mogadishu. A Blackhawk helicopter was hit by ground fire, however, and U.S. Rangers who came to protect wounded crewmen took fire. Twelve U.S. personnel were killed, 78 others were wounded, and six were taken hostage. The next day, the body of one of the killed Americans was dragged through the streets to cheering by Mogadishu residents.[8] The next day Clinton said he would withdraw all U.S. forces from Somalia.[9]

In the wake of the Somalia fiasco, the Clinton Administration adopted a policy directive in which it stated that the United States would participate in UN actions only if its own interests were involved. This was Presidential Directive 25 of May 4, 1994. In the directive, titled *Reforming Multilateral Peacekeeping Operations*, President Clinton set criteria for U.S. involvement that stressed U.S. interests as a prerequisite.[10]

The directive was at odds with the UN Charter, which calls on the Security Council, of which the United States is a permanent member, to act to preserve the international peace, even if the interests of a state are not involved. The directive heightened the perception that the United States acts to protect its own interests rather than collective interests.

Even with regard to Somalia, however, the interests of the United States may not have been irrelevant. The Somalia situation arose just after the U.S. military action against Iraq. "The Gulf War—'Desert Storm'— changed our strategic view of Somalia virtually overnight," wrote Herman Cohen, who served as Assistant Secretary of State for African Affairs under Bush.[11] Even though by late 1992 the Iraq intervention had ended, the Iraq situation remained problematic for the United States. Maintaining access through the Red Sea was key to achieving U.S. objectives in Iraq. As will be seen in chapter 33, the Red Sea would shortly become a launch area for missile attacks against Iraq.

Even before its military intervention in the Persian Gulf, Somalia's proximity to the Gulf had made Somalia an object of strategic interest for the United States. Somalia had been friendly to the Soviet Union in the 1970s. But when Somalia invaded the Ogaden region of Ethiopia in an effort to incorporate it, the Soviet Union backed Ethiopia. Somalia cut ties with the USSR, and the United States stepped in to befriend Somalia.[12] This was a cold war coup for the United States, which allowed the U.S. to make inroads in a country that had been in the Soviet camp. Somalia became, to the United States, a bulwark against communism in Africa.[13]

Somalia's geographic position was also key. Somalia lay just across the Red Sea from Saudi Arabia and Iraq. The Red Sea was an important highway for U.S. military vessels sailing to and from the Persian Gulf. Somalia had long been of strategic interest to European powers anxious for access via the Red Sea to India or southeast Asia.[14] In the 1970s, the USSR had operated a military base at Port Berbera, on the Gulf of Aden in northern Somalia.[15]

The United States quickly took over the base at Port Berbera, rewarding Barre with military aid in exchange. Sam Gejdenson, chair of the U.S. House of Representatives Subcommittee on International Economic Policy and Trade, wrote that Somalia's strategic significance for the United States lay both in its proximity to the Persian Gulf and in its air and naval facilities at the Port of Berbera. The United States viewed these facilities as "forward and rear deployment areas for operations in the Persian Gulf and the Straits of Hormuz."[16] From 1980, the United States stationed a rapid deployment force unit at Port Berbera.[17] When the situation in Somalia deteriorated in late 1990, however, the U.S. abandoned the base.[18]

At a Defense Department briefing on the Somalia intervention, reporters asked General Joseph Hoar, Commander of the U.S. Central Command, whether there might be a strategic motive behind the intervention. "There's been some cynical people that suggest," said a reporter, "our motivation behind this might be to get some kind of permanent military presence in the Horn of Africa, and it's long been known that Central Command has had the desire at some point to at least have a forward headquarters over there."

General Hoar replied: "During the Cold War, we had made arrangements with Somalia to use under some mutually agreeable circumstances the port and airfield at Berbera, which is all the way up north. That port . . . is about 165 miles from the Bab al Mandeb." Bab al Mandeb is the strait leading from the Red Sea into the Indian Ocean. It provides the only sea passage from Europe or North America to the Middle East without requiring vessels to go south around the African land mass.

"And our interest and our concern at that time," General Hoar continued, "was to be able to keep that very narrow strait open since there were Soviet forces on both sides. That threat has clearly diminished. I think it's fair to say that our principal national interest in the central region is focused on the Gulf, the free flow of oil, and the moderate Arab states with which we've worked every day."

Although General Hoar did not acknowledge a strategic motive to the Somalia intervention, in the same breath he acknowledged Somalia's geographic importance and the importance of Persian Gulf oil. The difficulties the United States encountered in Somalia kept it from reaping any strategic benefit it may have sought.

NOTES

1. Res. 794, SCOR, 47th yr., Res. & Decs., p. 63, UN Doc. S/INF/48 (1992).

2. UN SCOR, 47th yr., 3145th mtg., pp. 27–28, UN Doc. S/PV.3145 (1992).

3. "Mission to Somalia: Transcript of President's Address on Somalia," *New York Times*, December 5, 1992, p. A4.

4. SCOR, 47th yr., 3145th mtg., p. 24, UN Doc. S/PV.3145 (1992) (Mr. Noterdaeme, Belgium).

5. SCOR, 47th yr., 3145th mtg., p. 17, UN Doc. S/PV.3145 (1992) (Mr. Li Daoyu, China).

6. SCOR, 47th Sess., 3145th mtg., at 51, U.N. Doc. S/PV.3145 (1992) (Mr. Gharekan, India).

7. "Mission to Somalia: Transcript of President's Address on Somalia,"

New York Times, December 5, 1992, p. A4; Art Pine, "U.S. Boosts Somalia Troops after 12 Die," *Los Angeles Times*, October 5, 1993, p. A1.

8. Herman Cohen, *Intervening in Africa: Superpower Peacemaking in a Troubled Continent* (2000), p. 215.

9. Bureau of International Organization Affairs, U.S. Department of State, Pub. No. 10161 (1994), in *International Legal Materials* 33 (1994): 802.

10. Cohen, *Intervening in Africa*, p. 203.

11. Rajendra Ramlogan, "Towards a New Vision of World Security: The United Nations Security Council and the Lessons of Somalia," *Houston Journal of International Law* 16 (1993): 218–19.

12. Michael Binyon, "Wily Barre Played East against West," *Times* (London), January 28, 1991, Overseas news.

13. Ramlogan, "Towards a New Vision of World Security," p. 221.

14. Michael Binyon, "Wily Barre Played East against West."

15. Sam Gejdenson, "Congress Makes U.S. Foreign Policy: Somalia: A Case Study," *American University Journal of International Law & Policy* 5 (1990): 1089.

16. Rick Wells, "Battered Somalia Navigates Rocky Shoals of Reaganomics," *Financial Times*, December 8, 1982, p. 4.

17. Peter Godwin, "Somali Rebel Wages a War from Wimbledon," *Times* (London), June 5, 1988.

18. Richard Dowden, "Mystery of Soviet Arms Find in Somalia," *Independent* (London), May 27, 1991, p. 7.

33. BAGHDAD: MISSILES WITH A MESSAGE

It was not long before the Red Sea figured in a U.S. military action. On June 27, 1993, President William Clinton ordered the launch of twenty-three Tomahawk cruise missiles from vessels in the Red Sea and Persian Gulf. Most of the missiles struck their target, the headquarters building of Iraq's Intelligence Service in downtown Baghdad. Three hit nearby residential areas, where eight persons were killed and a dozen injured. Clinton expressed regret for the casualties.[1]

Clinton said the raid had accomplished its purpose: "It was a success. I feel quite good about what transpired. I think the American people should feel good."[2] To Clinton's bad fortune, however, one of the victims was Leila Attar, a well-known Iraqi painter, who was killed along with her husband when an errant missile hit their home. When Attar and the other victims were buried, a crowd of ten thousand joined the funeral procession, demanding revenge for the raid.[3]

Clinton explained the raid as a response to a plot by Iraq's intelligence agency to assassinate former U.S. President George Bush. No actual attempt had been made against Bush, but a group of men had been arrested in Kuwait with a Toyota Land Cruiser containing a car bomb. They had apparently come in from Iraq shortly before Bush was scheduled to visit Kuwait to make a speech.

The Clinton administration reported the June 27 raid to the UN Security Council. Military force can be used only in self-defense, and it must be reported to the Security Council. The United States claimed self-defense and presented evidence to substantiate a plot against Bush. Iraq, denying the plot, asked the Council to condemn the United States for aggression.[4]

The administration characterized the alleged attempt on Bush as an "armed attack" against the United States. "It is clear that this was no impulsive or random act," said President Clinton. "It was an elaborate plan devised by the Iraqi government and directed against a former president of the United States because of actions he took as president. As such, the Iraqi attack against President Bush was an attack against our country and against all Americans."

Clinton explained the rationale for the raids as protection and deterrence: "There should be no mistake about the message we intend these actions to convey to Saddam Hussein; to the rest of the Iraqi leadership; and to any nation, group, or person who would harm our leaders or our citizens. We will combat terrorism. We will deter aggression. We will protect our people."

Clinton also provided a detailed account of the evidence that he said showed Iraq was behind the alleged plot. He explained that the explosives "have been directly examined by FBI forensic experts. In the judgment of these experts," he said, "key components—including the remote-control firing device, the plastic explosives, the blasting cap, the integrated circuitry, and the wiring—were built by the same person or persons who built bombs previously recovered from the Iraqis. Certain aspects of these devices have been found only in devices linked to Iraq and not in devices used by any other terrorist groups. According to the forensic experts, other explosives seized in this plot, including 'cube bombs,' contained components built by the same person or persons who built similar devices recovered in the past from Iraqis."[5]

Kuwaiti police arrested sixteen persons, mostly Iraqis, connected with the Toyota, and charged twelve with plotting against Bush.[6] As UN ambassador Madeleine Albright told the Council, the U.S. Federal

Bureau of Investigation had examined the bomb and concluded that "key components, including the remote-controlled firing device, the plastic explosives, the blasting cap, the integrated circuitry and the wiring, were built by the same person or persons who built bombs previously recovered from the Iraqis. Certain aspects of these devices have been found only in devices linked to Iraq and not in devices used by any other terrorist group." Albright said that "the United States Department of Justice and the Central Intelligence Agency have concluded that Iraq planned, equipped, and launched the terrorist operation that threatened the life of an American President."[7] Albright held up a photograph of the front of the explosive device allgedly found in the Toyota next to a photograph of another device she claimed had previously been used by the Iraqi government. "Even an untrained eye," she said, "can see that these are identical except for the serial numbers." Then Albright did the same with interior photographs: "As you can see," she said, "the selection of the components and the construction techniques in the two devices, including soldering, the use of connectors and the wiring techniques, are also identical."[8]

To demonstrate motive, Albright cited statements by the Iraqi government suggesting that it planned to punish President Bush for having waged war against Iraq in 1991.[9] She said that U.S. officials had interviewed the sixteen suspects,[10] and that two Iraqis among them confessed having been recruited in Basra, Iraq, by "individuals associated with the Iraqi intelligence service," who provided them with the car bomb on April 10, 1993.[11]

According to the U.S. claim, the plotters had planned to blow up the Toyota alongside Bush's motorcade. Failing that, the Toyota was to be exploded during a public speech by Bush at a university campus. If that was not possible, then a suicide bomber wrapped in explosives would assault Bush.

Wali Ghazali, one of the Iraqi suspects, said he was approached by an Iraqi intelligence agent who provided the Toyota Land Cruiser outfitted with explosives and asked him to take it to Kuwait and to assassinate Bush.[12] Ghazali told the court in Kuwait that he had been asked to detonate the rigged Toyota near a university, where he was told Bush would give a speech, and, if that plan failed, to carry out a suicide bombing. U.S. officials said that the Toyota contained 175 pounds of plastic explosives, enough to injure persons within a four-hundred-yard radius when detonated.[13] Kuwaiti police said that they found the bomb-rigged Toyota parked in an agricultural area near Kuwait City at a sheep pen owned by one of the persons subsequently charged in the case.[14]

Iraqi Ambassador Nizar Hamdun, addressing the Security Council in reply, denied Iraqi involvement in any plot against President Bush: "The Government of Iraq has denied, and continues to deny, any role with respect to the alleged attempt." "That story was completely fabricated," he said, "by the Kuwaiti regime for well-known purposes relating to its policy towards Iraq and with a view to damaging and harming my country." Hamdun said "that for similar purposes certain organs within the United States Administration found in this story a pretext for an act of aggression against Iraq in pursuance of the United States policy of containment against Iraq." Hamdun challenged the United States "to come up with any clear evidence acceptable to an impartial third party." He said that the United States "has accused and sentenced Iraq, and has carried out its sentence, all without providing evidence against it or inviting it to clarify its position."[15]

No Security Council member introduced a resolution to condemn the United States. At the end of Albright's presentation and a brief discussion, the Security Council president adjourned the meeting, stating, "No proposal on this item has been submitted on which the Security Council is required to take action. Therefore, I understand that the Council has thus concluded its consideration of the item before it."[16] The Council never took up the matter again.

While Council members from Europe expressed approval of the missile strike, Council members Cape Verde, Djibouti, Morocco, Pakistan, and Venezuela urged "restraint by all States, consistent with the principles of the Charter and in particular for the maintenance of international peace and security and the avoidance of the use of force inconsistent with the purposes of the United Nations."[17] China said that disputes "should be settled through peaceful means of dialogue and consultation. We are opposed to any action that can contravene the Charter of the United Nations and norms of international relations."[18]

At the meeting, Albright presented evidence to show the discovery of a bomb in Kuwait at the time of Bush's visit there, but less evidence of a plot to assassinate Bush, and less still of Iraq's direction of such a plot. The alleged leader of the plotters, Ra'ad Assadi, was said by Kuwaiti officials to have admitted to being a colonel in the Iraqi secret service. However, in a security court in Kuwait, Assadi denied he held such a position and identified himself as a professional smuggler who had been asked to smuggle the group into Kuwait.[19] When the judge remarked to another of the suspects, Salem Nasser al-Shammari, that he looked familiar, the suspect replied he had been jailed fifteen times in Kuwait for smuggling.[20]

U.S. investigators visited Kuwait in May and apparently were unconvinced of an Iraqi plot against Bush, prompting them to make a second trip to Kuwait in June.[21] The administration did not explain what the investigators learned during the second trip that dispelled the doubts left after the first.

In the security court in Kuwait, two of the men arrested confessed to having participated in a conspiracy to assassinate Bush, while the others denied it.[22] Most of the men were apparently connected with the lucrative trade of smuggling liquor from Iraq, where liquor can legally be sold, into Kuwait, where it cannot. One reason for doubting an Iraqi plot against Bush was that whisky smugglers were neither a reliable group for such a project nor technically competent to carry it off.[23] One Clinton administration official said that the group looked like "the Keystone Kops."[24]

Even if the group had intended harm to Bush, the link to the Iraq Intelligence Service was not obvious. Defense lawyers claimed in the Kuwait court that the incriminating statements were the product of coercion by Kuwaiti interrogators. The State Department, in its annual human rights report for 1993, noted these claims and reported evidence of abuses by Kuwaiti State Security police, the very police that interrogated these suspects. "There were credible reports of abuse in Kuwaiti detention facilities, especially at the KSS facility," the Department said. "Reported abuses included blindfolding detainees, verbal abuse, and some physical abuse, particularly beating detainees on the soles of their feet and burning detainees with cigarettes. In some cases detainees were slapped, kicked, or shoved against walls. In one instance, Kuwaiti police and KSS personnel beat and used electrical shocks to torture a Kuwaiti man." The State Department noted that the judge trying the Bush plot case declined to exclude the confessions.[25] Even apart from possible torture, there was the possibility that the confessions were the product of a calculation that a conviction was inevitable, and that an admission might yield a more lenient sentence.

Wali Ghazali, in his incriminating statement, said that he had been told to set the bomb off during a Bush speech at Kuwait University. In fact, Bush was to speak at a different university in Kuwait. In addition, Bush would have been riding in an armor-plated vehicle, so setting off the bomb in the manner Ghazali said was planned, in the general vicinity of the speech, would likely not have harmed Bush.[26]

The Kuwaitis, moreover, had much to gain by pointing the finger at Iraq. Sami G. Hajjar, a former Army War College specialist on the Middle East, said it was possible that the plot was staged by the Kuwaitis "to pump up the Iraqi threat and to ingratiate themselves with the U.S." The *Baltimore Sun* asked a former CIA officer with long experience in the Middle East about this possibility. Without disclosing the name of the officer, the *Sun* quoted him as saying, "The Kuwaitis would not be reliable sources."[27]

The hostility between Kuwait and Iraq at the time did give the Kuwaitis a motive for giving a black eye to the government of Iraq. Kuwaiti officialdom was known for making up negative stories about Iraq, and for that reason many in the Clinton administration initially dismissed the Kuwaitis' claims of an anti-Bush plot. They remembered the false Kuwaiti claims in 1990 about babies being torn from incubators in a Kuwait hospital.

Clinton had strong reasons to go ahead with a missile strike, even if the evidence was less than airtight. Clinton had just entered office. A new president may view a military action as a demonstration that he is to be taken seriously. Clinton was perceived as soft on security.[28] The raid, moreover, was a limited military action, confined to a short time period, with no commitment of troops. So the downside risks were low. Presented with information that might or might not show an Iraqi plot against Bush, Clinton had more to gain by acting than by doing nothing. After the raid, his approval rating climbed.

By defending Bush, Clinton would potentially reap political rewards. He was defending a member of the opposition political party, moreover, one he had just defeated in an election. Additionally, he was defending a president, and he, after all, was himself a president.

On the other side, Clinton faced political trouble if he failed to act. From the time the Kuwaitis made public their information about the Toyota in April, major media had pilloried Clinton for not responding. Senior officials in Clinton's administration who wanted a stronger anti-Iraq policy leaked information to reporters, who in turn printed the information in a way that made Clinton appear weak or indecisive. On May 8, the *Washington Post* reported administration officials saying that the plot story was true. The *Post* named two officials as advocating retribution against Iraq: Sandy Berger, Clinton's deputy assistant for security, and CIA Director James Woolsey.[29]

Members of Congress responded to the leaks and called on Clinton to act. Lee Hamilton, chair of the House Foreign Affairs Committee, said, "We should retaliate." Senator Richard Lugar said that a military response "is the only thing that Iraq would understand.[30]

The *New York Times* cited officials as saying that the device found in the Toyota was similar to devices used by Iraqi agents during the Gulf war.[31] This leaked information put more pressure on Clinton.

The *Post* took up the story again in early June, repeating that the administration had evidence of a plot and of Iraqi involvement. It quoted an unnamed "senior intelligence analyst" saying, "You can look at the type of the devices that were used in this case and past cases and you can infer a connection."[32] By late June the fact that the FBI was about to give

Clinton a report that would point the finger at Iraq was leaked to the press. On June 23 a *Wall Street Journal* analyst reported that fact. Writing under the incendiary headline "For the President, It's Decision Time on Attacking Iraq," he called for broad military action: "It may be time to start building a case for renewed military action against Iraq, in which the plot to kill Mr. Bush could be the main exhibit."[33]

Clinton was backed into a corner. If he didn't act, he was weak. If he did, he could expect kudos. Attorney General Janet Reno gave Clinton the FBI report on June 24. Clinton decided on the attack on June 25, and it was carried out June 26.

Whatever the calculation may have been, information that became available after the missile strike made Clinton's case seem less convincing. A few months later, journalist Seymour Hersh showed Albright's photographs to seven explosives experts. They said, to a person, that the circuitry in the photographs was readily available commercially; the components could be found in ordinary walkie-talkies. They found nothing to connect the device to Iraq.[34]

More damaging still, the FBI chemist who analyzed the device found in the Toyota Land Cruiser said that Hersh's experts were right. Frederic Whitehurst was, in 1993, the FBI's top specialist on analysis of explosives. An FBI evaluation of his work said that he was "unequaled in any laboratory." Whitehurst had done the analysis on the World Trade Center bombing and other high profile cases.[35] Clinton had referred in his statement about the raid to "the forensic experts." Whitehurst was the main expert.

Whitehurst described his reaction when he heard Clinton and Albright saying that the explosives could be linked to the Iraqi government. "I thought 'The news has got this wrong.' I said specifically it wasn't a match." When Whitehurst later saw a document prepared by higher-ups in the FBI that, in his opinion, misstated his conclusion about the device, he filed an administrative protest.[36]

What Whitehurst had concluded in his report on the device was the following: "This laboratory therefore has no information to support the hypothesis that Iraqi agents were involved with the assassination attempt."[37] In his protest, Whitehurst wrote, "The truth of the matter is that Unit Chief Chris Ronay or someone reworded and/or purposely misinterpreted my report, despite my strong statements disavowing a relationship between the explosives used in the past by Iraqi agents and those used in the Bush assassination attempt." Christopher Ronay was the administrative head of the explosives unit in which Whitehurst worked.

Clinton had apparently not spoken with Whitehurst before attacking Iraq. Nor, apparently, had he asked to see Whitehurst's report.

FBI Inspector-General Michael Bromwich examined Whitehurst's claim that his report had been distorted in the higher echelons of the FBI before the information went to Clinton. Bromwich said that Whitehurst's finding on the explosives had indeed been distorted higher up the ladder. The higher officials justified their manipulation of Whitehurst's finding on the grounds that they had other information, unconnected to the analysis of the explosives, to implicate Iraq.[38]

Two possibilities emerge from the information that is publicly known. One is that Ronay or others altered Whitehurst's report and told higher-ups that the device did have an Iraqi "signature." The other is that Ronay or others told higher-ups that Iraq was involved without relying on the supposedly Iraqi character of the explosives device. In either event, the explosives device would seem to be irrelevant as evidence of Iraqi involvement.

What the "other evidence" was that was told to the Inspector-General is not known. Similarly, the "other evidence" that Albright mentioned to the Security Council but never disclosed has remained a mystery. The only publicly available evidence is the conviction and confessions in the court in Kuwait, and these, as indicated, are clouded in suspicion.

After these post-raid disclosures, no new investigation was undertaken by the Clinton administration. Clinton's successor apparently accepted Clinton's findings. In 2003, in the run-up to a new invasion of Iraq, President George W. Bush referred to Saddam Hussein as "a guy that tried to kill my dad."[39]

NOTES

1. John Lancaster and Barton Gellman, "U.S. Calls Baghdad Raid a Qualified Success: Intelligence Complex Hit Hard; 3 Errant Missiles Strike Houses," *Washington Post*, June 28, 1993, p. A1.

2. Patrick Cockburn, "Clinton Acclaims Iraq strike," *Independent* (London), June 28, 1993, p. 1.

3. "Funeral Crowd Demands Revenge," *Washington Post*, June 28, 1993, p. A12.

4. Letter dated 27 June 1993 from the Permanent Representative of Iraq to the United Nations addressed to the President of the Security Council, SCOR, 49th year, UN Doc. S/260004 (1993).

5. Department of State Dispatch, vol. 04, no. 27, July 5, 1993.

6. Martin Walker, "Attack on Baghdad: Forensic Findings Convinced Us of Men's Guilt," *Guardian* (London), June 28, 1993, p. 8; William Maclean, "Iraqi Accused in Bush Plot Says Was Only Smuggling," Reuter Library Report, July 5, 1993.

7. SCOR, 49th yr., 3245th mtg., p. 4, UN Doc. S/PV.3245 (1993).

8. SCOR, 49th yr., 3245th mtg., p. 5, UN Doc. S/PV.3245 (1993).

9. SCOR, 49th yr., 3245th mtg., p. 6, UN Doc. S/PV.3245 (1993).

10. SCOR, 49th yr., 3245th mtg., p. 5, UN Doc. S/PV.3245 (1993).

11. SCOR, 49th yr., 3245th mtg., p. 5, UN Doc. S/PV.3245 (1993).

12. Patrick Cockburn, "Did Iraq Really Plot to Kill Bush?" *Independent* (London), July 4, 1993, p. 12.

13. SCOR, 49th yr., 3245th mtg., pp. 4–5, UN Doc. S/PV.3245 (1993).

14. Scott Baldauf, "Defendants in Kuwait Deny Conspiracy in Trial of Attempt on Bush's Life," *Christian Science Monitor*, July 9, 1993, p. 7.

15. SCOR, 49th yr., 3245th mtg. p. 11, UN Doc. S/PV.3245 (1993).

16. SCOR, 49th yr., 3245th mtg. p. 25, UN Doc. S/PV.3245 (1993).

17. SCOR, 49th yr., 3245th mtg., p. 17, UN Doc. S/PV.3245 (1993).

18. SCOR, 49th yr., 3245th mtg., p. 21, UN Doc. S/PV.3245 (1993).

19. Walker, "Attack on Baghdad: Forensic Findings Convinced Us of Men's Guilt."

20. Maclean, "Iraqi Accused in Bush Plot Says Was Only Smuggling."

21. R. Jeffrey Smith and Ann Devroy, "Clinton Says U.S. Action 'Crippled' Iraqi Intelligence; Officials Decline to Release Further Details," *Washington Post*, June 29, 1993, p. A14.

22. Scott Baldauf, "Defendants in Kuwait Deny Conspiracy in Trial of Attempt on Bush's Life." 23. Cockburn, "Did Iraq Really Plot to Kill Bush?"

24. R. Jeffrey Smith, "U.S. Links Iraq to Bush Plot; Action May Be Taken after Kuwait Trial," *Washington Post*, June 10, 1993, p. A25.

25. US Department of State, *Country Reports on Human Rights Practices for 1993* (1994), p. 1225.

26. Cockburn, "Did Iraq Really Plot to Kill Bush?"

27. Scott Shane, "When the Threat of Hussein Hit Home for Bush; Plot: Ten Years Ago, the World Was Told Iraqi Agents Tried to Kill the President's Father. But Did It Actually Happen?" *Baltimore Sun*, February 23, 2003, p. 1A.

28. Michael Andrew Knights, *Cradle of Conflict: Iraq and the Birth of Modern U.S. Military Power* (2005), p. 142.

29. Barton Gellman, "U.S. Links Iraq to Plot to Assassinate Bush in Kuwait," *Washington Post*, May 8, 1993, p. A1.

30. Stephen Labaton, "Congressmen Urge Action if Iraq Hatched Plot to Assassinate Bush," *New York Times*, May 10, 1993, p. A9.

31. Douglas Jehl, "Car Bomb Found near Bush Said to Suggest Hand of Iraq," *New York Times*, May 11, 1993, p. A3.

32. Smith, "U.S. Links Iraq to Bush Plot; Action May Be Taken after Kuwait Trial."

33. Gerald F. Seib, "For the President, It's Decision Time on Attacking Iraq," *Wall Street Journal*, June 23, 1993, p. A16.

34. S. M. Hersh, "A Case Not Closed," *New Yorker*, November 1, 1993, pp. 85–86.

35. Sydney P. Freedberg, "Good Cop, Bad Cop," *St. Petersburg Times*, March 4, 2001, p. 1A.

36. Shane, "When the Threat of Hussein Hit Home for Bush; Plot: Ten Years Ago, the World Was Told Iraqi Agents Tried to Kill the President's Father. But Did It Actually Happen?"

37. Jeff Stein, "Bad Blood at the FBI: Has the FBI Found New Ways to Make the Crime Fit the Punishment? An Agent Turns Whistle-blower," *Playboy*, vol. 44, no. 4, p. 129 (April, 1997).

38. Shane, "When the Threat of Hussein Hit Home for Bush; Plot: Ten Years Ago, the World Was Told Iraqi Agents Tried to Kill the President's Father. But Did It Actually Happen?"

39. Ibid.

34. SUDAN: PHARMACEUTICAL FIASCO

News reports of the simultaneous bomb blasts at the U.S. embassies in Tanzania and Kenya in 1998 caught my attention, not only because of the high number of deaths—two hundred fifty—but for a personal reason. As I saw photographs of the Tanzania embassy, I realized that the car bomb that destroyed most of the building had been in a car parked in the parking space I used to use when I visited that embassy. My wife and I had lived in Tanzania sixteen years earlier, and we often parked our aging Audi in the space closest to the side door, which led to a mini-library where expatriates exchanged paperback books to read. That parking space was an obvious choice for a car bomber intent on destroying the embassy building.

The U.S. reaction to the bombings caught my attention as well. We attacked the Sudan and Afghanistan with missiles two weeks later. The Red Sea once again was the launch site. The missiles targeted the Osama bin Laden organization—a camp in Afghanistan and a factory in Khartoum, Sudan—which the US held responsible for the two bombings. The missiles in Afghanistan, aimed at a bin Laden encampment, fell in a remote area. Several dozen were killed, though not the top leaders who were the targets.[1] In the Sudan the missiles, fired at night, hit the capital city. No one was killed in Khartoum, but ten persons were reportedly hospitalized from injuries, some of them quite serious.[2]

The United States told the Security Council that the attacks were in self-defense.[3] Informing Congress of the attacks, Clinton said that they were based on "convincing information from a variety of reliable sources that the bin Ladin organization is responsible for the devastating bombings on August 7, 1998, of the U.S. Embassies in Nairobi, Kenya, and Dar es Salaam, Tanzania, that killed over 250 persons. United States forces struck a facility in Sudan being used to produce materials for chemical weapons."[4]

The Department of State claimed that the factory in Khartoum was in an area secured by the government of Sudan: "The U.S. is confident," said the Department of State, that "this Sudanese government-controlled facility is involved in the production of chemical weapons agents."[5]

The facts underlying the attacks would prove controversial, however.[6] The U.S. missile destroyed a manufacturing plant in Khartoum. The State Department claimed that the plant was producing a chemical called Empta, which is used to make the deadly VX nerve gas. The Department said that this plant was connected to Osama bin Laden, who was then operating a guerrilla group in Afghanistan, and that bin Laden had bombed the U.S. embassies in Kenya and Tanzania and was planning similar attacks elsewhere.[7] On these facts, the United States argued that it was defending itself from bin Laden by attacking the plant in the Sudan.

The Sudanese government disputed these facts, saying that the plant produced pharmaceuticals for use by humans and animals, and not anything dangerous like nerve gas. It said that the plant had been approved by the Iraq sanctions committee established by the Security Council to export medical products to Iraq under the Security Council's oil-for-food program. It denied any connection between bin Laden and the plant.

Sudan asked that the UN Security Council convene "to take its responsibility under the Charter of the United Nations by condemning this barbarous and iniquitous aggression."[8]

The United States replied that its evidence was solid: "We've made very clear—the Security Council took this up on Monday—we made clear that in our view . . . it wasn't necessary. We believe we have convincing evidence that satisfied us; and the Security Council didn't go further with it on Monday."[9]

U.S. officials said that the plant did not produce pharmaceuticals, but when the government of Sudan allowed journalists and UN officials to tour the rubble, television pictures showed packs of pharmaceuticals. U.S. officials soon acknowledged that elements of the Sudanese version were true, in particular that the plant, contrary to the initial U.S. assertion, did produce pharmaceuticals.

The bin Laden connection also proved problematic. Administration officials speaking on condition of anonymity acknowledged that they could show no connection between bin Laden and the plant.[10] They retreated to a claim that bin Laden had connections to persons in the Sudanese government, who in turn may have had connections to the plant.

The government of Sudan denied even these connections. Bin Laden had been in the Sudan until 1996, but in that year the government expelled him. Sudan said there was no longer any connection between bin Laden and anyone in the Sudanese government.[11]

As to what the plant was producing, a U.S. engineer had designed the factory; he said that it was built to produce pharmaceuticals, and that it did not have facilities or equipment to make nerve gas. An official of a Milan company that supplied powders for pharmaceuticals to the plant said that he had been in the plant recently and had seen neither equipment to produce chemicals nor any available space in which such equipment could be placed.[12]

U.S. officials also acknowledged that they had no solid evidence that Empta was being produced at the plant. The United States claimed to have soil samples from near the plant that showed Empta, but the officials admitted that the presence of Empta in the soil did not necessarily indicate that Empta had been produced at the plant, as opposed to having been stored there or transshipped through the plant.[13]

According to outside experts, other substances are closely related to Empta, and thus only quite careful reading of data could show conclusively whether Empta was present. Empta reacts quickly with other substances would break down once in the soil. Therefore, it is not likely that one could extract a sample of Empta from soil.[14] Scientists hired by the plant's owner tested nearby soil samples taken in October 1998 and found no traces of the Empa compound, which forms when Empta breaks down. Professor Thomas D. Tullius, chair of the Boston University chemistry department, reported that "What they found was that in those samples, to the practical limits of scientific detection, there was no Empta or Empa, its breakdown product."[15]

The Sudanese government asked the Security Council to investigate. Despite the serious factual questions raised by Sudan, the Security Council did not ask the United States for further explanation. It "shelved the discussion."[16]

The Organization of African Unity was upset at the Security Council's unquestioning acceptance of evidence that seemed flawed. It asked the Security Council to conduct an inquiry.[17] Not only was the plant a pharmaceutical factory, it was the major pharmaceutical factory in the country. Its destruction stopped the delivery of pharmaceuticals for a time in the Sudan.

Arab states at the United Nations presented a draft resolution to the Security Council to the same effect. The Council discussed the draft but adjourned without acting.[18] The Security Council's failure to hold any inquiry was attributed to pressure from the United States. Abraham Sofaer, who served as legal advisor in the Department of State under President Reagan, wrote that it is "disturbing . . . that the defense secretary announced (on the basis of erroneous intelligence) that the factory in Sudan did not make pharmaceuticals, and that the Clinton Administration has been unwilling to participate in a thorough evaluation of its factual premises concerning the plant."[19] The Clinton administration may have realized that its evidence would not withstand scrutiny and did not want the embarrassment of an airing of the evidence in the Security Council.

Clinton had managed to pull off the Baghdad bombing raid in 1993 with no ill consequences to himself. That success may have encouraged him to try again in Khartoum, just as Eisenhower's success in Guatemala encouraged him to undertake the Bay of Pigs invasion. The choice to attack backfired, however. The factual premises unraveled within a few weeks. Foreign affairs officials of European allies, including Germany, the United Kingdom, France, and Italy, questioned Clinton's evidence. Even though it successfully avoided a Security Council discussion, the Clinton administration did not avoid censure.

The reasons for a raid based on such faulty evidence are not easy to discern. The White House reportedly took the decision to bomb the Khartoum factory without consulting high-level civilian and military officials who normally would be involved in such a decision.[20] The Administration was under pressure to do something in reaction to the bombing attacks on the U.S. embassies in Kenya and Tanzania. As in 1993 with the Baghdad raid, Clinton ran the risk of appearing weak if he did not retaliate.

NOTES

1. Barry Bearak, "Estimates of Toll in Afghan Missile Strike Reach as High as 50," *New York Times*, August 23, 1998, p. A11, col. 1.

2. Jane Perlez, "In Sudan, Furor and a Warning Amid the Ruins," *New York Times*, August 22, 1998, p. A1, col. 5.

3. Letter dated 20 August 1998 from the Permanent Representative of the United States of America addressed to the President of the Security Council, UN Doc. S/1998/780 (1998).

4. Letter from the President to the Speaker of the House and the President of the Senate, August 21, 1998, White House Press Release, August 22, 1998, in *Foreign Policy Bulletin* 9, no. 5 (1998): 15.

5. Department of State Fact Sheet, Department of State Press Release (released by the Department of State's Coordinator for Counterterrorism), August 21, 1998, in *Foreign Policy Bulletin* 9, no. 5 (1998): 13.

6. Jules Lobel, "The Use of Force to Respond to Terrorist Attacks: The Bombing of Sudan and Afghanistan," *Yale Journal of International Law* 24 (1999): 543–46.

7. Steven Lee Myers, "Dozens of Ship-launched Cruise Missiles Strike at Same Moment," *New York Times*, August 21, 1998, p. A10; Address by the President to the Nation, White House Press Release, August 20, 1998, in *Foreign Policy Bulletin* 9, no. 5 (1998): 6; Excerpts from Press Briefing by Secretary of

State Albright and National Security Advisor Berger, White House Press Release, Aug. 20, 1998, in ibid., p. 8.

8. Letter from Sudanese State Minister for External Relations Roric to the President of the U.N. Security Council, U.N. Press Release S/1998/786, August 21, 1998, in *Foreign Policy Bulletin* 9, no. 5 (1998): 12.

9. Excerpts from Daily Press Briefing by Department of State Deputy Spokesman Foley, August 26, 1998, Department of State Press Release, August 26, 1998, in *Foreign Policy Bulletin* 9, no. 5 (1998): 17; "White House Rejects Jimmy Carter's Call for Testing at Bombed Factory Site," *Chicago Tribune*, September 20, 1998, p. 15.

10. Bryan Bender, "Poor US intelligence May Have Led to Sudan strikes," *Jane's Defence Weekly*, September 2, 1998; Tim Weiner and James Risen, "Decision to Strike Factory in Sudan Based on Surmise," *New York Times*, September 21, 1998, p. A1.

11. Tim Weiner and Steven Lee Myers, "Flaws in U.S. Account Raise Questions on Strike in Sudan," *New York Times*, August 29, 1998, p. A1.

12. Daniel Pearl, "More Doubts Rise over Claims for U.S. Attack—Test of Sudanese Factory Is Criticized as the U.N. Is Asked to Investigate, *Wall Street Journal*, October 28, 1998, p. A8; Hassan Ibrahim et al., "The Missiles, the Bungling Pentagon and the Nerve Gas Factory That Never Was," *Middle East Observer*, August 30, 1998, p. 4.

13. Tim Weiner and James Risen, "Decision to Strike Factory in Sudan Based on Surmise."

14. Seymour M. Hersh, "The Guns of August," *New Yorker*, October 12, 1998, p. 40.

15. James Risen and David Johnston, "Experts Find No Arms Chemicals at Bombed Sudan Plant," *New York Times*, February 9, 1999, p. A3.

16. Carter urges inquiry into U.S. raid on Sudan, *New York Times*, September 18, 1998, p. A4.

17. "OAU Demands Inquiry into US Bombing in Sudan," Agence France Presse, September 21, 1998.

18. "Security Council Meets on Resolution on U.S. Bombing on Sudan," Xinhua News Agency, September 28, 1998.

19. Abraham D. Sofaer, "U.S. Acted Legally in Foreign Raids," *Newsday*, October 19, 1998, p. A29.

20. Seymour M. Hersh, "The Guns of August," pp. 36–37.

35. IRAQ: LOW-INTENSITY INTERVENTION

Through the 1990s, the United States assumed control of the airspace over most of Iraq and on occasion fired missiles at Iraqi ground installations. The administration claimed a right to do this because of what the Security Council had authorized at the beginning and at the end of the Persian Gulf crisis of 1990–91. In the view of most Security Council members, however, these earlier resolutions on Iraq provided no such authorization. As they saw the matter, the Clinton administration had devised an interpretation of the earlier resolutions that was at odds with what the resolutions actually said. There was no full-scale ground attack on Iraq during this period, but the military action against Iraq was substantial.

The first step in this low-intensity campaign was the enforcement of air interdiction zones, commonly called "no-fly" zones. These were areas in Iraqi airspace in which the United States did not allow Iraq to fly aircraft. President Bush established the first such zone over Iraqi airspace north of the 36th parallel in 1991.[1]

In 1992, the United States, this time jointly with the United Kingdom and France, and with Russia's acquiescence, established a second interdiction zone south of the thirty-second parallel.[2] The two zones together covered most of Iraq's airspace, the southern zone touching the southern suburbs of Baghdad. In the zones, clashes developed, as Iraqi anti-aircraft installations would occasionally fire, and as US planes tried to take out these ground installations.

Iraq's government viewed the zones as an unlawful intrusion into its airspace, because the airspace above a country is under that country's control.[3] Others may use it only with permission. The stated purpose of the zones was to keep Iraq from suppressing population groups resident in those sectors: Kurds in the north and Sh'ia Muslims in the south. In the aftermath of the Persian Gulf war, the United States and allied forces began a program of humanitarian relief directed toward the Kurds in the north. The United States and allies had forces on the ground there delivering supplies.[4] In the south, the stated aim was to curb suppression of the Shi'ite population, which had acted against the Baghdad government in 1991 with President Bush's encouragement. Bush said that the zone would "enhance our ability to monitor developments in southern Iraq."[5] Iraq, it was said, had increased its use of aircraft to put down rebel activity in the Shi'ite areas around the city of Basra. The prohibition against Iraqi aircraft would limit Iraq's ability to repress rebels.[6]

Since Iraqi airspace belonged to Iraq, the Bush administration, and the Clinton administration after it, needed a rationale. They found one in two Security Council resolutions. Resolution 678 of November 1990, as we saw in Chapter 31, authorized military action against Iraq to get it out of Kuwait. Resolution 688, adopted by the Security Council in 1991, condemned "the repression of the Iraqi civilian population in many parts of Iraq, including most recently in Kurdish populated areas." The resolution demanded that Iraq "immediately end this repression." It further "insist[ed] that Iraq allow immediate access by international humanitarian organizations to all those in need of assistance in all parts of Iraq."[7]

The United States said that Resolution 688 allowed it to exclude Iraqi aircraft. As for the south, Resolution 688 did not specifically mention the Sh'ia, but Edward Perkins, the U.S. delegate, told the Security Council that the area south of the thirty-second parallel included "the areas where a majority of the most significant recent violations of Resolution 688 have taken place."[8] Perkins said that the southern zone was established "in response to graphic proof of brutality, including the strafing of villages. Operation Southern Watch monitors the implementation of resolution 688 (1991) and deters the most serious forms of repression by the Iraqi military authorities. Monitoring is facilitated by a no-fly zone."[9]

Resolution 688 said nothing about enforcement authority.[10] So the United States read Resolution 688 together with Resolution 678, which did contain an authorization for enforcement, but for another purpose.[11] Resolution 678 authorized UN member states to "use all necessary means to uphold and implement the Security Council Resolution 660 and all subsequent relevant Resolutions and to restore international peace and security in the area."[12]

The State Department read the two together, as if the authorization in Resolution 678 could apply to enforcing Resolution 688, which contained no authorization. The State Department relied on Resolution 688 for the authority to protect the Kurds and Sh'ia and on Resolution 678 for enforcement authority.[13]

The first missile strikes came just as Bush was about to leave office in January 1993. Bush sent missiles to enforce the no-fly zones. He also sent missiles into an industrial area near Baghdad as a response to restrictions Iraq imposed on the movement of UN weapons inspectors. Iraq said that forty-two persons were killed in the series of raids. Russia criticized these attacks as beyond the scope of Security Council resolutions, and as a usurpation of Security Council authority. The strikes were made after Iraqi troops reentered Kuwait briefly to retrieve supplies they had left behind.[14]

In September 1996, the US, under President Clinton, raised the stakes. It expanded the southern no-fly zone northward, from the thirty-second to the thirty-third parallel. It fired Tomahawk cruise missiles against Iraqi air defense installations in southern Iraq. These attacks came in response to Iraq's deployment of troops into northern Iraq at the apparent request of a Kurdish faction involved in a violent conflict with another Kurdish faction there.[15] The United States said that Resolution 688 prohibited Iraq from sending troops into northern Iraq. Resolution 688 "condemn[ed] the repression of the Iraqi civilian population in many parts of Iraq, including most recently in Kurdish-populated areas." In the U.S. view, Iraq had violated Resolution 688 by sending troops to inter-vene in an intra-Kurd dispute. But Resolution 688 said nothing about pro-hibiting Iraq from sending troops.

To justify the 1996 missile attacks, the United States used the same rationale it had used to justify the no-fly zones—Resolution 688, super-imposed on Resolution 678. The two resolutions taken together, said the United States, allowed any UN member state to use force to stop the threat to the peace reflected in Iraq's suppression of the Kurds.[16]

Other governments found this reasoning fanciful. A number said that there was no basis for the Clinton administration's reading of Resolutions 678 and 688. Resolution 688 did not authorize military action against Iraq.[17] Resolution 678 authorized UN member states to "use all necessary means to uphold and implement the Security Council Resolution 660 and all subsequent relevant Resolutions." The Clinton administration read that to include Security Council resolutions adopted even after Resolution 678, like Resolution 688. The Council could not, however, have author-ized force to implement future resolutions it might adopt on Iraq. The phrase "all subsequent relevant resolutions" must have meant only reso-lutions already adopted when Resolution 678 was passed.[18]

The UK, France, and Russia initially endorsed the no-fly zones, as had UN Secretary-General Boutros Boutros-Ghali.[19] British Foreign Sec-retary Douglas Hurd acknowledged, however, that the zones were not sanctioned by any UN resolutions. He thought they were justifiable on the basis of "extreme humanitarian need," even if they were not authorized by resolutions.[20]

In 1996, when the United States expanded the southern zone north-ward, it did so unilaterally, even though France and the United Kingdom were both participating in patrolling the southern no-fly zone. The UK acquiesced, but Herve de Charette, France's foreign minister, objected that the expansion was not based on any Security Council resolution.[21] France reversed its earlier view that the zones were lawful.

Russia criticized the expansion on the same grounds, also reversing its earlier position. Foreign Minister Evgenii Primakov said that the no-fly zone could not be extended without a Security Council resolution. Russia accused the United States of seeking to "substitute itself for the UN Security Council" in undertaking to implement Resolution 688 by launching missiles at Iraq.[22] The Arab League condemned the 1996 attacks as violations of Iraq's sovereignty.[23]

Three months later, France announced it would no longer fly missions in the northern no-fly zone either, because, it said, "the humanitarian component . . . is not part of the new arrangement."[24] France's point was that while the zone had been established to protect the Kurds through a humanitarian relief operation, that operation had ceased, and the original purpose was thus no longer being served. France's view undercut the United States in its reliance on Resolution 688, because the only possible basis for grounding the no-fly zone on Resolution 688 was that the aim was to protect the Kurds.

Resolution 688, moreover, did not recite that it was adopted on the basis of Chapter VII of the UN Charter, and it referred to international peace only obliquely, stating that the consequences of the violation, presumably the outflow of refugees, threatened international peace. That reference was too indirect to make Resolution 688 a binding resolution.[25] The United Nations Legal Department said that Resolution 688 was not adopted under Chapter VII and contained no enforcement provision.[26] Anthony Aust, the Legal Counsellor in the UK Foreign and Colonial Office, told Parliament the same: "Resolution 688 . . . was not made under Chapter VII."[27]

The U.S. reading of the Security Council resolutions was too convoluted to command much support. Resolution 678 authorized use of force against Iraq if Iraq, by January 15, 1991, did not comply with prior Security Council resolutions. The main point, of course, was Iraq's occupation of Kuwait. Resolution 678 authorized force in response to acts done by Iraq prior to the adoption of Resolution 678. It did not authorize force for possible future acts that Iraq might take.

Resolution 678 did, additionally, mention that force might be used "to restore international peace and security in the area," and the United States relied on this language as well. The reference to maintenance of peace was related, however, to reversing Iraq's aggression against Kuwait.[28] Action to reverse that aggression would, according to Resolution 678, serve to maintain peace in the region. Thus, the phraseology about peace in the region was not carte blanche to UN member states to determine that future acts by Iraq warrant unilateral force against it.

Moreover, nothing in Resolution 688 prohibited Iraq from inserting troops into northern Iraq. Resolution 688 merely demanded that Iraq not suppress the minority populations. Entry in response to a request from a major faction of the Kurds, with that faction alleging it was being attacked by another faction, hardly amounts to suppression, even if the Iraq government anticipated advantage to itself by acting.

In early 1998, the low-intensity campaign was stepped up again. The Clinton administration sent an armada to the Persian Gulf to pressure Iraq to permit greater access to UN weapons inspectors. The inspectors were checking to see whether Iraq was complying with Security Council Resolution 687, which incorporated cease-fire terms from the Persian Gulf war of 1991, in particular a term that required Iraq to dismantle weapons of mass destruction under outside supervision.[29]

Iraq complained of too many Americans among the inspectors, accusing them of gathering intelligence to use against Iraq. When the Security Council, at US insistence, rejected this objection, Iraq refused to allow the inspectors access to certain sites.

At that juncture, the United States sent naval vessels to the region, saying that it did not need a new Security Council resolution to use military force to compel Iraq to permit broader inspections. The Security Council was not willing to pass a new resolution to authorize military action.[30] Of the other permanent members, only the United Kingdom was in support. Security Council Resolution 687 of 1991 specified what should happen if Iraq were to violate its terms. The resolution recited in its concluding provision, paragraph 34, that the Council "[d]ecides to remain seized of the matter and to take such further steps as may be required for the implementation of the present resolution."

The UK tried to gain a new Security Council resolution to authorize military force against Iraq, but the Council was not inclined. The United States argued that it, or other states, was entitled to take action against Iraq to force it to comply with the weapons inspection regime even without any new Security Council resolution. Paragraph 34 required that any response to a future Iraqi breach be collective. As one analyst correctly noted, "Resolution 687 . . . does not authorize Member States to use all necessary measures (or force) to ensure compliance."[31]

Some Security Council members, like Russia, thought that Iraq was not in material breach of Resolution 687 as of early 1998 for refusing inspections.[32] Iraq had refused weapons inspection, it said, only in response to a UN refusal to change the composition of the inspection teams; Iraq was not refusing to comply with the inspection regime itself. As the United States appeared poised to take military action against Iraq in February 1998, UN Secretary-General Kofi Annan reached an understanding with Iraq about future inspections, and the United States decided not to act.[33]

The Clinton administration kept up pressure, however. In March it got the Security Council to threaten "severest consequences" if Iraq did not comply with its January understanding with Annan to allow access by UN inspectors.[34] In November, it got the Security Council to adopt another resolution ordering Iraq to cooperate with the UN inspectors.[35] In these two resolutions, the Security Council stopped short of authorizing force, instead retaining its own prerogative to determine how to deal with Iraq.[36]

In December 1998, the administration decided to attack Iraq even without Security Council authorization. The aim this time was to force Iraq to admit UN weapons inspectors. Cruise missiles were fired for four days in heavy barrages.[37] With France and Russia likely to veto, the administration had no chance of getting a Security Council resolution to authorize these strikes, so, as before, it claimed authority under prior Security Council resolutions. It got little support in that view from other states.[38] Saudi Arabia refused to let Saudi-based planes raid Iraq, because it thought that the raids were not authorized by Security Council resolutions.[39] Russia said that by attacking without such an authorization reso-lution the United States committed aggression.[40]

In selecting targets for the December 1998 attacks, the United States used information gathered by a sophisticated electronic eavesdropping system that tapped into conversations by Iraqi leaders.[41] The CIA had pre-pared listening devices to intercept Iraqi military communications.[42] The devices were secretly installed by U.S. members of the UN weapons inspection team, confirming Iraq's charge that the U.S. was abusing the inspections regime.[43] The United States had installed the listening devices without telling the Security Council or the non-U.S. members of the UN inspection team.

A final escalation of the low-intensity campaign came in January 1999. The administration claimed that Iraqi ground forces fired twenty missiles at U.S. planes.[44] A number of shooting incidents resulted, with U.S. pilots firing at air defense installations they identified as having fired on them or as having threatened them.[45]

The United States authorized its pilots—and this was the new ele-ment—to attack even air defense installations that "were not the immediate source of action against American planes."[46] The United States flew three thousand sorties during the early weeks of 1999, bombing Iraqi radar, mis-sile sites, communications centers, and other facilities. Overall the attacks by U.S. pilots destroyed one fourth of Iraq's air defense network.[47]

Significantly, a new rationale was put forward for the air interdiction zones that was unrelated to protecting minority populations. "The new American policy," it was reported, "reflects the new situation after the evacuation from Iraq of [weapons inspection] experts from the United Nations Special Commission. . . Now with little hope of resuming the commission's mission, the United States has fallen back on a policy of containing Iraq, to keep it from using its weapons against its neighbors."[48] The United States embarked, it was reported, on "a low-grade war, fash-ioned by the military and the administration without public debate, aimed at salvaging the administration's 'containment' policy toward Saddam Hussein and destabilizing his regime."[49]

Saudi Arabia again refused to let Saudi-based U.S. planes participate, saying, "We object to any nation taking matters into its own hands, and using bombing as an instrument of diplomacy."[50]

Acting against Iraq to keep it from threatening its neighbors could hardly be based on Resolution 688, which, as we saw, sought protection of minorities within Iraq. Although the United States did not publicly voice a new legal rationale for the overflights, legal counsel reportedly advised the administration that the attacks could be justified as self-defense.[51] Self-defense, however, would apply only if the U.S. planes had a right to be in the no-fly zones in the first place, which they did not.[52]

Russia reacted to the 1999 raids by saying that "the creation of no-fly zones was a unilateral action, taken without authorization from the UN Security Council and is thus unacceptable in the eyes of international law." It said that "references made by the USA and Great Britain to resolution 688 of the UN Security Council have no legal ground at all."[53] At a closed session of the Council on March 3, Sergei Lavrov, representing Russia, again said that the no-fly zones were unlawful. Qin Huasun, representing China, said that the zones were not based on Security Council resolutions.[54]

The low-intensity campaign, with its escalations in 1996, 1998, and 1999, was based on a manipulation of Security Council resolutions. The Security Council rebuffed the United States in its efforts to get new resolutions to authorize the escalations. That fact makes it clear that the Security Council did not view those escalations as necessary or appropriate. Council members did not view the prior resolutions as authorizing either the no-fly zones or the later bombing raids.

The manipulation of Security Council resolutions was a new form of deceptive military intervention. The deception related not to the facts, but rather to whether there was authorization for acts that otherwise would constitute aggression.

Further, the Clinton administration's claim that Iraq was violating the weapons inspection regime by excluding inspectors was disingenuous, since the administration had subverted the regime by using it to spy on Iraq. U.S. credibility suffered, as it became clearer with each escalation that it was acting outside Security Council authorization.

NOTES

1. Elaine Sciolino, "U.S. Warns against Attack by Iraq on Kurdish Refugees," *New York Times*, April 11, 1991, p. A10.

2. "No-Fly Zone" in Southern Iraq: Excerpt from a statement by President Bush released by the White House, Office of the Press Secretary, Washington, DC, August 26, 1992, in U.S. Department of State Dispatch 3 (1992): 682; Lucia Mouat, "West Refines Strategy to Safeguard Shiites," *Christian Science Monitor*, August 19, 1992, p. 1; Michael Wines, "U.S. and Allies Say Flight Ban in Iraq Will Start Today," *New York Times*, August 27, 1992, p. A1; Evelyn Leopold, "Allies Give Iraq List of Specifics in No-fly Zone," Reuters, August 26, 1992.

3. Letter dated 24 December 1992 from the Permanent Representative of Iraq to the United Nations addressed to the Secretary-General, UN Doc. S/25038 (1992); Letter dated 2 April 1993 from the Permanent Representative of Iraq to the United Nations addressed to the Secretary-General, UN Doc. S/25523 (1993).

4. Frank T. Csongos, "US Warns Iraq Not to Fly Missions near Refugees," U.P.I., April 10, 1991.

5. "No-Fly Zone" in Southern Iraq: Excerpt from a statement by President Bush released by the White House, Office of the Press Secretary.

6. "British, French and U.S. Agree to Hit Iraqi Aircraft in the South," *New York Times*, August 19, 1992, p. A1.

7. Res. 688, SCOR, 46th yr., *Resolutions and Decisions*, p. 31, UN Doc. S/INF/47 (1991).

8. "No-Fly Zone" in Southern Iraq: Excerpt from a statement by President Bush released by the White House, Office of the Press Secretary.

9. SCOR, 47th yr., 3139th mtg., p. 34, U.N. Doc. S/PV.3139 (1992).

10. "Don't Shoot down Iraq Aircraft," *New York Times*, August 19, 1992, p. A20.

11. Timothy P. McIlmail, "No-Fly Zones: The Imposition and Enforcement of Air Exclusion Regimes Over Bosnia and Iraq," *Loyola of Los Angeles International and Comparative Law Journal* 17 (1994): 50–51.

12. Res. 678, SCOR, 45th yr., *Resolutions and Decisions*, p. 27, UN Doc. S/INF/46 (1990).

13. Press briefing by Mike McCurry and Mark Parris, Washington DC, September 4, 1996.

14. "Warplanes Poised to Strike Iraq," *Advertiser*, January 14, 1993; Paul Lewis, "U.S.-led Raids on Iraq Strain Unity of Gulf War Coalition," *New York Times*, January 20, 1993, p. A1.

15. Robin Wright, "U.S. Forces Hit Iraq Again in 2nd Round of Missile Strikes," *Los Angeles Times*, September 4, 1996, p. A1.

16. Press briefing by Mike McCurry and Mark Parris, Washington DC, September 4, 1996; State Department briefing, September 4, 1996, Federal News Service.

17. Mary Ellen O'Connell, "Continuing Limits on UN Intervention in Civil War," *Indiana Law Journal* 67 (199

2): 905; Torsten Stein, "No-Fly-Zones," *Israel Year Book on Human Rights* 27 (1997): 209.

18. McIlmail, "No-Fly Zones: The Imposition and Enforcement of Air Exclusion Regimes Over Bosnia and Iraq," pp. 51–52.

19. "U.N. Chief Endorses Allied No-fly Zone over Iraq," Reuter Library Report, August 28, 1992.

20. Charles Richards, "Hurd Defends Flight Ban," *Independent* (London), August 20, 1992, p. 9; Robin Oakley and Michael Binyon, "Hurd Rejects Legal Doubts on Iraq Force," *Times* (London), August 20, 1992, Home news.

21. Evelyn Leopold, "France Raps U.S. on World Trade, U.N., Iraq," Reuters North American wire, September 25, 1996.

22. "Russia Warns Washington over Iraq," Agence France Presse, September 4, 1996.

23. "Arabs Refuse to Back US Strike," *Independent* (London), September 4, 1996, p. 9.

24. Craig R. Whitney, "France to Pull Its Planes out of Patrols over Northern Iraq," *New York Times*, December 28, 1996, p. A5.

25. Christine Gray, "After the Ceasefire: Iraq, the Security Council and the Use of Force," *British Year Book of International Law* 65 (1994): 161.

26. "EC's Parliament Hits U.S. strikes, Saddam Alike," *Washington Times*, January 22, 1993, p. A8.

27. *British Year book of International Law* 63 (1992): 827.

28. McIlmail, "No-Fly Zones: The Imposition and Enforcement of Air Exclusion Regimes Over Bosnia and Iraq," p. 52.

29. Res. 687, paras. 7 to 14, SCOR, 46th yr., *Resolutions and Decisions*, p. 11, UN Doc. S/INF/47 (1991).

30. Lyle Denniston, "Threat against Iraq Raises Legal Debate: Is Approval Required from U.N., Congress?" *Baltimore Sun*, February 17, 1998, p. 1A; "Russia Says Iraq Not Breaching U.N. Resolutions," Deutsche Presse-Agentur, February 4, 1998.

31. Stein, "No-Fly-Zones," p. 209.

32. Christopher Wren, "U.N. Resolutions Allow Attack on the Likes of Iraq," *New York Times*, February 5, 1998, p. A5.

33. David Hoffman, "World Leaders Hail Accord on Iraq," *Washington Post*, February 24, 1998, p. A18.

34. Res. 1154, SCOR, 53rd yr., UN Doc. S/RES/1154 (1998).

35. Res. 1205, SCOR, 53rd yr., UN Doc. S/RES/1205 (1998).

36. Jules Lobel and Michael Ratner, "Bypassing the Security Council: Ambiguous Authorizations to Use Force, Cease-Fires and the Iraqi Inspection Regime," *American Journal of International Law* 93 (1999): 152.

37. Eugene Robinson, "U.S. Halts Attacks on Iraq after Four Days," *Washington Post*, December 20, 1998, p. A1.

38. "US and UK Isolated over Iraq Bombing," *Middle East Economic Report*, December 25, 1998.

39. Douglas Jehl, "Saudis Admit Restricting U.S. Warplanes in Iraq," *New York Times*, March 22, 1999, p. A6.

40. "Iraq, Russia Call for Unconditional Halt to Attacks," Agence France Presse, December 16, 1998.

41. Tim Weiner, "U.S. Used U.N. Team to Place Spy Device in Iraq, Aides Say," *New York Times*, January 8, 1999, p. A1.

42. Barton Gellman, "U.S. Spied on Iraqi Military Via U.N.; Arms Control Team Had No Knowledge of Eavesdropping," *Washington Post*, March 2, 1999, p. A1.

43. Barbara Crossette, "Iraqi Official Criticizes U.N. Chief over Role in Arms Inspection," *New York Times*, September 16, 1998, p. A11.

44. Dana Priest and Howard Schneider, "Over Iraq, U.S. Fights a Quiet War; Pentagon Plays down Scope of Operations," *Washington Post*, March 7, 1999, p. A1.

45. Steven Lee Myers, "U.S. Jet Fires Missile at an Iraqi Battery after Being Targeted," *New York Times*, January 8, 1999, p. A8; Steven Lee Myers, "In 3d Day of Strikes, U.S. Jets Hit Iraqi Air Defense Sites," *New York Times*, March 2, 1999, p. A3.

46. Elizabeth Becker, "U.S. Pilots over Iraq Given Wide Leeway to Fight Back," *New York Times*, January 27, 1999, p. A6.

47. Priest and Schneider, "Over Iraq, U.S. Fights a Quiet War; Pentagon Plays down Scope of Operations."

48. Elizabeth Becker, "U.S. Pilots over Iraq Given Wide Leeway to Fight Back," *New York Times*, January 27, 1999, p. A6.

49. Priest and Schneider, "Over Iraq, U.S. Fights a Quiet War; Pentagon Plays down Scope of Operations."

50. Douglas Jehl, "Saudis Admit Restricting U.S. Warplanes in Iraq," *New York Times*, March 22, 1999, p. A6.

51. Priest and Schneider, "Over Iraq, U.S. Fights a Quiet War; Pentagon Plays down Scope of Operations."

52. Stein, "No-Fly-Zones," p. 211; Gray, "After the Ceasefire: Iraq, the Security Council and the Use of Force," p. 168.

53. "Foreign Ministry Condemns No-fly Zones over Iraq," Interfax news agency, Moscow, in Russian 1506 gmt, February 12, 1999, BBC Summary of World Broadcasts, February 15, 1999.

54. "Chinese, Russian UN Envoys Condemn Continued Air Strikes on Iraq," BBC Summary of World Broadcasts, March 6, 1999; Elizabeth Becker, "Turks Assail Strikes on Iraq that Disabled Oil Pipeline, *New York Times*, March 4, 1999, p. A14.

36. KOSOVO: CREDIBILITY ABOVE ALL

The bombing of Serbia in 1999 again saw the Clinton administration pushing Security Council resolutions in implausible directions, the same technique it had used with Iraq. In March 1999, the United States along with NATO allies bombed Serbia in connection with Serbia's efforts to keep hold of Kosovo, which was inhabited by a majority Albanian population.

Announcing that he would begin bombing in Serbia, Clinton said, "We should remember what happened in the village of Racak back in January—innocent men, women, and children taken from their homes to a gully, forced to kneel in the dirt, sprayed with gunfire—not because of anything they had done, but because of who they were. Now, roughly 40,000 Serbian troops and police are massing in and around Kosovo. Our firmness is the only thing standing between them and countless more villages like Racak—full of people without protection, even though they have now chosen peace. Make no mistake, if we and our allies do not have the will to act, there will be more massacres."

Clinton also referred to "our stake in peace in the Balkans and in Kosovo. This is a humanitarian crisis, but it is much more. This is a conflict with no natural boundaries. It threatens our national interests. If it continues, it will push refugees across borders and draw in neighboring countries. It will undermine the credibility of NATO, on which stability in Europe and our own credibility depend."[1]

NATO, with the United States in the lead, sought to force Yugoslavia to accept a plan for Kosovo, using military force if necessary. The United States promoted a plan that would have seen autonomy for Kosovo and possible eventual separation from Serbia, with NATO troops entering the territory. Yugoslavia refused to sign onto this agreement, seeing it as a foreign occupation of its territory.

Through 1998, the United States pushed NATO toward military action as the way ahead in the situation. NATO allies held back. White House spokesperson James Rubin said, "We are continuing to push to military action against the Serbs . . . NATO is not there yet."[2]

Lacking a Security Council resolution authorizing the use of force, the Clinton administration said that existing Security Council resolutions provided such authorization. It listed Security Council resolutions 1199 and 1203, among others, as resolutions being violated by Yugoslavia.[3] National Security Advisor Sandy Berger specified Security Council Resolution 1199 as authorization for military action.[4] When the United States began the bombing, the State Department, too, said the action was authorized by Security Council Resolution 1199.[5]

Resolution 1199 called for a cease-fire between Yugoslav and Kosovo forces, for political dialogue between the two parties, for autonomy for Kosovo, and for a return of refugees.[6] It did not suggest military force as a means to achieve these objectives. Russia, which voted for Resolution 1199, objected to the bombing on the ground that the resolution did not authorize military intervention.[7] Yugoslavia called the bombing campaign an "unprecedented defiance of the authority and prestige of the [Security] Council by one regional organization," a reference to NATO.[8]

As in the Iraq situation, the United States had wanted a new Security Council resolution authorizing the use of force over Kosovo if the parties did not come to terms.[9] Russia appeared likely to veto such a resolution, however.[10] The most the United States could gain from the Security Council was a statement by its president urging Yugoslavia to comply with the demands of a six-state contact group to come to a settlement. A statement by the Security Council president is a procedure the Council uses when it is unable to adopt a resolution but can reach agreement on certain points.

A six-nation contact group held talks between the Kosovo Albanian element and the government of Yugoslavia. The statement by the Security Council president did not suggest the use of military force if such a settlement could not be reached.[11]

Foreseeing what would actually happen when the bombing began, some US officials in late 1998 feared "that military force by the United States and its reluctant NATO partners might only embolden Serb forces into a more violent campaign in Kosovo."[12]

Yugoslavia sued the NATO countries in the International Court of Justice over the bombing campaign to try to stop it. The court said it had no jurisdiction and therefore did not rule on the campaign's legality.[13]

Although the Clinton administration argued that the bombing was necessary to convince Yugoslavia to devise an appropriate status for Kosovo that would involve self-government for its Albanian population, it backed off that rationale in the final days before it actually began to bomb.

The United States had been at the fore in threatening Yugoslavia with bombing from mid-1998. NATO, with the U.S. as the prime moving force, issued a threat in October 1998, and another in January 1999.[14] Neither threat seemed to gain any action from Yugoslavia. In the final days before the bombing campaign began, a major reason to bomb was said to be the credibility of NATO. Threats had been made against Yugoslavia, and if NATO did not carry through, then NATO would not be believed in the future if it made a threat. Javier Solana, Secretary General of NATO was said to be "disturbed about the credibility of NATO as the threats of air strikes have lost their punch."[15]

As NATO leaders conferred about whether to bomb Serbia, "the principal reasons cited by government leaders were the need to stave off a humanitarian catastrophe and to salvage NATO's credibility." British Prime Minister Tony Blair, making the case for bombing before the House of Commons, said, "To walk away now would destroy NATO's credibility."[16]

Senator John Warner, Chair of the Armed Services Committee, said, "The credibility of NATO is on the line." Warner added that "the credibility of the United States working with its European partners in NATO is on the line and, equally important, the credibility of the U.S. military to perform a task as directed by the commander in chief."[17] Kosovo and its situation seemed to have become less the issue than the future credibility of NATO.

A group of British parliamentarians who opposed the bombing campaign complained that the reasons for the NATO action changed: "First we were told that bombing was necessary to force Slobodan Milosevic to sign the Rambouillet document. Then bombing was supposed to be necessary to defend Kosovo Albanians. We are now told that NATO's credibility is at stake to justify the extension of bombing from military to commercial and industrial targets throughout Yugoslavia."[18]

An intervention may, in theory, have multiple reasons behind it. But when multiple reasons are put forward, suspicion is always raised that none of them is truly valid. Clinton, as we saw, stressed the Racak village killings of January 1999 as an indication of the need for intervention. The Organization for Security and Cooperation in Europe had indeed called this a killing of civilians. The European Union sent a team of Finnish pathologists who performed autopsies on some of the victims at a morgue in Pristina, Kosovo. They reported that the dead wore clothing that appeared to be civilian and concluded, "There were no indications of the people being other than unarmed civilians."[19] Yugoslavia claimed, to the contrary, that no mass killing of civilians had occurred at Racak. What happened, it said, was a military action involving Yugoslav and Kosovo Liberation Army forces.

The killings at Racak were later included in an indictment for crimes against humanity issued by the Hague tribunal against Slobodan Milosevic, the Serbian leader. Racak was also included in an indictment of six other top Serbian officials. At the Hague, witnesses testified on both sides of the issue. Milosevic died before his trial ended, so there was no verdict about Racak. In 2006, after Milosevic's death, the tribunal dropped the Racak allegation from the indictment of Milosevic's lieutenants. A three-judge trial panel said that the Racak incident, even if it were a massacre of civilians, was not associated deportation, since population was not being forcibly displaced from Racak.[20]

Of what were apparently forty-five persons killed at Racak, forty bodies were taken to Pristina for autopsy, the remaining five having been taken for burial by relatives. The indictment of the six Serbian officials named the forty and gave their ages. All but one were male. One was a boy of thirteen, and there was one man eighty-one years old, and another aged sixty-eight. Several were in their fifties and early sixties. Most of those killed were of military age.[21] Clinton, by referring to the victims as "innocent men, women and children" gave an impression of the victims that did not conform to the reality. They might have been "innocent," but except for one woman and one child, all were adult males.

Nor did Clinton acknowledge that there had been military action in Racak shortly before the discovery of the bodies. Human Rights Watch, which reported on Racak soon after the event, said there had been military action in the village that very day. It said that Serbian police entered Racak, where the Kosovo Liberation Army was apparently operating. There had been a firefight there three days earlier between KLA and Yugoslavian government elements.[22]

The initial alarm over Racak was sounded by William Walker, a U.S. official who headed the OSCE's Kosovo Verification Mission. The mission gained access to Racak in the afternoon of January 15, shortly after the killings occurred. Walker reported the incident as an unjustified massacre of civilians. Yugoslavia declared him persona non grata.

Walker's assessment drew criticism, and not only from the Yugoslav government. Walker had a checkered history on such matters. His prior government service had included a stint as U.S. ambassador in El Salvador. In 1989, six Salvadoran Jesuit priests, opponents of the U.S.–supported government, were killed by Salvadoran army personnel. Walker said that the Salvadoran army had not been the perpetrators. The incident potentially jeopardized Congress-funded aid to the Salvadoran military.[23] The UN Truth Commission for El Salvador later established the army's responsibility for the killings.[24]

A member of Walker's Kosovo Verification Mission questioned Walker's methodology. Heinz Loquai, a retired German brigadier general, was deputy to Walker at the time. Loquai viewed the declaration of Walker as persona non grata to be a justifiable action, since the agreement between OSCE and the government required notification before Walker could make a visit . Loquai also questioned Walker for not having secured the area of Racak to prevent disturbance of the crime scene. He questioned how Walker could so quickly conclude that the victims were civilians. He noted that Walker arrived only after the reported firefight that might have accounted for the killings had ended. Loquai therefore concluded Walker had insufficient information about the circumstances of the killings. Finally, Loquai pointed out that the bodies of the slain had been left in place. To Loquai, that fact was inconsistent with a massacre of civilians, an action that perpetrators would likely have wanted to cover up by concealing the bodies. Loquai surmised that if this had been a killing of civilians, those responsible would have moved the bodies to a different location.[25]

When NATO began air strikes, Russia initiated a Security Council session, at which Russia and China said that NATO was not empowered to act alone. China said that it "oppose[d] interference in the internal affairs of other States, under whatever pretext or in whatever form."[26] The United States, with the UK and France backing it, cited prior Security Council resolutions: "Security Council resolutions 1199 (1998) and 1203 (1998) recognized that the situation in Kosovo constitutes a threat to peace and security in the region and invoked Chapter VII of the Charter. In resolution 1199 (1998), the Council demanded that Serbian forces "take immediate steps to improve the humanitarian situation and avert the impending humanitarian catastrophe."[27]

The Clinton administration did not claim, as it could not, that the resolutions called for use of military action to enforce them. It did not explain how one could extrapolate an authorization to use force from a series of demands made on Yugoslavia. The Kosovo Albanians had, to be sure, been subjected to atrocities. But they, too, had been fighting, and their army had committed its own atrocities. The Kosovo Liberation Army had, in fact, been regarded by U.S. officials as a terrorist group.

Many Albanians were displaced. Yet the efficacy of bombing was unclear. When the bombing began, it led Yugoslavia, as some had expected, to intensify rather than to ease its pressure on the Albanians. Only after the bombing started did the Yugoslav government force large numbers of Albanians out of Kosovo.

Yugoslavia denied even that. It claimed that the outflow of Albanians that occurred shortly after the bombing started was a reaction to the bombing, that the Albanians were fleeing the bombs. The displacement did, however, seem to be precipitated by Yugoslavia. Within a matter of days, eight hundred thousand Albanians fled from or were forced out of Kosovo and into neighboring Albania or Macedonia.[28]

When the bombing campaign started, it was not clear whether it would help or hurt the Albanians. In the short term, given the reaction of Yugoslavia, it hurt them. Only after the bombing ended did the bulk of the displaced return.

Two weeks into the bombing campaign, NATO began referring to a Serb plan to ethnically cleanse Kosovo of Albanians, a plan code-named Horseshoe. CNN reported that President Clinton was "convinced that if he had not launched the air campaign, Slobodan Milosevic would have enacted plans to wipe out Kosovo anyway. In fact, the CIA had warned Clinton that Milosevic was going to unleash a huge offensive to ethnically cleanse the entire province. At Rambouillet, France in March, the Kosovo Liberation Army leadership presented documents to U.S. diplomats that the KLA had stolen from the Serb forces. These stolen documents laid out the battle plans for Operation Horseshoe.[29] State Department spokesperson James Rubin cited Operation Horseshoe to justify the bombing.[30]

But General Loquai later said that the documents showing an Operation Horseshoe plan were fakes. The documents were fabricated, he said, from Bulgarian intelligence reports: "I have come to the conclusion that no such operation ever existed." Loquai said that the German defence ministry turned a vague report from Sofia into a "plan," and itself coined the name Horseshoe. The Bulgarian intelligence report, Loquai said, was that the Yugoslav military was out to destroy the Kosovo Liberation Army, not to expel the Albanian population.[31]

"Operation Horseshoe" complemented the account of Racak, Loquai wrote. "There is a connection between the 'Racak massacre' and 'Operation Horseshoe,'" he said. "The head of the [OSCE] Kosovo Monitoring Team, Walker, ignited with his unproven version of 'Racak' the spark for war against Yugoslavia." Then "Operation Horseshoe" served to put out any criticism of the war.[32]

NOTES

1. Press conference, March 19, 1999, *Weekly Compilation of Presidential Documents* 35, no. 12 (March 29, 1999): 471.

2. Philip Smucker, "No Easy Answers to Crisis: Kosovo Conflict Is Even Thornier Than Others in Balkans," *Washington Times*, October 11, 1998, p. A1.

3. "US welcomes OSCE statement," Federal Document Clearing House, January 18, 1999.

4. Press Briefing by National Security Advisor Sandy Berger, March 26, 1999, M2 Presswire.

5. USIA Foreign Press Center briefing, April 8, 1999.

6. Res. 1199, SCOR, 53rd yr., UN Doc. S/RES/1199 (1998).

7. "Russia: NATO Cannot Act in Kosovo without U.N. Clearance," Interfax Russian News, September 24, 1998.

8. SCOR, 54th yr., 3989th mtg., UN Doc. S/PV.3989 (1999) (Mr. Jovanovic, Yugoslavia).

9. "British FM Confident of New UN Resolution on Kosovo," Agence France Presse, October 22, 1998.

10. Sergei Baibakov, "UN Security Council Discusses Draft Resolution on Kosovo," TASS, October 23, 1998.

11. "Full text of UN Security Council statement on Kosovo," Agence France Presse, January 30, 1999.

12. Philip Shenon, "Kosovo's Crisis Is Bad, and Getting Worse: Clinton Administration Appears to Be Undecided on What to Do," *New York Times*, September 16, 1998, p. A8; John Kifner, "The Ravaging of Kosovo, a Special

Report; How Serb Forces Purged One Million Albanians," *New York Times*, May 29, 1999, p. A1.

13. Case Concerning Legality of Use of Force (Serbia and Montenegro v. Belgium), International Court of Justice, Judgment (preliminary objections), December 15, 2004.

14. Marc Weller, "Forcible Humanitarian Action: The Case of Kosovo," in Michael Bothe, Mary Ellen O'Connell, and Natalino Ronzitti, eds., *Redefining Sovereignty: The Use of Force after the Cold War* (2005), p. 286, 295.

15. Jane Perlez, "U.S. Hope Is Slim as Talks Restart on Kosovo Crisis," *New York Times*, March 15, 1999, p. A1.

16. William Drozdiak, "NATO Rewrites History with Attack on Kosovo," *Kitchener-Waterloo Record*, March 26, 1999, p. A19.

17. Roy Gutman, "Clinton, NATO Warn Milosevic 'Clock Is Ticking,'" *Newsday*, March 20, 1999, p. A5.

18. "UK MPs Demand Parliament Be Recalled for NATO Bombing," Xinhua News Agency, April 5, 1999.

19. Report of the EU Forensic Expert Team on the Racak Incident, 17 March 1999, in Heike Krieger, ed., *The Kosovo Conflict and International Law: An Analytical Documentation 1974–1999* (2001), p. 198.

20. International Criminal Tribunal for Former Yugoslavia, Decision on Application of Rule 73 *Bis*, Case No. IT-05-87-T, July 11, 2006; "'Direct Cause' of NATO Bombing of Serbia Dropped by Hague Tribunal," BBC Monitoring Europe (report by Belgrade Radio B92), BBC Monitoring Europe, July 8, 2006.

21. Prosecutor v. Milutinovic et al., Case No. IT-05-87-PT, International Criminal Tribunal for Former Yugoslavia, Indictment dated May 12, 2006, Annex A: Victims identified at Racak, January 15, 1999.

22. Human Rights Watch: Report on the Massacre in Racak, January 1999, in Krieger, *The Kosovo Conflict and International Law: An Analytical Documentation 1974–1999*, p. 192.

23. Noam Chomsky, *The New Military Humanism: Lessons from Kosovo* (1999), p. 41.

24. Douglass Cassel, "Guardian of Truth, Decency," *Chicago Daily Law Bulletin*, May 31, 2001, p. 5.

25. Heinz Loquai, *Der Kosovo-Konflikt—Wege in einen vermeidbaren Krieg: Die Zeit von Ende November 1997 bis März 1999* (2000), pp. 50–51.

26. SCOR, 54th yr., 3988th mtg., p. 3, 12, UN Doc. S/PV.3988 (1999) (Mr. Lavrov, Russia; Mr. Qin, China).

27. SCOR, 54th yr., 3988th mtg., p. 4, UN Doc. S/PV.3989 (1999) (Mr. Burleigh, USA).

28. Weller, "Forcible Humanitarian Action: The Case of Kosovo," p. 300.

29. "Forced out," CNN, April 4, 1999.

30. John Goetz and Tom Walker, "Serbian Ethnic Cleansing Was a Fake, General Says," *Sunday Times*, April 2, 2000, Overseas News.

31. Loquai, *Der Kosovo-Konflict—Wege in einen vermeidbaren Krieg: Die Zeit von Ende November 1997 bis März 1999*, pp. 138–44; Goetz and Walker, "Serbian Ethnic Cleansing Was a Fake, General Says."

32. Loquai, *Der Kosovo-Konflict—Wege in einen vermeidbaren Krieg: Die Zeit von Ende November 1997 bis März 1999*, p. 144.

37. AFGHANISTAN: END TO TERROR?

After the suicide airliner attacks in the United States on September 11, 2001, the country enjoyed broad sympathy. The UN Security Council adopted Resolution 1368, referring to "the horrifying terrorist attacks" and expressing "its deepest sympathy and condolences to the victims and their families and to the people and Government of the United States of America." The resolution called the attacks "a threat to international peace and security" and expressed the Council's "readiness to take all necessary steps to respond."[1] On September 28, the Security Council adopted Resolution 1373, calling for measures against international terrorism, and again referred to the September 11 attacks as a threat to the peace. A finding of a "threat to the peace" can, under the UN Charter, lead to economic or military sanctions.[2] The United States thus was in a position to obtain assistance from the international community in dealing with Afghanistan and the al-Qaeda organization.

The United States pursued a number of routes to avert the threat. It sought to shut off financing to al-Qaeda. In Resolution 1373, the UN Security Council called both for the prosecution of anyone who finances terrorism and for the prevention of the movement of terrorists across borders.

Nonetheless, the Bush administration decided to act militarily, and to do so on its own. It invaded Afghanistan on October 7, 2001, accompanied by only one other country, the UK. In a letter to the Security Council, the United States said that it was acting in self-defense.[3] International sympathy held. The European Union sent the Security Council a letter expressing its "wholehearted support for the action that is being taken in self-defence."[4] Even Russia and China voiced support.

Afghanistan itself, of course, was not the direct source of the threat. But al-Qaeda operated in Afghan territory, and the Taliban government of Afghanistan was not stopping it.

To properly claim self-defense for a military action, there must be no alternative to the use of force. Military action must be a last resort. On this aspect, the United States was not fully forthcoming. In its letter to the Security Council, it claimed self-defense but did not explain why military force was the only measure that would protect it.

In announcing the invasion of Afghanistan, President Bush said, "More than two weeks ago I gave Taliban leaders a series of clear and specific demands: close terrorist training camps; hand over leaders of the Al Qaeda network; and return all foreign nationals including American citizens unjustly detained in your country."[5]

The United States did make demands on the Taliban government to turn over al-Qaeda figures that it said were responsible for the September 11 attacks. The United States did not, however, make this demand in accordance with the way a government normally asks for the surrender of a person sought for commission of a crime. With the exception of Osama bin Laden, it did not name the persons whose surrender it was demanding.

President Bush told Congress on September 20 of a list of U.S. demands on the Taliban, the first of which was to "deliver to United States authorities all the leaders of Al Qaeda who hide in your land." After listing this and other demands, he said, "These demands are not open to negotiation or discussion. The Taliban must act and act immediately. They will hand over the terrorists or they will share in their fate."[6] Consistent with this stance, the United States engaged in no discussion with the Taliban about a surrender.

The normal international procedure for the surrender of a suspect is extradition. The government that seeks surrender provides information to show probable cause that the person sought committed a crime. A court in the country from which extradition is requested hears the evidence in open court and decides whether there is sufficient evidence that the accused person committed the crime in question. In requesting evidence, the Taliban was thus adhering to accepted international standards.

With regard to Osama bin Laden, the Taliban was not dismissive of the U.S. request. Both before and after the beginning of the U.S. invasion, it indicated willingness to discuss a surrender. But the Bush administration refused to talk to the Taliban government. The Taliban suggested the possibility of surrendering bin Laden to a third country. The Bush administration did not respond.[7] "The Administration," wrote the *National Journal*, "has rejected Taliban efforts to frame the terrorist attacks as law enforcement matters."[8] Yet the administration was making a law enforcement demand.

The Taliban said that its security people had bin Laden under their control and that they were thus in a position to deliver his surrender.[9] The Taliban ambassador to Pakistan, Abdul Salam Zaeef, said that only an Afghan court could decide on an extradition request, and that the United States would need to provide evidence of bin Laden's guilt. The Bush administration refused to provide evidence or to enter discussions with the Taliban about a turnover, demanding instead that the Taliban surrender bin Laden outside of normal extradition procedures: "We've made clear what needs to be done with him, and it's time for them to act," said an administration official.[10]

To those familiar with extradition procedures, the Bush administration's stance was hard to justify. "The United States," wrote M. Cherif Bassiouni, an extradition expert, "never formally sought bin Laden's extradition from Afghanistan, nor did it present to Afghanistan's government any evidence of his criminal involvement in the terrorist attacks on New York and Washington." Because of this failure, Bassiouni characterized the U.S. armed action in Afghanistan as an "over-reaction."[11] The refusal to pursue the peaceful surrender of al-Qaeda figures casts doubt on the Bush administration's assertion that the refusal to surrender al Qaeda figures was a reason to invade Afghanistan.

The Bush administration, moreover, portrayed the attacks in New York and Washington in a way that opened up the possibility of a military invasion, but which was more than a trifle questionable. It said that the attacks constituted an act of war and that the war pitted the United States against the forces of terrorism. The September 11 attacks were crimes under the laws of New York and of the United States, but there was little basis for characterizing them as an invasion of the United States. One legal analyst examined the UN Charter rules on use of force in relation to the Afghanistan invasion and concluded that "the 11 September attack more closely approximates a criminal attack than an armed attack."[12] Carrying one step further, the administration held Afghanistan responsible for having facilitated the activity of al-Qaeda, thus justifying an invasion of Afghanistan.

This sleight of hand allowed the Bush administration to depict itself as engaged in a "war," hence entitled to self-defense. Even if self-defense is open, a state may not rush to war. UN Charter Article 51, the self-defense provision, allows defensive force only until the Security Council acts. If the Security Council is in a position to act, a state under attack has no need to resort to armed force on its own. The Security Council, as indicated, was more than solicitous of the United States in the wake of the September 11 attacks. The Bush administration ignored the Security Council's receptivity to collective measures that might have provided protection to the United States.

Another factual element in the picture was missing from the Bush administration's analysis. It conveniently ignored recent history that would have put the United States less in the role of innocent victim, and more in the position of losing out on a policy that had backfired. Al-Qaeda became a significant fighting force only because of the Reagan administration's funding of it as a counterweight to the pro-Soviet government that ruled Afghanistan in the 1980s. At the time, Afghanistan was ruled by a government allied to the USSR. We funded al-Qaeda as a way of drawing the USSR into a "Vietnam" situation. We did not think ahead to what al-Qaeda might become in the future.

From a practical standpoint, it was not clear that capturing al-Qaeda operatives in Afghanistan would protect the United States. The Bush administration argued that it would, but it provided little substantiation. The anti-U.S. fury that drove al-Qaeda's adherents was a product of interference by successive U.S. administrations in the Middle East. One instance was Lebanon, where President Eisenhower intervened in 1958, as we saw in chapter 8, to ensure that Lebanon would remain pro-Western. Again in 1984, President Reagan intervened, as we saw in chapter 22, for the same reason. In 1953, as recounted in chapter 19, the CIA helped overthrow a democratically elected prime minister in Iran. Bush's father only made matters worse when, as we saw in chapter 31, he stationed U.S. troops in Saudi Arabia, the first time the United States had inserted a military force into the region without a clear objective and with no anticipated withdrawal time.

President Bush's thinking in the-run up to the invasion of Afghanistan is revealed in public statements following the September 11, 2001, attacks. "America was targeted," Bush said, "because we're the brightest beacon for freedom and opportunity in the world."[13] "Freedom and democracy are under attack," he said. We are engaged in "a monumental struggle of good versus evil."[14]

In a speech to Congress, Bush raised the question: "Why do they hate us?" He answered: "They hate what they see right here in this chamber, a democratically elected government. . . . They hate our freedoms: our freedom of religion, our freedom of speech, our freedom to vote and assemble and disagree with each other."[15]

But it was precisely our denigration of democracy in the Middle East that generated animosity. Bush's misreading of the history of relations between the U.S. and the Middle East set the stage for yet another episode of intervention that carried the potential of generating even more hostility.

Apart from self-protection, the perennial desire to keep control in the Middle East may have played a role in the decision to invade Afghanistan. In early 2001, the administration was in contact with the Taliban over possible construction of a north-south pipeline to carry natural gas from Turkmenistan through Afghanistan and then to Pakistan.

This project had been pursued by the Clinton administration in the mid-1990s, when U.S.-based UNOCAL was actively pursuing it. UNOCAL, at the time, was in a consortium of companies proposing a central Asia gas pipeline project. The project was abandoned in 1998, but Bush revived it shortly after taking office, leading some to think that his invasion of Afghanistan was aimed at getting a friendly government in place so that the pipeline could proceed.[16]

After overthrowing the Taliban, the Bush administration promoted for the position of president of Afghanistan Hamid Karzai, who had worked for UNOCAL on the pipeline project. In 2006, at an intergovernmental meeting in Turkmenistan, the pipeline project was seriously discussed and seemed to be en route to resuscitation. Afghanistan's minister for mines and industry reported that President Karzai backed the project.[17]

NOTES

1. Res. 1368, SCOR, 56th yr., UN Doc. S/RES/1368 (2001).

2. Res. 1373, SCOR, 56th yr., UN Doc. S/RES/1373 (2001).

3. Letter dated 7 October 2001 from the Permanent Representative of the United States of America to the United Nations addressed to the President of the Security Council, SCOR, 56th yr., UN Doc. S/2001/946 (2001).

4. Letter dated 8 October 2001 from the Permanent Representative of Belgium to the United Nations addressed to the Secretary-General: Annex: Statement of the General Affairs Council of the European Union issued on 8 October 2001, on behalf of the European Union, on action against the Taliban following the terrorist attacks in the United States, SCOR, 56th yr., UN Doc. S/2001/967 (2001).

5. "Bush's Remarks on U.S. Military Strikes in Afghanistan," *New York Times*, October 8, 2001, p. B6.

6. "President Bush's Address on Terrorism before a Joint Meeting of Congress," *New York Times*, September 21, 2001, p. 4.

7. Genaro C. Armas and Pauline Jelinek, "Bush Brushes off Latest Taliban Offer; Rejects Bid to Hand bin Laden to Third Country," *Record* (Bergen County,

N.J.), October 15, 2001, p. 1; Charles Osgood, "President Bush Rejects Taliban Offer to Negotiate," CBS News Transcripts, October 15, 2001.

8. Elisabeth Frater and Shawn Zeller, "The Legal Battleground," *National Journal*, September 29, 2001.

9. "Taliban Say bin Laden under Their Control," CNN.com, September 30, 2001, http://archives.cnn.com/2001/WORLD/asiapcf/central/09/30/ret.taliban.bin-laden/index.html.

10. "No Negotiations, U.S. Tells Taliban," CNN.com, October 1, 2001, http://archives.cnn.com/2001/WORLD/asiapcf/central/10/01/ret.us.taliban/.

11. M. Cherif Bassiouni, "Legal Control of International Terrorism: A Policy-Oriented Assessment," *Harvard International Law Journal* 43 (2002): 87.

12. Mark A. Drumbl, "Judging the 11 September Terrorist Attack," *Human Rights Quarterly* 24 (2002): 332.

13. "Bush's Remarks to the Nation on the Terrorist Attacks," *New York Times*, September 12, 2001, p. A4.

14. Bill Sammon, "Bush Will Lead Battle against 'Evil,'" *Washington Times*, September 13, 2001, p. A10.

15. "President Bush's Address on Terrorism before a Joint Meeting of Congress," *New York Times*, September 21, 2001, p. B4.

16. Salim Muwakkil, "Nightmares of Reason: Sorting Fact from Fiction in 9/11 Conspiracy Theories," *In These Times*, June 24, 2002, p. 14.

17. Scoff Baldauf, "Afghan Gas Pipeline Nears Reality," *Christian Science Monitor*, February 15, 2006, p. 4.

38. Iraq: Regime Change

In 2002 and 2003, the Bush administration took up the Clinton theme of prior UN Security Council resolutions on Iraq as providing a basis for military action. In November 2002, even while claiming authority based on prior resolutions, the administration pressed the Council for a resolution authorizing an attack on Iraq over weapons of mass destruction and weapons inspection issues. Bush said that Iraq had chemical, biological, and nuclear weaponry it was not disclosing.

In response, the Security Council adopted Resolution 1441, in which it stated as a factual conclusion that Iraq was out of compliance with its obligations under Resolution 687, the 1991 cease-fire resolution. The noncompliance the Security Council had in mind related to disclosure of evidence of destruction of stockpiles of weaponry, not to building or maintaining weaponry. The resolution also said that the Council would afford Iraq "a final opportunity to comply with its disarmament obligations" and threatened unspecified "serious consequences" as a result of Iraq's "continued violations."[1]

The Security Council adopted Resolution 1441 as much to deter the United States from invading as to encourage Iraq to comply. Council members feared that if they adopted no resolution, Bush would invade. It was a risky approach, however, because of the U.S. history of claiming a unilateral right to enforce Council resolutions. Resolution 687, of course, reserved to the Council the power to decide whether to take enforcement action against Iraq, but the United States had not respected that power of the Council in the past.

By saying Iraq was out of compliance, the other members were able to wrest from the United States another opportunity for inspections. The United States would not attack Iraq, at least for the time being.

When the Security Council adopted Resolution 1441, the U.S. representative informed it that the United States did not view the resolution's lack of an authorization to attack Iraq to mean that the United States was not authorized to do so. John Negroponte, the U.S. delegate, told the Council that the United States thought that prior resolutions already provided such authorization. Speaking to the possibility that Iraq might continue to violate Resolution 687, he said, "If the Security Council fails to act decisively in the event of further Iraqi violations, this resolution," by which he meant Resolution 1441, "does not constrain any Member State from acting to defend itself against the threat posed by Iraq or to enforce relevant United Nations resolutions and protect world peace and security."[2] Negroponte did not specify Resolution 678, but other members doubtless understood that by "relevant United Nations resolutions" he had Resolutions 678 and 687 in mind.

This was an extraordinary position for the United States to take, since the Council had adopted Resolution 1441 specifically to stop the United States from invading Iraq. Negroponte was restating the position the U.S. had taken both under Clinton and under the first Bush, but which had little basis.

The Bush administration next raised the stakes by saying that Iraq had weaponry and was trying to figure out how to use it. In his State of the Union address to Congress in January 2003, President Bush said, "Saddam Hussein recently sought significant quantities of uranium in Africa."[3] Despite the U.S. position that it already had authority to attack Iraq, Bush wanted a new resolution. A major reason was that the British government was skittish about invading Iraq without a new resolution, and Bush wanted the UK to participate.

Bush sent Secretary of State Colin Powell to the Security Council to say that Iraq had weapons of mass destruction and the launching material to use them at secret locations in Iraq. Powell delivered this account to the Security Council in dramatic fashion on February 5, 2003.

Powell made the U.S. case with CIA Director George Tenet sitting behind him, as if to add weight to the facts he related. Iraq was out of compliance not only by failing to account for destroying weaponry, said Powell, but by keeping and hiding weaponry. Powell said that Iraq was concealing launching equipment for nuclear missiles.

Saddam Hussein, said Powell, was "so determined" to get nuclear weapons capability that he "made repeated covert attempts to acquire high-specification aluminum tubes from 11 different countries." Such tubes, Powell said, "can be used as centrifuges for enriching uranium." Powell acknowledged that such tubes might have other uses, but then he invoked his military background: I am no expert on centrifuge tubes, but just as an old army trooper I can tell you a couple of things. First, it strikes me as odd that these tubes are manufactured to a tolerance that far exceeds United States requirements for comparable rockets."

According to Powell, chemical weapons were abundant in Iraq: "Iraq today has a stockpile of between 100 and 500 tons of chemical weapons agent. That is enough agent to fill 16,000 battlefield rockets." Powell said that Iraq was hiding mobile biological weapon factories in trucks: "We know that Iraq has at least seven of these mobile biological agent facto-ries." Putting images on a screen, Powell explained, "Here you see both truck-mounted and railcar-mounted mobile factories." Then he projected drawings: "As these drawings based on their [intelligence sources] descriptions show, we know what the fermentors look like. We know what the tanks, pumps, compressors and other parts look like. We know how they fit together. We know how they work." In short, Iraq was por-trayed as a serious menace to the region, and perhaps beyond. The overall picture was ominous. Iraq had already attacked its weaker neighbor, Kuwait. It had the capacity to go global with its destruction.[4]

Powell's performance did not, however, convince the other members of the Security Council to adopt a new resolution to authorize force against Iraq. Behind the scenes, the United States lobbied other Council members for a resolution authorizing force. It particularly targeted Council members from Third World countries that were dependent on the United States for economic aid.[5] The pressure tactics did not work. Bush had so little backing in the Council for a new resolution that he had to abandon the effort.

Powell's case against Iraq quickly unraveled. Hans Blix, who headed the UN inspection team in Iraq, told the Security Council that inspectors had looked for mobile biological laboratories but had found none.[6] Mohamed el-Baradei, head of the International Atomic Energy Agency, refuted Powell on the aluminum tubes. He told the Council that the IAEA had investigated, and that the tubes were not for use in centrifuges. El-Baradei also refuted President Bush's claim that Iraq had tried to get nuclear material in Africa. El-Baradei said that the IAEA had investigated that matter as well and had concluded that the documents that supposedly showed such a transaction were "not authentic."[7]

After the United States invaded Iraq, Powell's claim that Iraq was concealing stockpiles of prohibited weapons could not be substantiated. U.S. troops scoured Iraq unsuccessfully trying to find them.[8] Joseph Wilson, who had been dispatched to Africa to see if Iraq had obtained fissionable material there, went public and confirmed el-Baradei's refutation of President Bush's information. Wilson said that it was "highly doubtful" that any transaction took place for Iraq to receive such material.[9]

Investigations in Congress refuted all Powell's main points. Charles Duelfer, who headed the CIA's Iraq Survey Group, told the U.S. Senate Armed Services Committee that Iraq had destroyed its chemical and biological weapons shortly after the Persian Gulf war and that it had made no further efforts towards nuclear weapons capability.[10]

Much of Powell's evidence had come from Iraqi defectors anxious to convince the United States to invade. Powell eventually had to admit that his evidence was faulty, but that was only well after the invasion had been launched. A CIA agent told the U.S. Senate Intelligence Committee that Powell's main source on biological weapons in trucks was an Iraqi defector code named "Curve Ball," whose reliability was suspect. Other "sources" that supposedly confirmed "Curve Ball's" account either were suspect themselves or did not in fact provide confirmation.[11]

The weakness of Powell's evidence had been apparent within the U.S. intelligence community. It was at the leadership level that the decision was made to run with it.

When the United States invaded, it still needed to provide an explanation to the Security Council. The Council had just rejected its bid for an authorization resolution. Would the United States argue that it was under threat of attack by Iraq, in other words, invoke the preventive self-defense of the neo-conservatives in the Bush administration? Would it fall back on its previous argument that prior Security Council resolutions were adequate to provide authorization?

As it entered Iraq, the United States sent a letter to the Security Council. To the surprise of many, it did not base the invasion on preventive self-defense.[12] Instead it opted for the prior resolution argument. This was a difficult line to take, for, as we saw, most members of the Security Council had rejected the argument when Clinton made it. So, too, had Council members when the Bush administration unsuccessfully sought a new resolution in late 2002 and early 2003. If prior resolutions sufficed, a new resolution should not have been needed.

The U.S. letter referred to Resolution 678 authorizing action against Iraq and Resolution 687, the 1991 cease-fire resolution. "The actions being taken," the letter recited, "are authorized under existing Council resolutions, including its resolutions 678 (1990) and 687 (1991)."

"Resolution 687 (1991)," the letter continued,

imposed a series of obligations on Iraq, including, most importantly, extensive disarmament obligations, that were conditions of the cease-fire established under it. It has been long recognized and understood that a material breach of these obligations removes the basis of the cease-fire and revives the authority to use force under resolution 678 (1990). This has been the basis for coalition use of force in the past and has been accepted by the Council, as evidenced, for example, by the Secretary-General's public announcement in January 1993 following Iraq's material breach of resolution 687 (1991) that coalition forces had received a mandate from the Council to use force according to resolution 678 (1990). Iraq continues to be in material breach of its disarmament obligations under resolution 687 (1991), as the Council affirmed in its resolution 1441 (2002).[13]

This was an implausible line of reasoning for the United States to pursue. It had just lobbied the Security Council heavily for a new resolution. Even though, as Negroponte had told the Council in November 2002, the U.S. position was that such a resolution was not needed, the pressure tactics the U.S. used to get a new resolution made it seem that it did not really believe that the prior resolutions sufficed.

The U.S. letter explained that we were implementing Security Council Resolution 678, adopted in November 1990, which authorized military force to remove Iraq from Kuwait if Iraq did not depart before January 15, 1991 and if military force was the only possible means to secure Iraq's departure from Kuwait. Resolution 678, as the letter explained, was followed by a cease-fire in April 1991, the terms of which were embodied in Resolution 687. One of the terms of the cease-fire was that Iraq would eliminate chemical, biological, and nuclear weaponry and permit inspection to that end.[14]

Taking that postulate, the letter reasoned that the cease-fire embodied in Resolution 687 was no longer binding. Given Iraq's noncompliance, the cease-fire was in effect nullified. On that basis, member states were authorized to implement the resolution that preceded the cease-fire, namely, Resolution 678.

Curiously, the Bush administration made no public statement referring to its letter to the Security Council, or even to the rationale expressed in the letter. It did not advertise its formal rationale for the action. Instead it spoke about Iraq as a threat.

A few days into the invasion, Iraq sent a letter to the Security Council on behalf of the Arab Group, less Kuwait, asking the Council to convene "with regard to halting the American-British aggression."[15] The Council did not convene. Nor did the Council discuss the validity of the

U.S. position on Resolution 678. There was little the Council could do to stop Bush.

The Security Council, to be sure, was in disarray as a result of the difference in view between the UK and U.S. on the one side, and France, Russia, and China on the other. After the military action began, Council members focused on the post-military situation, because that was a matter on which they might play a role. For one Council member, Germany, a discussion of the legality of the action would have been dangerous. Germany had allowed the United States to use bases in Germany to prepare the attack on Iraq. Thus, despite Germany's expressed opposition to the action, it was a participant. Under international law, a state that knowingly facilitates a violation by another state renders itself complicit.

The U.S. letter repeated many of the inaccuracies U.S. delegates had recited during the 1990s. Its reliance on Resolution 687 had no basis. As we saw in chapter 35, Resolution 687, the cease-fire resolution of 1991, included a final clause that recited that the Council "decides to remain seized of the matter and to take such further steps as may be required for the implementation of the present resolution and to secure peace and security in the area." By this clause, the Security Council reserved to itself the right to decide what to do if Iraq did not comply with any of the terms of Resolution 687.

Another difficulty with the Resolution 687 argument was that Resolution 687 was between Iraq and the UN, not between Iraq and the United States.[16] The terms of the cease-fire were spelled out in Resolution 687, not in a document signed by the United States. As one analyst stated, "this was clearly a cease-fire imposed by the Security Council, not an arrangement arrived at between the parties."[17]

As for Resolution 678, the 1990 resolution authorizing use of force, it predated Iraq's acceptance of disarmament obligations. It made little sense to say that the Security Council, in Resolution 678, authorized the use of force against Iraq for a purpose that was not at issue at the time Resolution 678 was adopted.

The U.S. letter, as quoted above, relied on a statement made in January 1993 by UN Secretary-General Boutros Boutros-Ghali. In January

1993, the U.S. and UK had just undertaken bombing raids against Iraq, and the statement was with regard to their legality. Boutros-Ghali had said at that time that a breach Iraq had just committed of Resolution 687 might legalize unilateral use of force under Resolution 678.

The January 1993 statement was one of very few from an authoritative source that the United States might find to cite. The U.S. used military force on its own against Iraq all through the 1990s, and it rarely gained favorable reaction statements from UN organs.

The January 1993 instance, in any event, did not support the U.S. position. The breach by Iraq that led to the January 1993 U.S.–UK bombing raids, as we saw in chapter 35, was a re-entry by Iraq into Kuwait to collect supplies it had abandoned in February 1991. Thus, the breach related to the essence of Resolution 678, which required Iraq to abandon Kuwait.

Deceptively, the U.S. letter referred to the Secretary-General's statement as an "announcement." In fact, the Secretary-General was corralled by reporters in Paris, where he happened to be at a conference, and they asked him what he thought about the U.S.–UK raids. He made the statement in response to their questions.[18] Neither before nor after did he or any other Secretary-General make a similar statement.

In addition, in referring to the January 1993 statement, the U.S. letter stated that the rationale based on Resolutions 678 and 687 had been "accepted by the Council," as "evidenced" by the Secretary-General's statement. That suggested that the remark of the Secretary-General reflected a view of the Security Council. Since the Secretary-General does not speak for the Security Council, this claim made no sense. Members of the Security Council through the 1990s, as we saw, prominently France, Russia, and China, viewed unilateral force by the United States against Iraq as unauthorized by existing Security Council resolutions.

U.S. forces in Iraq never found chemical, biological, or nuclear weapons, although not for lack of trying. The public was left to wonder whether Bush really thought he would find such weapons, or whether other factors prompted the invasion. In an unguarded moment, Bush had, as we saw in chapter 33, referred to Saddam Hussein as "a guy that tried to kill my dad." Bush might, thought some, have viewed the invasion as a favor to Israel, with which he had developed a close relationship. Or perhaps it was another effort, like those dating back to the mid-twentieth century, to control the politics of an oil-rich nation.

NOTES

1. Res. 1441, SCOR, 57th yr., UN Doc. S/RES/1441 (2002).

2. SCOR, 57th yr., 4644th mtg., p. 3, UN Doc. S/PV.4644 (2002).

3. "President's State of the Union Message to Congress and the Nation," *New York Times*, January 29, 2003, p. 12.

4. SCOR, 58th yr., 4701st mtg., pp. 8–14, UN Doc. S/PV.4701 (2003).

5. Tom Zeller, "How to Win Friends and Influence Small Countries," *New York Times*, March 16, 2003, p. 3.

6. SCOR, 58th yr., UN Doc. S/PV.4714, p. 3.

7. SCOR, 58th yr., UN Doc. S/PV.4714, p. 7.

8. Editorial, "The Quest for Illicit Weapons," *New York Times*, April 18, 2003, p. 14.

9. Joseph Wilson, "What I Didn't Find in Africa," *New York Times*, July 6, 2003, p. 9.

10. Jim Landers, "Iraq Didn't Pose Serious Weapons Threat, CIA Adviser Says," *Dallas Morning News*, October 7, 2004.

11. "The Weapons That Weren't," *Economist*, July 17, 2004.

12. Guglielmo Verdirame, "International Law and the Use of Force Against Iraq," in Paul Cornish, ed., *The Conflict in Iraq 2003* (2004), p..

13. Letter dated 20 March 2003 from the Permanent Representative of the United States of America to the United Nations addressed to the President of the Security Council, SCOR, 57th yr., UN Doc. S/2003/351 (2003).

14. Res. 687, paras. 7–14, SCOR, 46th yr., *Resolutions and Decisions*, p. 11, UN Doc. S/INF/47 (1991).

15. Letter dated 24 March 2003 from the Permanent Representative of Iraq to the United Nations addressed to the President of the Security Council, UN SCOR, 57th yr., UN Doc. S/2003/362 (2003).

16. Jules Lobel and Michael Ratner, "Bypassing the Security Council: Ambiguous Authorizations to Use Force, Cease-Fires and the Iraqi Inspection Regime," *American Journal of International Law* 93 (1999): 150.

17. Christine Gray, "After the Ceasefire: Iraq, the Security Council and the Use of Force," *British Year Book of International Law* 65 (1994): 141.

18. Alan Ferguson, "Vigilance or Vendetta? How Far Can You Stretch," *Toronto Star*, January 23, 1993, p. D1; Mark Tran, "Attack on Iraq: UN Gives Official Backing after Ceasefire Violations," Guardian, January 15, 1993, p. 8.

39. WHY NOT TELL THE TRUTH?

The fact that successive administrations have been less than candid with the public when intervening abroad raises troublesome questions. With the cold war covert operations, the pattern was fairly uniform. An operation was undertaken clandestinely, and if word leaked to the press, the administration denied involvement. It would give the press a cover story, as Eisenhower did with regard to Indonesia when his administration told the press that the U.S. agents involved were private mercenaries. With open interventions, a public explanation would be provided. Even though the reasons given were not genuine, the media typically did not probe, and the public accepted them.

Beginning in the 1990s, a new form of disingenuous conduct appeared, as the UN Security Council, freed from the cold war stalemate, began to adopt resolutions relating to conflict situations. The United States used these resolutions as a basis for interventions not contemplated by those who drafted the resolutions. The U.S. might distort facts to explain how a resolution justified a particular action, or it might interpret a resolution in a manner that would allow an intervention contrary to the resolution's intention.

The matter of lack of government candor on military action needs to be placed in some perspective. The United States is not the only country to lie upon initiating military action. Governments always seek to put themselves in the best possible light. When Germany invaded Poland in September 1939, it did not say that it was out to spread the Nazi philosophy. It said that Poland attacked first.

In 1956, after Egypt nationalized the Suez Canal from its French and British owners, Israel invaded. Britain and France said that the fighting between Israel and Egypt might jeopardize free passage through the Canal, so they sent troops into Egypt.[1] In fact, the invasion of Egypt had been planned jointly in advance by Israel, the UK, and France. The three of them agreed that Israel would attack first. The UK and France would join in, claiming that they were trying to stop the fighting.[2] The cover story did not hold up, however. It was quickly laid bare.[3]

Just at that same time, the Soviet Union sent troops into Hungary, after a reform-oriented administration assumed power there. The Soviet government claimed that it had been invited by the Hungarian administration, but it could show no evidence of an invitation, and its intervention was widely condemned.[4]

In 1967, Israel was successful with a false story when it attacked Egypt, reporting that Egypt had attacked three Israeli towns, which it named. In fact, Egypt had taken no military action against Israel. At the United Nations, Israel's story was challenged by Arab and Soviet-bloc countries, but it was accepted by most others. After a few weeks, Israel changed its story to say that Egypt had been about to launch an attack, and that it attacked first to prevent it. That story, inconsistent with the first, also gained wide acceptance, but it, too, was false. Although belligerent rhetoric was exchanged between Egypt and Israel, Israel did not expect an attack when it invaded Egypt, as a number of Israeli officials later acknowledged.[5]

In 1968 the Soviet Union found less success with a story it gave for sending troops into Czechoslovakia. Unnamed "party and Government leaders of the Czechoslovak Socialist Republic" had invited the intervention, it said.[6] The Soviet Communist Party newspaper *Pravda* published a letter explaining the reasons for the request, purportedly from a "group of members of the Central Committee of the Communist Party of

Czechoslovakia, of the government and National Assembly who asked for the assistance of the governments and communist parties of the fraternal countries."[7] Immediately, the Czech Communist Party issued a denial that the Czech government had asked for intervention.[8] Finding little acceptance of its request story, the Soviet government shifted to a different justification, namely, that socialism in Czechoslovakia was being undermined by outside forces, and that it must protect Czechoslovakia from a possible invasion by Western countries.[9] This rationale, which came to be called the Brezhnev doctrine, was apparently not based on any actual or threatened external actions against Czechoslovakia.

The United States is by no means unique in disguising the reasons for sending troops abroad. We have intervened more often than any other nation in recent history, and we have been more successful in convincing observers that our cover stories have been truthful. When a country uses its troops abroad, a favorable version of events is necessary for three reasons. First, the country must convince its own troops of the need to fight. A cause perceived to be just is essential if troops are to pursue their activity vigorously.

Second, the country must gain the support of its public. Even for countries that are not particularly democratic, it is hard to maintain a war effort for long if the public is against it. The public, too, must believe that the cause is just.

Third, the country must neutralize opposition from other countries and the world community. If it is a strong country, that will be easier, but for any country, military action is more easily carried to completion if outside states approve, or at least do not strenuously object.

If governments send troops to overthrow a foreign government for ideological reasons, they usually avoid mentioning them, because countries are expected to act under the neutral principles stated in the United Nations Charter. If they give an ideological justification, like the Johnson administration in the Dominican Republic, or the Soviet Union in Czechoslovakia, they may do so only as a last resort. Johnson first tried a rescue rationale for the Dominican Republic, and the Soviet Union first tried an invitation story for Czechoslovakia. The Reagan administration was less chary about saying that it was intervening for ideological purposes, arguing that it was permissible to give military support to what it called "freedom fighters" opposing a communist government. Nicaragua was the case par excellence where the Reagan administration used this theory. But even with Nicaragua, the administration at the same time made arguments on the basis of the universally accepted neutral principles, claiming that it was opposing Nicaraguan aid to El Salvador insurgents.

With ideological motivations, a government may believe that what it is doing is for the best, and therefore that it is justified in inventing a cover story. With the Dominican Republic and Czechoslovakia, both Johnson and Brezhnev probably believed they were doing the right thing.

For the United States, the cold war provided a powerful rationale for misrepresenting the facts. A report prepared in 1954 for President Eisenhower said that "we are facing an implacable enemy whose avowed objective is world domination by whatever means and at whatever cost. There are no rules in such a game. Hitherto acceptable norms of human conduct do not apply. If the U.S. is to survive, long-standing American concepts of 'fair play' must be reconsidered."[10] President Eisenhower doubtless slept with a clear conscience after being less than forthcoming about our operations in Guatemala, Indonesia, Lebanon, and Cuba.

Some U.S. officials have analyzed prevarication and have said that it is ethically permissible. In 1962 Assistant Secretary of Defense Arthur Sylvester said that lying is sometimes necessary to serve the national security.[11] Sylvester said that in crisis situations, he believed in "the inherent right of the Government to lie." He spoke of lying euphemistically as "generation" of news, and said that "news management" was "part of the arsenal of weaponry" of government.[12] Sylvester's position recalls the classic definition of a diplomat as one who is willing to lie for his country.

In 1986, as we saw, the Reagan administration planted false press stories about terrorist activity by Libya, and when this disinformation campaign was revealed, National Security Advisor John Poindexter justified it in terms similar to Sylvester's. Poindexter said that "deception" was a "tool that the government can use in combatting a very significant national security problem."[13] The public apparently did not appreciate the deceptions over Libya, however. A *New York Times*/CBS poll asked for opinions about government deception. It found that 73 percent thought that the government has no right to lie, even on foreign policy matters. The poll showed that the prevarication by successive administrations had left the public skeptical. Only 34 percent said that they thought the government told the truth "most of the time."[14]

Thus, ethical considerations aside, lying may not always be as efficacious as it appears to an administration that practices it. Even if false stories suffice to keep the public at bay while a military action proceeds to its conclusion, the public may in the long run turn against the administration. Although President Johnson scored initial success with his version of the Gulf of Tonkin incident, once the public perceived that he was not being forthright in explaining our actions in Vietnam, confidence in his leadership eroded, and he decided not to run for re-election.[15] In the next presidential election, that of 1968, the "credibility gap" was a central issue.[16] In 1971, the publication of the *Pentagon Papers* gave further evidence of falsehoods about Vietnam; public cynicism developed, and even a sense of alienation from government.[17] The prevarication also undermined public confidence in the press, which was held responsible for passing along the administration's untruths.[18]

Still, this lack of confidence has not led the public to rise up, as government lying about military actions overseas does not seem to be a priority issue to most people. The public has often been willing to overlook the lying, perhaps because it has perceived that the prevarication has been employed to fight stated threats, such as communism or terrorism.

Our prevarication about military actions has, as we have seen, typically drawn a harsher reaction abroad. Many of our interventions have been condemned at the United Nations or the Organization of American States. We are perceived as a country that throws its weight around to serve its own interests.

NOTES

1. GAOR, Emergency Session I, Plenary, p. 7, UN Doc. A/PV.561 (1956) (Britain); GAOR, Emergency Session I, Plenary, p. 30, UN Doc. A/PV. 562 (1956) (France).

2. Donald Neff, *Warriors at Suez* (1981), pp. 309–310.

3. Res. 997, GAOR, ES-I, *Resolutions*, p. 2, UN Doc. A/3354 (1956); Res. 1002, GAOR, ES-I, *Resolutions*, p 3.

4. Report of Special Committee on the Problem of Hungary, June 7, 1957, GAOR, 11th yr., Supplement No. 18, p. 137, UN Doc. A/3592 (1957).

5. John Quigley, *The Case for Palestine: An International Law Perspective* (2005), pp. 163–65.

6. "Statement by T.A.S.S.," *Pravda*, August 21, 1968, p. 1, col. 1; Raymond H. Anderson, "Soviet Explains: Says Its Troops Moved at the Request of Czechoslovaks," *New York Times*, August 21, 1968, p. A1, col. 5.

7. "Letter of the Group of Members of the Central Committee of the Communist Party of Czechoslovakia, of the Government and National Assembly of the C.S.S.R.," *Pravda*, August 22, 1968, p. 1, col. 6.

8. Declaration of the Presidium of the Central Committee of the Czechoslovakian Communist Party, August 21, 1968, in *International Legal Materials*, vol. 7, p. 1285 (1968).

9. S. Kovalev, "Sovereignty and the International Obligations of Socialist Countries," *Pravda*, September 26, 1968, p. 4, col. 1, translated as "Text of Pravda Article Justifying Invasion of Czechoslovakia," *New York Times*, September 27, 1968, p. A3, col. 1. (The *Times* gave the date of the *Pravda* article incorrectly as September 25).

10. *Final Report: Foreign and Military Intelligence*, U.S. Senate, Select Committee to Study Governmental Operations with Respect to Intelligence Activities, Book I, 94th Cong., 2d sess, April 26, 1976, p. 9.

11. James Deakin, *Lyndon Johnson's Credibility Gap* (1968), p. 54.

12. "U.S.-'Generated' News Defended by Sylvester," *Washington Post*, December 7, 1962, p. A2, col. 8.

13. Norman Kempster, "Poindexter Defends Deception on Security Issues," *Los Angeles Times*, October 15, 1986, p. A16, col. 4.

14. "Poll Finds Anger on Official Lies," *New York Times*, October 31, 1986, p. A3, col. 2.

15. Davis Wise, *The Politics of Lying: Government Deception, Secrecy, and Power* (1973), p. 26.

16. John Mueller, *War, Presidents and Public Opinion* (1973), pp. 112–13.

17. Wise, *The Politics of Lying: Government Deception, Secrecy, and Power*, pp. 14–15; Deakin, *Lyndon Johnson's Credibility Gap*, p. 52.

18. Haynes Johnson, "The Irreconcilable Conflict between Press and Government: 'Whose Side Are You On?'" in Thomas M. Franck and Edward Weisband, eds., *Secrecy and Foreign Policy* (1974), pp. 165, 173–74.

40. Why Intervene at All?

A more basic question than why to lie about intervention is why to intervene in the first place. No other country sends its troops so often to fight in distant locations as does the United States. Our country has developed a set of interests around the globe, largely stemming from our commercial activity. Our companies are everywhere, buying and selling, making investments, digging mines, setting up assembly lines, and cultivating cash crops. By early in the century we needed raw materials unavailable at home to fuel the mass-assembly production system we had mastered. Our industry, the most robust in the world, needed markets to sell the fruits of that system of production.

We spread first through regions close to home, as our companies set up shop in Latin America. Our banana plantations were the most visible activity. Previously, of course, the home of the world's major companies had been Europe, but early in the nineteenth century Spain and Portugal lost their Latin colonies, and President James Monroe declared that Europe was not to recolonize in our hemisphere. This was the Monroe Doctrine.

During the rest of the century, our business activity in Latin America increased, and our government began to intervene militarily to ensure that the rights of our companies were respected. By 1895, Secretary of State

Richard Olney could say that the United States was "practically sover-eign" in the western hemisphere, because "its infinite resources combined with its isolated position render it master of the situation."[1] Many Latin Americans doubtless agreed with Olney's assessment, although they may not have viewed our role as so benign.

Exercising our role of "master of the situation," President Theodore Roosevelt claimed a right to intervene in any Latin country that defaulted on its public debt. To put a country's finances in order, we would operate its customs houses and put its finances back on a proper footing. Roo-sevelt first used this rationale to intervene in the Dominican Republic in 1905, and his rationale became known as the Roosevelt corollary to the Monroe Doctrine.[2]

Over the next three decades, we intervened in many Latin American countries, anxious to see governments at the helm that would let our com-panies operate without major restriction. In our strategic thinking, secu-rity and economic considerations became intertwined.[3] After World War II, with Europe weakened, we spread out to the rest of the world. As Europe's colonial empires declined, our companies became the main out-side financial force in Asia and Africa. As with Latin America, we wanted friendly governments in power so that we could extract their minerals, employ their labor force, and sell our products.

We set up a worldwide apparatus, the first country ever to do so. We sent naval fleets to all the world's oceans and stationed ground troops in far-flung locations. We could intervene anywhere. We preserved friendly governments and displaced the unfriendly, giving the Monroe Doctrine and its Roosevelt corollary a global reach.[4]

In Third World areas formerly dominated by Europe, we came into a power broker role, taking Indochina from France, and the Middle East from Britain and France. Our companies saw nothing wrong in what they were doing, and in some ways they benefited the populations of the coun-tries where they operated. The companies were simply doing good busi-ness; they were looking for the cheapest raw materials and labor and for new markets.

Our preeminence in the financial life of weaker countries was accompanied by a similar role in their politics. Our companies, whose assets often exceeded those of the countries where they operated, could control events. In return for payoffs, politicians in those countries, whether disguised or openly, let the companies operate as they liked. In reaction to this phenomenon, opposition to our preeminence developed in Asia and Africa, as it already had in Latin America. Often this opposition was led by leftist parties on close terms with the Soviet Union or China.

Fighting communism became a rationale for the effort to gain economic control. When in 1949 the communists won the Chinese civil war and the Soviet Union developed atomic weaponry, the Truman administration found it that much easier to convince Congress and the public of the danger of communism, even though China was caught up in its own problems, and we were the ones who developed atomic weapons first. The Truman administration spelled out its new policy of permanent militarization in 1950 in the National Security Council directive 68, which we encountered earlier in the context of the Korean war. The Truman administration used the three years of war in Korea to implement NSC 68, raising the annual military budget from $13 billion to $50 billion. Although Eisenhower cut the military budget somewhat in the years that followed, the course of high-level militarization had been set.

NSC 68 also addressed the question of when to use our armed forces. It said that "it is important that the United States employ military force only if the necessity for its use is clear and compelling and commends itself to the overwhelming majority of our people."[5] Presidents have not followed that injunction. We have used military force in situations in which the public probably did not perceive a need. Senator Frank Church said that as for the CIA and its efforts abroad, it targeted "small, weak countries."[6] Two former CIA operatives said that the CIA's overall objective was to keep us "the dominant arbiter of social, economic, and political change in the awakening regions of Asia, Africa, and Latin America."[7]

In influencing the political direction in Third World nations, our efforts were directed less toward keeping them from orienting toward the Soviet Union than toward encouraging them to orient themselves toward our interests. Nationalism and neutralism were seen as just as serious a threat to our control as was Leftism, because what we sought was access to the economy. That is why we overthrew President Arbenz in Guatemala in 1954 and tried to overthrow President Sukarno in Indonesia in 1958. Both men were nationalists and neutralists, with only the marginal connection to the Soviet Union or China. It is why the Eisenhower Doctrine, promulgated in 1957 as a policy of opposing communism in the Middle East, was applied in 1958 in the Lebanon-Iraq-Jordan situation to counter Arab nationalism. In Korea and Indochina, our efforts were aimed less at keeping the Russians and Chinese out than at drawing those areas into the market-economy sphere that included Japan, which we were also trying to orient in our direction.[8]

One can speculate about whether administration officials believed what they were saying about a communist threat. With Korea, for example, many of them doubtless believed, despite the contrary evidence, that we were being challenged by the Soviet Union or China. Soon, in any event, the red menace was accepted administration doctrine, and fighting communism became the accepted rationale for government policy. After a time, policy makers stopped thinking too deeply about the reasons, so entrenched became the cold war mode of thinking.

Fighting communism gave philosophical rectitude to a fight to maintain access to markets and foreign labor and resources. We appeared to be fighting not for material gain but for freedom of conscience, representative democracy, and the rule of law. The fact that we supported authoritarian governments as long as they let us access their economies was not noticed. In the Nicaragua of Anastasio Somoza, the Cuba of Fulgencio Batista, and the Dominican Republic of Rafael Trujillo, there was little democracy, yet we supported these men. Our backing of such men may have led to more of the Leftism we were supposedly fighting.

From a financial standpoint the policy worked. We prospered during the 1950s and 1960s as we expanded our control. Politically, however, the policy had serious costs. It is doubtful that even the interventions considered successful at the time were in our best interest in the long term. The Guatemala coup of 1954 left that impoverished country with seemingly endless violence and civil war. Its governments were so repressive that in the 1970s the Carter administration virtually disowned the country. With Grenada and Panama, the populations eventually turned against us when we did not come through with the financial aid they thought would flow from our intervention.

NOTES

1. "Mr. Olney to Mr. Bayard," July 20, 1985, FRUS 1895, p. 558.

2. "Message from the President of the United States, Transmitting a Protocol of an Agreement between the United States and the Dominican Republic, Providing for the Collection and Disbursement by the United States of the Customs Revenues of the Dominican Republic, Signed on February 7, 1905," February 15, 1905, FRUS 1905, pp. 334–42.

3. Piero Gleijeses, *The Dominican Crisis: The 1965 Constitutionalist Revolt and American Intervention* (1978), p. 15.

4. Thomas J. McCormick, *America's Half-Century: United States Foreign Policy in the Cold War* (1989), p. 75.

5. "A Report to the President Pursuant to the President's Directive of January 31, 1950," April 7, 1950, FRUS 1950, vol. 1, p. 267.

6. Frank Church, "Covert Action: Swampland of American Foreign Policy," *Bulletin of the Atomic Scientists*, February 1976, p. 9.

7. Victor Marchetti and John Marks, *The CIA and the Cult of Intelligence* (1974), p. 4.

8. McCormick, *America's Half-Century*, pp. 100, 111.

41. WON'T THE MEDIA
   PROTECT US?

This book began with Hugo Black's exhortation to the press to protect our youth from dying in foreign wars for reasons hidden from them. Our media has remarkable technical capability, bringing instantaneous reports from any point on the globe. Yet many reporters and editors have not been inclined to inquire behind official stories. When the U.S. intervened in the Dominican Republic, many journalists reported as fact what they were told by U.S. Embassy officials. Others wrote skeptically.[1]

With Grenada, again, a few media outlets challenged official stories, but most reported the government version as fact, which meant they gave a false picture. What came across in most media about Grenada was that it was a rescue mission, that it was done jointly with other countries, that the Cubans there were "troops" that attacked us, and that the airport under construction in Grenada was for military use.[2]

In an intervention situation, the administration is aware that accurate media reporting may jeopardize its ability to convince the public of its version of the facts, so typically an administration tries to keep the media from contrary information.[3] On occasion, newspapers that have come upon contrary information suppress it out of considerations of patriotism. In 1954, just before the CIA overthrew the Guatemalan government, a *New York Times* reporter was writing about Guatemala in a way that CIA Director Allen Dulles found too sympathetic to President Arbenz. After Dulles complained, the *Times* editors decided to keep the reporter out of Guatemala during the overthrow. When the Bay of Pigs landing was in the planning stage, a *Miami Herald* reporter discovered that the CIA was training Cuban exiles at secret locations in Florida and submitted an article saying so. The editor made the reporter show his draft to CIA Director Dulles, who asked the *Herald* not to publish the piece. The *Herald* killed it.[4] A few days before the landing at the Bay of Pigs, a *New York Times* reporter found out that the invasion was about to jump off and submitted a story saying so. A *Times* editor consulted President Kennedy and edited the story to obscure the fact that an invasion was imminent.[5]

The CIA, of course, has taken direct action to influence the news. As we saw with the Angola operation, it has planted false news stories.[6] Beginning in the 1950s, the CIA established a media and publishing empire that owned wire services, newspapers, and magazines. It recruited U.S. journalists abroad. It convinced news organizations to hire CIA agents to provide them "cover."[7] According to CIA insiders, the aim was to deceive the public both abroad and in the United States to shape opinion in favor of CIA objectives. This objective was pursued with false information the CIA planted regarding the Vietnam war; a major aim was to influence public opinion in the United States and to thwart the public campaign against our involvement. Planted CIA stories were run by major newspapers.[8] The Senate intelligence committee said that such CIA efforts to abuse the media "for clandestine operations is a threat to the integrity of the press."[9]

In a more subtle vein, administration officials place a "spin" on events in order to influence public opinion. They may feed trusted reporters with background information that puts events in a particular light, and the reporter, considering the "inside" information a scoop, will print it, with attribution to a "senior official."[10] During the 1965 intervention in the Dominican Republic, the U.S. embassy, seeking to discredit the pro-Bosch forces, told reporters in a not-for-attribution briefing that the main pro-Bosch military officer had met with communists the previous day. After the officer denied the meeting, Ambassador Tapley Bennett acknowledged that the information was untrue.[11]

That the media generally follow the State Department or Defense Department lead is not surprising. What these agencies say is news. They flood the media with press statements through their public information services, which employ thousands and spend millions to get their messages across.[12] With regard to secret operations, the media has no ready access to information. Thus, it is largely dependent on tips from inside sources, but even an insider who talks may have a motive to distort the reality.[13]

When reporters have insisted on writing material objectionable to administration officials, administration officials have tried to discredit them. President Nixon put certain journalists on an "enemies list." Repeating, without questioning, the government's version of facts may be safer.[14] From El Salvador, *New York Times* reporter Raymond Bonner wrote graphic accounts of the bombing of rural villages by the U.S.–backed El Salvador government. His accounts were accurate, from what can be determined, but they threatened the Reagan administration's efforts to convince Congress that El Salvador was improving its human rights record. The U.S. embassy in San Salvador barred Bonner from press briefings and kept him from interviewing embassy personnel. When the *Times* saw that Bonner did not have access to these sources, it pulled him from El Salvador.[15]

Even when reporters are skeptical of the government's facts, it may take time to figure out whether the government lied. For the government, what is important is that the public back an intervention while it is in progress. Typically, once a short-term operation is over, the media loses interest. So if, as with the Panama intervention in 1989, it later turns out that we killed many more people than originally reported, the media will not give that fact great prominence.

Increasingly, the television networks, news magazines, and leading newspapers are owned by corporations and financial institutions with far-flung financial interests.[16] These are the very entities that may benefit from military intervention. The media may have a conflict of interest in reporting on interventions.

The media can play one of several roles in a developing situation. It can be compliant in feeding the public the information the Pentagon wants it to get. During the run-up to the Persian Gulf war, the media did not cover the inconsistencies in Bush's statements about a threat to Saudi Arabia. It did not cover Saddam Hussein's conciliatory responses to peace feelers by third parties. It made little effort to expose the false atrocity stories about the babies on incubators. That lack of coverage made it easier for Bush to insert troops into Saudi Arabia, and then to attack Iraq.

Again in 2003, the media did little to inquire into the validity of the false information Colin Powell gave to the Security Council about Iraq Even though the holes in Powell's evidence were apparent from the outset, even without access to classified information. Analysts whose work was not picked up by the major media communicated on Websites to refute Powell.

I gave a public speech March 1, 2003, that I titled "Colin Powell's Evidence." Even though I did not have the specific information that later became available that called Powell's material into question, it was obvious that his information was from suspect sources. The photographs he showed did not show what he claimed.

Powell put satellite photographs on a screen and said: "Here we see that cargo vehicles are again at this trans-shipment point, and we can see that they are accompanied by a decontamination vehicle associated with biological or chemical weapons activity."[17] I could not see anything in the images other than trucks. Had the media probed Powell's evidence, the administration would have had a more difficult time launching an attack. As matters stood, when it invaded on March 20, it acted on unrefuted evidence that Iraq was a menace to the world community.

More damaging still than passivity, the media may publicize false information that forces a president's hand. The *New York Times* and *Washington Post*, as we saw in chapter 33, backed President Clinton into a corner by leaking information on the alleged plot to assassinate former President George H.W. Bush. They made Clinton appear weak if he did not act. It was, of course, Clinton's own people who were feeding the information, so the newspapers can say they were simply reporting important information. And it was ultimately Clinton's call as to whether to launch missiles at Baghdad.

The picture, fortunately, is not entirely bleak. Many journalists are able to get accurate information into wide-circulation publications. On the matter of the supposed Iraqi build-up in 1990 to invade Saudi Arabia, the *St. Petersburg Times* purchased satellite photographs that showed there was no build-up and published information about them. It even did so, and this has been quite rare, before the intervention began. The major media were not interested in this inconvenient detail.

Veteran White House journalist Helen Thomas finds the media too accepting of the executive branch's interpretation of events. Thomas wrote that as the 2003 war began in Iraq, a pool of reporters were invited into the Oval Office at the White House. "Most of the media present," Thomas said, "didn't challenge Bush's decision or ask him how he could justify the invasion especially when so many of our allies, with the exception of Great Britain and Australia, had expressed their reservations about the war."[18]

Often when journalists inclined to uncover deception are able to piece together the necessary information, they are able to publish it only after the fact, as with Seymour Hersh's informative exposé on the 1993 missile raid against Baghdad. Still, the media does constitute an obstacle to false portrayals. The notes in this book reference hundreds of press stories that drew an official version of facts into question. The media is a force with which the government has to contend.

NOTES

1. Tad Szulc, *Dominican Diary* (1965), p. 202.

2. Michael Parenti, *Inventing Reality: The Politics of the Mass Media* (1986), pp. 182–83.

3. David Wise, *The Politics of Lying: Government Deception, Secrecy, and Power* (1973), p. 27.

4. John M. Crewdson, "The C.I.A.'s 3-Decade Effort to Mold the World's Views," *New York Times*, December 25, 1977, p. A1, col. 1.

5. Peter Wyden, *Bay of Pigs: The Untold Story* (1979), pp. 153–55; Arthur M. Schlesinger, Jr., *A Thousand Days* (1965) p. 261; William Colby, *Honorable Men: My Life in the CIA* (1978), pp. 181–82.

6. U.S. Senate, Select Committee to Study Governmental Operations with Respect to Intelligence Activities, *Final Report: Foreign and Military Intelligence*, Book I, 94th Cong., 2d sess, April 26, 1976, pp. 198–200, 454; Stuart H. Loory, "The CIA's Use of the Press: A 'Mighty Wurlitzer,'" *Columbia Journalism Review*, September–October 1974, p. 9.

7. Colby, p. 182.

8. Parenti, p. 233. John M. Crewdson, "The C.I.A.'s 3-Decade Effort to Mold the World's Views," NY Times, Dec. 25, 1977, p. A1, col. 1. John M. Crewdson, "Worldwide Propaganda Network Built by the C.I.A.," NY Times, Dec. 26, 1977, p. A1, col. 1. John M. Crewdson, "C.I.A. Established Many Links to Journalists in U.S. and Abroad," NY Times, Dec. 27, 1977, p. A1, col. 5.

9. *Final Report: Foreign and Military Intelligence*, p. 455.

10. Theodore Draper, *The Dominican Revolt: A Case Study in American Policy* (1968), p. 89.

11. Draper, pp. 89-90.

12. Edward S. Herman & Noam Chomsky, *Manufacturing Consent: The Political Economy of the Mass Media* (1988), p 19, 23.

13. Loch K. Johnson, *America's Secret Power: The CIA in a Democratic Society* (1989), p. 246.

14. Haynes Johnson, "The Irreconcilable Conflict between Press and Government: "Whose Side Are You On?," in Thomas M. Franck & Edward Weisband, eds., *Secrecy and Foreign Policy* (1974), p. 165, 176-177.

15. Parenti, p. 57.

16. Benjamin Compaine, "Who Owns the Media Companies?" in Benjamin Compaine, ed., *Who Owns the Media? Concentration of Ownership in the Mass Communication Industry* (1982), pp. 451-465.

17. UN SCOR, 58th yr., 4701st mtg., p. 10, UN Doc. S/PV. 4701 (2003).

18. Helen Thomas, Watchdogs of Democracy? The Waning Washington Press Corps and How It Has Failed the Public (2006), pp. 156-157.

42. WON'T CONGRESS PROTECT US?

The Constitution gives Congress vast authority over foreign affairs, most significantly the power of the purse. The president gets not a farthing unless Congress allocates it. So an administration cannot wage a war of any duration unless it gets funding from Congress. Besides, the Constitution says that Congress is supposed to make the important decisions when it comes to war and peace. The framers of the Constitution did not envisage a president who could commit the country to war under his own authority. They gave Congress the all-important power to declare war as an exclusive power of Congress. Under the Constitution, a president may not make war without a declaration by Congress.

The framers were also concerned about military actions short of full-scale war, like many of those recounted in this book. Although a military action may be minor in scope, or of short duration, it has the potential of getting us into a larger war. The framers were concerned that a president might evade Congress's prerogatives by starting a minor military action that would lead to war, so they wrote into the Constitution a clause giving Congress the power to issue so-called letters of marque and reprisal.[1] These were documents issued by eighteenth century sovereigns to their military officers or to private persons to authorize them to carry out a military attack on the sovereign's behalf. They were typically issued when the sovereign had been affronted and wanted to take reprisal. Thomas Jefferson said that the Constitution gave this power to Congress, because minor attacks could lead to war. President John Adams approached Congress more than once to ask it to issue letters of marque and reprisal.

Congress, however, has not invoked its power of issuing letters of marque and reprisal to object to interventions. By failing to insist on this power, and by letting presidents carry out military operations on their own authority, Congress, in the words of one scholar of the Constitution, "has abdicated its constitutional responsibilities."[2]

Although the Constitution seems to give Congress the upper hand when it comes to military action abroad, the executive has practical advantages that undermine Congress's power. With covert operations, Congress cannot exercise its power of the purse if it does not learn of the action. The CIA may camouflage funding for an action in general budget categories, so Congress does not know what it is funding. Congress has not insisted on budget accountability.[3]

Also, the executive controls access to information, because it commands our intelligence-gathering agencies and gets reports from embassies around the world. If Congress and the administration argue over agricultural subsidies, a member of Congress can get information from the folks back home, but if the issue is whether to invade Ruritania, a member of Congress may be dependent on the executive for information. Commanding sources of information, the executive can present foreign policy options to Congress in a light favorable to its own plans. Regarding clandestine intervention, the Senate committee on intelligence said that Congress is "almost totally dependent on the executive branch for information on covert operations."[4]

One other advantage for the executive is Congress's size. With one hundred senators and 535 members in the House of Representatives, and with half of Congress, more or less, being of the president's party, it is difficult to muster a majority to stop a president. With most interventions, as we have seen, Congress has "rallied around the flag." Many members of Congress are afraid to criticize a president who commits troops into combat, for fear of sounding unpatriotic or unsupportive of our soldiers.

Many members of Congress have expressed concern about executive branch obfuscation and secrecy. U.S. Representative David Bonior complained that paramilitary operations ordered by a president "commit us to a specific foreign policy that has never been openly defended and supported, and whose outcome cannot be guided by our own democratic institutions."[5] After the secret bombing of Cambodia in 1969-70, Senator Harold Hughes said that if the Defense Department continued to withhold information about military operations, "there will never be a moment in the history of this country in the future when the people will have a hand in the declaration of war or the conduct of war over international borders."[6]

The Senate committee on intelligence expressed the same concern: "The secrecy covert actions requires means that the public cannot determine whether such actions are consistent with established foreign policy goals. This secrecy also has allowed covert actions to take place which are inconsistent with our basic traditions and values."[7] The committee might have made the same comment about overt military operations that the government justifies with false reasons, because there, too, the public and Congress are deprived of a say.

Congress, on the whole, has been half-hearted in extracting information from the executive branch on military operations. The CIA, when it began undertaking covert operations, did not volunteer information on them to Congress, and Congress has not been demanding of the CIA about them.[8] CIA Director William Colby, during his time in office, found that Congress was "in the thrall of the Agency's mystique" and was prepared to let it act on the quiet.[9]

In the 1970s, after a number of covert operations were publicly revealed to Congress's embarrassment, it passed the Hughes-Ryan Amendment, which required the administration to report to it on covert operations.[10] The amendment did not, however, require prior notification of covert operations, so Congress was making no effort to exert a veto power over them. Two years after the amendment went into effect, the Senate committee on intelligence said that the amendment was only marginally effective.[11]

Since the mid-1970s, however, each house of Congress has had a permanent committee to oversee covert operations. The Hughes-Ryan language was tightened in 1980 to require prior notification of these committees of a covert operation, but with a loophole that let the president limit the notification to Senate and House leaders, rather than to the committees.[12] Congress tried to close that loophole in 1990, but President Bush vetoed the bill.[13]

At times, the Senate and House committees have pursued information diligently, but they have rarely been a match for the more experienced State Department and CIA personnel. Officials have tried to avoid appearing when called by congressional committees.[14] One CIA official claimed that the CIA doctored its files to keep sensitive material from Congress,[15] and that CIA Director William Colby routinely lied to Congress during briefings.[16]

In one Congressional debate over our involvement in Vietnam, members of both the House and Senate quoted from what they said was a Vietnamese periodical, citing passages that made our involvement seem appropriate. What they did not know was that the periodical had been produced by the CIA.[17] Whether the blame should rest more on Congress, or more on the executive, oversight by Congress has hardly been effective.[18] With the 2003 Iraq war, the Senate did eventually inquire and determine that the executive's factual claims were invalid. But that came only a year after the intervention.

In giving the executive money for military operations, Congress, to be sure, shared the administration's cold war assumptions. During the Korean war, convinced by the administration that we were being threatened by world communism, Congress let military spending skyrocket. Korea cost so much that Congress stopped funding the Marshall Plan for Europe. With the Kennedy administration and the Indochina war, military spending shot up higher still. In the 1980s, at the urging of the Reagan administration, Congress ratcheted military spending up another notch.

The monetary aspect of the interventions raises a serious question of public policy. The taxpayers give Congress the money to run the country, and Congress gives it to the executive. With military interventions undertaken secretly or for reasons other than those stated, the administration spends the public's money fraudulently. It tells them that it is spending it for certain reasons, but it is spending it for different reasons.

Administration prevarication about military intervention brings a major breakdown in the democratic process. The public elects the representatives, deciding whom to elect, in part, on how they vote on budget matters. When the administration conceals from Congress what it is spending money on and why, the public is deprived of its role in the budget process.

In some instances the public might, if it knew the true facts, agree with what is being done, but in others it might not. In either case it is being forced to pay for something it does not know about. While the blame is not entirely on Congress, or entirely on the administrations, Congress has not protected the public from administrations that commit us to combat under false pretenses.

NOTES

1. Constitution of the United States, art. 1, sec. 8, para. 11.

2. Jules Lobel, "Covert War and Congressional Authority: Hidden War and Forgotten Power," *University of Pennsylvania Law Review* 134 (1986): 1041.

3. *Final Report: Foreign and Military Intelligence*, U.S. Senate, Select Committee to Study Governmental Operations with Respect to Intelligence Activities, Book I, 94th Cong., 2d sess., April 26, 1976, p. 384.

4. *Final Report: Foreign and Military Intelligence*, p. 447.

5. *Congressional Record*, vol. 128, p. H9158, December 8, 1982.

6. *Bombing in Cambodia*, Hearings before the Committee on Armed Services, U.S. Senate, 93rd Cong., 1st sess. (1973), p. 157.

7. *Final Report: Foreign and Military Intelligence*, p. 445.

8. Ibid., p. 150; Victor Marchetti and John Marks, *The CIA and the Cult of Intelligence* (1974), pp. 345–47.

9. William Colby, *Honorable Men: My Life in the CIA* (1978), p. 182.

10. U.S. Congress, *Statutes at Large*, vol. 88, p. 1804 (1974); US Code, Title 22, §2422.

11. *Final Report: Foreign and Military Intelligence*, p. 151.

12. U.S. Congress, *Statutes at Large*, vol. 94, p. 1981 (1980); US Code, Title 50, §413.

13. Michael Wines, "Bush, to Guard Secrecy, Kills Espionage Agencies' Budget," *New York Times*, December 1, 1990, p. A10, col. 5.

14. Aaron Latham, "Introduction to the Pike Papers," *Village Voice*, February 16, 1976, p. 70.

15. John Stockwell, *In Search of Enemies: a CIA Story* (1978), p. 273.

16. "Should the U.S. Fight Secret Wars?" *Harper's* magazine, September 1984, p. 43.

17. *Final Report: Foreign and Military Intelligence*, p. 454.

18. Loch K. Johnson, *America's Secret Power: The CIA in a Democratic Society* (1989), pp. 108, 247.

43. INTERVENTIONS OF THE FUTURE

The U.S. military interventions to the end of the cold war were rationalized as necessary to fight communism. The most recent interventions have been rationalized as necessary to fight terrorism. Some others had still different rationales.

In the 1980s, the Reagan administration examined the question of when and how we should intervene. President Reagan established the Commission on Integrated Long-Term Strategy, which issued a report in 1988. The report called for devoting more attention and resources to minor wars in Asia, Africa, and Latin America. "Nearly all the armed conflicts of the past forty years," the report said, "have occurred in what is vaguely referred to as the Third World: the diverse countries of Asia, the Middle East, Africa, Latin America, and the Eastern Caribbean."

Third World conflicts, the report said, "have had and will have an adverse cumulative effect on U.S. access to critical regions, on American credibility among allies and friends, and on American self-confidence." The report said that "if this cumulative effect cannot be checked or reversed in the future, it will gradually undermine America's ability to defend its interests in the most vital regions, such as the Persian Gulf, the Mediterranean and the Western Pacific. In the coming decades the United States will need to be better prepared to deal with conflicts in the Third World."

The wars the report envisioned represented what it called "low intensity conflict," insurgencies that would operate at a modest level over an extended period. In most instances, the report said, we would not be involved with our troops but would provide "security assistance" to a government. We also might support an insurgency, the report said, if it is anticommunist. This kind of support, it said, may embarrass neighboring countries that provide base areas for "freedom fighters," so our support should be done as "covert action." In that way, "the U.S. Government can maintain official silence." This can be done either by the military or by the CIA, it said. In any event, the report concluded, security assistance should be increased substantially.[1] Despite the reference to "freedom fighters," the report implicitly acknowledged that U.S. control, rather than fighting communism, was our objective. The phrase "access to critical regions" was the most telling line in the report.

When the cold war ended, fighting communism no longer could be used as a justification for intervention. President George H.W. Bush had to explain why we would intervene in a world of only one superpower. He said that our interests might require military intervention, despite the end of the cold war. "Notwithstanding the alteration in the Soviet threat," he said in 1990, "the world remains a dangerous place with serious threats to important U.S. interests wholly unrelated to the earlier patterns of the U.S.–Soviet relationship."[2] General A.M. Gray, Commandant of the Marine Corps, wrote, "If we are to have stability in these [Third World] regions, maintain access to their resources, protect our citizens abroad, defend our vital installations, and deter conflict, we must maintain within our active force structure a credible military power projection capability with the flexibility to respond to conflict across the spectrum of violence throughout the globe."[3] General Carl Vuono, Army chief of staff, said that "because the United States is a global power with vital interests that must be protected throughout an increasingly turbulent world, we must look beyond the European continent and consider other threats to our national security."[4]

These officials were not suggesting anything new in terms of our practice, since, as they acknowledged, our military interventions have generally been in the Third World. But with the cold war over, the administration was hard pressed to convince Congress of the need to keep military spending at the high levels of the 1980s. The rationale President Truman had used in 1950 to raise military spending no longer applied. So the (first) Bush administration acknowledged what had been true all along, namely, that our military takes the Third World as its main focus.[5] It was remarkably frank in stressing access to resources, virtually admitting that the rationale of fighting communism had been used as a fig leaf.

Top military brass explained the kinds of conflicts that might break out. General Vuono wrote,

> Regional rivalries supported by powerful armies have resulted in brutal and devastating conflicts in the Third World.... The proliferation of advanced military capabilities has given an increasing number of countries in the developing world the ability to wage sustained, mechanized land warfare. The United States cannot ignore the expanding military power of these countries, and the Army must retain the capability to defeat potential threats wherever they occur. This could mean confronting a well-equipped army in the Third World.[6]

Iraq's invasion of Kuwait in 1990 presented an opportunity to put this new theory into practice. Vital resources, the administration said, were threatened by a Third World war. "What is at stake economically," explained Secretary of State James Baker, "is the dependence of the world on access to the energy resources of the Persian Gulf."[7]

President Bush presented the issue in more apocalyptic terms, saying that our goal in the Persian Gulf was "maintaining access to energy resources that are key—not just to the functioning of this country but to the entire world. Our jobs, our way of life, our own freedom, and the freedom of friendly countries around the world would all suffer if control of the world's great oil reserves fell into the hands of Saddam Hussein."[8]

Baker, too, depicted the stakes as high: "It is not just a narrow question of the flow of oil from Kuwait and Iraq. It is about a dictator who, acting alone and unchallenged, could strangle the global economic order, determining by fiat whether we all enter a recession or even the darkness of a depression."[9] Bush argued that if Iraq were to control Saudi Arabia's oil, and perhaps that of the Gulf emirates, it would have 60 percent of the world's oil reserves.

This analysis reads like a prescription for the interventions that followed into the new century. The post-cold-war warriors acknowledged access to resources and free flow of commerce as the reason for intervention. As before, they overlooked the negative consequences, one might call it "collateral damage," of military intervention.

In the Middle East, particularly, our policy makers ignored the impact of intervention. They failed to draw lessons from our previous interventions. In 1953, as we saw, the CIA engineered the overthrow of an elected leader in Iran and put in his place a man who became unpopular for aligning Iran with the West, and who ultimately was overthrown. He was replaced by elements intensely hostile to the West as a result of this experience, and the immediate result was the taking of hostages at the U.S. embassy in Iran. The moral we should have drawn is that meddling is hazardous.

The troop deployment in the Persian Gulf in 1990–91 held the prospect of inspiring just such a negative reaction. Analysts said that "anti-American Islamic extremism in the region was likely to be fueled by the crisis."[10] Islamic fundamentalism had grown in the Arab world, taking Iran as the model, largely as a reaction to Western penetration. Our support for Israel and our opposition to Palestinian nationalism discredited the Arab nationalist politicians we called "moderate" and created the political space for Islamic fundamentalism.

When he invaded Kuwait, Saddam Hussein capitalized on this sense of grievance by saying that negotiations over Iraq's withdrawal from Kuwait could be held only if they included discussion of Israel's withdrawal from the Arab territories it occupied. Hussein's position was approved by many Arabs, who viewed him as the first Arab leader in a generation to stand up to the humiliation represented by the continuing U.S. support for Israel. Thus, although cold war considerations were absent, the United States still failed to consider local issues. From the beginning of the twentieth century we set our military sights on weaker countries for their markets, cheap labor, and minerals. The end of the cold war did not end that orientation.

Opposing a supposed outside enemy was not a new rationale for intervention when the cold war began. In 1916, President Woodrow Wilson sent the Marines to occupy the Dominican Republic, arguing that Germany might take it over if we stayed out, although there was little evidence of any such possibility. Our real aim was control. Before the Marines left the Dominican Republic eight years later in 1924, our military administration had let U.S. sugar companies gain title to much of the sugar-growing land there, driving off Dominican peasants and burning their villages in the process.[11]

Far from eliminating interventions, the end of the cold war removed one factor that stood in their way. During the cold war, the Soviet Union called us to account when we gave a false reason for an intervention. It denounced our interventions and challenged our portrayal of the facts. The end of the cold war made intervention under false pretenses easier. "The end of the Cold War and the United States's position as the world's sole and unchallenged superpower renders opposition to U.S. actions even more difficult," wrote Jules Lobel.[12]

Preventive self-defense, the theory popularized by the (second) Bush administration, opened the path even wider to intervention on contrived reasons. Under the traditional self-defense doctrine, an intervening state had to claim that an armed attack had occurred. Under preventive self-defense, it would need only say that an attack might occur some time in the future. Preventive self-defense would authorize military action based on information about a potential enemy's future acts; it would be based not on an attack that everyone could see but on suppositions. The doctrine thus fit well with the way in which successive U.S. administrations had been intervening all along. If one's practice is to intervene for reasons other than what one publicly states, it makes sense to espouse a theory of self-defense that facilitates prevarication.

The (second) Bush administration's espousal of a concept of preventive self-defense was a central feature of its foreign policy. The doctrine seemed to fit the military action the United States initiated against Iraq in March 2003, even if the administration did not use this justification in its formal statement of reasons to the United Nations. President George Bush spoke of a threat posed by Iraq to the United States. Even if Iraq was not an immediate danger to the United States, so the argument ran, it might attack at some point, and it would be better to stop Iraq when the opportunity presented itself.

The concept of preventive self-defense, of course, runs counter to the precepts viewed by the international community as necessary to limit the use of force between states. If states may use force out of a concern for future danger, then the rule against aggression could be evaded quite easily.

In many situations, states may be able to make a credible case that another state poses a danger. When India and Pakistan were involved in a standoff, with each having weapons in place to attack the other, either could probably have attacked and argued, plausibly, that the other was going to attack it.

Even if the concept were sound as a matter of principle, its implementation might be so fraught with difficulty as to make it unworkable. The information that a state would put forward to make out such a case would be based on intelligence gathering. It might be of the type that Colin Powell gave the UN Security Council on February 5, 2003, in his effort to establish that Iraqi weaponry posed a threat, namely, information provided by informants, or photographs that can be interpreted in different ways. Still worse, information might be manipulated, as was done with the information about Iraq supposedly seeking to buy fissionable material from Niger.

NOTES

1. *Discriminate Deterrence: Report of the Commission on Integrated Long-Term Strategy* (Fred C. Iklé and Albert Wohlstetter, co-chairmen) (prepared for Secretary of Defense and Assistant to the President for National Security

Affairs), January 1988, pp. 13–17; "More Vietnams; The Federal Commission on Integrated Long-Term Strategy's Report Is Likely to Cause an Increase in U.S. Conventional Forces," *Nation*, January 23, 1988, p. 75.

2. Maureen Dowd, "Backing Pentagon, Bush Says Military Can Be Cut 25% in 5 Years," *New York Times*, August 3, 1990, p. A13, col. 3.

3. Gen. A. M. Gray, "Defense Policy for the 1990s," *Marine Corps Gazette*, May 1990, p. 18.

4. Michael Klare, "Policing the Gulf—and the World," *Nation*, October 15, 1990, p. 420, 418.

5. Michael Klare, "The U.S. Military Faces South," *Nation*, June 18, 1990, p. 841.

6. Klare, "Policing the Gulf—and the World," p. 418.

7. James A. Baker, "America's Stake in the Persian Gulf Crisis," Statement to House Foreign Affairs Committee, September 4, 1990, U.S. Department of State, *Current Policy* No. 1297 (1990).

8. George Bush, "Against Aggression in the Persian Gulf," August 15, 1990, U.S. Department of State, *Current Policy* No. 1293 (1990).

9. James A. Baker, "America's Stake in the Persian Gulf Crisis."

10. Judith Miller, "Gulf Impact: Experts See U.S. Gain, but a Long-Range Threat to Interests," *New York Times*, October 11, 1990, p. A8, col. 1.

11. Piero Gleijeses, *The Dominican Crisis: The 1965 Constitutionalist Revolt and American Intervention* (1978), pp. 17–18.

12. Jules Lobel, "The Use of Force to Respond to Terrorist Attacks: The Bombing of Sudan and Afghanistan," *Yale Journal of International Law* 24 (1999): 557.

44. THE PRICE OF FRAUDULENT INTERVENTION

Beyond violating the rights of Congress and the people, many of our military interventions violated the rights of the people against whom we fought. Governments are not free to roam the planet with tanks, using them wherever their interests are threatened. The people of each country are entitled to determine what kind of government to have and who should rule. When a civil war rages in a country, outside governments are supposed to stay out of it. When a government is peacefully in control, others are not permitted to stir up an insurgency or invade to remove the government.

All this has been decided by the countries of the world, working through the United Nations, which was set up after World War II to keep countries from using force against each other. The world body's founding treaty, the UN Charter, says that each country agrees not to commit aggression against others. A country may use force only if it is attacked by another and has to defend itself, or if another country is attacked and asks for help in its defense.

Along with its World War II allies, the United States put forward the idea for a United Nations, and the Charter was negotiated and signed at a meeting we hosted in San Francisco in 1945. The Charter binds all the countries that have joined the United Nations, including the United

States. Under our own Constitution, when we conclude a treaty, it becomes part of the law of the United States. The Constitution says that a treaty, like a bill enacted by Congress, is the "law of the land." Thus, it must be followed by our own government, by Congress, and by the president.

So what of our various military interventions in other countries? If we were to review all of them in light of the UN Charter, we would find little room for arguments in their support. That is why, as we went through the interventions in this book, we often saw the UN objecting.

Although on occasion when we used military force we said we were helping another country to defend itself, generally that was not the case. We said that South Vietnam asked us to defend it against North Vietnam, but, as we saw, that was a civil war, not a war between two countries. We said that El Salvador asked us to defend it against Nicaragua, but Nicaragua had not attacked El Salvador, so we were not entitled to defend El Salvador. In both cases, we had our own reasons for attacking.

Our covert paramilitary operations were typically aimed at removing a government we didn't like, or at keeping in power a government we did like. The UN Charter prohibits this kind of operation, because each country is sovereign in its own territory and has the right to determine its own form of government.

Much of the activity recounted in this book was unlawful under the United Nations Charter, and therefore unlawful under the United States Constitution. That means, among other things, that these operations were illegal for the presidents who ran them. The Constitution says that a president who violates the law is to be impeached. The founding fathers thought it was only natural that a president who violated the Constitution should be thrown out of office. Congress, however, has rarely had the political stomach for impeachment.

Although there is little one can do after the fact to undo a military intervention, we would do well not to let our past interventions languish in a kind of perpetual purgatory. It might serve a salutary purpose for our relations with the rest of the world if we would state on the record that we will not do this kind of thing again.

Apologizing for past interventions might not be too extreme. Japan apologized to both North Korea and South Korea for its occupation of Korea from 1910 to 1945, an occupation that involved considerable repression of the Koreans, and that left a deep wound even after Japan's withdrawal.[1]

The Soviet Union apologized for the forced resettlement of ethnic groups for collaborating with Germany during World War II.[2] The Soviet government, shortly before its demise, said that the secret protocols to the Soviet-German nonaggression pact of 1939, which set up spheres of Soviet and German influence in eastern Europe, were "in contradiction to the sovereignty and independence of a number of third countries."[3] It said that "the decision to introduce Soviet troops into Afghanistan" in 1979 "deserves both moral and political condemnation."[4] "The bringing of armies of five socialist countries into Czechoslovak territory in 1968," it said, was "unfounded" and "erroneous."[5]

These are unusual actions, because while governments are quick to act, they are not so quick to admit their mistakes. Such self-criticism would cost us little, however. It might be of considerable importance to the peoples of the countries affected. It might engender good will in countries like Guatemala, Laos, and Grenada. A public apology would be a recognition of the right of those peoples to order their own affairs.

The legacy we left in the Third World was not one calculated to make friends. The Soviet Union, with a message of antineocolonialism, was viewed with suspicion but often got a better reception than we did. Asia came out of World War II anxious to rid itself not only of the Japanese, but of the former European rulers. Asians did not want us or anyone else to take the role of power broker. In the Middle East, the Arabs and Persians were not happy about our efforts to take over from France and Britain. Regarding our secret interventions, Senator Frank Church said that "we have lost, or grievously impaired, the good name and reputation of the United States." We are "regarded with distrust."[6]

Now that the cold war has ended, the United States is able to attack anywhere in the world without fear of reprisal and without significant risk to our own personnel. "Technology now permits the United States," writes Ramsey Clark, "to destroy nearly any country on earth without the risk of casualties from enemy fire. It can send missiles and planes that cannot be intercepted, and bomb at will."[7]

That ability, and the uses we have made of it, account for even greater distrust of us than when Senator Church spoke. A 2006 "global attitudes" poll by the Pew Research Center showed an appallingly low opinion of the United States abroad. In earlier surveys the Middle East stood out as the region whose inhabitants held a low opinion of the United States. The 2006 survey showed a lower opinion of the United States in countries that are traditionally allies. In France, 63 percent held a favorable view of the United States in 2002. In 2006, only 39 percent did. The 2003 Iraq war and its aftermath was apparently the main factor.[8] We are consistently characterized as being "arrogant," "unilateralist," and "dangerous."

Our freewheeling use of military power has kept the collective system of international order from functioning effectively. The UN Security Council, which was to be the guardian of the peace, has been degraded. The United States has repeatedly given it false information to justify interventions that would not have been supported had the true facts been known. When an intervention has been covert, the deception has been in denying involvement. When an intervention has been overt, the deception has been in the reasons for the action. The Security Council is not able to cope with these types of deception. It lacks independent fact-finding capacity. The membership of the Council typically relies on what member states tell it.

Another way in which the Security Council has been degraded is that it has ceded its functions to the United States. The Council "authorizes" unilateral action in situations in which a more prudent course might be a collectively run action. Or it makes threats, as in Resolution 1441 against Iraq, as a way of pacifying the United States, to keep it from acting unilaterally.

Under the UN Charter, the Security Council has "primary responsibility for the maintenance of international peace and security."[9] "[T]he members of the United Nations," writes one analyst, "have conferred the responsibility for maintenance of the peace on the Security Council and not on any other entity that the Council may imagine. All the procedural rules governing the exercise of this responsibility would be circumvented if there were such a power of delegation."[10]

Under the UN Charter, the Security Council is charged not only with deciding when military action is needed, but also with controlling military actions, including the important determination of when to stop military action that it has commenced. The delegation technique, which was invented by the United States for use in the Persian Gulf war and was implemented in Resolution 678, allowed the Security Council to absolve itself from the operational command and control of the coalition action.[11] It also gave the United States greater opportunity to use military force for its own unstated purposes. The Security Council adopted Resolution 678 in the expectation that diplomacy would be attempted and military force would be the last resort. President Bush proceeded full speed ahead to military action.

The forms of intervention by deception have increased. Neither the media nor the legislative branch of government has presented a serious obstacle. As consumers of food products, the American public has demanded, and gained, a list of ingredients on food labels. As consumers of foreign policy decisions, we have yet to demand or gain the same truth in labeling. Yet as citizens, we are the last line of defense.

NOTES

1. "South Korean Leader Accepts Japanese Emperor's Apology," *New York Times*, May 27, 1990, p. A17, col. 6; Steven R. Weisman, "Japan and North Korea Set Talks on Ties," *New York Times*, September 29, 1990, p. A3, col. 4.

2. Declaration of the Supreme Soviet of the U.S.S.R. On Recognizing as Illegal and Criminal the Repressive Acts against Peoples Subjected to Forced Resettlement and on Ensuring Their Rights, *Vedomosti s'ezda narodnykh deputatov SSSR i verkhovnogo soveta SSSR* [Gazette of the Congress of People's Deputies of the U.S.S.R. and the Supreme Soviet of the U.S.S.R.], no. 23, item 449 (1989).

3. Decree of the Congress of People's Deputies of the U.S.S.R. Regarding

a Political and Legal Evaluation of the Soviet-German Nonaggression Treaty of 1939, *Vedomosti s'ezda narodnykh deputatov SSSR i verkhovnogo soveta SSSR* [Gazette of the Congress of People's Deputies of the U.S.S.R. and the Supreme Soviet of the U.S.S.R.], no. 29, item 579 (1989).

4. Decree of the Congress of People's Deputies of the U.S.S.R. On a Political Evaluation of the Decision to Introduce Soviet Troops into Afghanistan in December 1979, *Vedomosti s'ezda narodnykh deputatov SSSR i verkhovnogo soveta SSSR* [Gazette of the Congress of People's Deputies of the U.S.S.R. and the Supreme Soviet of the U.S.S.R.], no. 29, item 582 (1989).

5. "Prague 1968: Views Now in East Bloc," *New York Times*, December 5, 1989, p. A15, col. 1.

6. Frank Church, "Covert Action: Swampland of American Foreign Policy," *Bulletin of the Atomic Scientists*, February 1975, p. 11.

7. Ramsey Clark, *The Fire This Time: U.S. War Crimes in the Gulf* (1992), p. 143.

8. Mark Silva, "Bush Defends U.S. Agenda," *Chicago Tribune*, June 22, 2006, p. C9.

9. United Nations Charter, art. 24 (1).

10. Michael Bothe, Les limites des pouvoirs du Conseil de sécurité, in R. J. Dupuy, ed., *Le Développement du rôle du Conseil de sécurité* (1993), p. 73.

11. Martti Koskenniemi, "The Place of Law in Collective Security," *Michigan Journal of International Law* 17 (1996): 461.

Bibliography

Acheson, Dean. *Present at the Creation*. New York: Norton, 1969.

Albertson, Ralph. *Fighting without a War: An Account of Military Intervention in North Russia*. New York: Harcourt, Brace, and Howe, 1920.

Allison, John M. *Ambassador from the Prairie: Or Allison Wonderland*. Boston: Houghton Mifflin, 1973.

Appleman, Roy E. *United States Army in the Korean War: South to the Naktong, North to the Yalu (June-November 1950)*. Washington, D.C.: Office of the Chief of Military History, Department of the Army, 1961.

Barnet, Richard. *Intervention and Revolution: The United States in the Third World*. New York: World Pub. CO, 1968.

Bassiouni, M. Cherif, "Legal Control of International Terrorism: A Policy-Oriented Assessment," *Harvard International Law Journal* 43 (2002): 83–103.

Berry, William. "Ten Days of Urgent Fury," *All Hands*, May 1984, pp. 18–29.

Bennett, Ralph Kinney. "Grenada: Anatomy of a 'Go' Decision." *Reader's Digest*, February 1984, pp. 72–77.

Bennouna, Mohammed. *Le consentement à l'ingérence militaire dans les conflits internes*. Paris: Librarie générale de droit et de jurisprudence, 1974.

Bill, Alfred Hoyt. *Rehearsal for Conflict: The War with Mexico 1846–1848*. New York: Knopf, 1947.

Bonner, Raymond. *Weakness and Deceit: U.S. Policy and El Salvador*. New York: Times Books, 1984.

Bothe, Michael, Mary Ellen O'Connell, and Natalino Ronzitti, eds., *Re-Defining*

Sovereignty: The Use of Force after the Cold War. Ardsley, NY: Transnational, 2005.

Branfman, Fred. *Voices from the Plain of Jars: Life under an Air War*. New York: Harper and Row, 1972.

Burns, Richard Dean, and Milton Leitenberg. *The Wars in Vietnam, Cambodia, and Laos, 1945–1982: A Bibliographic Guide*. Santa Barbara, CA: ABC-Clio Information Services, 1984.

Buergenthal, Thomas, ed., *Contemporary Issues in International Law: Essays in Honor of Louis B. Sohn*. Kehl: N.P. Engel, 1984.

Cabot, John Moors. *First Line of Defense*. Washington, D.C.: Georgetown School of Foreign Service, 1979.

Caro, Robert A. *The Years of Lyndon Johnson: Means of Ascent*. New York: Knopf, 1990.

Carr, Edward Hallett, *The Bolshevik Revolution 1917–1923*. Baltimore: Penguin, 1966.

Cavelier, German. *La política internacional de Colombia*. Bogota: Editorial Iqueima, 1960.

Chomsky, Noam. *The New Military Humanism: Lessons from Kosovo*. Monroe, ME: Common Courage Press, 1999.

Church, Frank. "Covert Action: Swampland of American Foreign Policy," *Bulletin of the Atomic Scientists*, February 1975, pp. 7–11.

Clark, Ramsey. *The Fire This Time: U.S. War Crimes in the Gulf*. New York: Thunder's Mouth Press, 1992.

Cobban, Helena. *The Making of Modern Lebanon*. London: Hutchinson, 1985.

Cockburn, Leslie. *Out of Control: The Story of the Reagan Administration's Secret War in Nicaragua, the Illegal Arms Pipeline, and the Contra Drug Connection*. New York: Atlantic Monthly Press, 1987.

Colby, William. *Honorable Men: My Life in the CIA*. New York: Simon and Schuster, 1978.

Colby, William, et al. "Should the U.S. Fight Secret Wars?" *Harper's*, September 1984, pp. 33–47.

Commander in Chief, U.S. Atlantic Command. *Operation Urgent Fury Report*. Norfolk, VA: U.S. Department of Defense, 1984.

Compaine, Benjamin, ed. *Who Owns the Media? Concentration of Ownership in the Mass Communcation Industry*. White Plains, NY: Knowledge Industry Pubs., 1982.

Conference for a New Direction in U.S. Korea Policy. New York: Committee for a New Direction for U.S. Korea Policy, 1977.

Cormier, Frank. *LBJ: The Way He Was*. Garden City, NY: Doubleday, 1977.

Cornish, Paul, ed. The Conflict in Iraq 2003. Basingstroke, NH: Macmillan, 2004.

Cudahy, John. *Archangel: The American War with Russia*. Chicago: A.C. McClurg, 1924.

Cumings, Bruce. *Liberation and the Emergence of Separate Regimes, 1945–1947*. Vol. 1, *The Origins of the Korean War*. Princeton, N.J.: Princeton University Press, 1981.

——. *The Roaring of the Cataract, 1945–1950*. Vol. 2, *The Origins of the Korean War*. Princeton, N.J.: Princeton University Press, 1990.

Davis, Nathaniel. "The Angola Decision of 1975: A Personal Memoir." *Foreign Affairs* (Fall 1978): 109–24.

Deakin, James. *Lyndon Johnson's Credibility Gap*. Washington, D.C.: Public Affairs Press, 1968.

DeNike, Howard, John Quigley, and Kenneth Robinson, eds. Genocide in Cambodia: Documents from the Trial ofPol Pot and Ieng Sary. Philadelphia: University of Pennsylvania Press, 2000.

Discriminate Deterrence: Report of the Commission on Integrated Long-Term Strategy. Fred C. Ilké and Albert Wohlstetter, co-chairmen. Prepared for Secretary of Defense and Assistant to the President for National Security Affairs. Washington, D.C., January 1988.

Donovan, Robert J. *Tumultuous Years: The Presidency of Harry S. Truman 1949–1953*. New York: Norton, 1982.

Draper, Theodore. *The Dominican Revolt: A Case Study in American Policy*. New York: Commentary, 1968.

Drumbl, Mark A., "Judging the 11 September Terrorist Attack," *Human Rights Quarterly* 24 (2002): 323–60.

Dupuy, René-Jean. "Agression indirecte et intervention sollicitée à propos de l'affaire libanaise." *Annuaire Français de Droit International* (1959): 431–67.

Edwards, Albert. *Panama: The Canal, the Country, and the People*. New York: Macmillan, 1912.

Eisenhower, Dwight D. *Mandate for Change 1953–1956*. Garden City, N.Y.: Doubleday, 1963.

Eveland, Wilbur Crane. *Ropes of Sand: America's Failure in the Middle East.* New York. Norton, 1980.

Fall, Bernard B. *Vietnam Witness 1953–66.* New York: Praeger, 1966.

Foot, Rosemary. *The Wrong War: American Policy and the Dimensions of the Korean Conflict, 1950–1953.* Ithaca, NY: Cornell University Press, 1985.

Franck, Thomas M. "Who Killed Article 2(4)? or Changing Norms Governing the Use of Force by States." *American Journal of International Law* 64 (1970): 809–37.

Franck, Thomas M., and Edward Weisband, eds. *Secrecy and Foreign Policy.* New York: Oxford University Press, 1974.

Gettelman, Marvin E. Vietnam: *History, Documents, and Opinions on a Major World Crisis.* Greenwich, Conn.: Fawcett Pubs., 1965.

Gettelman, Marvin, E., et al., eds. *El Salvador: Central America in the New Cold War.* New York: Grove Press, 1986.

Geyelin, Philip. *Lyndon B. Johnson and the World.* New York: Praeger, 1966.

Gibson, James William. *The Perfect War: Technowar in Vietnam.* Boston: Atlantic Monthly Press, 1986.

Gilbert, Martin. *The Second World War: A Complete History.* New York: Henry Holt, 1989.

Gleijeses, Piero. *The Dominican Crisis: The 1965 Constitutionalist Revolt and American Intervention.* Baltimore, MD.: Johns Hopkins University Press, 1978.

Gott, Richard. *Rural Guerrillas in Latin America.* Harmondsworth, England: Penguin, 1973.

Goulden, Joseph C. *Truth Is the First Casualty: The Gulf of Tonkin Affair—Illusion and Reality.* Chicago: Rand McNally, 1969.

Grant, Ulysses S. *Personal Memoirs of U.S. Grant.* New York: C.L. Webster, 1894.

Gray, Christine, "After the Ceasefire: Iraq, the Security Council and the Use of Force," *British Year Book of International Law* 65 (1994): 135–74.

Grenada. Whose Freedom? London: Latin America Bureau, 1984.

Grenada. The World against the Crime. Havana: Editorial de Ciencias Sociales, 1983.

Gunther, John. *The Riddle of MacArthur.* New York: Harper, 1950.

Handy, Jim. Gift of the Devil: A History of Guatemala. Boston: South End Press, 1984.

Hastings, Max. *The Korean War.* New York: Simon and Schuster, 1987.

Herman, Edward S., and Noam Chomsky. *Manufacturing Consent: The Political Economy of the Mass Media*. New York: Pantheon, 1988.

Hernandez, Manuel Arteaga, and Jaime Arteaga Carvajal. *Historia política de Colombia*. Bogota: Intermedio Editores, 1986.

Hersh, Seymour. "Target Qaddafi," *New York Times*, February 22, 1987, p. F17, col. 1.

Hitchcock, Wilbur. "North Korea Jumps the Gun." *Current History* 20 (March 1951): 136–44.

Howarth, David. *Panama*. New York: McGraw Hill, 1966.

Hoyt, Edwin C. *Law and Force in American Foreign Policy*. Lanham, MD: University Press of America, 1985.

Hughes, Emmet John. *The Ordeal of Power: A Political Memoir of the Eisenhower Years*. New York: Atheneum, 1963.

Immerman, Richard H. *The CIA in Guatemala: The Foreign Policy of Intervention*. Austin: University of Texas Press, 1982.

Johnson, Loch K. *America's Secret Power: The CIA in a Democratic Society*. New York: Oxford University Press, 1989.

Johnson, Lyndon B. "An Assessment of the Situation in the Dominican Republic." *Department of State Bulletin* (1965): 19–21.

Kalb, Madeleine. *The Congo Cables: The Cold War in Africa from Eisenhower to Kennedy*. New York: Macmillan, 1982.

Kennan, George. *The Decision to Intervene*. New York: Atheneum, 1967.

Kirkpatrick, Lyman B., Jr. *The Real CIA*. New York: Macmillan, 1968.

Knights, Michael Andrew. *Cradle of Conflict: Iraq and the Birth of Modern U.S. Military Power*. Annapolis, MD: Naval Institute Press, 2005.

Knightley, Philip. *The First Casualty: From the Crimea to Vietnam: The War Correspondent as Hero, Propagandist, and Myth Maker*. New York: Harcourt Brace Jovanovich, 1975.

Kolko, Joyce. *The Limits of Power: The World and United States Foreign Policy, 1945-1954*. New York: Harper and Row, 1972.

Krieger, Heike (ed.), *The Kosovo Conflict and International Law: An Analytical Documentation 1974–1999*. Cambridge: Cambridge University Press, 2001.

Kwitny, Jonathan. *Endless Enemies: The Making of an Unfriendly World*. New York: St. Martin's Press, 1984.

Laffin, John. *The War of Desperation: Lebanon 1982–85*. London: Osprey, 1985.

Liebenow, J. Gus. *Liberia: The Quest for Democracy*. Bloomington: Indiana University Press, 1987.

Lobel, Jules, and Michael Ratner. "Bypassing the Security Council: Ambiguous Authorizations to Use Force, Cease-Fires, and the Iraqi Inspection Regime," *American Journal of International Law* 93 (1999): 124–54.

Loquai, Heinz, *Der Kosovo-Konflikt—Wege in einen vermeidbaren Krieg: Die Zeit von Ende November 1997 bis März 1999.* Baden-Baden: Nomos, 2000.

Lowenthal, Abraham F. *The Dominican Intervention.* Cambridge, MA: Harvard University Press, 1972.

MacArthur, John R. *Second Front: Censorship and Propaganda in the Gulf War.* New York: Hill and Wang, 1992.

McClintock, Michael. *The American Connection.* Totowa, NJ: Zed, 1985.

McCormack, Gavan. *Cold War Hot War: An Australian Perspective on the Korean War.* Sydney Hale and Iremonger, 1983.

McCormick, Thomas J. *America's Half-Century: United States Foreign Policy in the Cold War.* Baltimore, MD: Johns Hopkins University Press, 1989.

McCoy, Alfred W. *The Politics of Heroin in Southeast Asia.* New York: Harper and Row, 1972.

McGehee, Ralph. *Deadly Deceits: My 25 Years in the CIA.* New York: Sheridan Square Pubs., 1983.

Malone, Linda A. "The Kahan Report, Ariel Sharon and the Sabra-Shatilla Massacres in Lebanon: Responsibility Under International Law for Massacres of Civilian Populations." *Utah Law Review* (1985): 373–433.

Marchetti, Victor, and John Marks. *The CIA and the Cult of Intelligence.* New York: Knopf, 1974.

Marcum, John. "Lessons of Angola." *Foreign Affairs* (April 1976): 407–425.

Martin, David, and John Walcott. *Best Laid Plans: The Inside Story of America's War against Terrorism.* New York: Harper and Row, 1988.

Martin, John Bartlow. *Overtaken by Events: The Dominican Crisis from the Fall of Trujillo to the Civil War.* New York: Doubleday, 1966.

Martinez, Milton. *Panama 1978–1990: Una Crisis sin Fin Panama.* Centro de Estudios y Acción Social Panameño, 1990.

May, Brian. *The Indonesian Tragedy.* London: Routledge and Kegan Paul, 1978.

Miller, Merle. *Lyndon: An Oral Biography.* New York: Putnam, 1980.

Mosley, Leonard. *Dulles: A Biography of Eleanor, Allen, and John Foster Dulles and Their Family Network.* New York: Dial Press, 1978.

Mossman, James. *Rebels in Paradise: Indonesia's Civil War.* London: Cape, 1961.

Mueller, John E. War, *Presidents and Public Opinion.* New York: Wiley, 1973.

Murray, Robert. *Red Scare: A Study of National Hysteria, 1919–1920*. New York: McGraw-Hill, 1964.

Neff, Donald. *Warriors at Suez: Eisenhower Takes America into the Middle East*. New York: Simon and Schuster, 1981.

Normand, Roger, and Chris af Jochnick. "The Legitimation of Violence: A Critical Analysis of the Gulf War," *Harvard Journal of International Law* 35 (1994): 387–416.

O'Ballance, Edgar. *The Wars in Vietnam, 1954–1980*. New York: Hippocrene Books, 1981.

O'Shaughnessy, Hugh. *Grenada: Revolution, Invasion and Aftermath*. London: Observer, 1984.

O'Toole, G. J. A. *The Spanish War: An American Epic—1898*. New York: Norton, 1984.

Paige, Glenn D. *The Korean Decision June 24–30, 1950*. New York: Free Press, 1968.

Panikkar, K. M. *In Two Chinas: Memoirs of a Diplomat*. London: George Allen and Unwin, 1955.

Parenti, Michael. *Inventing Reality: The Politics of the Mass Media*. New York: St. Martin's Press, 1986.

The Pentagon Papers As Published by the New York Times. New York, Toronto: Bantam Books, 1971.

The Pentagon Papers: The Defense Department History of United States Decision making on Vietnam (Senator Gravel ed.). Boston: Beacon Press, 1971.

Phillips, David Atlee. *The Night Watch*. New York: Atheneum, 1977.

Piller, Charles, and Keith R. Yamamoto. *Gene Wars: Military Control over the New Genetic Technologies*. New York: Beech Tree Books, 1988.

Potter, Pitman B. "Legal Aspects of the Beirut Landing." *American Journal of International Law* 52 (1958): 727–30.

Powers, Thomas. *The Man Who Kept Secrets: Richard Helms & the CIA*. New York: Knopf, 1979.

Prados, John. *Presidents' Secret Wars: CIA and Pentagon Covert Operations since World War II*. New York: Quill, 1986.

President's Special Review Board. *Report of the Special Review Board* (Tower Commission Report). New York: Bantam Times Books, 1987.

Prouty, Col. L. Fletcher, U.S. Air Force, Ret. *The Secret Team: The CIA and Its Allies in Control of the United States and the World*. Englewood Cliffs, NJ: Prentice-Hall, 1973.

Public Papers of the Presidents of the United States: Harry S. Truman, 1950. Washington, D.C.: U.S. Government Printing Office, 1965.

Quigley, John. *The Case for Palestine: An International Law Perspective.* Durham, NC and London: Duke University Press, 2005.

——. "The Legality of the United States Invasion of Panama." *Yale Journal of International Law* 15 (1990): 276–315.

——. *Palestine and Israel: A Challenge to Justice.* Durham, NC, and London: Duke University Press, 1990.

——. "Parachutes at Dawn: Issues of Use of Force and Status of Internees in the United States-Cuban Hostilities on Grenada, 1983." *University of Miami Inter-American Law Review* 17 (1986): 199–248.

——. "The United States Invasion of Grenada: Stranger than Fiction." *University of Miami Inter-American Law Review* 18 (1986–87): 271–352.

Randal, Jonathan. *The Tragedy of Lebanon: Christian Warlords, Israeli Adventurers and American Bunglers.* London: Chatto & Windus, 1983.

Rauch, Georg von. *A History of Soviet Russia.* New York: Praeger, 1958.

Rickover, H. G. *How the Battleship Maine Was Destroyed.* Washington, D.C.: U.S. Department of the Navy, 1976.

Ridgway, Matthew. *The Korean War and How We Met the Challenge, How All-Out Asian War Was Averted, Why MacArthur Was Dismissed, Why Today's War Objectives Must Be Limited.* Garden City, NY: Doubleday, 1967.

Roosevelt, Kermit. *Countercoup: The Struggle for the Control of Iran.* New York: McGraw-Hill, 1979.

Salinger, Pierre, and Eric Laurent. *Secret Dossier: The Hidden Agenda Behind the Gulf War.* New York: Penguin Books, 1991.

Sayers, Michael, and Albert E. Kahn. *The Great Conspiracy against Russia.* New York: Boni & Gaer, 1946.

Schapp, Bill. "Disinforming the World on Libya." *Covert Action Information Bulletin,* No. 30 (Summer 1988): 71–76.

Schlesinger, Arthur B., Jr. *A Thousand Days.* Boston: Houghton Mifflin, 1965.

Schroeder, John H. *Mr. Polk's War: American Opposition and Dissent, 1846–1848.* Madison: University of Wisconsin Press, 1973.

Searle, Christopher. *Grenada: The Struggle against Destabilization.* London: Writers and Readers Pub. Cooperative Society, 1983.

Shawcross, William. *Sideshow: Kissinger, Nixon and the Destruction of Cambodia.* New York: Simon and Schuster, 1979.

Simons, Geoff. *The Scourging of Iraq: Sanctions, Law and Natural Justice.* New York: St. Martin's Press, 1998.

Smith, Joseph Burkholder. *Portrait of a Cold Warrior.* New York: Putnam, 1976.

Sorensen, Theodore C. *Kennedy.* New York: Harper and Row, 1965.

Stein, Torsten. "No-Fly-Zones," *Israel Year Book on Human Rights* 27 (1997): 193–214.

Sterling, Claire. *The Terror Network: The Secret War of International Terrorism.* New York: Holt, Rinehart, and Winston, 1981.

Stevenson, Charles A. *The End of Nowhere: American Policy toward Laos since 1954.* Boston: Beacon Press, 1972.

Stockwell, John. *In Search of Enemies: A CIA Story.* New York: Norton, 1978.

Stone, I. F. *The Hidden History of the Korean War.* New York: Monthly Review Press, 1952.

Szulc, Tad. *Dominican Diary.* New York: Delacorte Press, 1965.

Talbott, Strobe, ed. *Khrushchev Remembers.* Boston: Little Brown & Company, 1970.

Treverton, Gregory F. *Covert Action: The Limits of Intervention in the Postwar World.* New York: Basic Books, 1987.

Tully, Andrew. *CIA: The Inside Story.* New York: Morrow, 1962.

Turley, William S. *The Second Indochina War: A Short Political and Military History, 1954–1975.* Boulder, CO: Westview Press, 1986.

Ulam, Adam. *A History of Soviet Russia.* New York: Praeger, 1976.

United States-Vietnam Relations 1945–1967: Study Prepared by the Department of Defense. Washington, D.C.: U.S. Government Printing Office, 1971.

Uribe, Antonio Jose. *Colombia, Estados Unidos y Panamá.* Libreria colombiana, 1976.

U.S. Congress. House. *Mutual Security Appropriations for 1959.* Hearings before the Subcommittee of the Committee on Appropriations. 85th Cong., 2d sess., 1958.

——. *Situation in Lebanon and Grenada.* Hearing before a Subcommittee of the House Committee on Appropriations. 98th Cong., 1st sess., 1983.

——. *United States Policy on Angola.* Hearing before the Committee on International Relations. 94th Cong., 2d sess., 1976.

——. *U.S. Aid Operations in Laos.* Seventh Report by the Committee on Government Operations. House Report 546, 86th Cong., 1st sess., 1959.

——. *U.S. Military Actions in Grenada: Implications for U.S. Policy in the Eastern Caribbean.* Hearing before the Subcommittees on International

Security and Scientific Affairs and on Western Hemisphere Affairs of the House Committee on Foreign Affairs. 98th Cong., 1st sess., 1983.

U.S. Congress. Senate. *Alleged Assassination Plots Involving Foreign Leaders: An Interim Report of the Select Committee to Study Governmental Operations with Respect to Intelligence Activities.* 94th Cong., 1st sess., 1975. Report no. 94-465.

——. *Angola.* Hearings before the Subcommittee on African Affairs of the Committee on Foreign Relations. 94th Cong., 2d sess., 1976.

——. *Bombing in Cambodia.* Hearings before the Committee on Armed Services. 93rd Cong., 1st sess., 1973.

——. *Final Report: Foreign and Military Intelligence.* Select Committee to Study Governmental Operations with Respect to Intelligence Activities, Book 1. 94th Cong., 2d sess., 1976.

——. *Military Situation in the Far East.* Hearings before the Armed Services and the Committee on Foreign Relations. 82d Cong., 1st sess., 1951.

——. *Mutual Security Appropriations for 1955.* Hearings on H. R. 10051, an Act Making Appropriations for Mutual Security for the Fiscal Year Ending June 30, 1955, and For Other Purposes. Committee on Appropriations. 83rd Cong., 2d sess., 1954.

——. *Refugee and Civilian War Casualty Problems in Indochina.* Staff Report Prepared for the Use of the Subcommittee to Investigate Problems Connected with Refugees and Escapees of the Committee on the Judiciary. 91st Cong., 2d sess., 1970.

——. *Situation in Grenada.* Hearings Before the Senate Committee on Foreign Relations. 98th Cong., 1st sess., 1983.

——. *United States Security Agreements and Commitments Abroad: Kingdom of Laos.* Hearings before the Subcommittee on United States Security Agreements and Commitments Abroad. Comm. on Foreign Relations. 91st Cong., 1st sess., 1969.

——. *War-Related Civilian Problems in Indochina. Part II: Laos and Cambodia.* Hearings before the Subcommittee to Investigate Problems Connected with Refugees and Escapees of the Committee on the Judiciary. 91st Cong., 1st sess., 1971.

U.S. Department of State. "Communist Interference in El Salvador." Special Report, no. 80, February 23, 1981. Washington, D.C.: U.S. Government Printing Office, 1981.

The U.S. Invasion of Panama: The Truth Behind Operation 'Just Cause.' New York: Independent Commission of Inquiry on the U.S. Invasion of Panama, 1990.

Walker, Thomas, ed. *Reagan versus the Sandinistas: The Undeclared War on Nicaragua.* Boulder, CO, and London: Westview Press, 1987.

Weems, John Edward. *The Fate of the Maine.* New York: Holt, 1958.

Weissman, Stephen R. *American Foreign Policy in the Congo 1960–1964.* Ithaca, NY: Cornell University Press, 1974.

——. "CIA Covert Action in Zaire and Angola: Patterns and Consequences." *Political Science Quarterly* 94 (Summer 1979): 263–86.

Wise, David. *The Politics of Lying: Government Deception, Secrecy, and Power.* New York: Random House, 1973.

Wise, David, and Thomas B. Ross. *The Invisible Government.* New York: Random House, 1964.

Woodward, Bob. *The Commanders.* New York: Simon and Schuster, 1991.

——. *Veil: The Secret Wars of the CIA 1981–1987.* New York: Simon and Schuster, 1987.

Wright, Quincy. "United States Intervention in Lebanon." *American Journal of International Law* 53 (1959): 112–25.

Wyden, Peter. *Bay of Pigs: The Untold Story.* New York: Simon and Schuster, 1979.

Yant, Martin. *Desert Mirage: The True Story of the Gulf War.* Buffalo, NY: Prometheus Books, 1991.

Name Index

Abreu Cruz, Roberto, 243

Acheson, Dean, 35, 50, 56, 60, 62, 194

Adams, John, 398

Adams, Tom, 224

Agnew, Spiro, 164, 166

Aidid, Mohammed, 313

Alarcón, Ricardo, 249

Albright, Madeline, 318–25

Allison, John, 80–83

Annan, Kofi, 341

Aquino, Corazon, 263–66

Arafat, Yassir, 209

Arbenz, Jacobo, 71–75, 388, 392

Armitage, Richard, 266

Aspin, Les, 295

Assadi, Ra'ad, 321

Attar, Leila, 317

Austin, Warren, 43, 48, 56

Baker, James, 283, 287, 304, 306, 405

Ball, George, 120

Baradei, Mohammed el-, 370

Barre, Siad, 310, 314

Barrow, Gen. Robert, 293

Bassiouni, M. Cherif, 361

Batista, Fulgencio, 97, 388

Beckwith, Col. Charles, 193

Bennett, Tapley, 148–50, 156–57

Benoit, Pedro, 148

Berger, Sandy, 323, 350

Bevin, Ernest, 57

Biden, Joseph, 178

Bin Laden, Osama, 329–31, 360–61

Bishop, Maurice, 221, 229–31, 247–50

Bissell, Richard, 138

Black, Hugo, 17, 391

Blix, Hans, 370

Bonner, Raymond, 393

Borah, William, 28

Bosch, Juan, 147–49, 155–58

Bourne, Geoffrey, 230

Bourne, Peter, 231, 243

Boutros-Ghali, Boutros, 338, 373–74
Bradley, Gen. Omar, 62
Brezhnev, Leonid, 379–80
Bromwich, Michael, 325
Brooks, Capt. Thomas A., 215
Brown, Harold, 193
Brzezinski, Zbigniew, 185–88
Budeit, James, 230–31
Bunker, Ellsworth, 164
Bush, George H.W., 207, 263–66,
    273–77, 283–90, 293–95,
    299–307, 311–15, 317–25,
    335–37, 394, 400, 404–406, 415
Bush, George W., 13, 20, 325,
    359–64, 367–75, 395, 407–408

Cabot, John Moors, 76
Carter, Jimmy, 184–88, 191–95,
    197–200, 236, 271–72, 289, 389
Casey, William, 199, 257, 272
Castillo Armas, Carlos, 72–75, 97
Castro, Fidel, 97, 100, 158, 186–87,
    247–48
Chamorro, Edgar, 198, 200
Chamorro, Violeta, 288
Chamoun, Camille, 87–92, 215–16
Chapelier, George, 111
Charette, Herve de, 338
Cheney, Richard, 301
Chicherin, George, 26
Christopher, Warren, 193
Church, Frank, 113, 387, 413–14
Clark, Joseph, 151
Clark, Ramsey, 414
Clinton, William J., 290, 313, 317–25,
    330–33, 335–43, 349–55,
    367–68, 371, 394–95

Cohen, Herman, 294, 313
Colby, William, 110, 173–77,
    399–400
Cornwall, Leon, 228, 230
Cumings, Bruce, 39
Curtis, Col. Donald McB., 39

Dam, Kenneth, 230, 240
Davignon, Etienne, 132
Davis, Nathaniel, 174–75
Devlin, Lawrence, 138–43
Díaz, Alberto, 241
Díaz, Col. Carlos, 74
Diem, Ngo Dinh, 123
Dillon, C. Douglas, 141
Doe, Samuel, 291, 293
Duarte, Napoleon, 203
Duelfer, Charles, 370
Dulles, Allen, 73, 82, 138–41
Dulles, John Foster, 37, 47, 73, 75,
    79–83, 92, 106–107

Eagleburger, Lawrence, 274, 276
Eisenhower, Dwight, 71–76, 79–83,
    87–92, 97–102, 106–108, 117,
    138–39, 142, 159, 186, 209, 215,
    242, 330, 361, 375, 378, 385, 386
Endara, Guillermo, 271, 274–76,
    283–84, 287–88
Eveland, Wilbur Crane, 88

Federspiel, Howard, 84
Ferch, John, 242–43, 246
Fitzwater, Marlin, 301
Ford, Gerald, 169, 173–79
Fortier, Donald, 254
Fox, J. Edward, 270

Francis, David, 25
Fulbright J. William, 120–21, 151, 156, 158

Gejdenson, Sam, 314
Gemayel, Amin, 208–210
Gemayel, Bashir, 207–208
Gemayel, Pierre, 207
Ghazali, Wali, 319, 322
Gillespie, Charles, 224
Gizenga, Antoine, 137, 140–41
Glaspie, April, 302–303
Glassman, Jon D., 199–201
Grant, Ulysses, 24
Gray, Gen. A. M., 402
Green, Marshall, 84
Gromyko, Andrei, 50, 191
Guevara, Che, 247

Hajjar, Sami G., 322
Hamdun, Nizar, 320
Hamilton, Lee, 323
Handal, Shafik, 200
Harriman, Averell, 134
Hart, Gary, 243
Hersh, Seymour, 252, 256, 322, 393
Hillenkoetter, Roscoe, 49
Hoar, Gen. Joseph, 314–15
Hoare, Michael, 132
Ho Chi Minh, 110, 117, 124
Hodge, Gen. John R., 40–41, 65
Hoffman, Fred, 283
Holt, Maj. Jim, 243
Howe, Geoffrey, 222
Hughes, Harold, 165, 397–98
Hussein, King, 90, 92
Hussein, Saddam, 293, 300–301,

304–305, 307, 316, 323, 340,
366–67, 373, 392, 403–404

Ieng Sary, 168

Jefferson, Thomas, 396
Jessup, Philip, 35
Jimenez, Raul, 245
Johnson, Hiram, 23, 27–28
Johnson, Lyndon, 110–11, 118–25,
129, 133–34, 142, 147–51,
155–58, 284, 377–79
Johnson, Prince, 292–93

Karzai, Hamid, 364
Kasavubu, Joseph, 139–43
Kelly, Gen. Thomas, 304
Kennedy, Edward, 112
Kennedy, John, 99–102, 109, 118,
121–22, 142, 189, 390, 398
Khrushchev, Nikita, 37, 39, 49,
100–102, 139, 159
Kim IlSung, 37, 40, 49
Kirkpatrick, Lyman, 99
Kissinger, Henry, 101, 173–79, 188
Knight, Harold, 165
Kozak, Michael G., 287

Lansdale, Gen. Edward G., 109
Lansing, Robert, 27
Lavrov, Sergei, 343
Lenin, V.I., 208
Lobel, Jules, 407
Lodge, Henry Cabot, 73, 89–91
Lon Nol, 164–67
Loquai, Heinz, 354–56
Lovett, Robert, 58

Lugar, Richard, 323
Lumumba, Patrice, 137–42

MacArthur, Gen. Douglas, 36, 38–39, 51, 55–64
McDonald, Adm. Wesley, 221, 223, 234, 241–43
McKinley, William, 24–25
MacMichael, David, 210
McNamara, Robert, 119
McPeak, Gen. Merrill, 305, 307
Manglapus, Raul, 266

Mao Tsetung, 166
Marcos, Ferdinand, 263–64
Martens, Robert J., 84
Marx, Karl, 208
Milosevic, Slobodan, 352, 355
Mobutu, Joseph, 139–43, 173–75, 183–88
Mobutu Sese Seko. See Mobutu, Joseph
Monroe, James, 21–23, 173–79, 385–86
Monzón, Col. Elfego, 74–75
Morales, George, 202
Morse, Wayne, 119
Mossadegh, Mohammed, 194–95
Mubarak, Hosni, 256
Mulcahy, Edward, 176
Mulele, Pierre, 140
Murphy, Robert, 81
Myers, Robert J., 232

Nasser, Gamel Abdul, 88
Negroponte, John, 368, 372
Neto, Agostinho, 186

Nidal, Abu, 258
Nixon, Richard, 75, 111–112, 126, 163–66, 393
Noriega, Gen. Manuel, 271–75
Noyes, Charles, 33

Olney, Richard, 21, 386
Ortega, Daniel, 201–202

Pahlavi, Shah Muhammed Reza, 194
Parsons, J. Graham, 106
Pastor, Robert, 236
Perez de Cuellar, Javier, 305
Perkins, Edward, 336
Peurifoy, John, 74–75
Phillips, David Atlee, 76
Poindexter, John, 256–57, 380
Pol Pot, 168
Polk, James, 23–24
Pope, Allen Lawrence, 81–83
Powell, Colin, 369–71, 394, 408
Primakov, Evgenii, 338

Qaddafi, Col. Moammar, 253–59
Qin Huasun,, 343

Reagan, Ronald, 198–202, 205–212, 215–18, 221–27, 229–35, 249–50, 253–58, 263–64, 272–73, 288, 332, 362–63, 379–80, 393, 400, 403
Reno, Janet, 324
Rhee, Syngman, 36–38, 41
Rickover, Adm. Hyman, 25
Ridgway, Gen. Matthew, 56
Robertson, Walter, 106
Rodriguez, Ramón Milian, 272

Ronay, Christopher, 325
Roosevelt, Franklin, 22
Roosevelt, Kermit, 194–95
Roosevelt, Theodore, 21–23, 194, 269–70, 386
Rubin, James, 350, 355
Rusk, Dean, 47, 58, 60, 134, 148–49, 155

Sandino, Augusto, 197
Schaufele, William, 175, 177–78
Schwarzkopf, Norman, 234
Scoon, Sir Paul, 223–25
Scowcroft, Brent, 306
Shultz, George, 254–59
Sihanouk, Norodom, 164–65
Simonet, Henri, 186
Slim, Sir William, 60
Smith, Joseph Burkholder, 82
Solarz, Stephen, 266
Somoza Debayle, Anastasio, 197–99, 388
Somoza Garcia, Anastasio, 197
Soumialot, Gaston, 137
Souvanna Phouma, 107
Spaak, Paul Henri, 131–33
Stalin, Joseph, 37, 48–49
Stennis, John, 134
Stevenson, Adlai, 102, 133, 137, 142
Stiner, Gen. Carl, 289
Stockdale, James B., 119
Sukarno, Ahmed, 79–83, 388
Sylvester, Arthur, 380
Symington, Stuart, 112, 165

Taft, Robert, 35
Taylor, Charles, 295

Tempelsman, Maurice, 143
Tenet, George, 369
Thatcher, Margaret, 224
Thomas, Cmdr. David, 293
Timberlake, Clare, 138–39
Tindemans, Leo, 184
Trujillo, Rafael, 388
Truman, Harry, 35, 38–40, 47–51, 55–65, 73, 117, 125, 387, 405
Tsarapkin, Semyon, 73–76
Tshombe, Moise, 141–43, 183–84
Tullius, Thomas D., 332
Tunney, John, 178
Tweedy, Bronson, 138, 140

Ulmer, Al, 82
Ungo, Guillermo, 206

Vance, Cyrus, 185–87
Vessey, Gen. John. W., Jr., 245
Vuono, Gen. Carl, 404–405

Walker, William, 353–56
Warner, John, 352
Weinberger, Caspar, 232–33, 241–43, 254, 259
Wessin y Wessin, Elias, 148, 156
White, Robert, 208
Whitehurst, Frederic, 324–25
Williams, Pete, 293, 295
Wilson, Joseph, 370
Wilson, Woodrow, 22, 26–28, 407
Woolsey, James, 323
Wrong, Hume, 58

Ydígoras Fuentes, Miguel, 72, 97–98
Young Woon Lee, Adm., 32